Lecture Notes in Computer Science 8892

Commenced Publication in 1973
Founding and Former Series Editors:
Gerhard Goos, Juris Hartmanis, and Jan van Leeuwen

T0212766

Andreas Jedlitschka   Pasi Kuvaja
Marco Kuhrmann   Tomi Männistö
Jürgen Münch   Mikko Raatikainen (Eds.)

Product-Focused Software Process Improvement

15th International Conference, PROFES 2014
Helsinki, Finland, December 10-12, 2014
Proceedings

 Springer

Volume Editors

Andreas Jedlitschka
Fraunhofer Institute for Experimental Software Engineering
Fraunhofer-Platz 1, 67663 Kaiserslautern, Germany
E-mail: andreas.jedlitschka@iese.fraunhofer.de

Pasi Kuvaja
University of Oulu
Department of Information Processing Science
90014 Oulu, Finland
E-mail: pasi.kuvaja@oulu.fi

Marco Kuhrmann
University of Southern Denmark
The Maersk Mc-Kinney Møller Institute
Campusvej 55, 5230 Odense, Denmark
E-mail: kuhrmann@mmmi.sdu.dk

Tomi Männistö
Jürgen Münch
University of Helsinki
Department of Computer Science
00014 Helsinki, Finland
E-mail: {tomi.mannisto, juergen.muench}@cs.helsinki.fi

Mikko Raatikainen
Aalto University
Department of Computer Science and Engineering
00076 Aalto, Finland
E-mail: mikko.raatikainen@aalto.fi

ISSN 0302-9743   e-ISSN 1611-3349
ISBN 978-3-319-13834-3   e-ISBN 978-3-319-13835-0
DOI 10.1007/978-3-319-13835-0
Springer Cham Heidelberg New York Dordrecht London

Library of Congress Control Number: Applied for

LNCS Sublibrary: SL 2 – Programming and Software Engineering

Typesetting: Camera-ready by author, data conversion by Scientific Publishing Services, Chennai, India

Printed on acid-free paper

Springer is part of Springer Science+Business Media (www.springer.com)

Preface

On behalf of the PROFES Organizing Committee, we are proud to present the proceedings of the 15th International Conference on Product-Focused Software Process Improvement (PROFES 2014) held in Helsinki, Finland.

Since 1999, PROFES has established itself as one of the recognized international process improvement conferences. The main theme of PROFES is professional software process improvement (SPI) motivated by product, process, and service quality needs. PROFES 2014 addressed both quality engineering and management topics, including processes, methods, techniques, tools, organizations, and enabling SPI. Solutions found in practice and relevant research results from academia were presented.

A committee of leading experts in SPI, software process modeling, and empirical software engineering selected the technical program.

This year, 45 full papers were submitted. At least three independent experts reviewed each paper. After a thorough evaluation, 18 technical full papers were finally selected (40% acceptance rate).

Furthermore, we received 22 short paper submissions. Each submission was reviewed by three members from the PROFES Program Committee. Based on the reviews and overall assessments, 14 short papers were accepted for presentation at the conference and for inclusion in the proceedings.

The topics addressed in this year's papers indicate that SPI is still a vibrant research discipline, but is also of high interest for industry. Several papers report on case studies or SPI-related experience gained in industry.

The papers addressed the following topics:

- Agile Development
- Decision-Making
- Development Practices and Issues
- Product Planning
- Project Management

Since the beginning of the PROFES conference series, the purpose has been to highlight the most recent findings and novel results in the area of process improvement. We were proud to have with Günther Ruhe (University of Calgary) and Ville Tikka (Wecolve), two renowned keynote speakers from research and industry at the 2014 edition of PROFES. Furthermore, the PROFES Doctoral Symposium now has established its place in the community. In addition, PROFES provided tutorials addressing themes relevant for industry.

We are thankful for the opportunity to have served as chairs for this conference. The Program Committee members and reviewers provided excellent support in reviewing the papers. We are also grateful to the authors, presenters, and session chairs for their time and effort in making PROFES 2014 a success.

Particular thanks go to the keynote speakers for giving their insightful speeches at the conference. We would also like to thank the doctoral symposium chair Maria Paasivaara (Aalto University), the tutorial chair Fabian Fagerholm (University of Helsinki, Finland), and the local arrangements chair Simo Mäkinen. Last but not least, we would like to thank our social media chairs Daniel Graziotin (Free University of Bozen-Bolzano) and Daniel Méndez Fernández (Technische Universität München), the publicity chair Kari Liukkunen (University of Oulu), the website chair Max Pagels (University of Helsinki), and the head of the conference secretariat Mary-Ann Wikström (Aalto University).

October 2014

Andreas Jedlitschka
Pasi Kuvaja
Marco Kuhrmann
Tomi Männistö
Jürgen Münch
Mikko Raatikainen

Organization

General Chair

Jürgen Münch   University of Helsinki, Finland
Tomi Männistö   University of Helsinki, Finland

Program Co-chairs

Andreas Jedlitschka   Fraunhofer IESE, Germany
Pasi Kuvaja   University of Oulu, Finland

Short Papers and Posters Chair

Marco Kuhrmann   University of Southern Denmark, Denmark

Tutorial Chair

Fabian Fagerholm   University of Helsinki, Finland

Doctoral Symposium Chair

Maria Paasivaara   Aalto University, Finland

Proceedings Chair

Mikko Raatikainen   Aalto University, Finland

Local Arrangements Chair

Simo Mäkinen   University of Helsinki, Finland

Publicity Chair

Kari Liukkunen   University of Oulu, Finland

Social Media Chair

Daniel Graziotin   Free University of Bozen-Bolzano, Italy
Daniel Méndez Fernández   Technische Universität München, Germany

Website Chair

Max Pagels   University of Helsinki, Finland

Head of Conference Secretariat

Mary-Ann Wikström   Aalto University, Finland

Program Committee

Silvia Abrahão   Universitat Politècnica de València, Spain
Sousuke Amasaki   Okayama Prefectural University, Japan
Maria Teresa Baldassarre   University of Bari, Italy
Andreas Birk   SWPM, Germany
Luigi Buglione   Engineering.IT/ETS Montréal, Canada
Gerardo Canfora   University of Sannio, Italy
Marcus Ciolkowski   QAware GmbH, Germany
Maya Daneva   University of Twente, The Netherlands
Oscar Dieste   Universidad Politécnica de Madrid, Spain
Tore Dybå   SINTEF/University of Oslo, Norway
Christof Ebert   Vector, Germany
Davide Falessi   Fraunhofer Center Experimental Software
                                      Engineering Maryland, USA
Xavier Franch   Universitat Politècnica de Catalunya, Spain
Daniel Graziotin   Free University of Bozen-Bolzano, Italy
Noriko Hanakawa   Hannan University, Japan
Jens Heidrich   Fraunhofer IESE, Germany
Yoshiki Higo   Osaka University, Japan
Frank Houdek   Daimler, Germany
Martin Höst   Lund University, Sweden
Hajimu Iida   Nara Institute of Science and Technology
                                      (NAIST), Japan
Janne Järvinen   F-Secure, Finland
Petri Kettunen   University of Helsinki, Finland
Ricardo Jorge Machado   Universidade do Minho, Portugal
Lech Madeyski   Wroclaw University of Technology, Poland
Vladimir Mandic   University of Novi Sad, Serbia
Kenichi Matsumoto   Nara Institute of Science and Technology
                                      (NAIST), Japan
Sebastian Meyer   Leibniz Universität Hannover, Germany
Maurizio Morisio   Politecnico di Torino, Italy
Daniel Méndez Fernández   Technical University Munich, Germany
Makoto Nonaka   Toyo University, Japan
Paolo Panaroni   INTECS, Italy
Oscar Pastor   Universitat Politècnica de València, Spain

Dietmar Pfahl   University of Tartu, Estonia
Reinhold Plösch   Johannes Kepler University Linz, Austria
Daniel Rodriguez   Universidad de Alcalá, Spain
Barbara Russo   Free University of Bozen-Bolzano, Italy
Klaus Schmid   University of Hildesheim, Germany
Kurt Schneider   Leibniz Universität Hannover, Germany
Michael Stupperich   Daimler, Germany
Marco Torchiano   Politecnico di Torino, Italy
Guilherme Travassos   COPPE/UFRJ, Brazil
Adam Trendowicz   Fraunhofer IESE, Germany
Burak Turhan   University of Oulu, Finland
Sira Vegas   Universidad Politécnica de Madrid, Spain
Stefan Wagner   University of Stuttgart, Germany
Hironori Washizaki   Waseda University, Japan

Additional Reviewers

Asim Abdulkhaleq   University of Stuttgart, Germany
Carmine Giardino   Free University of Bozen-Bolzano, Italy
Javier Gonzalez-Huerta   Universitat Politècnica de València, Spain
Erica Janke   University of Applied Sciences Neu-Ulm,
                            Germany
Ana Lima   Instituto Politécnico de Viana do Castelo,
                            Portugal
Lucy Ellen Lwakatare   University of Oulu, Finland
Marta López Fernández   Universidad Complutense de Madrid, Spain
Paula Monteiro   Instituto Politécnico de Viana do Castelo,
                            Portugal
Jasmin Ramadani   University of Stuttgart, Germany
Juliana Teixeira   Instituto Politécnico de Viana do Castelo,
                            Portugal
Xiaofeng Wang   Free University of Bozen-Bolzano, Italy

Table of Contents

Product Planning

Project Management

Short Papers

A Comparative Study of Testers' Motivation in Traditional and Agile Software Development

Anca Deak

Department of Computer Science
Norwegian University of Science and Technology Trondheim, Norway
deak@idi.ntnu.no

Abstract. The future software engineers looking for positions in the software industry tend to lean towards software development/coding rather than software testing. Our study investigates what factors cause software testing professionals working both in agile and traditional methodologies, to choose and remain in this career path. Using a qualitative survey among software development companies we retrieve information about the difference between the traditional and agile testers. In addition we identify information about the motivating and de-motivating factors in current testing practices. The results could help the companies in their recruiting processes, in the transition from traditional to agile within a company and in motivating their testers, which will lead to better job satisfaction and productivity.

Keywords: software testing, agile, waterfall, motivation, testers, human factors.

1   Introduction

The aim of this paper is to investigate the motivational factors impacting a software tester, observing them from the perspective of working methodology and comparing them with the existing results developed for the software engineer category. Motivation has been repeatedly cited as an important factor in productivity, quality and the successful delivery of a project within budget and time constraints [1] with several motivation theory emphasizing the importance of employee motivation such as Herzberg [2] and Mayo [3]. In this study we are looking at the positive and negative factors which influence professional software testers' motivation when working in traditional and agile methodologies. The subject of motivation within software engineers was the scope of an extensive systematic literature review performed by Beecham et al. [4] and updated by Franca et al. [5]. The two studies provided us with groups of motivators and de-motivators for a software engineer, as they were identified in their literature reviews.

Although there is extensive work on motivation in IT personnel [6] and on motivation agile teams [7] and [8], to our knowledge there is a lack of research focusing specifically on motivation in software testing. A tester's position can be similar to a software engineer, but there is a particularity of the testing jobs which is

A. Jedlitschka et al. (Eds.): PROFES 2014, LNCS 8892, pp. 1–16, 2014.

prone to situations where discussions or diplomacy might be required. The results of a survey looking at the human factors which have a negative influence on real practice of software testing in software companies in Spain identified the following factors: instability of testers positions (48 %), lack of attractiveness of testing (48 %) and poor career development for testers (41,7 %), [9]. The study advises us to seriously take into consideration these factors due to the high percentage of respondents. The human and social aspects of working in testing, or inside a testing team, as well as the attitude towards the testing team in a company, were studied from the testers' perspective in a case study by Shah and Harrold [10]. These lead us to believe that it is worthwhile to make specific investigations about motivation among software testers. The research will be guided by the investigation of these factors, their relationships and effects on job outcomes.

While there is a documented lack of interest in choosing and pursuing a testing career [11] with development positions seen as more rewarding from career and financial perspective, there is still little research on why professional software testers choose to remain in their position. Our research is focusing on retrieving the motivation for those who chose to remain in software testing as a profession, while observing them in two different working environments, the agile and traditional settings. The final results will be compared to the factors in [4] and [5], which will enable us to observe if there are specific motivational factors for a software tester. With the framework of these criteria in mind we retrieved information about the difference between the traditional and agile testers, which could help the companies in their recruiting processes or in the transition from traditional to agile within a company. The study can also provide recommendations to companies and management for motivating the testing personal, which will lead to a better job satisfaction, productivity and quality of the developed product.

The rest of the paper is organized as follows: Section 2 presents the related research while the research question and methods used are described in Section 3 together with the research design and data collection process. In Section 4 we described and examined the results, while in Section 5 we examine the findings of the study and discuss the implications and the future work for this research.

2   Research Context

2.1   Traditional and Agile Testing

Software testing is a process through which the functionality of a software program is assessed during the development process. The investigation conducted for the assessment will focus both on verification and validation [12]. During the verification, the testers ensure that the software correctly implements a specific function and otherwise formulated, that it answers the question: are we building the product right? Validation ensures that the software has been built in order to satisfy customer's requirements. Validation answers the question: are we building the right product? The software testing process is also used to evaluate the nonfunctional quality of a system, by assessing aspects such as performance, security or usability.

For the traditional methodology, the software development lifecycle is constructed from a sequential set of stages: starting with a feasibility study at the top level and finishing with the implementation of the product. One trait of this methodology is the placing of testing towards the end of the project life cycle, which leads to defects being discovered close to the production deployment stage. In the requirement stage, the software tester can check if the requirements are according to the client's wishes, while during the design phase, the tester can verify if the design document covers all the requirements and review the design document from the architecture perspective. In the coding phase the testing team can execute test cases, as well as generating testing data. In the testing stage running the system test cases can verify whether the system operates according to the stated requirements. Once the product reaches the maintenance stage, the tester can retest new fixes and patches and afterwards use regression testing to ensure that the new changes do not impact functionality in an unintended manner.

In an Agile Environment there would be more emphasis on collaboration and face to face interaction. The testers will be involved earlier into the development process and the development team will have write unit tests first and then code, rather than code first and then create a test plan which tends to occur in traditional environments. Members of an agile team are expected to be cross-functional so they may have to write code, do requirements elicitation or work closely with the customer. No QA/Testing department will be present and the person involved in the testing activities will be seen as "a team member who has most testing experience" rather than "a tester".

2.2 Studies on Testing Practice

Software testing and industrial surveys of testing practices such as [13] and [14] have been central themes in the specialized literature. Brain and Labiche [15] have emphasized the importance of testing research in an industrial setting, by arguing that the human influence and experience are important factors to be considered when performing testing related research and that the most applicable results are the ones obtained by observing professional testers at work.

A certain ad-hoc practice was underlined in [14], while the importance of experience and domain knowledge in testing was emphasized by Beer and Ramler [16]. Their multiple-case study, covering three industrial software projects, classified two categories of experience: experience in testing and experience with the product domain. Having a degree of experience in software testing proved to be useful for those involved in general management of the testing and particularly for those working with test automation. Product domain knowledge also proved valuable when working with test case design, planning regression testing and requirement's engineering. Those results reinforced Turley and Bieman's conclusion that experience is a valued asset for software engineers [17], and those of the ethnographic study conducted by Martin et al. [18] on testing processes and practices in a small start-up company. The Martin et al. [18] study, which focused on integration and acceptance testing done in the company, showed that testers working in contexts where requirements were not defined in detail and without any strict processes, needed understanding of the business and experience in the domain and techniques that were used to test the product. In addition, testers were also required to possess good skills in test automation.

The perceptions of software testing were in the focus of an industrial survey conducted by Causevic et al. [19] and in that of the empirical study of a testing team in a vendor organization conducted by Shah, Harrold and Sinha [20]. The survey conducted by Causevic et al. [19], which uses both qualitative and quantitative methods, organized the results into four distinct categories: safety-criticality, agility, distribution of development and application domain. Their findings revealed the discrepancies observed between the current practices and the perceptions of respondents which could prove beneficial in shaping future research on software testing. One notable result from the quantitative analysis on satisfaction level of practitioners is related to Test Driven Development (TDD), which registered the most significant difference between the preferred practice and the current practice.

Among the findings of the empirical study conducted by Shah, Harrold and Sinha [20], is the enthusiasm showed by the testers about their job and their positive attitude toward testing, which is the opposite of the common attitude towards testing: where a software development job is preferred over a testing one. A desire for innovation and a high value among the testers were also observed in the same study. In addition, the results of this study show that the quality of testing is affected by motivation of testers and emphasizes the need for appreciating testers' efforts. Taipale and Smolander conducted a qualitative study [21], which explored the software-testing practices and suggested improvements in this process based on the knowledge acquired during their study. Their improvement proposition include adjusting testing according to the business orientation of the company, enhanced testability of software components, efficient communication, early involvement of testers and increased interaction between developers and testers.

2.3   Existing Motivation Models in Software Engineering

Motivation in Software Engineering was the scope of a systematic literature review conducted by Beecham et al. [4], in which 92 papers published between 1980 and June 2006 were analyzed. The result of this study provided 16 characteristics of the software engineer together with 21 motivators and 15 de-motivators identified in the literature, which are available in the Appendix. Another, subsequent study by Franca et al. [5] extended and updated this results by analyzing 53 papers published between March 2006 to August 2010. As a result, another 8 additional motivators were identified: team quality, creativity/innovation, fun, professionalism, having an ideology, non-financial benefits, penalty policies and good relationship with users/customer, as well as a new de-motivator: task complexity. The study also shows that two of the motivators discovered in [4] were no longer present: appropriate working conditions and sufficient resources. The change noticed in the motivators and de-motivators also illustrates the evolving nature in the motivation of software engineers and this is expected to change even more as the software engineering field is evolving.

Most of the studies involved in these two literature reviews were quantitative survey studies and they provided important insights into characterizing the factors and results related to motivation. One limitation of the mentioned studies, which we need to consider, is that the majority of the studies are referring to the job itself as being the main motivational factor. Since the title of software engineer can contain multiple roles and responsibilities which can greatly vary from one position to another, more information about the job that motivates the software engineer is required. Our study focuses on software testers, who are often considered as software engineers in job title terminology, but have different responsibilities than developers. Based on the results presented in systematic literature review conducted by Beecham et al. [4], same group of authors have studied different models of motivation and proposed a new model which was compared with the previous models and refined based on this comparison in Sharp et al. [22]. A systematic review of motivators in the agile context conducted by de O. Melo et al. [23], highlights differences between the overall view of motivation in software development and the motivation in an agile context. The study, which in addition includes three case studies in agile companies, suggests that certain motivators have an increased importance in agile teams and provides new motivators. The same study also claims that motivation seems to be higher for agile development teams which were previously exposed to other working methods.

3   Research Method

The scope of this paper is to investigate the motivational factors impacting a software tester, observing them from the perspective of traditional and agile working methodology and comparing them with data analyzed for the software engineer category. These objectives are reflected by the following research question:

- **RQ**: *How do motivational and de-motivational factors for software testers differ in agile environments versus traditional type environments?*

3.1   Survey Design

The population of our study is made by software testing professionals with testing experience. In the software testers' category we will refer to all software engineers who have software testing as their main job responsibility. In addition, we discussed with few developers who were involved with testing as part of their responsibilities.

A total of 26 participants were interviewed from six companies, from which 13 interviews were performed in agile working teams, while the other 13 interviews occurred in teams following the traditional development methodology. The interviewees included testers and testing managers who face the daily problems of software testing activities. In company F we talked with members of two teams involved in testing activities, one agile working team and one team following the traditional development methodology. The companies and interviewees are described in Table 1.

During the interviews we used a semi-structured guideline and open questions to encourage the respondents to provide us with their own reflections and use their own terms. The interview guideline included both closed questions, for which responses will be easier to analyze and compare, and open questions which will allow the participants to point out issues that were not mentioned in the closed-form questions. The open questions were themes' based and concerned problems of testing, collaboration within their team and relationships with fellow colleagues. In addition we enquired about positive and negative aspects of their daily activities, working environment, schedules and the influence of the business domain orientation. In parallel with this process we will check if all the motivators and de-motivators of software engineers present in literature can be applied for software testers as well. The same set of questions will enable us to see if there is a difference in the priority of these motivators and de-motivators between traditional and agile testers and for testers in relation to the more general category of software engineers.

Table 1. Companies and interviewees

Company	Business	Size	Methodology	Interviewees
A	Software producer & service provider	medium international	Agile, TDD	Testing manager(1) Tester (2) Developer (1)
B	Software producer & testing provider	medium international	Agile, Scrum	Testing manager(1) Tester (2)
C	Software producer	large national	Traditional	Section manager (1) Testing manager (1) Tester (2)
D	Software producer	large international	Traditional	Section manager (1) Testing manager (2) Tester (3)
E	Software producer	medium international	Agile	Testing manager (1) Tester (1) Developer (1)
F	Software producer	large international	Agile/Traditional	Testing manager(1) Tester (3) Developer (2)

The duration of the interviews varied between 30 minutes and 90 minutes, and they were performed on the premises of each company, in quiet meeting rooms where each participant was interviewed individually. During the interviews the respondents were encouraged to express their opinions freely, by guaranteeing their anonymity and assuring them that the records will be accessible only to the researchers involved in this study. As recommended by Myers and Newman [24], we used a mirroring technique in questions and answers in order to encourage the respondents to share their stories. During the interviews we asked the participants to talk about both current events and to reflect retrospectively on previous scenarios. All interviews were recorded and transcribed, and the transcription was sent to each participant for final checking and approval. Notes were also taken with the prominent issues for each interview. The transcribed interviews were coded in several rounds. All data has been anonymised, which included changing names and removing unnecessary details.

Starting the process of analyzing the research data available, we first identified the segments of text relevant to the research question and discarded those having no relation to it. Afterwards, we proceeded with the coding phase and labeled each segment (or sub-segment) by means of one or more easily recognizable terms or categories, using a software tool designed for qualitative analysis (NVivo 10). The codes were analyzed and similar codes were aggregated into more general codes in order to reduce the number of codes utilized and retrieve the emerging categories. The transcripts were revisited several times, and the coding process was performed in repeated rounds and the results were reviewed and discussed with my senior colleagues. Each category and code can be linked to quotations from the interviews and these are used to strengthen and enhance the results. The categories were derived based on the results provided in the studies by Beecham et al. [4] and [5] as a model for constructing a list of motivators and de-motivators for software testers. Two tables, one combining the de-motivators, and another one combining the motivators from both studies and the ones emerging from our study, are available in the Appendix.

4   Results and Discussion

In this section we present and describe the concepts for negative and positive factors, and we present a comparison between these factors based on the working methodology for traditional and agile testers.

4.1   Concepts for Negative Factors

In Table 2 we can observe the relationship between codes and concepts for negative factors derived from the study after the qualitative analyze process. The negative factors are presented in descending order starting from the one who was most frequently mentioned in the interviews:

Table 2. Relationships between codes and concepts for negative factors

Concepts	Codes linked to concept
Negative factors	
Lack of influence and recognition	late involvement in the project, testing is underestimated in the company, afraid of opening defects, no control over the schedule
Unhappy with management	insufficient resources, unrelated tasks
Technical issues (NEW)	versioning, insufficient number of test environments, poor quality, integration issues with simulators
Lack of organization	lack of clear processes, tasks, redundant meetings
Time pressure (NEW)	squeeze, long days, short periods, overloaded schedule
Boredom	routine, repetitive tasks, unchallenging work
Poor relationships with developers	bugs related friction, stereotypic view of testing, slow defect fix rate, late changes to the code
Working environment issues	colleagues with no social antenna, open plan landscape related issues

Concept - Lack of influence and recognition
The concept which appeared most often as a factor with negative impact was the **lack of influence and recognition.** Under this concept we gathered the segments referring to the irregular working flow, and lack of control over an unstable schedule. Testers' late involvements in the development cycle, together with the struggle for recognition are also frequently cited by the participants *"When I as a tester or test manager enter a project too late in the process to get a reasonable contribution to the quality with the testing."* (Tester, Company C). When the focus of testing activities is more on testing issues, like retesting defects, rather than testing the product or requirement, testers are not provided with a sense of accomplishment, but rather with a frustration of not performing their real job. Under the same **no sense of recognition** concept we aggregated the worries for an unattractive career path development, with a low likelihood of promotion, in comparison with other roles, such as the ones for developers. *"The developing projects and the daily operations have to realize how important software testing is. The testing area has to be lifted up as an important part of the company's work."* (Testing Manager, Company C)

Concept - Unhappy with management
The second most mentioned concept addresses participants' dissatisfaction with the management related policies, the unrealistic schedules and the scarcity of resources. An unsupportive management can lead to tester being reluctant when they need to log in new defects: *"testers use a lot of time, they are afraid of opening defects".* (Testing Manager, Company D) Opening a critical bug can be a stressful scenario even for an experienced tester, it can lead to frictions with the fellow developers or with conflicts with the management: *"I found bugs which stopped or hold a release, which on one hand is a good thing, because if the bug will have go into production it will have created serious problems, but is also a little bit like putting your reputation in line. The release is stopped because of you."* (Tester, Company A) Raising defects which prove to be invalid can be detrimental for a tester but it is a natural part of his or her career but can lead to a lack of respect from the developers or pressure from managers.

Concept - Technical issues
Technical issues within testing context are referring to problems with testing tools, development environments or a weak infrastructure. An insufficient number of test environments, poor quality or insufficient fidelity to the actual system being tested, together with integration party with 3rd party tools or simulators were mentioned as hindering factors of a technical nature. *"It takes a lot of time to get the tests started, not everything works correctly, setting up an environment and also installing the software on our test servers."* (Tester, Company B). In some companies the participants complained about the weak infrastructure which was proving to be the root cause in many false defects and required time and effort in investigations. *"My main frustration is that we don't have good enough tools to do our work and we have to use tools that make our work a lot more difficult than it should be."* (Developer, Company F)

Concept – Lack of organization
The interviewees were not pleased with the continuously changing plans or bad planning from the beginning. In addition some of the participants were having an increasing number of tasks which were not related with testing or outside their focus

area. *"We fill a lot of time until we don't have any left space, but often we want to update the plan."* (Tester, Company F). Participants related the **lack of organization** or carefully planning as a strong source for the repeating time pressure problem for members of the testing team. A high number of meetings which were considered redundant or irrelevant to their work tasks were also mentioned as a time consuming negative factor.

Concept - Time pressure
Another concept which appears often as a factor with negative impact was the **time pressure** associated with testing execution. Traditional working teams often delay testing until the end of projects, squeezing it in the process. Unfortunately, projects often fall behind schedule, so the testing teams need to compress and sacrifice the activities due to their shrinking time frame. *"I've been in this business for many years and testing is at the end of this lifecycle, and always pressed to so short periods, long days, and shortcuts. It's always like that."* (Testing Manager, Company D). Testing time is sacrificed to recover the delays in other processes and by doing so there is often a compromise on the quality of the delivered product. *"I don't like that we are the last link in the chain, and we don't always get the time that was promised in the beginning. Give us more time to finish our testing and do it properly."* (Tester, Company D).

The concept appears also in the interview with testers from agile teams where the testing is occasionally facing similar time pressure. The company has sprints with unbreakable deadlines, but since the first half is allocated to test case designs, issues are often discovered late in the sprint. This situation gives little time to fix the issues. *"Sometimes it's difficult to plan because they don't really know when they are ready. They want testing done immediately as they are ready, but they themselves don't really know when they are ready."* (Tester, Company A)

Concept - Boredom
Some of the participants mentioned the routine of some testing activities and the feeling of **boredom** associated with maintenance testing. *"Everything is routine, there is no surprises after the system is in production"* (Testing Manager, Company D)

Concept - Poor relationships with developers
The second most mentioned concept is the **relationship between testers and developers**, which can be problematic at times. Most of these frictions results from discussions related to bugs. *"I do remember having discussions about bugs: Is it really a bug or is it really important enough to be included in the release."* (Tester, Company A). Another factor quoted by many participants was the stereotypic view of testing by the developers, *"the classical view that they are developing and finally we are testing and then it's coming back with us saying <<that is not good, that is not good>>"* (Testing Manager, Company A).

Two testers from different companies described their co-workers' view of testing as *"a necessary evil"*. The slow defect fix rate and developers making unannounced late changes to code were also mentioned as a factor of concern and conflict between developers and testers. *"It's a lot of things, challenges that take time, sometimes it can take time to get environments, sometimes you raise bugs and they don't take them quickly enough"* (Testing Manager, Company D)

Concept - Working environment issues
Several participants complained about working in open space landscape which is considered noisy due to the nature of the office design but also due to colleagues with no social antenna. *"When it comes to office conditions it can be quite noisy in this open landscape thing."* (Tester, Company F)

4.2   Concepts for Positive Factors

The relationship between codes and concepts for positive factors derived from the study are presented in Table 3. The positive factors are presented in descending order starting from the one which was most frequently mentioned in the interviews.

Table 3. Relationships between codes and concepts for positives factors

Concepts	Codes linked to concept
Positive factors	
Enjoy challenges (NEW)	Enjoy challenging yourself, every day you never know what's coming up, like the chaos, need challenges
Focus for improving the quality (NEW)	finding bugs, to investigate, making things better, personal goal on improving the quality
Variety of work	work variation, combine testing and programming,
Recognition	ensure that testing tasks are important in the company, send testers to courses and conferences, get the support I need to a good job
Good management	good communication in the team, with developers, enough resources
Technically challenging work	technically challenging work

Concept - Enjoy challenges
Most of the interviewed participants **enjoyed challenges** represented by the testing activities, challenging themselves or simply thriving on the chaos which can sometimes accompany the daily activities of a tester. *"When I perform my test and it works, I'm thinking: Am I doing something wrong? Is the test doing what it's supposed to? When it fails, I'm also thinking: Is it really doing things correctly?"* (Tester, Company A) and *"There is always something new, new challenges towards different test scenarios."* (Tester, Company D)

Concept - Focus for improving the quality
The second most occurring concept related to testers **passion for improving the quality** of the software, the pleasure in investigating and finding defects which will lead to a better product. *"I do have a passion for improving the quality and finding defects. And there I have learned that I have different focus than the developers, maybe the right focus for testing. I'm happy when I find bugs. Of course, I'm also happy when things are working."* (Tester, Company A)

Concept - Variety of work
On several occasions the concept of **variety of work** was mentioned and it referred to being included in the testing activities associated with the whole development cycle, not just a specific phase. Another contribution to the variety was considered having a combination of programming and testing tasks as part of job responsibilities. *"The biggest factor for me is that you do different things, it's very varied and you get to see the whole picture. You can participate from the start of a project to the end doing various things, that's the biggest thing for me."* (Tester, Company B)

Concept – Recognition
The concept of recognition included awarness of testing importance in the company both from management and developmet teams as well as positive feedback received from developers in relation to discovering and fixing bugs. *"When we heard feedback from engineers, when we hear they say <<thank you, this test helped us to pick something that is wrong>>"* (Tester, Company F) Under the same category we included participants expresing the pride they experience by working in a company known for delivering high-end products. *"I believe I work in a company that is delivering high end embedded software for the worldwide. I want to make sure that the software we deliver has high quality. "* (Testing Manager, Company E)

Concept - Good management
Under the concept **Good management** we aggregated all the positive references to relations and communication with the managers, between the testers and with developers. *"I think is important to be on good terms with the developers; if they are having some Agile approach, you as a tester or test manager will get invited to their daily Scrum, so you get a feel for the modules they are struggling with and so on. It can help you prioritize, when you start to test."* (Testing Manager, Company D)

Concept - Technically challenging work
Another positive concept **Technically challenging work** was associated with the participants need to have allocated tasks reflecting their technical competencies. *"The most interesting thing that you can have is interesting technology to work with."* (Developer, Company D)

If we look at the list of concepts from which we derived the factors available in Table 4 and Table 5, we see that while both types of testers enjoy having a degree of variety in their work, the lack of influence and recognition is a major negative factor for most of the participants involved in this study. If we compare the concepts emerging from this study with the list of de-motivators and motivators available in the Appendix we noticed that several new factors emerged from our study: **Time pressure** and **Technical issues** within testing context for the negative factors. On the positive side we identified new factors **Enjoy challenges** and **Focus for improving the quality**. All these concepts are specific to the nature of testing activities with **Technical issues** within testing context involving large quantities of effort and time invested in items which should be readily available at the beginning of testing. The **Time pressure** concept is referring to the tendency of testing time to shrink from the original estimate until the actual execution period is taking place.

Table 4 and Table 5 show a comparison of positive and negative factors between the testers from the two groups, based on the number of respondents mentioning these factors. If we look at how the factors are distributed among traditional and agile testers, we easily observe a higher time pressure factor for the traditional testers, while the Lack of organization tends to score higher in the agile teams. The lack of influence and recognition is present in both type of working environments with the traditional teams having a slightly higher occurrence. When discussing with general managers in companies working in the traditional way, they signaled several problems with the testing position, such as a struggle for recognition as a valuable team and also frustration coming from the lack of influence when suggesting recommendation or requests related to their working activities. Whatever methodology is followed, all the participant companies are interested in providing Product Quality. What differs from traditional to agile is that testing is started early in the sprint and the emphasis on testing has improved with practices such as TDD.

Table 4. Positive factors for traditional and agile testers grouped by methodology

Positives factors group by methodology	Agile	Traditional	Total
Enjoy challenges	3	8	11
Focus for improving the quality	7	4	11
Variety of work	6	5	11
Recognition	4	5	9
Good management	2	5	7
Technically challenging work	3	3	6

Table 5. Negative factors for traditional and agile testers grouped by methodology

Negatives factors	Agile	Traditional	Total
Lack of influence and recognition	9	12	21
Unhappy with management	9	10	19
Technical issues	9	7	16
Lack of organization	8	5	13
Time pressure	3	10	13
Boredom	7	5	12
Poor relationships with developers	5	2	7
Working environment issues	1	4	5

Testers working in Agile do not belong to a separate testing group, but work within the development team. They consider testing an ongoing process that happens throughout the development process, not just something that happens in a separate phase after development is done. Another point is that testing is done by the whole team, rather than just by testers and the relationship between testers and non-testers tends to be collaborative rather than adversarial. It was interesting to notice that more agile testers were unhappy about their relationship with developers since testers get more respect on agile teams where they are seen as colleagues, and are involved much earlier in the process, making it easier to ensure a system is produced that's easy to test. It might be related to a situation where a company applies customized version of agile methods "for good organizational reasons" [18]. Participants form both categories complained about the heavy load and unrealistic schedules which is in concordance with earlier research results [6].

Both categories of testers face the time pressure issue and although the initial model proposed by Beecham includes stress as a strong de-motivational factor, we feel that time pressure is such a specific and persistent problem during testing activities that we can assign it a separate category. A complete list of motivating and de-motivating factors for software testers, including the ones proposed during this study are available in the Appendix.

Limitations and Threats to Validity
The results of our study should be treated with some caution since there are other factors which may impact the motivation of a tester such as the organization structure, internal policies and processes. In addition, motivation can be influence by human factors such as personality types [25], and individual characteristics such as age [26]. In order to avoid the threats to validity presented by Robson [27] in this kind of research, we ensured observer triangulation by having the data analyzed by three researchers. In addition, the collected data and the results of this study were compared with our earlier quantitative study [28], which allowed us to apply both data and method triangulation. We are aware that the low number of participants is a limitation and given the high number of variables playing an important role in the survey, the results of this study should be considered as preliminary, but since the focus was on depth instead of breadth we still think that the participants provided a typical sample giving us with a lot of inputs and perspective. Since increasing the number of participants could reveal more details or strengthen the conclusion of this study, our plan is to further expand our research by engaging with other companies and increase the total number of interviewees. A longitudinal study may provide further insights into the motivational and de-motivation factors of software testing personal. Our qualitative analysis spanned across six companies using traditional and agile methodologies, performing functional and non-functional testing, which could give better generalizability than performing interviews in just one company [24].

5   Conclusion and Further Work

The extensive research about motivation in software engineering has added to the body of knowledge characterizing the factors behind the motivation at the workplace. In this study, we looked at a specific branch of software engineering, namely software testing and we presented the main results of a qualitative study about motivation of testers in four software development companies.

We provided a set of factors with negative and positive influence on the daily activities of software testers and added additional categories to the ones already presented and published in the software engineering world. We look at the differences between testers working in traditional and agile development and noticed a higher degree of stress and a positive approach towards the challenges of testing activities for those engaged in the waterfall approaches, while the agile testers, although expressing more problems in communication with developers seemed to be better integrated into their teams. To further our research we plan to extend this study by involving more companies and in addition to look into the characteristics of testers and the relationships with their fellow coworkers.

References

1. DeMarco, T., Lister, T.: Peopleware: Productive Projects and Teams. Dorset House (1999)
2. Herzberg, F.: One More Time: How Do You Motivate Employees. Harv. Bus. Rev. 46, 53–62 (1968)
3. Mayo, E.: The social problems of an industrial civilization. Routledge & Kegan Paul, London (1949)
4. Beecham, S., Baddoo, N., Hall, T., Robinson, H., Sharp, H.: Motivation in Software Engineering: A systematic literature review. Inf. Softw. Technol. 50, 860–878 (2008)
5. Franca, A.C.C., Gouveia, T.B., Santos, P.C.F., Santana, C.A., da Silva, F.Q.B.: Motivation in software engineering: A systematic review update. In: 15th Annual Conf. on Evaluation & Assessment in Softw. Eng. (EASE 2011), pp. 154–163. IET (2011)
6. Boehm, B.W.: Software Engineering Economics. Prentice Hall (1981)
7. Whitworth, E., Biddle, R.: Motivation and Cohesion in Agile Teams. In: Concas, G., Damiani, E., Scotto, M., Succi, G. (eds.) XP 2007. LNCS, vol. 4536, pp. 62–69. Springer, Heidelberg (2007)
8. McHugh, O., Conboy, K., Lang, M.: Using Agile Practices to Influence Motivation within IT Project Teams. Scand. J. Inf. Syst. 23 (2011)
9. Fernández-sanz, L., Villalba, M.T., Hilera, J.R., Lacuesta, R.: Factors with Negative Influence on Software Testing Practice in Spain: A Survey 2 Analysis of Testing Practices in Organizations, pp. 1–12
10. Shah, H., Harrold, M.J.: Studying human and social aspects of testing in a service-based software company. In: Proceedings of the 2010 ICSE Workshop on Cooperative and Human Aspects of Software Engineering, CHASE 2010, pp. 102–108. ACM Press, New York (2010)
11. Deak, A., Stålhane, T., Cruzes, D.: Factors Influencing the Choice of a Career in Software Testing among Norwegian Students. In: Software Engineering, p. 796. ACTA Press, Calgary (2013)
12. Boehm, B.W.: Verifying and validating software requirements and design specifications. IEEE Softw. 1, 75–88 (1984)
13. Grindal, M., Offutt, J., Mellin, J.: On the Testing Maturity of Software Producing Organizations. In: Test. Acad. Ind. Conf. Pract. Res. Tech. (TAIC PART 2006), pp. 171–180 (2006)
14. Runeson, P., Andersson, C., Host, M.: Test processes in software product evolution: a qualitative survey on the state of practice. J. Softw. Maint. Evol. Res. Pract. 15, 41–59 (2003)
15. Briand, L., Labiche, Y.: Empirical studies of software testing techniques. ACM SIGSOFT Softw. Eng. Notes. 29, 1 (2004)
16. Beer, A., Ramler, R.: The Role of Experience in Software Testing Practice. In: 2008 34th Euromicro Conf. Softw. Eng. and Advanced Applications, pp. 258–265. IEEE (2008)
17. Turley, R.T., Bieman, J.M.: Competencies of exceptional and nonexceptional software engineers. J. Syst. Softw. 28, 19–38 (1995)
18. Martin, D., Rooksby, J., Rouncefield, M., Sommerville, I.: "Good" Organisational Reasons for "Bad" Software Testing: An Ethnographic Study of Testing in a Small Software Company. In: 29th Int. Conf. Softw. Eng. (ICSE 2007), pp. 602–611. IEEE (2007)
19. Causevic, A., Sundmark, D., Punnekkat, S.: An Industrial Survey on Contemporary Aspects of Software Testing. In: 2010 Third International Conference on Software Testing, Verification and Validation, pp. 393–401. IEEE (2010)

20. Shah, H., Harrold, M.J., Sinha, S.: Global software testing under deadline pressure: Vendor-side experiences. Inf. Softw. Technol. 56, 6–19 (2014)
21. Taipale, O., Smolander, K.: Improving software testing by observing practice. In: Proc. 2006 ACM/IEEE Int. Symp. Int. Symp. Empir. Softw. Eng., ISESE 2006, p. 262 (2006)
22. Sharp, H., Baddoo, N., Beecham, S., Hall, T., Robinson, H.: Models of motivation in software engineering. Inf. Softw. Technol. 51, 219–233 (2009)
23. De, O., Melo, C., Santana, C., Kon, F.: Developers Motivation in Agile Teams. In: 2012 38th Euromicro Conf. Softw. Eng. Adv. Appl., pp. 376–383 (2012)
24. Myers, M.D., Newman, M.: The qualitative interview in IS research: Examining the craft. Inf. Organ. 17, 2–26 (2007)
25. Kanij, T., Merkel, R., Grundy, J.: An empirical study of the effects of personality on software testing. In: 2013 26th Int. Conf. Softw. Eng. Educ. Train., pp. 239–248 (2013)
26. Boumans, N.P.G., de Jong, H.J., Janssen, S.M.: Age-Differences in Work Motivation and Job Satisfaction. The Influence of Age on the Relationships between Work Characteristics and Workers' Outcomes. Int. J. Aging Hum. Dev. 73, 331–350 (2011)
27. Robson, C.: Real World Research, 2nd edn. Blackwell Publ., Malden (2002)
28. Deak, A., Stalhane, T.: Organization of Testing Activities in Norwegian Software Companies. In: 2013 IEEE Sixth International Conference on Software Testing, Verification and Validation Workshops, pp. 102–107. IEEE (2013)

Appendix

Table 6. List of de-motivating factors from previous work

Nr.	De-motivating factors for Software Testers
Proposing study Beecham et al.	
1	Stress
2	Inequity
3	Interesting work going to other parties
4	Unfair reward system
5	Lack of promotion opportunities
6	Poor communication
7	Uncompetitive pay/unpaid overtime
8	Unrealistic goals/phony deadlines
9	Bad relationship with users and colleagues
10	Poor working environment
11	Poor management
12	Producing poor quality software
13	Poor cultural fit/stereotyping/
14	Lack of influence/
Proposing study Franca et al.	
15	Task Complexity (too easy or too difficult)

Table 7. List of motivating factors

Nr.	Motivating factors for Software Testers
Proposing study Beecham et al.	
1	Rewards and incentives
2	Testing needs addressed (training opportunities; opportunity to specialize)
3	Variety of work
4	Career path (opportunity for advancement, promotion prospect, career planning)
5	Empowerment/responsibility (responsibility is assigned to the person not the task)
6	Good management (sr. management support, team-building, good communication)
7	Sense of belonging/supportive relationships
8	Work/life balance (flexibility in work times, caring manager/employer)
9	Working in successful company (e.g. financially stable)
10	Employee participation/involvement/working with others
11	Feedback
12	Recognition (for a high quality, good job done based on objective criteria
13	Equity
14	Trust/respect
15	Technically challenging work
16	Job security/stable environment
17	Identify with the task (clear goals, personal interest, know purpose of task)
18	Autonomy
19	Appropriate working conditions/environment/good equipment/tools/physical space
20	Making a contribution/task significance
21	Sufficient resources
Proposing study Franca et al.	
22	Team quality
23	Creativity/Innovation
24	Fun (playing)
25	Professionalism (high professional environment)
26	Having an Ideology
27	Non-financial benefits
28	Penalty Policies
29	Good relationship with users/customers

Challenges When Adopting Continuous Integration: A Case Study

Adam Debbiche[1], Mikael Dienér[1], and Richard Berntsson Svensson[2]

[1] Department of Computer Science and Engineering, Chalmers,
Gothenburg, Sweden
{adam.debbiche,mikael.diener}@gmail.com
[2] Department of Computer Science and Engineering,
Chalmers, University of Gothenburg,
Gothenburg, Sweden
richard@cse.gu.se

Abstract. The complexity of software development has increased over the last few years. Customers today demand higher quality and more stable software with shorter delivery time. Software companies strive to improve their processes in order to meet theses challenges. Agile practices have been widely praised for the focus they put on customer collaboration and shorter feedback loops. Companies that have well established agile practices have been trying to improve their processes further by adopting continuous integration - the concept where teams integrate their code several times a day. However, adopting continuous integration is not a trivial task. This paper presents a case study in which we, based on interviews at a major Swedish telecommunication services and equipment provider, assess the challenges of continuous integration. The study found 23 adoption challenges that organisations may face when adopting the continuous integration process.

Keywords: continuous integration, software, challenges.

1 Introduction

Software organizations today face a market with ever changing requirements and pressure to release more often. The use of agile practices has increased because of the emphasis they put on customer collaboration and embracing change [14]. Still, companies have been looking into shortening the feedback loop further and releasing more often to the customer by embracing continuous integration [14].

Continuous integration (CI) relates to the frequency at which changes are checked in [19]. Each check in results in a new working build of the software provided that all tests are passed. Continuous integration emphasizes multiple code check-ins on a daily basis as opposed to nightly builds. It is the next step in the evolution of an agile R&D company that has established agile practices in place [14]. It has been suggested that CI increases the frequency of software releases and shortens the feedback cycle [6]. Additionally, Miller [13] state that

A. Jedlitschka et al. (Eds.): PROFES 2014, LNCS 8892, pp. 17–32, 2014.

CI reduces the time developers spend on checking in new code while maintaining the same level of product quality.

In order to support more frequent integration, requirements need to be small enough in order for developers to test them separately then integrate multiple times a day. This is not always a trivial task in the context of CI [6]. Breaking down large user stories into small enough stories with the right level of detail and visible business and customer value has been identified as a challenge [6].

The purpose of this study is to gain in-depth understanding of challenges with organisational adoption of CI. Understanding the challenges faced by an organisation that have adopted CI will help increase both academic and practitioner understanding of the adoption of CI. This paper achieves its aim through a case study on a single organisation to identify challenges faced by that organisation when adopting the CI process. Data was collected through in-depth interviews with 13 practitioners.

The remainder of this paper is organized as follows. In Section 2, related work is presented, while the research methodology is described in Section 3. Section 4 presents the results, while Section 5 discusses and relates the findings to previous studies, and Section 6 gives a summary of the main conclusions.

2   Related Work

Continuous Integration has its roots in the eXtreme Programming (XP) agile method [11]. The goal for each developer is to commit new code several times a day then build and test the software. A successful test run results in a new build that the team can deploy. A CI system often involves using a CI server that automates the building process [5]. When a developer has added a feature or fixed a bug then the code is tested locally and built before being pushed to a CI server. At this stage, the server merges the new code with the latest version on the server. A new version of the software is built provided that the merge is successful. Otherwise, the developer is directly notified of the conflicts.

Fowler [5] presents a set of benefits related to the implementation of CI. First, the risk of integration errors decreases since integration is no longer a daunting and unpredictable task that is done at the end of each sprint. Second, bugs are discovered and fixed earlier due to the frequency of builds and tests. Bugs are also easier to catch since each small change to the code is checked in and tested separately before being integrated into the mainline [5]. Despite the advantages of adopting CI, several organisations have faced challenges when migrating to CI, e.g. challenges related to moving from agile practices to CI [14]. In [14], CI challenges were identified in relation to problems with handling component dependencies during development and integration. Moreover, automatic testing in the context of CI was also a barrier since it involved testing code running on embedded hardware [14].

The practice and implementation of CI varies in industry [17]. This is due to the fact that the concept is interpreted differently. Sthal and Bosch [17] developed a descriptive model that facilitates the documentation of CI practices and implementations. The model consists of an Integration Flow Anatomy which is essentially a directed acyclic graph (DAG) that shows the activities of a CI process. The graph consists of two types of nodes: input (e.g. source code) and activity (e.g. executing test cases) [17]. While the model has not been fully validated due to the small sample size, it has nevertheless been tested on a real project and the authors were able to identify areas of future improvement for the project and team [17].

Holck and Jorgensen [7] studied the use of a decentralized CI process in the open source community (FreeBSD and Mozilla) where developers are often distributed. The authors found that developers working on open source projects are often free to pick any tasks or bugs they want to work on. Deciding when to integrate changes is also delegated to the developer. This is an advantage when compared to the more plan-driven work assignment process of traditional projects [7]. Breaking down tasks into smaller pieces is also prevalent in open source. However, breaking down large tasks is not trivial. For instance, adding support for Symmetric Multi-Processing (SMP) to the FreeBSD kernel resulted in multiple build errors and severely disrupted the work of other developers [7].

3   Research Methodology

For this study we aim to understand and explain the challenges faced by an organisation when adopting CI. The research question that provided the focus for the empirical investigation is:

- **RQ:** What are the challenges of implementing a continuous integration process in practice?

Since the purpose of this study is to gain an in-depth understanding of the challenges an organisation may face when adopting CI, it is important to study software development teams in practice. The investigation presented in this paper was carried out using a qualitative research approach because it allows the researcher to understand the studied phenomenon and its context in more depth [20]. Due to the potential richness and diversity of data that could be collected, semi- structured interviews [16] would best meet the objectives of this study. Semi-structured interviews help to ensure common information on predetermined areas is collected, but allow the interviewer to probe deeper where required.

This study was conducted as a single case study with an interpretive perspective [9]. That is, to better understand social and organizational contexts where each individual's interpretation is of importance [9]. In addition, this study follows the explanatory-descriptive purpose as classified by Robson [15]. The explanatory-descriptive purpose does not only focus on describing a situation and how things work but also on finding causal relationships between problems and situations.

3.1   Case Company

This research was conducted at one case company located in Sweden. The case company is a world leading provider of telecommunication equipment and services. It offers a wide range of products such as base stations, radio access networks, microwave networks as well as products for television and video. The case company has more than 100.000 employees and offers its services to customers in 180 countries. The products developed by the case company consist of both hardware and software modules.

A number of cross functional teams have adopted CI as part of their development process, albeit with a varying degree of maturity. The teams working on the product use multiple branches for development and integration with different quality assurance policies. Once a team begins working on a new feature or a bug fix, changes are first pushed to their work branch (WB). When a feature is finished then the changes are pushed to the team's Latest Local Version (LLV) where the new functionality is tested. If the LLV tests are successful then the new changes are delivered to the Pre-Test Build (PTB) branch where full regression tests are run. Finally, the new code is integrated with the Latest Stable Version (LSV) branch where the system is tested as a whole.

3.2   Data Collection

Semi-structured interviews [16] were used as the method of collecting data in this study. The research instrument was designed with respect to the different areas of interest and inspiration from [2]. In order to identify relevant subjects for this study, the selection process was carried out with help from a "gatekeeper" at the case company. That is, the researchers did not influence the selection of subjects, nor did the researchers have any personal relationship with the subjects. A total of 13 interviews were performed for this study, eight subjects from Sweden and five subjects from China (see Table 1). Prior to conducting interviews, a pilot interview was conducted to improve the interview instrument (the pilot interview is not part of the collected data). In order to facilitate and improve the data analysis process, for all interviews (which varied in length from 25 to 65 minutes) we took records in the form of audio recordings and then transcribed the interviews using NVivo.

The interviewees were asked to talk about their understanding of, and their views on, the CI process, as well as challenges that they faced in CI. A number of additional demographic and open-ended questions were added to ensure subjects could disclose all knowledge relevant to the research.

3.3   Data Analysis

Data analysis in this study was done using thematic analysis [1]. It follows a six steps method presented by Braun and Clarke [1]. The first two authors took part in all the steps as described below while the results from the analysis was validated and discussed with the third author:

Table 1. Study subjects

Team	Number of months using CI	Subjects
T1	18-24	2 developers
T2	2	1 developer
T3	12	1 developer
T4	0	2 developers
T5	2-3	1 developer
T6	12	1 developer
T7	8	1 CI driver
No team	N/A	1 Line Manager, 1 Agile Coach
		1 Configuration Manager, 1 Product Owner

Step 1 - Familiarize yourself with the data: The goal of this step is for the researchers to get acquainted with the data collected. For this study it meant translating interview recordings into extensive notes.

Step 2 - Generating initial codes: This phase involves creating the initial codes from the data set [1]. Open coding as described by Robson [15] was used throughout the analysis phase. For this study, the answers in the extensive notes obtained from the interviews were coded into categories. It is important to note that none of the categories were obtained prior to coding as this is highly discouraged when using open coding [15]. The extensive notes were imported into NVivo and then initial codes were generated.

Step 3 - Searching for themes: This step entails classifying the codes initially generated into broader themes. For this study, the initial codes were put into a main category based on the research question. The main category was in turn divided into sub-categories containing sub-themes.

Step 4 - Reviewing themes: In this phase, the themes identified in the preceding step are refined. In this study, the focus was on determining whether the identified categories were appropriate and reflective of the actual data. This was decided based on recurring patterns found in the data and whether they are supported by multiple subjects. New codes were created as well as renamed or removed.

Step 5 - Defining and naming themes: This step requires the scope of the main category to be clearly defined. For this study, all the codes in each category were verified in order to make sure that they were consistent with the overall theme of the category. As part of this step, the final name of each theme was decided before producing the results.

Step 6 - Producing the report: Results of this study are reported in section 4.

3.4 Validity Threats

In this section, threats to validity in relation to the research design and data collection are discussed. We consider the four perspectives of validity and threats as presented in [16].

Construct validity reflects to what extent the research methodology captures studied concepts and what is investigated according to the research questions. The interview protocol was designed based on work done by Claps [2] and tested during one pilot interview. Minor revisions were made based on the feedback from the pilot interview. To reduce bias during the selection of subjects, a "gatekeeper" at the case company was used. That is, the researchers did not influence the selection of subjects. In order to obtain a true image of the subjects' opinion, anonymity was guaranteed, both within the company and externally.

Internal validity refers to the risk of interference in causal relations within the research. Since this study is of empirical nature, incorrect data is a validity threat. In case of the interviews, the recordings and the written extensive notes assured the correct data. In addition, the researchers had the chance to validate the questions and answers with the subjects lessening the chances of misunderstandings.

External validity refers to what extent the findings of the research can be generalised and of interest to other cases. This study included interviews with different roles and teams to benefit the external validity of this research, on the other hand, only performing interviews at one company affects the generalisability of the results negatively. However, the purpose of qualitative studies puts more focus on describing and understanding a contemporary phenomenon and less on the ability to generalize the findings beyond the boundaries of the studied settings. Nevertheless, results from this study may benefit the investigation of phenomena within similar contexts.

Reliability threats relate to what extent the findings of the study are dependent on the researchers that executed the research. This study has been performed by two researchers which increases the reliability and reduces the risk of single researcher bias. In addition, all research design artifacts, findings and each step of the research have been reviewed by the third author.

4   Results

This section answers the RQ, challenges of adopting CI in an organisation. The identified challenges are shown in Figure 1. The most frequent mentioned challenge is Tools & Infrastructure which was mentioned by 13 practitioners, followed by Domain applicability (mentioned by 11 practitioners), and Mindset and Understanding (both were mentioned by 10 practitioners). The challenges in Figure 1 are discussed in the following sections.

4.1   Mindset

The results of this study found that challenges related to the developer mindset play an important role when transitioning to CI.

Scepticism. One of the mindset challenge identified at the case company is being convinced about the benefits that come from adopting CI. Interviewees (7 out of 13) report that they are positive about the concept of CI but need

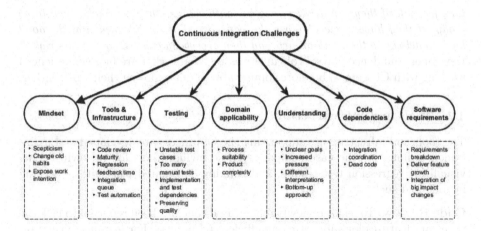

Fig. 1. Continuous integration challenges

to, by themselves, experience the benefits that comes with the change. This to be fully convinced and furthermore promote the adoption. Introducing such a big process change to about 30 teams can be a challenge, as described by a CI driver: *"In the summer of last year, when we started to pilot CI we introduced this change to the team. However, not all of the people are buying the change, not all of them like this change."*

Some developers that were interviewed are not fully persuaded about the benefits that CI might bring to the product described by agile coach: *"From the very beginning, the team they question about the value for that, how much benefit we can get from the CI because actually, we have already the streamline and we have already monthly delivery and they just want to know what's the benefit, if we want to improve delivery frequency to a weekly delivery. what's the benefit for that."* Similarly, a CI Driver involved in coaching and helping teams with transitioning to CI highlights the importance of questioning a change.

Change Old Habits. Developers often get used to working in a certain way. The introduction of CI challenged those habit. Consequently, some developers found it hard to give up their old habits. A line manager mentioned that people that have been working at the company for a long time are harder to change compared to junior people because they got used to working in a certain way.

Exposing Work Intention. Continuous integration emphasises early and frequent integrations. As a result, developers are compelled to expose their work earlier. Some interviewees (4 out of 13) found this to be challenge because they were used to big bang integrations at the end of a sprint. This gave them enough time to polish their code before integrating it. With the adoption of CI and the increase in integration frequencies, developers are worried about integrating low quality code that could be questioned by experts and managers, as an agile coach put it, *"some teams they are not familiar or used to frequent delivery, because* *they feel safe if they can deliver once a month because they can make everything ready, if they have some changes, he can correct it on his own branch, don't have to deliver to the main branch and then everybody can see your faults right."* Developer confidence plays a role in this issue. Teams that are more experienced working with CI seem to be more comfortable about exposing their work earlier.

4.2   Tools and Infrastructure

The tools and infrastructure supporting the CI process are developed and maintained in-house at the case company. These include tools for reviewing code, visualising regression test results, and running automated test suites, checking in code and such.

Code Review: Tools for reviewing integrated code has been reported to lack the necessary features for supporting an efficient CI process. For instance, visualisation of the "bigger picture" while performing a code review has been requested. However, current code review tools only support visualisation of each integrated change separately. This limits the ability to see the impact of smaller changes and how they related to the "bigger picture".

Maturity: The maturity of the tools and their surrounding infrastructure that developers use when integrating code has been reported as a challenge. These tools are often seen as not ready for an efficient CI process. Currently, it takes a long time for developers to integrate their work, especially to the PTB and LSV branches. This in turn prevents them from reaching the desired integration frequency. The build framework and the delivery tools are lacking in terms of maturity and new ways for developers to integrate their codes need to be developed, as one configuration manager puts it, *"after years of developing a product, process and tools tend to be tightly intertwined. When new processes come along then you need to adopt the tools for it."* This highlights the challenge that the introduction of CI has placed on the tools used at the moment. They need to be better adopted to facilitate CI.

Regression Feedback Time. One common opinion at the case company is that the feedback loops from the automated regression tests are too long. Regression feedback times are reported to take anywhere from four hours to two days. This highlights the problem of getting feedback from regression tests up to two days after integrating code. By then, it could already be out of date. According to one developer, in order to fully derive the efficiency benefits that could come with the change of process, fast feedback loops are important when adopting CI. Nevertheless, long feedback loops, in contrast to "big bang integrations" are still preferable as mentioned by one software developer: *"I think that doing it every day actually is better than doing it in a big bang as we used to do."*

Integration Queue. The process of managing the integration queue has been difficult due to the nature of the product. There are hundreds of developers working on common and different parts at the same time from different locations. This means that new code is constantly added to the integration queue.

Consequently, two issues emerge. First, keeping track of all the deliveries while preserving quality becomes difficult. Second, the chance of blocking the integration queue increases due to the surge in integrations which can lead to the branch being blocked for several days. These two challenges manifest themselves primarily when integrating to the Pre-Test Branch.

Test Automation. The support of test automation is lacking in the current infrastructure. This makes maintaining the quality of the product difficult according to one developer. There are a lot of manual steps involved in integrating new code. Some system tests are run manually. The ability to automate tests is highly sought after by developers when checking in new code.

4.3 Testing

Challenges associated with testing at the case company are the lack of automated tests along with a stable test framework according to developers.

Unstable Test Cases. Test cases are sometimes unstable (i.e. likely to break or not reflecting the functionality to be tested) and may fail regardless of the code. This makes the evaluation of the results difficult. The varying test coverage between different branch levels, for instance the LLV and the PTB, further complicates the evaluation of the integrated code. Since the PTB covers more tests that are stricter, teams may not be able to guarantee that integrated code will not break the PTB branch, based solely on LLV test results.

Too Many Manual Tests. Automated tests are considered a prerequisite for CI according to an interviewee. The current amount of manual tests is an obstacle to the efforts of adopting CI. Many developers state that there are a lot of tests that need to be run manually before the code can be integrated. This resulted in gaps in the current testing frameworks. The problem is more prevalent on the platform level of the product. This means that teams working closer to the hardware suffer from more manual tests compared to the teams working on the application level.

Implementation and Test Dependencies. A problem related to writing test cases is syncing them with the code they are supposed to test. Often, code is implemented before its test cases are written (or vice versa). This makes it complex to coordinate the integration of new code with its corresponding test cases. Developers do not always know what to do with new code that has no corresponding tests yet or test cases without implemented code.

Preserving Quality. Maintaining the right level of quality while adopting CI has been a concern. According to a CI driver, there has been too much focus on how to introduce CI but not so much on how to retain the quality of the product to be delivered. Additionally, the large amount of people working on the product means that guaranteeing the quality of the increased integrations becomes challenging. Finding an appropriate integration frequency without threatening quality is currently an issue. This is closely related to another identified challenge while adopting CI, more specifically the increased pressure regarding higher integration frequencies. Pushing the integration frequency goal too eagerly could jeopardise the quality of each individual integration.

4.4   Domain Applicability

The challenges related to the suitability of CI at the case company and the related product are presented in this sub-section.

Process Suitability. While taking a step towards more frequent integrations using CI, the case company has been experiencing problems using the same desired frequency throughout all parts of the product. Additionally, some subjects (6 out of 13) are of the opinion that CI is not feature, domain and task independent. Meaning, the possible integration frequency differs depending on what kind of work being carried out. Several software developers highlight the problem of using CI for all parts of the product and features. Another identified challenge related to the suitability of CI is the ability to break down software requirements (described in Section 4.7)

Product Complexity. Product complexity is something that the developers struggle with when transitioning to CI. As a result, many think that CI is difficult to adopt in regards to the product and that it cannot be followed by the book. Compared to smaller products, where all code is merged to a single branch, the development makes use of many branches which adds to the complexity.

Some believe that the complexity is due to how the product is designed: some changes (sometimes minor) require the node to be rebooted which is not appreciated by the customer. The use of quick workarounds rather than fixing the main problem also contributes to the complexity of the product. While the size of the organisation, product and people involved in it has been recognized as a challenge by most interviewees (7 out of 13). Some think that the complexity of the product and the difficulty of transitioning to CI is more related to the confidence of the teams and the tools at their disposal.

4.5   Understanding

The results indicate that teams and management interpret the concepts and objectives of CI differently. These challenges are described below.

Unclear Goals. Lack of setting up clear goals for the teams migrating towards CI is currently an impediment for the teams. Pilot teams are used to explore the possibilities of working with CI. These pilot teams later help other teams migrating. How the teams adopt CI has been up to them. While this freedom is generally welcome, some interviewees (5 out of 13) still believe that the overall goals are unclear. One line manager thinks that there are often some differences in how teams work with CI which can lead to coordination problems and that a more general way ought to be developed. Some developers indicated that they want the organisation to provide clearer instructions on how to proceed with the adoption of CI. Another CI coach believes that more feedback from the pilot teams is needed before any clear goals can be established while emphasising that the aim should be to maximize integration frequencies while enabling teams to set their own pace and goals.

Increased Pressure. The initiative to adopt CI has resulted in increased pressure on the teams according to some interviewees (4 out of 13). Despite the positive support and attitude towards the concept of CI, teams feel that management would like it to happen faster than currently possible which leads to increased pressure. Some developers feel that they lack the confidence and experience to reach desired integration frequencies. There seems to be a general consensus among developers that transitioning to CI carries risks, a period of chaos and increased pressure. Hence, the frequency of integrations and how to proceed should be done in steps in order to minimize the risk of increased pressure.

Bottom-Up Approach. A pilot team was initially established to pilot the CI concept. Currently, the pilot team members act as CI drivers. They provide assistance and training through meetings, workshops and discussions to the other teams. It seems that both management and the teams are mostly happy with the work done by the pilot teams. Most think that they are committed to helping other teams transition to CI. However, the bottom up approach seems to have led some to believe that management could be more involved in the overall process of transitioning to CI.

4.6   Code Dependencies

A consequence of more frequent integrations when adopting CI is that work needs to be divided into smaller pieces. This could mean that work that would otherwise benefit from being developed in one single integration, now might need to be split up into several integrations. Additionally, by dividing work into several integrations, development might be carried out by several developers instead of a single one. This stresses the importance of considering code dependencies and how this affects the integration process.

Integration Coordination. The results from this study indicate that the task of coordinating integration dependencies has been more difficult since the adoption of CI. Consequently, four different issues were reported by developers:

- Component interfaces need to be more clearly defined.
- It is harder to locate the source of errors during integration, because code is delivered from different teams.
- More failures have been experienced during integration.
- Need to wait until other components/parts are done before integrating work.

It has been suggested that a solution to some of the issues presented above could be the use of "dead code", which is described further in the next paragraph.

Dead Code. Integrating partial code for a feature, user story or delivery is currently an issue for the case company. This due to the testability of such integrations. Tests will fail until all parts are in place. A suggestion presented by multiple developers could be to create a test framework that allow integration of so called "dead code". Meaning, code that is activated and tested when all parts are in place. However, making code support this type of activation/deactivation might be more costly, according to one software developer.

4.7   Software Requirements

Software requirements were identified as a challenge when adopting CI. It has increased the frequency at which teams integrate their code. Consequently, requirements that previously could be integrated on sprint basis now need to be broken down to allow more frequent integrations.

Requirements Breakdown. Interviewees report that since the adoption of CI, breaking down requirements to enable more frequent integrations, has been challenging. These challenges are related to finding a balance between size, testability and assuring quality on the integration line. In addition, one developer reports on the lack of experience, constant re-prioritisation and new decisions on requirements, which makes the task of finding a balance even more challenging.

Deliver Feature Growth One of the issues reported by developers with breaking down requirements when using CI is delivering feature growth. It is difficult to know whether small changes that do not directly add value to a feature are worth integrating. Some developers feel this is inevitable. For instance, sometimes you need to re-factor code or make minor changes. These changes do not necessarily contribute growth to the feature itself but are still needed. This means that teams need to be prepared for integrations that do not automatically add feature growth to the customer per say.

5   Discussion

The findings indicate that adopting the mindset aligned with CI is a challenge. Interviewees were skeptical about the benefits that they could gain from adopting CI. Similarly, Claps [2] found that teams adopting continuous deployment need to adopt the mindset needed for it. This means that there needs to be a shift towards a single and united organisational culture that adopts the principles of CI. The case company is transitioning to CI in order to be able to integrate more often and deliver better quality software according to the interviewees. This implies that adopting CI can be seen as introducing a change to an existing software process. Also, bringing change to an existing process in an organisation with the aim of improving software quality is considered a software process improvement (SPI) endeavor [4]. As such, CI is a SPI initiative undertaken by the studied company in a bid to further increase the efficiency of the software development process. Mathiassen et al. [12] argue that improving a process (such as implementing CI) involves changing people. They argue that people do not change simply because processes change. As such resistance to change should be expected. This could explain why some developers express some degree of scepticism towards the adoption of CI. Another reason could be the lack of motivation to change, due to the complexity of adopting a new process, especially if the change is perceived as being too complex [3].

Results show that all of the 13 interviewees mentioned challenges related to tools and infrastructure such as code review, regression feedback time when adopting to CI. The maturity of the tools and infrastructure was found to be a major issue. This has been mentioned in earlier literature. For instance, Olsson et al. [14] identified tools with support for automated tests as a barrier when adopting CI in two companies. Similarly, they argue that developing a fully automated infrastructure remains the key focus when adopting CI [14]. At the case company, the tools and the infrastructure are not entirely ready to accommodate CI. Many developers feel that the current tools available are holding them back. This means that teams are still not able to fully exploit the benefits of CI. That said, a lot of progress is being made such as developing new tools to better support automated tests and the reduction in the amount of branches which is a challenge in itself [14]. The maturity issue is most likely due to the fact that CI is a new concept that is still being adopted. Also, the ongoing responsibility shift means that tools and infrastructure need more time to adapt.

Another issue is the tests themselves. The need for automated tests when transitioning to CI has been recognized in previous research [5], [8]. While organisations realise the importance of automated tests when moving towards CI, they still struggle with it [14]. Improving the testing tools and the infrastructure is not enough according to the interviewees. Olsson et al [14] have also identified automated tests as a key barrier when transitioning from agile to CI. In order to mitigate this problem, two companies facing this issue, have made it their priority to greatly increase the number of automated tests [14] since this is important for CI [5]. Doing this at the case company might not be a trivial task due to the nature of the requirements they are facing. Some are too large and cannot be tested separately. Therefore, writing automated tests might not currently be an option. For instance, one issue mentioned by some of the developers is automating the tests for some features that are part of the Linux kernel used in the product. This issue is similar to the problem encountered by the developers of the FreeBSD project when they were implementing the Symmetric Multi-Processing (SMP) module in the Linux kernel using CI [7]. The ongoing struggle with manual tests could be due to to the complexity of the product itself, which has been developed for well over a decade. Hence, updating the old and large test cases could be a tedious and time consuming task.

Results from this study show that there is an ambiguity regarding the goals and the organisational vision for the implementation of CI. More than half (7 of 13) of the interviewed subjects had a hard time answering questions due to their lack of knowledge of what was expected from them personally. According to Kotter [10], successful cases of process change all share a common denominator, which is divided into 8 steps, liable for their success of change implementation. Kotter [10] highlights the importance of spending the necessary amount of time on each step, and failing to do so will lead to undesired results. For instance, lacking and under-communicating a vision might lead to confusion and incompatible results, which will take the organisation in the wrong direction. This might be a reason to the unclear goals and expectations regarding CI at the case company. Another reason could be the use of a bottom-up approach where directions and guidance come from experience gained in pilot teams. This might have led to the confusion regarding a vision, since the most expected communication channel for organisational visions ought to be management. According to research done by Stahl and Bosch [17] there is no general consensus regarding the practice of CI. Besides the fact that this makes the comparison between different CI practitioners difficult, it could be a reason for the ambiguity at the studied company as well.

Findings from this study show that the suitability of CI is questioned by the majority of subjects interviewed (11 of 13 interviewees). Interviewees mentioned the complexity of the product and the industry in which the case company operates as not being ideal for CI. Research done by Olsson et al [14] describes barriers identified in hardware oriented companies moving towards CI. These companies are used to hardware oriented processes and are struggling with adopting a software oriented process such as CITherefore a shift in culture is needed. Additionally, research done by Turk et al. [18] on the suitability of agile development methods shows that assumptions (e.g. face-to-face communication, quality assurance, changing requirements) made by such methods are not appropriate for all organisations, products and projects. The authors [18] highlight important limitations of said methods, where two is of particular interest for this research, namely limited support for large complex software and large teams. Agile development methods are considered a prerequisite for CI [14], therefore findings by Turk et al. [18], might apply to the applicability of CI. Therefore, the suitability issues of CI raised by interviewees are most likely due to the complexity of the product and t he number of people working on it.

6   Conclusion

This research presents the results of an empirical study that examines the adoption of the CI process at a case company. Understanding the intricacies of this complex phenomenon is critical for framing research directions that aim to improve CI practices. Through a case study, 13 semi-structured interviews were conducted and a set of challenges related to the adoption of CI were identified.

A number of adoption challenges were uncovered by the case study in this research, where the most dominant results include: 1) The mindset is an important factor in the success of implementing CI. Scepticism towards the introduction of a new process needs be considered in order to win over non believers. 2) Testing tools and the maturity of the infrastructure supporting the CI process is required in order to facilitate the daily tasks involved. Continuous integration advocates the use of automated tools to allow more frequent and efficient integrations. 3) Similar to Agile, assumptions made by the concept of CI may not apply to all organisations, products and projects, especially those of larger dimensions. Some of the identified challenges such as mindset, tools and infrastructure maturity and testing have been mentioned in previous literature when transitioning to continuous integration. However, this study also identified software requirements as a challenge when adopting CI.

For practitioners, knowing how to address the challenges an organisation may face when adopting CI provides a level of awareness that they previously may not have had. These challenges can be used as a checklist by companies that are about to adopt CI. The findings of this study can be extended by observing an increased sample of practitioners and companies using CI.

References

1. Braun, V., Clarke, V.: Using thematic analysis in psychology. Qualitative Research in Psychology 3(2), 77–101 (2006)
2. Claps, G.: Continuous Deployment: An Examination of the Technical and Social Adoption Challenges. diploma thesis, The University of New South Wales (2012)
3. Conboy, K., Coyle, S., Wang, X., Pikkarainen, M.: People over process: Key challenges in agile development. IEEE Software 28(4), 48–57 (2011)
4. Deependra, M.: Managing change for software process improvement initiatives: A practical experience-based approach. 4(4), 199–207 (1998)
5. Fowler, M.: Continuous integration @ONLINE (May 2006), http://martinfowler.com/articles/continuousIntegration.html
6. Goodman, D., Elbaz, M.: It's not the pants, it's the people in the pants, learnings from the gap agile transformation what worked, how we did it, and what still puzzles us. In: Agile Conference AGILE 2008, pp. 112–115 (August 2008)
7. Holck, J., Jørgensen, N.: Continuous integration and quality assurance: A case study of two open source projects. Australasian J. of Inf. Systems 11(1) (2003)
8. Humble, J., Farley, D.: Continuous Delivery: Reliable Software Releases Through Build, Test, and Deployment Automation, 1st edn. Addison-Wesley Professional (2010)
9. Klein, H., Myers, M.: A set of principles for conducting and evaluating interpretive field studies in information systems. MIS Quarterly 23(1), 67–93 (1999)
10. Kotter, J.P.: Leading change: Why transformation efforts fail. Harvard Business Review 85(1), 96 (2007)
11. Lacoste, F.: Killing the gatekeeper: Introducing a continuous integration system. In: Agile Conference, AGILE 2009, pp. 387–392 (2009)
12. Mathiassen, L., Ngwenyama, O., Aaen, I.: Managing change in software process improvement. IEEE Software 22(6), 84–91 (2005)
13. Miller, A.: A hundred days of continuous integration. In: Agile Conference, AGILE 2008, pp. 289–293 (August 2008)
14. Olsson, H., Alahyari, H., Bosch, J.: Climbing the "stairway to heaven" – A multiple-case study exploring barriers in the transition from agile development towards continuous deployment of software. In: 38th EUROMICRO Conference on Software Engineering and Advanced Applications, pp. 392–399 (September 2012)
15. Robson, C.: Real World Research: A Resource for Social Scientists and Practitioner-Researchers. Regional Surveys of the World Series. Wiley (2002)

16. Runeson, P., Höst, M.: Guidelines for conducting and reporting case study research in software engineering. Empirical Software Engineering 14(2), 131–164 (2009)
17. Ståhl, D., Bosch, J.: Modeling continuous integration practice differences in industry software development. J. Syst. Softw. 87, 48–59 (2014)
18. Turk, D., France, R., Rumpe, B.: Assumptions underlying agile software-development processes. Journal of Database Management 16(4), 62–87 (2005)
19. Van Der Storm, T.: Backtracking incremental continuous integration. In: 12th European Conference on Software Maintenance and Reengineering, CSMR 2008, pp. 233–242 (2008)
20. Yin, R.K.: Case study research: Design and methods. Sage (1994)

Agile Development in Automotive Software Development: Challenges and Opportunities

Brian Katumba and Eric Knauss

Department of Computer Science and Engineering
Chalmers| University of Gothenburg
Gothenburg, Sweden
katsbriol@hotmail.com, eric.knauss@cse.gu.se

Abstract. In modern cars, most of the functionalities are controlled by software. The increased significance of software-based functionality has resulted in various challenges for automotive industry, which is slowly transitioning towards being a software centric industry. Challenges include the definition of key competencies, processes, methods, tools, and organization settings to accommodate combined development of software and hardware. Based on qualitative research, this paper aims at understanding the applicability of agile methods to automotive software development. Our explorative case study with one of the development sections at Volvo Car Cooperation identified challenges in their software development process related to process perception and reactive mode, multi-tasking and frequent task switching, individualism and lack of complete knowledge, as well as long communication chains and low cross-function mind set. Moreover it prepares a transition of software development at this multinational automotive company towards agile by relating agile principles and practices to automotive software process challenges.

Keywords: agile software development, automotive software development, software process improvement, embedded systems, challenges.

1 Introduction

Agile software development methods have changed the way software is developed in many domains. They promise better ability to cope with changing requirements, shorter time to market, and faster release cycles [1]. In contrast to earlier assumptions, agile principles have successfully implemented in large-scale software development and it has been reported that advantages of agile methods can be realized even in such environments [2–4].

In the domain of automotive software development, introduction of agile methods is hindered by the fact that software development has to be in sync with hardware development, which has been used as a strong argument to use a plan-driven approach. Yet, increased complexity and interdependency of automotive software challenges the ability to create an accurate plan upfront. In addition, automotive companies face an increased pressure to shorten their time to market and their release cycles. In this context, we performed a qualitative study with the following objective.

A. Jedlitschka et al. (Eds.): PROFES 2014, LNCS 8892, pp. 33–47, 2014.

Research Objective: This paper aims at i) understanding to what extent agile methods are applicable to the software development at Volvo Car Cooperation (VCC) and ii) preparing the transition of software development at this multinational automotive company towards agile by relating agile principles and practices to automotive software process challenges.

We approach this objective based on a qualitative explorative case study with one development section in the powertrain department of VCC. The development section under investigation is characterized by doing part of the software development in house. We performed 29 semi-structured interviews with members of the development section and triangulated this data with internal documents.

Our main finding is that today, complexity of software, need to shorten release cycles, and pressure to cut development costs has led to a situation where plan-driven development starts to fail. Our interviewees mention critical challenges they encounter today, including process perception and reactive mode, multi-tasking and frequent task switching, individualism and lack of complete knowledge, and long communication chains and low cross function mind set. All of these challenges can be considered waste from the perspective of Lean software Development [5–7].

2   Agile Software Development and Related Work

2.1   Agile Software Development

Agile software development approaches emerged in the mid-1990s as a new solution to well-known problems experienced by traditional software development methods, including exceeding budgets, poor code quality and exceeded development schedules [6], [8], [9]. Agile methods intend to solve the persistent problems of traditional development by taking an iterative and incremental approach to software development. All agile methods have in common that requirements and solutions evolve through collaboration between self-organizing and cross sectional teams. Agility focuses on new ways of running business and casting off old ways of doing things, and the concept involves exploration, opportunity exploitation [10], acquiring new competencies, developing new product lines, and opening up new markets [11].

Agile development is guided by the agile manifesto, which declares the main values and purpose of agile software development in the form of the agile principles [12]. Although these principles are suitable and have been widely used for smaller software development organizations, evidence indicates that they can be adapted to large software-intensive organizations operating in complex global development environments [2], [4], [13]. Therefore these organizations are indeed in the process of deploying agile methods as part of their de-facto approach to software development, for example telecommunication companies, automotive industries, medical industries. Hence, in representing the values mentioned above, agile methods may very well pave the way for the future of software development also within large multi-national software organizations [14]. This paper aims at identifying how i) to check whether agile methods are applicable to the software development at Volvo Car cooperation and ii) to use these principles to transition software development at this multinational automotive company towards agile.

Among the agile software development methods, we discuss Scrum [15], eXtreme Programming (XP) [16], Lean Software Development [6].

2.2   Related Work

The study of agile software development is currently persuasive in software organizations [2], however its application and context for several years has often been to smaller organizations where development teams are involved in the product from development to product release [17].   While seemingly incompatible in embedded software development industry [18], introducing agile software development and agile practices is a challenge undertaken by many automotive industries producing embedded software. In this study we report the challenges of introducing agile software development practices in large automotive software development industry, where development involves the production of both hardware and software at the same time some of the requirements are realized by the suppliers.

Paasivaara et al. report the successful use of agile practices in large software projects [17]. Their case study is carried out on a 40-person development organization that is geographically distributed between Norway and Malaysia. They base their results on qualitative interviews to come up with a description on how Scrum practices were successfully applied by for example the use of teleconference and web cameras for daily meetings, frequent visits, unofficial distributed meetings, and annual gathering among others.

Abrahamsson explains the need of having a cost efficient development process in embedded software development [19]. He points out the increase of software in embedded devices that has resulted into challenges in the European industry. His ITEA agile project for application of agile processes in complex embedded systems concludes that the application of agile practices in embedded software development methods and process can reduce lead time and cost by 70% throughout the different industry sector [19]. Abrahamsson also explores the actual use and usefulness of Extreme Programming and Scrum in complex embedded software development [20].

The increasing use of embedded software in a wide range of products is causing a considerable impact to the society. Some of these products deal directly with human lives such as in automobiles, because of this their production need to go through rigorous process. Albuquerque presents in a systematic review [18] how agile methods have been used in the production of embedded systems. In addition they describe their benefits, challenges, and limitations to different industries including automotive industries.

Ulrik and Bosch present a set of factors that should be considered when implementing agile software development in mass produced automotive embedded software where development is governed by a stage gate process for hardware and product development as a whole is driven by a plan-driven process [2]. In addition they list agile measures to be considered by the original equipment manufacturer (OEM).

Besides applying agile in the actual automotive software development, agile has also been used to enhance supply chain management between suppliers and in-house development in the automotive industry [21].

It is worth noting that agile introduction comes with different perceptions in an organization. Dybå and Dingsoyr present an empirical study of agile software development [22]. As part of their results, they present the perception of agile development from a customer, developer and an organization perspective [22].

3   Background and Research Methodology

3.1   Research Site: Volvo Car Cooperation (VCC)

Volvo Car Cooperation is a Swedish automotive company operating on the global market. For this particular study, one development section was studied. This section is part of the department of Complete Powertrain Engineering within R&D. As part of the Volvo Car Corporation organization, the studied section contributes to system development of complete powertrains, developing and optimizing of the powertrain control system and assessing the powertrain attributes in VCC's vehicles.

In specific, the studied section delivers SW and electronic HW to VCC production line, after market, and to different departments at VCC for development purposes. The section develops parts of the software in house (focus in this paper) and specifies software requirements for other parts that are then developed by a variety of suppliers. At the development section, most of the software is developed in MATLAB's Simulink in addition to following MISRA-C/C++ guidelines. To confirm that a supplier delivers what the specification stated, VCC does the validation and verification of the software. The software developed is embedded in nature and is massively produced.

Because of the complexity of the system development within the car industry, this section has seen a need to investigate more effective and reliable methods of system development. In every new car model, manufacturers are introducing new advanced functionality due to customer demands and competition from the market. Often, suppliers delegate development tasks to sub-suppliers that are specialized on certain features. This considerably adds to the complexity of integration, making software development in the automotive industry even more complex in terms of development, time and cost.

By transitioning to agile, the development section in our case study aims at further improving the end-to-end process flow. Specifically the goal is to cut lead times, to be more customers focused, and to make better use of limited resources. At the time of initiation of this study one of four groups at the section had unsuccessfully tried using Scrum for in-house software development. Motivated by this experience, we conducted our case study to systematically explore the possibilities of adopting agile practices at the section.

3.2   General Overview of Current Process

The development section under research consists of about 60 engineers who are divided in four groups. The first group is responsible for the architecture &

non-propulsive control, while the remaining three groups are responsible for the engine control modules and transmission. For software development, there are various roles involved at the section. Intentionally, the specific names of the roles are left out but rather the roles are categorized in seven categories as shown in Table 1; managers, software responsible, test engineers, software coordinators, trouble shooter (not part of this study), system responsible/ architects, system developers/designers, Hardware responsible (not part of the study), and internal software responsible.

Table 1. Roles and Responsibilities

Roles	Experience(Years)	Tasks and Responsibilities
Manager	> 10	Spearheading group activities and project related communication
System Responsible/ Architects	>10	Architects have the key role to control architectural part of the model. The architect is responsible for all elements in the architecture and communication between the elements. This involves both hardware and software architecture
Software responsible	$2 <= 7$	Responsible for both in-house and supplier software production, software deliveries, Technical questions of the project, Project Planning
SPM(Software Plugin Module) Developer	$2 <= 8$	Responsible for SPM(Software Plugin Modules) development(in-house software development)
Software Coordinator	$5 <= 9$	Responsible for controlling and coordinating software versions and releases, Compiling software together as well as managing change orders, uploading software to DTECS- Development Tool for Embedded Control Systems, and handling special deliveries internally
Tester	$2 <= 7$	Verify and validate software on both component and system level, software calibration

The development section follows a traditional stage-gate process (V-Model), where the gates are driven by decisions and investment in the manufacturing of the product, i.e. driven by the hardware. The gates progress as the project grows and their progression corresponds to software artefacts such as user requirements, system requirements, software architecture, component requirements, and software implementation. At this development section, the big part of software requirements comes from the electrical department as a result of system engineering work while the other requirements come from other departments, e.g. system safety, engine and transmission department, and legal department. Requirements are collected and documented in a special purpose tool (Elektra), which acts as a requirement repository. System architects refine these requirements and break them down to support the decision on which requirements are developed in house and which requirements are sent to the suppliers or subcontractors.

There are three different development paths a requirement can take: i) hardware developed by a supplier, ii) software developed by a supplier, and iii) software developed in house. In case i) and ii), the supplier decides which development process to follow, but for software process improvement, the supplier is required to use one of the following software process improvement models: ISO/IEC15504, Automotive SPICE, and CMM/CMMI. In case iii), a traditional V-model approach is followed according to the architects.

In this study various roles at the development section where interviewed (see table 1), and based on the results from the interviews we came up with different development challenges.

3.3   Research Method

We investigated the applicability of agile methods based on an exploratory qualitative case study [23]. In this exploratory research, the researchers studied the current development method at VCC development section and then sought new insights and generated new ideas and hypotheses for the study.

By definition, a case study is "an investigation of a contemporary phenomenon in depth and within a real life context, where the boundaries between the phenomenon and the context are unclear" [24]. With the aforementioned definition, the study is based on real life experiences of the researchers at Volvo Cars' Power Train section. It was unclear if agile methods could be applied at this section; therefore it was the purpose of the research to bring out the clarity of the phenomenon and context for the section in question.

A case study method has been chosen because identifying a suitable development process requires an in-depth investigation of the current process from the beginning to the end to understand the underlying principles and the problem that may be involved. In addition, Yin suggests that case studies allow investigators to retain the holistic and meaningful characteristics of real life events such as individual life cycles, group behaviors, organizational and managerial processes which can be augmented to fit the domain of this research [24]. Similarly, Andersson and Runeson argue that case studies in the software engineering discipline often take an improvement approach, similar to action research [25]. The purpose of this study is to improve the working process at the section under question.

According to [24], there are six main sources of data: documentation, archival records, interviews, direct observations, participant observations and physical artifacts. For this particular study, semi-structured interviews were the primary source of data and complemented by company presentations, company documentations and literature reviews as the secondary data source to allow triangulation of results. Interviews where transcribed and coded by highlighting and labeling important parts. We then grouped resulting codes into themes and derived opportunities and challenges in workshops. While we used all collected data to derive our conclusions, we can only partly disclose it to protect the company's sensitive data.

3.4   Research Setting

During the study, and as a significant starting-point for acquiring an insider's view of the research phenomenon, one of the authors of this paper spent three or four days every week during a four-month period at Volvo cars' site involved in this study. In supporting engagement between researchers and research subjects, this in-depth study as well as the observational studies that were carried out as part of it, were important impetus for developing an understanding of the research setting. While observational studies, and the documentation of these, were the main activity during this time, data sources such as meeting minutes and organizational documents were also used to get an enhanced understanding of the development teams and the development unit in which they operate.

As a starting point, 2 project managers introduced a vague project topic to the researchers that showed a need to become agile at the development section. The researcher had to narrow down the topic to make it feasible in the short time that was available. Never the less, it was not so easy since many things had to be put in consideration i.e. the time frame available, the nature of the organization and resources at the section.

The researchers took observational studies at the premises and, 29 semi-structured qualitative interviews[1] were conducted as the primary data source. During these interviews, questions focused around areas such as; 'requirements', 'Roles and competence', 'communication', 'process and phases', agile understanding, 'quality improvement' and 'co-location'.

In focusing the interviews around areas that had been identified as important by the researchers, there were reasons to believe that the research would attract attention and that the managers were even more motivated to participate actively, and on a continuous basis, in the study. The aim of the interviews was to reach an understanding of the current process at the section, to check for the suitability of agile development, and to initiate a new working method based on agile principles.

As in exploratory research, the findings generated emerged as an iterative process between theoretical conceptions and empirical data [26]. In accordance to this, collection and analysis of empirical data was undertaken as a concurrent activity, with an important part of the analysis conducted also after the empirical work. The initial conceptual apparatus – encompassing certain assumptions, beliefs, and rationale – transformed over time. Thus, our notions, our empirical data and the transformations of our interpretations of this worked as entangled elements in the process of analyzing the case.

4   Results: Process-Related Challenges in Relation to Agile

In this section, we present the results from our qualitative study and relate the finding to the research objectives: Firstly, to check whether agile methods are applicable to

---

[1] See interview guide at https://dl.dropboxusercontent.com/u/13255493/ Katumba-Agile_in_Automotive-Profes14-Interview_guide.pdf

the software development at Volvo Car cooperation and secondly to use these principles to prepare for the transition of software development towards agile. Specifically, we collected opportunities for agile methods, e.g. challenges that can be addressed or overcome by an agile method work in this context, and challenges for agile methods, i.e. characteristics of automotive software development that make it hard to introduce agile methods. We categorized these opportunities and challenges in five categories: *Process ability, workload management, domain specifics and supplier network, working context*, and *culture of sharing information and knowledge*. For each category, we include the perspective of different roles at the development section.

4.1   Process Ability

As discussed in our research background, development is supposed to follow the V-Model, as clearly indicated by introductory interviews from two managers and internal training documents. However, our interviewees indicated a lack of structure when it comes to developing software in house. Tasks are started as they hit the engineer's desktops and development seems to be driven by sudden urgencies rather than by a long term plan. One interviewee explicitly noted this *reactive mode* approach by saying:

> "[For developing software in house,] *There is no working process at the section, it may be there but I have not used it nor do I know how it looks like. What I know are the milestones and when I am supposed to deliver*"
> "*We had a process but we stopped using it since it required a lot of resources and hence it lacked the practicability of the project*",

This *perceived lack of an accepted process* by our interviewees is related to the fact that each member may have more than three or four roles. Not having a clear methodology to follow causes confusion and is seen as a challenge by our interviewees:

> "*...we are in a confusing situation and nothing [...] works in this confusing state of working. If this agile thing works out, you would have [helped us a lot]."*

We assume that the perceived lack of structure is the consequence of VCC aiming at increasing their flexibility with in-house software development. Agile methods might be helpful in this situation by adding just enough structure while still offering flexibility.

4.2   Workload Management

Heavy workloads is one of the main challenges faced at the VCC section, as supported by all interviewees irrespective of their roles. For example, the role of the *software responsible* was merged with another role in order to improve development efficiency. Initially, this role was to work on project planning activities, cost estimation, and supplier communication. Today, this role is also responsible for answering technical questions, prioritizing requirements for both internal and supplier software, breaking requirements down, as well as ensuring accuracy of test and calibration results. This *multitasking* is seen as challenging by our interviewees and it affects other roles as well. For example in internal software development, one engineer is responsible for all phases of development, including requirements, design and testing. This leads to a loss of focus of developers and ultimately can affect the quality of the feature.

A related challenge is *task switching*: people are participating in many projects at the same time and often need to jump from one task to the next, which might be in the context of a completely different project. A resulting problem mentioned in our interviews is the lack of time for continuous learning. Specifically, the testers at the section claimed to serve many software responsible with a ratio of 1:3 i.e. one tester can test software from three software responsible with each software responsible working on more than three projects. This results in *unbalanced workloads* and hinders the performance of the group members. In addition, *schedule synchronization* becomes a problem, because engineers are working on many projects, on multiple tasks, which they frequently switch. Synchronizing schedules of team members in this context becomes challenging, as indicated by the following quote from our interviews:

"*.. you may be in one meeting yet at the same time you needed at another meeting....*"

As agile methods rely to a large extent to oral face-to-face communication, such context switching might be problematic when introducing agile methods.

4.3   Domain Specifics and Supplier Network

The domain of automotive software development involves both in-house and supplier software development and VCC is no exception to this setting. At VCC, the big part of software requirements come from the electrical department as a result of system engineering work while the other requirements come from other departments; system safety, engine and transmission department and legal department. They usually collect and gather requirements in a tool called Elektra, which acts as a requirement repository. These requirements are further broken down at the section, of which some are developed in house while other requirements are sent to the suppliers or subcontractors. It is however important to note that these requirements may be hardware, internal software or supplier software requirements. For supplier requirements, the supplier decides which development process to follow, and is required to produce working software fully tested and integrated with the in house software. For software produced internally, according to the architects it has some elements of following a traditional V-model where specifications are done first, before design, integration, and validation. The domain of the network of in-house, supplier and hardware results into *inventory and motion*. In this, all requirements sent to the supplier are fully managed by the supplier till integration. This means if anything is missing or not done even if the in house team can work on it, the software is sent back to the supplier, the interviewees mentioned this *rework* could result in bottlenecks caused by *process dependencies*, if the software is needed for further activities to take place. One of the software responsible mentioned:

> "*We keep sending back the software modules to the supply in case there is something missing, even if it is something small which we can fix internally.*"

While this is a perfectly normal workflow in traditional automotive development, it seriously impacts the effectivity of (agile) in house development.

4.4   Working Context

In this category, we discuss challenges in the context of knowing what a function or feature should do. The interviewees claimed that at times they do not know the *context* of the functions or features they are developing, mainly due to the fact that they do not participate in the requirement elicitation phase of the project. This is a consequence of the multitasking challenge above, as one interviewee indicates:

> "*There are many projects running at the same time, meaning that each person is participating in more than one project*".

An example, one system responsible claimed to be participating in four projects at the same time. In this situation, engineers tend to focus on the projects close to deadline instead of working in projects that are in early stages. Also, this leads to a lack of competence and knowledge. For example, a system architect might only have a helicopter view of a function, whereas a tester is limited to knowledge about testing activities. This *separation of concern* and *lack of end-to-end knowledge* was perceived as problematic in the context of agile in house software development.

Challenges around working context are intensified when *requirements are vague* and not easy to understand. An example given during an interview was "*the engine should run fast and smooth*", leaving it to the developer to find out what smoothness is and at what level of smoothness needs to be reached.

Finally, the *ramp-up* challenge relates to bringing new recruits up to speed. Because of the complexity and lack of structure of the current development process, new recruits take long time to get to know their ways. The high workload means that they get limited support from the old 'group' members, who are always busy working on their tasks. This further reinforces individualism, where instead work should aim to achieve a common goal. Also, problems like lack of continuity and low knowledge about the features and their functions are a consequence of this.

4.5   Culture of Sharing Information and Knowledge

The different roles at VCC section under consideration are challenged with sharing information and knowledge. This challenge is mainly caused by their working culture that encompasses on individuals to achieve a common goal. Although each role is placed in a group, when it comes to actual work, the group influence is minimal. In addition, the chain of communication at times is long since information has to pass through different channels to reach a person who is really going to use it. For example, if a tester wants to clarify unclear requirements, information has to go through the software responsible, to the architects, to the electrical department and so on. This in the end leads to low continuity in development since by the time the information comes back to the person who initiated it, it may be late as that person may be already engaged with other activities in a different project. This again explains the problem of participating in more than one project as already mentioned.

5 Discussion

In this section we discuss the themes we found in the qualitative interview study and outline agile practices that can be adopted in automotive. For this, we map each theme to a set of relevant agile methods, principles, and practices. From our interviews, it is clear that the division under investigation is facing challenges that prevent them to fully leverage the potential of developing software in-house. The opportunities and challenges we found were grouped into themes: process related challenges, workload management, domain specifics, working context as well as information and knowledge sharing. In Table 2 we summarize opportunities and challenges for agile methods at the company and suggest agile practices that can be adopted.

The process related challenges seem to be caused by the nature of the organizational structure, which focuses more on the finished product than on the way the product is developed. By this all interviewees were less concerned about the process but instead more concerned on what they have to deliver.

Moreover, the organizational setting and the available competences are characterized by low agile knowledge as well as low general software development knowledge in comparison to the excellent knowledge in hardware development. We triangulated these results with responses to the agile questionnaire from interviewees and additional managers that showed that, although the teams know the term "agile", they lack the full context of it. This can be explained that the automotive industry has traditionally been characterized more by hardware production than software [2]. Relating this challenge to the agile methodology, it can be mitigated by having a flexible, holistic product development strategy as for example in Scrum [27]. With Scrum, there is a defined product strategy and structure, which accommodate changes at higher level at the same time leaving room for flexibility and innovativeness. Besides, the process ability challenges can also be explained by the domain specifics and supplier network. Automotive companies produce cars in-house by integrating their suppliers' deliveries of hardware and software. This means there should be a strategy that can accommodate both the in-house process and the supplier process to reduce the inventories and motions involved. From a lean perspective, the unnecessary motions are referred to as waste and so lean calls for an absolute elimination of waste in the production process [6], [7].

Table 2. Automotive challenges and opportunities for agile in-house software development

Theme	Opportunities for agile in automotive	Challenges for agile in automotive	Agile Practices
Process ability	Perceived lack of software development methodology and structure	Low agile competence, Reactive mode	Flexible, holistic product development strategy[1],
Workload management	Heavy workloads, Unbalanced workloads	Multi-tasking, Task switching, Schedule synchronization	Task boards[1,2] Sprint planning[1], Commitment phase[2] Defer Commitment[3] Frequent releases, short development cycles[2]
Domain specifics and supplier network	Inventory and motion, Rework	Process dependencies	Eliminate waste[3]
Working context	Vague requirements, Lack of end-to-end knowledge	Feature context, Separation of concerns, Ramp-up	Requirement Prioritization[1,2], Emergent Design and Metaphor[2] Product Backlog[1] User stories/ Product vision[1,2] Sprint Planning[1] System metaphor[2] Relying on a product owner[1]
Culture of sharing information and knowledge	Low knowledge sharing, Individualism, No team work	Long communication chains, Low cross function mind set	Retrospective[1,2,3] Cross function Teams[1] Self-organizing teams by encouraging colocation of all team members[1,2] Daily stand up[1], Pair programing[2] Continuous learning[3]

NOTE: 1 – Scrum, 2- Extreme Programming, 3- Lean

The heavy workloads mentioned in the interviews by almost all interviewees have resulted in multi-tasking, task switching, and poor schedule synchronization. These challenges indeed affect production since they are bottlenecks to the development chain. Management also confirmed these effects: the nature of the organization is set that way. A similar case is also discussed and experienced in another multinational cooperation in the telecommunication sector where task switching was one of the bottlenecks at their development section [4]. Looking at some of the agile practices that can be adopted to solve this issue were; using task boards to show the work to be done [28], sprint planning to solve product planning issues [29] and having short iterations that can result into frequent releases [20].

The working and feature context showed that teams sometimes lack the domain knowledge of the products they are working on. This was however explained by the vague requirements they get from the requirement engineers who mainly have hardware and electronics knowledge than software knowledge. In addition the separation of concerns where for example architects are doing only architectural work and testers do only the testing, is also seen as a cause of low domain understanding. Ramp up was also mentioned and refers to the fact that new comers find it difficult to find their way around development. This can be related to the process ability challenges as well. Working context challenges are suggested to be solved by having a product backlog for requirements [27]. The requirements in the backlog should be prioritized and each requirement should have a user story that explains what the requirement should do [28]. Moreover in the development, the use of design metaphors are encourages and relaying a competent product owner to share the knowledge of requirements [2].

The culture of sharing information and knowledge is something that is vital in software development[30]. It is in this that teams learn new tools, know each other, and to improve the process as well as innovativeness [4], [3]. However at the development section it was affirmed that there is low knowledge sharing, high level of individualism and not much teamwork. This results in long communication chains where people take long to communicate or provide feedback to those who need it. The lack of teamwork can be explained by teams having a low cross-functional mind-set and can result into individualism where everyone is concerned about him/herself to do the work. We suggest retrospectives, a self-organized cross-functional team setting, team colocation, working in pairs, and daily stand-ups to cub these challenges.

All the challenges mentioned were validated by the management at the section and are seen to overlap each other. The process related challenges could be the cause of low domain understanding at the same time can be argued to be the cause of workload related challenges. On the other hand the domain specific and supplier network challenge can be the cause of process related challenges, which can explain the working context challenges. And also having a complex development structure can explain why there is low knowledge sharing and no team interactions. In other words, these challenges are intertwined and one can result into the other.

6   Conclusion and Outlook

In this paper we presented our findings from a qualitative study with one of the development sections at Volvo Car Cooperation. Challenged by its transition towards being a software-centric company, which shows in the increased need for in-house software development. The department is looking for ways to improve their software development processes and decrease their time to market. Based on semi-structured interviews, we discovered specific challenges with the current way of developing their software. We discuss the applicability of agile methods to these challenges. For VCC, this study can serve as a first step towards transition to agile methods. Future work should focus on quantifying and measuring the current challenges so that potential improvements from switching to agile methods can be proven. We hope that others find our insights useful for understanding challenges that arise from software and software development pervading more and more products.

References

1. Cockburn, A.: Agile software development: The cooperative game, vol. 113, pp. 2000–2001. Addison-Wesley (2001)
2. Eklund, U., Bosch, J.: Applying Agile Development in Mass-Produced Embedded Systems. In: Wohlin, C. (ed.) XP 2012. LNBIP, vol. 111, pp. 31–46. Springer, Heidelberg (2012)
3. Holmström, H.O.: Acting Agile in Streamline Development. Inf. Syst. Res. Semin. Scand. (2009)
4. Katumba, B., Antanovich, A.: Bottlenecks in the Development Life Cycle of a Feature- A case study conducted at Ericsson AB. In: 7th Annual International Conference on Computing and ICT Research, pp. 472–490 (2011)
5. Poppendieck, M., Poppendieck, T.: Lean Software Development: An Agile Toolkit. Addison Wesley, Boston (2003)
6. Shalloway, A., Beaver, G., Trott, J.R.: Lean-Agile Software Development, Achieving Enterprise Agility. Addison Wesley, Upper Saddle River (2010)
7. Womack, J.P., Jones, D.T., Roos, D.: The Machine that Changed the World: The Story of Lean Production, pp. 1–11. Harper Collins, New York (1990)
8. Hafterson, T.: Incorporating Agile Methods into the Development of Large-Scale Systems. In: UMM CSsci Senior Conference, Moris, MN
9. Salo, O., Abrahamsson, P.: Agile methods in European embedded software development organisations: A survey on the actual use and usefulness of Extreme Programming and Scrum. IET Software 2(1), 58 (2008)
10. Yusuf, Y.Y., Sarhadi, M., Gunasekaran, A.: Agile manufacturing: The drivers, concepts and attributes. Int. J. Prod. Econ. 62(1–2), 33–43 (1999)
11. Dismukes, J.P., Uppal, M., Vonderembse, M.A., Huang, S.H.: Designing supply chains: Towards theory development. International Journal of Production Economics 100(2), 223–238 (2006)
12. Beck, K., Beedle, M., Van Bennekum, A., Cockburn, A., Cunningham, W., Fowler, M., Grenning, J., Highsmith, J., Hunt, A., Jeffries, R., Kern, J., Marick, B., Martin, R.C., Mellor, S., Schwaber, K., Sutherland, J., Thomas, D.: Manifesto for Agile Software Development. The Agile Alliance (2001), http://agilemanifesto.org/ (accessed: May 30, 2014)
13. Harrison, R., West, A., Lee, L.: Lifecycle Engineering of Future Automation Systems in the Automotive Powertrain Sector. In: 2006 IEEE Int. Conf. Ind. Informatics, pp. 305–310 (August 2006)
14. Abrahamsson, P., Warsta, J., Siponen, M.T., Ronkainen, J.: New directions on agile methods: A comparative analysis. In: Proceedings of the 25th International Conference on Software Engineering, pp. 244–254 (2003)
15. Schwaber, K., Beedle, M.: Agile Software Development with Scrum, vol. 18(9), p. 158. Prentice-Hall (2001)
16. Beck, K.: Extreme Programming Explained: Embrace Change, p. 224. IEEE (1999)

17. Paasivaara, M., Durasiewicz, S., Lassenius, C.: Distributed Agile Development: Using Scrum in a Large Project. In: 2008 IEEE Int. Conf. Glob. Softw. Eng., pp. 87–95 (August 2008)
18. Albuquerque, C.O., Antonino, P.O., Nakagawa, E.Y.: An investigation into agile methods in embedded systems development. In: Murgante, B., Gervasi, O., Misra, S., Nedjah, N., Rocha, A.M.A.C., Taniar, D. O., Apduhan, B.O. (eds.) ICCSA 2012, Part III. LNCS, vol. 7335, pp. 576–591. Springer, Heidelberg (2012)
19. Abrahamsson, P.: Speeding up embedded software development. ITEA Innov. Rep. (2007)
20. Salo, O., Abrahamsson, P.: Agile methods in European embedded software development organisations: A survey on the actual use and usefulness of Extreme Programming and Scrum. IET Software 2(1), 58 (2008)
21. Tarokh, M.J., Ghahremanloo, H., Karami, M.: Agility in Auto Dealers SCM. In: IEEE International Conference on Service Operations and Logistics, and Informatics, SOLI 2007, August 27-29, pp. 1–6 (2007)
22. Dybå, T., Dingsøyr, T.: Empirical studies of agile software development: A systematic review. Inf. Softw. Technol. 50(9–10), 833–859 (2008)
23. Robson, C.: Real world research: A resource for social scientists and practitioner-researchers, vol. 2, p. 624. Blackwell (2002)
24. Yin, R.K.: Case Study Research: Design and Methods, vol. 5(5), p. 219. Sage Publications (2009)
25. Andersson, C., Runeson, P.: A spiral process model for case studies on software quality monitoring method and metrics. Softw. Process Improv. Pract. 12(2), 125–140 (2007)
26. Klein, H.K., Myers, M.D.: A Set of Principles for Conducting and Evaluating Interpretive Field Studies in Information Systems. MIS Q. -Spec. Issue Intensive Res. Inf. Syst. 23(1), 67 (1999)
27. Julian, B.M.: Scrum Master Activities: Process Tailoring in Large Enterprise Projects. In: 2014 IEEE 9th International Conference on Global Software Engineering (ICGSE), August 18-21, pp. 6–15 (2014)
28. Guang-yong, H.: Study and practice of import Scrum agile software development. In: 2011 IEEE 3rd International Conference on Communication Software and Networks (ICCSN), May 27-29, pp. 217–220 (2011)
29. Schwaber, K., Sutherland, J.: The scrum guide (October 2011)
30. Sekitoleko, N., Evbota, F., Knauss, E., Sandberg, A., Chaudron, M., Olsson, H.H.: Technical Dependency Challenges in Large-Scale Agile Software Development. In: Cantone, G., Marchesi, M. (eds.) XP 2014. LNBIP, vol. 179, pp. 46–61. Springer, Heidelberg (2014)

Organization-Wide Agile Expansion Requires an Organization-Wide Agile Mindset

Hidde van Manen and Hans van Vliet

Computer Science Department, VU University Amsterdam, The Netherlands
hiddevanmanen@hotmail.com, hans@cs.vu.nl

Abstract. While agile methods are widely used, large organizations still struggle with the implementation thereof throughout the whole organization. The objective of our study is to identify factors that affect the expansion of agile software development in large organizations. We performed a multiple-case study to do so. We found agile software development in large organizations is more than implementing Scrum. In particular, we identified "agile mindset" as a crucial topic that deserves attention when expanding agile methods in large organizations.

Keywords: agile expansion, Scrum, agile mindset.

1 Introduction

Since their origin in February of 2001, agile software development methods have become immensely popular. While Forrester research from 2010 indicated that agile methods were practiced in more than a third of all projects [1], this percentage has kept growing strongly in the last few years and is now well over eighty percent of all projects [2]. Surely this cannot be the case in every organization? No. A quick internet search teaches us that large, international organizations all over the globe are still in the process of transforming their development organization towards agile software development – and that this change is not realized overnight. An example is the U.S. Postal Service, which has spent well over three years rolling out agile in its organization and recently announced that agile has officially replaced the waterfall methodology in March 2013[1].

Agile Methods, when referred to in this paper, encompass software development methodologies characterized by a continuous readiness to rapidly realize change, pro-actively or reactively embrace change, and learn from change while contributing to customer value. In particular, Scrum, the development methodology used in the environments studied in this paper, fits this definition. A focus on working code right from the beginning, delivery cycles of 2-4 weeks (so-called Sprints), and having business representatives on the team are but three practices to achieve the above benefits [3].

---

[1] http://fcw.com/articles/2013/06/13/usps-agile-development.aspx - accessed on June 25, 2013.

A. Jedlitschka et al. (Eds.): PROFES 2014, LNCS 8892, pp. 48–62, 2014.

The introduction and adoption of agile methods within organizations is a popular subject of research into agile methods [4]. The number of anecdotal and qualitative studies into the challenges of such adoption is large and studies have been performed both over short and long periods of time [5–13]. The findings of these studies are not always consistent [7]. On the other hand some factors are commonly accepted as being critical to the success of agile adoption, such as "management support" and "customer collaboration" [7, 9, 11].

One of the items on the current research agenda is to study agile software development within organizations that have left the so-called adoption phase [14]. Recently a few publications on this topic have seen the light, e.g. [15], but a lot of questions remain open. There is an increasing need for knowledge about this topic, as *"many organizations have completed the adoption stage and agile methods start to become well-established processes of these organizations"* [16]. The expansion of agile methods in large organizations is another one of the issues to be addressed and this is also the topic of our research.

Already in the early days of agile, some publications report practitioners struggling with scaling agile methods, e.g. [17]. What they describe is the demand to balance the new agile methods with the document-driven (waterfall) approach that large organizations require. Boehm, Beck and Turner [18, 19] were involved in a discussion on balancing agile methods with traditional document-driven methods in large organizations, in order to achieve the benefits of both. They state: *"both approaches have shortcomings that, if left unaddressed, can lead to project failure. The challenge is to balance the two approaches to take advantage of their strengths and compensate for their weaknesses"* [18, 19]. It seems rather hard to adopt agile methods on an enterprise-wide scale in large organizations. Agile methods in general, including Scrum, focus more on the team level and less on organizational issues. When large organizations try to adopt agile methods, they face a myriad of issues that are different compared to individual teams adopting agile and which make the organizational adoption a complex and hard journey. In every organization agile methods are implemented in a unique context that is the result of a combination of organizational, process, human and technological factors. Also, the challenges concerning the use of agile methods change when agile transforms from being a small experiment to being the main method used company-wide.

When we speak of agile expansion or scaling, we mean that agile methods are for example extended from one organizational unit to other organizational units, or from an initial small project to larger and more complex projects, which results in challenges of a new kind [15, 20]. Multiple authors describe and suggest that there are many issues and challenges that arise when agile is implemented and adopted at the organizational level, such as synchronization of agile and non-agile (document-driven) functions [15, 16, 21, 22].

Beyond Budgeting is complementary to the agile way of working. It is a performance management method oriented to fast changing environments, rather than strict control mechanisms [23]. Traditional management adopts a command-and-control way of thinking, whereas Beyond Budgeting adopts a sense-and-control way of thinking. The complementarities between Beyond Budgeting and Agile software development are discussed in [24].

Agility can also be linked to Lean Software Development. Lean manufacturing was introduced in the 1990's in the Japanese car industry. The concepts of lean manufactoring and agile software development were combined by Mary and Tom Poppendieck [25]. Lean software development is built around seven principles: eliminate waste, build quality in, create knowledge, defer commitment, deliver fast, respect people, and optimize the whole. Williams [26] gives an elaborate comparison of agile and lean production, while [27] gives an experience report on the application of lean approaches in agile software development.

The research question we aim to answer is: *Identify factors that affect the expansion of agile development in large organizations.* We performed a multiple-case study to do so. We found agile software development in large organizations encompasses more than implementing Scrum. We identified a number of issues that deserve attention when expanding agile methods in large organizations. We grouped them in two broad categories: "agile mindset" and "contextual dependencies". For lack of space, we only discuss the "agile mindset" issues in this paper. Example contextual dependencies identified are: "agility of partner organizations", "governance procedures", and "top management agile vision".

2   Research Method

The research we have performed was a multiple-case study. The case study method is best suited to develop an understanding of the interactions among information technology innovations and organizational context [28]. Multiple-case designs enable generalizability and the ability to extend theory through cross-case analyses [29]. Some argue with this, because the characteristics of each case are unique and this limits the external validity of comparing cases and making generalizations [30]. However, Walsham [31] argues that generalization is not necessarily the primary goal of studying multiple cases. More important is the deep insight that enables the researcher to develop concepts and theory based on information from many sources and understanding of the context.

2.1   Data Collection and Analysis

Since the focus of our research was on the expansion of agile methods in large organizations, we needed to study organizations of a certain scale that were in the process of expanding agile software development activities within their organization. We selected organizations that had been working on this expansion for quite some time, so they could discuss their previous efforts, struggles and results with us, because we were unable to perform a longitudinal study. Stepping in and following their efforts and progress over time was not an option. Thus, we selected two large multi-nationals based in the Netherlands which had both been expanding agile methods for at least 1,5 years at the time of our research. Besides the fact that both companies met our requirements of scale and being in the process of expansion, our selection of companies and sub-units was opportunistic. Due to time constraints, we have selected the first two companies that were positive about participating in our research. We selected two different types of organizations, a consumer electronics company and a bank, to increase diversity of the organizational and business context. Within the companies we limited the scope of our research to respectively a change program and a business line, because of the limited resources (one researcher and two months time) that were available for our research. The companies themselves selected the program and business line. The characteristics of the two companies are listed in Table 1.

Table 1. Case company characteristics

	Company A	Company B
Company background	Consumer electronics	Bank
Unit type	Program	Business line
Size	12 teams, 90 persons	7-8 teams, 80 persons
Direct organizational environment	100 teams, separated in three sectors and cross-sector	400 employess, spread over five business lines
Type of system developed	Internal profitability measuring system for controlling department	Internal back-office systems for global financial markets
Location	Co-located teams spread over several floors	Co-located teams on one big floor
Development method	Scrum	Loose Scrum
Years of experience with agile	1,5 years	Three years ago Open UP, one year ago "agile the next step"

The main source of data collection for our research was through face-to-face interviews. In both organizations we interviewed participants that have different roles within the organization in order to collect information from different angles and perspectives. We selected participants who were part of the agile development teams themselves or were directly involved with the teams that went through the transformation. We interviewed eight persons in Company A, and ten in Company B. Table 2 lists the interviewees, their role, and their experience with agile. For Company B, the business line that was subject to our research adopted several agile practices over a period of two years, such as standup meetings and work boards, but not others, such as iteration development or planning meetings. For that reason, a clear starting point for the experience with agile often cannot be given. All participants are from Dutch sites, except for the Operations Team Lead of Company A. The interviews took place in Spring 2013.

The interviews were semi-structured and conducted following the same template. The interviews lasted between 42 and 82 minutes with an average duration of approximately 62 minutes. The interviewer prepared an interview guide containing topics to discuss with participants. The interview guide served as a

Table 2. Participants overview

Company	Role	Experioence with Agile
Company A	Delivery manager	18 months
	Business analyst	12 months
	Member agile work group, agile coach	36 months (18 at another company)
	Business stakeholder	18 months
	Scrum master, agile coach, product owner support	18 months
	Account manager	n.a.
	Operations team lead	n.a.
Company B	Environment manager	3.5 years (1.5 Scrum master at another company)
	Agile coach	1 year
	Manager projects	Not clear
	Team manager support	Not clear
	Business manager	Not clear
	Team maneger development	Not clear
	Lead business analyst	Not clear
	Change & release manager	1 year Scrum master
	Tester	1 year
	Business line manager	Not clear

structure for the interview, as well as to make sure that the interviewer covered all topics and kept the right scope. What follows is a list of the topics that were on the interview guide:

- Description of the employees role in the organization, his/hers experience with agile software development and general information about the project and organization he/she is currently working on;
- Benefits of agile software development that the participant has (and has not) seen in the organization;
- Expansion of agile - what differences does the participant experience between agile at small (team) and large (organizational) scale;
- What challenges has the organization encountered in the expansion of agile. Possible topics: (organizational) processes, people, business, agile method, tools and (change) management;
- In case the participant had not made clear what he/she deemed to be most important, we asked that if the participant could suggest one change or give one advice to his/her CIO regarding the expansion of agile software development, what it would be.

The interview concluded with a summary of highlights from the interview, based on the interviewer's notes, on which the interviewee could make remarks. Then each participant was given the possibility to add anything to the record without the researcher's possible bias. The questions in the interview were mostly open-ended, to stimulate interviewees to tell a story in its context, which is important in the context of agile software development. The interview setting allowed the interviewer to explain questions or ask follow-up questions in case this was necessary and thus prevent inaccurate answers. Closed questions were used to confirm facts or statements that were made to the researcher in earlier interviews or to challenge initial analyses of the researcher.

In addition to the data gathered through personal interviews, the researcher has made on-site observations during daily stand-ups, retrospective and Scrum review meetings and walking around the office locations on several occasions. These observations and meetings were not recorded, but notes were taken. Also, we received some files from interviewed persons, including (but not limited to) organizational diagrams, documents about the agile vision, an agile maturity (evaluation) model, weekly report forms and a dashboard for reporting agile expansion KPI's. The last source of data came from sketches made during interviews by interviewees, e.g. about the project initiation process or to illustrate a timeline of events.

From the initial transcripts of the interviews, analysis went through the following steps:

- Initial coding: assigning codes to all relevant statements, catching the essence of what was said. The result was close to 100 codes per company.
- Focused coding, developing "concepts": eliminating, combining, or subdividing codes, looking for repeating ideas and concepts. This approach was based on [32]. We first grouped codes per person, and next merged similar concepts from multiple interviewees.
- Pattern coding, developing "categories": This step aims to aggregate and summarize the previous coding, identifying themes across all.
- Constructing theory: based on a comparison of the results for the two cases, two findings emerged: the importance of an "agile mindset" and "contextual dependencies". The researcher then went back to consult relevant literature on these two topics.

3 Results and Discussion

We identified two broad topics that are, according to participants of our research, important in order to successfully expand agile software development within a large organization: "agile mindset" and "contextual dependencies". We next went back to the codes and concepts from our research to identify factors that are positively or negatively related to the topics agile mindset or contextual dependencies. In this section we will go through this analysis for the "agile mindset" topic and relate our observations to existing literature.

Throughout our interviews participants in both companies deemed an agile mindset crucial to the successful expansion (i.e. the potential benefits of the agile way of working are obtained) of agile methods through the organization as a whole. At Company A participants mainly stated that although the development teams had adopted agile quickly and started to think more and more in agile ways, the business client and partner companies had more trouble changing their mindset. In Company B we heard often that the general resistance employees had towards working agile was partially based on a lack of an agile mindset, which in turn was influenced by an extensive experience with non-agile methods. In both companies participants said that managers had too little knowledge of agile or lacked an agile mindset.

We analyzed our interview records to identify factors that participants described in relation to an agile mindset. In this analysis three issues emerged, which form an important part of the agile mindset. These are 'collaboration', 'trust' and 'continuous improvement'. In other words, if there is no collaboration, trust or wish for continuous improvement, then there exists no agile mindset within an organization.

Figure 1 shows the result of our analysis on how these three issues are influenced by organizational and cultural factors. The numbers between brackets indicate how often these factors were mentioned during our interviews (multiple instances per participant are counted separately) and the symbols along the arrows illustrate if a relation is positive (+) or negative (-). We only include factors that were mentioned more than once. We discuss each issue and its constituent factors:

Collaboration

- **Competing "partners" structure (−):** Having multiple competing partner companies in the development process negatively affects collaboration. These partners have a separate goal and that is to win more contracts than other partners. Also this construction demotivates knowledge sharing across the organization, as a participant from Company A explained to us: *"'It would be stupid to share all our knowledge with [the other partner companies], because then what will our advantage over them be? Why would Company A choose us for the next project?"* On the other hand, a participant from Company B told us that having a "real" partnership with for example your support organization could boost collaboration. A "real" partnership means that you discuss both positive and negative things with each other. By doing this, the relationship is not only made up by discussions about what is going wrong, but can be enriched by talking about the progress you made together.
- **Serial work process (−):** A serial work process negatively affects collaboration, because during each step of the process, someone who is part of the process usually has less contact with other contributors of the process, but instead just waits until he gets something delivered from the person that precedes him in the chain.
- **Individual thinking (of people, teams, departments) (−):** Individual thinking was the factor most mentioned as influencing collaboration. When for example a team is focused too much on itself and not on the other teams they are working with to complete a product, this can lead to misalignment

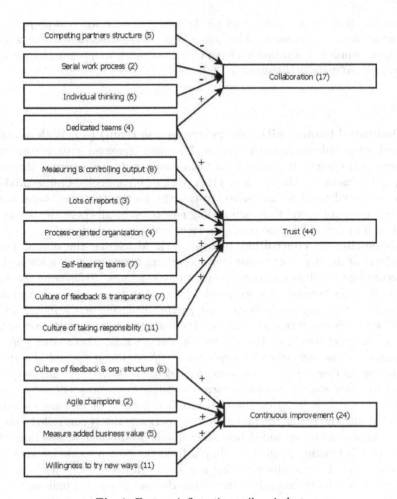

Fig. 1. Factors influencing agile mindset

of activities. Another example comes from Company A, where it is clear that the development organization and support organization are both pursuing their own goals, while they could improve their collaboration by working together as DevOps teams. One has to balance one's identity as a team member versus one's role in the organization at large [33].

– **Dedicated teams (with experience as one team) (+):** Having a team fully dedicated to one development stream increases collaboration, because team members are always available and do not have to switch between teams, environments and scopes. Also, experience as a team increases collaboration, because team members get to know each other's strengths and weaknesses. Participants from both companies condemned the first period of agile development, because they did not have dedicated teams then, as the following quote illustrates: *"After a few months of successful Scrumming, they dis-*

banded all the teams and spread all the members over different projects. We had to start all over again. That was a huge loss of knowledge." The reorientation required in a transition from individual work to a self-managing agile team is extensively discussed in [34].

Trust

- **Dedicated teams (with experience as one team)** (+): With increased dedication and experience as a team also comes increased trust, according to some participants. It is harder for team members to build trust if they only spend a fraction of their time together working on one collaborative product. A dedicated team is also more trustworthy for management, because the team need not spend time onboarding new team members at the beginning of each project. This also results in more stable output of work.
- **Measuring & controlling output** (−): Measuring the output (story points) of development teams and accounting teams on it, is a wrong idea according to multiple participants of both companies."*Beforehand [management] states how many story points a team has to earn in each Sprint. If the team does not reach its goal, the partner company gets a fine. I do not think that is not very agile-minded. The team needs to earn at least 80% of your contract points, or the partner will not get paid. This has an effect on teams. [At the start of agile] people were enthusiastic at the end of a sprint, picking up new stories to work on. Now developers are more anxious about starting new stories, because if they cant finish them, they will not get paid. This has definitely affected peoples mindset.* Instead of focusing on points and giving the teams the idea that their performance is controlled, companies should focus on added business value and customer satisfaction. Part of trust is trusting teams that they will do the best possible job they can. Misra et al [10] also observed that a more qualitative control leads to more success in agile projects. In terms of the Beyond Budgeting philosophy [35]: "*The main goal of Beyond Budgeting is not to get rid of budgets [. . .] but it is more the budgeting mindset we need to get rid of.*
- **Lots of reports** (−): The amount of reports that a team has to file is a nice indicator for trust, say participants. "*The fact that I have to report to approximately ten different managers each week, does not give me the feeling that they trust our team*", is how a participant explained the importance of reports to us.
- **Process-oriented organization** (−): If teams have to follow extensive processes and cannot change them this does not positively affect the feeling of trust in the organization. *Our organization needs a planning. When we file a project plan, we still need a Project Initiation Document (PID) with a decent reasoning on how long your project will take. And you cannot deviate from that too much. Another example is that IT development now wants to count with story points, but we are paying in euros, so you still need a translation back from story points, to working hours, to budgets. Although we are working agile, our planning is still waterfall, with all related phases. I*

believe it will stay that way. In an agile organization, there should be room to adjust processes and for teams to make their own choices, instead of having an extensive process in place for each particular situation.

- **Self-steering teams & facilitating management style** (+): On the other hand, if an organization allows teams to steer themselves and management has a facilitating attitude towards teams, this has a positive effect on trust in the organization. This is corroborated by [34] and [36], amongst others. Moe et al [37] identify several organisational barriers to self-management at the team level, such as the quest for organizational control and a culture of specialization. One important aspect of the facilitating management style is need for support and budget from the business to put qualified product owners on all development teams.

- **Culture of feedback & transparency** (+): Having a culture of feedback in the organization and being transparent across teams and departments positively influences trust. *We had our CIO at a product demo, and it was a Sprint in which not everything had gone right. I showed him [our problems] and he said he was happy to see that, because [he said:] all the demos that I go to, everything goes flawless. Apparently people do not dare and want to show what goes wrong. I think this is company culture. Everyone reports to his/her manager that things go well. For some reason, it is not done to report that something is not going well here, while I have seen this differently at other companies Ive worked for.* One participant explained how her organization lacks this: *"I think that at this moment there is no attention for organizational impediments at higher levels, because these impediments are not brought up in the first place. A lot of people are anxious about reporting impediments, because they have experiences where bringing up these issues was ... not well received."*

- **Culture of taking responsibility** (+): The agile mindset element of trust relies heavily on employees taking responsibility, say participants. *Agile is a certain mindset. It means that you give responsibility to employees and [management] has to be open to that. You have to reduce the amount of controls, and give people empowerment to take action and responsibility. If you keep all your control structures and your blame culture in place that will conflict with agile. Only following the method is not enough, you have to look at the idea behind the method and adjust your controls accordingly.* Instead of hiding behind processes people should build ownership over development processes and take responsibility of emerging problems. This helps to solve these issues quicker and more effectively, while it also increases people's trust in each other. Creating such a culture is both seen as a challenge [33] and as a success factor [10]. Taking responsibility also is one of the leadership principles of Beyond Budgeting [24].

Continuous Improvement

- **Culture of feedback and organizational structure** (+): A culture of feedback accompanied by appropriate organizational structures to cultivate this feedback and use it will positively affect continuous improvement. If these organizational structures are not in place, it can lead to disappointment among teams that spend time evaluating their work and providing constructive feedback about processes, say participants. Open constructive feedback is essential to the continuous improvement of the organization.

- **Agile champions** (+): The role of the business line management should be to address the resistance among employees, solve problems that hinder the agile expansion, change processes that do not fit the new way of working, train and coach people and facilitate the coordination with parties that the development depends on. However, multiple participants of our research mentioned that they miss a clear vision of the management. It is clear that agile is the way to go, but how, why, when and in what way the agile expansion should take place is unclear for them. Small changes are pervasive, but there is no coherent story. *There is no clear vision, no clear line. I think it is messy; some practices are picked and we are only doing agile partially. We are not rallying behind a choice and clearly going somewhere. We need someone to say: this is where we are going and this is how we are going to get there. I miss such a vision.* People that support the agile mindset and put effort in spreading it through the organization can have a lasting positive effect on continuous improvement[38].
- **Measure added business value** (+): Measuring added business value over costs focuses attention on continuous improvement of products, thus increasing the overall attention of continuous improvement in the organization. Continuous improvement is a key characteristic of both Beyond Budgeting and Lean Software Development.
- **Willingness to try new way of working** (+): Finally, the willingness of employees to try a new way of working also influences the continuous improvement of the organization. If employees are less willing to innovate their work processes, this reduces the possibilities for continuous improvement. The importance of continuous learning is also noted in [10, 39]. In the business line of one of the companies, there was a lot of resistance against agile among employees. This is partially a consequence of not making the change completely (but step-by-step), because this allows people to challenge the working method and its benefits. Improvements are not attributed to agile, while all issues give opponents more reason to complain. As a primary reason for the resistance, employees say that the why of the agile scaling was never clearly explained, as the following participant explained: *Change is not a problem as long as it is clear why it is needed. I hear a lot of people ask: Why? Did things go bad? Are there complaints? What is the goal of implementing agile? Is the goal to work agile, or are we trying to achieve certain benefits? That is not really clear.* To educate employees about agile and to create support, all employees had to follow an Agile Awareness training and make an Agile Foundation Exam, but they perceived these to be rather useless and not applicable in their work. There is disunity in teams, because some team members are opponents while other oppose agile. This resistance is not unwillingness; it is mostly habituation of the old way of working.

In our team we started to rollout agile. There are supporters and opponents. I have the idea that people are not yet convinced and that makes it hard to implement. () We have been discussing this for three weeks now, but if only the testers want to do it, we cannot do it. It only works when the whole team is behind it. Others do not think it is efficient, that it will not save them time. There also seems to be a difference between more and less experienced employees, where less experienced employees have a more positive attitude towards the agile expansion, which is also found in earlier research [40].

It is interesting to see that something intangible as "trust" seems to be at the core of the agile mindset, as is also observed by Moe [34], McHugh [41] and Strode [39]. The importance of trust was named even more than the other two main elements combined. More than the other two elements, trust is also affected by or reflected in organizational structures; one has to carefully balance control and flexibility [20]. This indicates that while the agile mindset is primarily a psychological issue, it is in fact quite related to organizational elements such as the reporting processes.

In order to successfully expand agile throughout the organization, the organization should foster an agile mindset among its employess. This involves developers, managers, and other stakeholders. Whitworth [42] researched the social nature of agile teams, and identified several characteristics of agile teams that stand out: (1) oppenness and respect, (2) a strong inclination for whole team consideration and involvement, and (3) highly value action, initiative and continuous improvement. Such is also reflected in the three core values of the agile mindset as identified in our research.

This agile mindset should exceed the agile team. Van Waardenburg [43] already mentions the importance of an agile mindset amongst business representatives. When the agile culture is limited to the IT department, it will only lead to frustration when working with other, non-agile, parts of the organization.

4   Limitations

Our research was more of a snapshot than an image of the organizations over time. A longitudinal study would have given us the chance to further validate our findings. This was not a possibility, as only limited time and resources were available to perform the research.

Both organizations that participated in our research used the Scrum method as their agile method. While Scrum is the most-used method in the world of agile, this limits the external validity of our researchs findings to organizations using other methods. Organizations that use other methods, which for example more directly address issues discussed in this thesis, may differ from our findings.

5   Conclusion

In this paper, we studied the expansion of agile methods in large organizations. We found the impact of agile on the organization goes much further than just the development teams that practice Scrum (or a variant). If an organization wants to become completely agile and achieve all the potential benefits of an agile way of working, this requires a certain mindset of people throughout the organization and an adaption of the agile implementation based on the contextual dependencies along three perspectives The latter is not further elaborated in the present paper). This conclusion is in line with results from a recent global survey on agile development by VersionOne. When asked what barriers existed to further adoption of agile methods in the enterprise, ranked one (selected by 52% of the participants) was the "ability to change organizational culture", followed in third place (35%) by "trying to fit agile elements into a non-agile framework" [2].

Through analysis of both our participants thoughts on the agile mindset and existing literature on this subject, we claim that the agile mindset's main elements are:

- **Trust:** all employees should take responsibility for changes and issues, as they are empowered and trusted by the management to make their own decisions, while the organizational structure and processes reflect this trust;
- **Continuous improvement:** everyone in the organization strives for continuous improvement of all processes, people, and products, by maintaining an open attitude towards each others feedback, and
- **Collaboration:** all results and improvements are achieved trough intensive collaboration of everyone in the organization.

Being a truly agile organization requires more than the implementation of an agile method such as Scrum. Being agile is a mindset based on trust, collaboration and continuous improvement. We would like to end our conclusions with a quote from Ivar Jacobson:

> *Agility should penetrate everything you do. It penetrates the way you should manage and do requirements, architecture, design, coding, integration and testing, and in the way that you should document and track what you do. () It reaches all levels in the company from upper level managers down to the developers. () Agile is an attitude that everyone must embrace.* [2]

Acknowledgement. We gratefully acknowledge the constructive feedback of Torgeir Dingsøyr on an earlier version of this paper.

References

1. West, D.: Water-Scrum-Fall is the Reality Of Agile for Most Organizations Today. Forrester (2011)
2. VersionOne: 7th annual state of agile development survey (2013)

---

[2] Ivar Jacobson International, Scaling Agile WP,
http://www.ivarjacobson.com/resource.aspx?id=402, accessed May 17th, 2013

3. Schwaber, K., Sutherland, J.: The Scrum Guide: The official rulebook. Technical Report (October 26, 1991), http://www.scrum/scrumguides/
4. Dybå, T., Dingsøyr, T.: Empirical studies of agile software development: A systematic review. Information and Software Technology 50(9-10), 833–859 (2008)
5. Boehm, B.: Get Ready for Agile Methods, with Care. Computer 35, 64–69 (2002)
6. Bottani, E.: Profile and enablers of agile companies: An empirical investigation. International Journal of Production Economics 125, 251–261 (2010)
7. Chow, T., Cao, D.B.: A surevy study on critical success factors in agile software projects. Journal of Systems and Software 81, 961–971 (2008)
8. Cockburn, A., Highsmith, J.: Agile software development, the people factor. Computer 34, 131–133 (2001)
9. Livermore, J.: Factors that significantly impact the implementation of an agile software development methodogy. Journal of Software 3, 31–36 (2008)
10. Misra, S.C., Kumar, V., Kumar, U.: Identifying some important success factors in adopting agile software development practices. The Journal of Systems and Software 82, 1869–1890 (2009)
11. Nerur, S., Mahapatra, R., Mangalaraj, G.: Challenges of Migrating to Agile Methodologies. Communications of the ACM 48, 73–78 (2005)
12. Schmidt, C.T., Venkatesha, S.G., Heymann, J.: Empirical Insights into the Perceived Benefits of Agile Software Engineering Practices: A Case Study from SAP. In: Companion Volume Proceeding 36th International Conference on Software Engineering (ICSE), pp. 84–92. IEEE Computer Society (2014)
13. Laanti, M.: Agile Methods in Large-Scale Software Development Organizations – Applicability and Model for Adoption. PhD thesis, University of Oulu, Oulu, Finland (2012)
14. Dingsøyr, T., Nerur, S., Balijepally, V., Brede Moe, N.: A decade of agile methodologies: Towards explaining agile software development. Journal of Systems and Software 85, 1213–1221 (2012)
15. Senapathi, M., Srinivasan, A.: Understanding post-adoptive agile usage: An exploratory cross-case analysis. Journal of Systems and Software 85, 1255–1268 (2012)
16. Abrahamsson, P., Conboy, K., Wang, X.: 'lots done, more to do': The current state of agile systems development research. European Journal of Information Systems 18, 281–284 (2009)
17. Reifer, D.: Scaling agile methods. IEEE Software 20(4), 12–14 (2003)
18. Beck, K., Boehm, B.: Agility through discipline: A debate. Computer 36(6), 44–46 (2003)
19. Boehm, B., Turner, R.: Balancing Agility and Discipline. Addison Wesley (2002)
20. Mishra, D., Mishra, A.: Complex software project development: Agile methods adoption. Journal of Software Maintenance and Evolution: Research and Practice 23(8), 549–564 (2011)
21. Mangalaraj, G., Mahapatra, R., Nerur, S.: Acceptance of software process innovations – the case of extreme programming. European Journal of Information Systems 18(4), 344–354 (2009)
22. Moe, N.B., Dingsøyr, T.: Research Challenges in Large Scale Agile Software Development. ACM SIGSOFT Software Engineering Notes 38(5) (2013)
23. Bogsnes, B.: Implementing Beyond Budgeting: Unlocking the Performance Potential. Wiley (2008)

24. Lohan, G., Conboy, K., Lang, M.: Beyond Budgeting and Agile Software Development: A Conceptual Framework for the Performance Management of Agile Software Development Teams. In: Proceedings of the 31st International Conference on Information Systems (ICIS 2010) (2010)
25. Poppendieck, M., Poppendieck, T.: Implementing Lean Software Development: From Concept to Cash. Addison-Wesley (2007)
26. Williams, L.: Agile Software Development Methodologies and Practices. In: Advances in Computers, vol. 80, pp. 4–44. Elsevier (2010)
27. Wang, X., Conboy, K., Cawley, O.: "Leagile" software development: An expereince report analysis of the application of lean approaches in agile software development. Journal of Systems and Software 85(6), 1287–1299 (2012)
28. Seaman, C.: Qualitative Methods in Empirical Studies of Software Engineering. IEEE Transactions on Software Engineering 25(4), 557–572 (1999)
29. Miles, M., Huberman, A.: Qualitative Data Analysis: An Expanded Sourcebook. Saga, London (1994)
30. Kitchenham, B.A., Pfleeger, S.L., Pickard, L.M., Jones, P.W., Hoaglin, D.C., Emam, K.E.: Preliminary Guidelines for Empirical Research in Software Engineering. IEEE Transactions on Software Engineering 28, 721–734 (2002)
31. Walsham, G.: Interpretive Case Studies in IS Research: Nature and Method. European Journal of Information Systems 4(4), 74–81 (1995)
32. Bogdan, R., Biklen, S.: Qualitative Research for Education: An introduction to Theories and Methods, 4th edn. Pearson (2003)
33. Moore, E., Spens, J.: Scaling Agile: Finding your Agile Tribe. In: Agile 2008 Conference, pp. 121–124. IEEE Computer Society (2008)
34. Moe, N.B., Dingsøyr, T., Dybå, T.: A teamwork model for understanding an agile team: A case study of a Scrum project. Information and Software Technology 52, 480–491 (2010)
35. Bogsnes, B.: Keynote: Beyond Budgeting in a Lean and Agile World. In: Abrahamsson, P., Marchesi, M., Maurer, F. (eds.) XP 2009. LNBIP, vol. 31, pp. 5–7. Springer, Heidelberg (2009)
36. Vidgen, R., Wang, X.: Coevolving Systems and the Organization of Agile Software Development. Information Systems Research 20(3), 355–376 (2009)
37. Moe, N.B., Dingsøyr, T., Dybå, T.: Overcoming Barriers to Self-Management in Software Teams. IEEE Software 26(6), 20–26 (2009)
38. Benefield, G.: Rolling out Agile in a Large Enterprise. In: Proceedings of the 41st Hawaii International Conference on System Sciences (HICSS 2008), p. 462. IEEE Computer Society (2008)
39. Strode, D.E., Huff, S.L., Tretiakov, A.: The Impact of Organizational Culture on Agile Method Use. In: Proceedings of the 42nd Hawaii International Conference on System Sciences, pp. 1–9. IEEE Computer Society (2009)
40. Vijayasarathy, L., Turk, D.: Drivers of agile software development use: Dialectic Interplay between benefits and hindrances. Information and Software Technology 54(2), 137–148 (2012)
41. McHugh, O., Conboy, K., Lang, M.: Agile Practices: The Impact on Trust in Software Project Teams. IEEE Software 29(3), 71–76 (2012)
42. Whitworth, E., Biddle, R.: The Social Nature of Agile Teams. In: Agile 2007, pp. 26–36. IEEE Computer Society (2007)
43. Waardenburg, G.V., van Vliet, H.: When Agile meets the Enterprise. Information and Software Technology 55(12), 2154–2171 (2013)

The Effects of Gradual Weighting
on Duration-Based Moving Windows
for Software Effort Estimation

Sousuke Amasaki[1] and Chris Lokan[2]

[1] Okayama Prefectural University,
Department of Systems Engineering, Soja, Japan
`amasaki@cse.oka-pu.ac.jp`
[2] UNSW Canberra,
School of Engineering and Information Technology, Canberra, Australia
`c.lokan@adfa.edu.au`

Abstract. Several studies in software effort estimation have found that
it can be effective to use a window of recent projects as training data
for building an effort estimation model. Windows can be defined as having a fixed size (containing a fixed number of projects), or as having a
fixed duration. A recent study extended the idea of windows, by weighting projects differently according to their order within the window, and
found that weighted moving windows could significantly improve estimation accuracy. That study used fixed-size windows. This study examines
the effect on effort estimation accuracy of weighted moving windows that
are based on fixed duration. We compare weighted and unweighted moving windows under the same experimental settings. Weighting methods
are found to improve estimation accuracy significantly in larger windows,
and the methods also significantly improved accuracy in smaller windows
in terms of MRE. This result contributes further to understanding properties of moving windows.

1 Introduction

A software effort estimation model is developed from past project data. Most
studies evaluate a model's accuracy with a hold-out or cross-validation approach.
These approaches split project data into training data and testing data randomly.

In reality, software projects can be ordered chronologically. Using past projects
as training data to predict future projects, instead of forming training and testing
sets randomly, is more reasonable. Intuitively, it also seems appropriate to use
only recent projects as a basis of effort estimation, because older projects might
be less representative of an organization's current practices.

Lokan and Mendes [1, 2] examined whether using only recent projects improves estimation accuracy. They used a window to limit the size of training
data so that an effort estimation model uses only recently finished projects. As
new projects are completed, old projects drop out of the window. They used
two types of window policies: fixed-size and fixed-duration. A fixed-size window policy determines the window size by the number of projects: the training

A. Jedlitschka et al. (Eds.): PROFES 2014, LNCS 8892, pp. 63–77, 2014.

set is the last N projects to finish before the target project starts. A fixed-duration policy determines the window size by calendar months: the training set is projects whose whole life cycle occurred during the last w months before the target project starts. Intuitively, we believe that a fixed-duration policy makes more sense: that estimators are more likely to think of "recent projects" in terms of calendar time rather than a given number of projects.

Lokan and Mendes found that estimation accuracy could improve by using either window policy, but the policies affected the accuracy differently.

Their studies assumed that projects within a window are all equally useful as training data. However, the chronological order of projects can be exploited further, by giving projects different importance according to their relative age to the target project, so that recent projects receive higher importance than older projects. Amasaki and Lokan examined this idea, and found that weighting the importance of training projects according to their order within the window of most recent projects affected estimation accuracy [3]. However, that study only used the fixed-size window policy.

In this paper, we turn to the fixed-duration policy, and explore the effects of weighted moving windows for software effort estimation with this approach. We address the following questions:

RQ1. Is there a difference in the accuracy of estimates between unweighted and weighted moving windows, when the definition of window size is based on duration?

RQ2. Can insights be gained from difference of trends in accuracy among weighted and unweighted moving windows as the window size varies?

RQ3. How do these results compare with results based on fixed-size windows (windows containing a fixed number of projects)?

2   Related Work

Research in software effort estimation models has a long history. However, few software effort estimation models were evaluated with consideration of the chronological order of projects.

Auer and Biffl [4] evaluated dimension weighting for analogy-based effort estimation, considering the effect of a growing data set. However, the authors used datasets having no date information. Thus, this evaluation method did not consider chronological order.

Mendes and Lokan [5] compared estimates based on a growing portfolio with estimates based on leave-one-out cross-validation, using two different data sets. In both cases, cross-validation estimates showed significantly superior accuracy. With cross-validation, all other projects in the data set — even some that were still in the future — are used as training data for a given project. Thus estimates using cross-validation are based on unrealistic information. If estimates based on unrealistic information are significantly more accurate than estimates considering chronology (based on realistic information), the implication is that the apparent accuracy achieved when ignoring chronology does not reflect what an estimator would achieve in practice.

Some studies such as [6, 7] used a project year in software effort estimation model construction. However, these studies did not consider chronological order in evaluation. Maxwell [8] demonstrated the construction and evaluation of a software estimation model with the consideration of chronology. A candidate effort estimation model selected a year predictor. She also separated project data into training and test data according to a year.

Lokan and Mendes [1] studied the use of moving windows with linear regression models and a single-company dataset from the ISBSG repository. Training sets were defined to be the N most recently completed projects. They found that the use of a window could affect accuracy significantly; predictive accuracy was better with larger windows; some window sizes were 'sweet spots'. Later they also investigated the effect on accuracy when using moving windows of various durations to form training sets on which to base effort estimates [2]. They showed that the use of windows based on duration can affect the accuracy of estimates, but to a lesser extent than windows based on a fixed number of projects.

This study builds on both [2] and [3]. The same data set is investigated again. This study extends [2] by exploring the use of weighting functions. It differs from [3] in using duration as the basis for defining window size.

3 Research Method

3.1 Dataset Description

The data set used in this paper is the same one analyzed in [1–3]. This data set is sourced from Release 10 of the ISBSG Repository. Release 10 contains data for 4106 projects; however, not all projects provided the chronological data we needed (i.e. known duration and completion date, from which we could calculate start date), and those that did varied in data quality and definitions. To form a data set in which all projects provided the necessary data for size, effort and chronology, defined size and effort similarly, and had high quality data, we removed projects according to the following criteria:

- The projects are rated by ISBSG as having high data quality (A or B).
- Implementation date and overall project elapsed time are known.
- Size is measured in IFPUG 4.0 or later (because size measured with an older version is not directly comparable with size measured with IFPUG version 4.0 or later). We also removed projects that measured size with an unspecified version of function points, and whose completion pre-dated IFPUG version 4.0.
- The size in unadjusted function points is known.
- Development team effort (resource level 1) is known. Our analysis used only the development team's effort.
- Normalized effort and recorded effort are equivalent. This should mean that the reported effort is the actual effort across the whole life cycle.
- The projects are not web projects.

Table 1. Summary statistics for ratio-scaled variables

Variable	Mean	Median	StDev	Min	Max
Size	496	266	699	10	6294
Effort	4553	2408	6212	62	57749
PDR	16.47	8.75	31.42	0.53	387.10

In the remaining set of 909 projects, 231 were all from the same organization and 678 were from other organizations. We only selected the 231 projects from the single organization, as we considered that the use of single-company data was more suitable to answer our research questions than using cross-company data. Preliminary analysis showed that three projects were extremely influential and invariably removed from model building, so they were removed from the set. The final set contained 228 projects.

We do not know the identity of the organization that developed these projects.

Release 10 of the ISBSG database provides data on numerous variables; however, this number was reduced to a small set that we have found in past analyses with this dataset to have an impact on effort, and which did not suffer from a large number of missing data values. The remaining variables were size (measured in unadjusted function points), effort (hours), and four categorical variables: development type (new development, re-development, enhancement), primary language type (3GL, 4GL), platform (mainframe, midrange, PC, multi-platform), and industry sector (banking, insurance, manufacturing, other).

Table 1 shows summary statistics for size (measured in unadjusted function points), effort, and project delivery rate(PDR). PDR is calculated as effort divided by size; high project delivery rates indicate low productivity. In [1], the authors examined the project delivery rate and found it changes across time. This finding supports the use of a window.

The projects were developed for a variety of industry sectors, where insurance, banking and manufacturing were the most common. Start dates range from 1994 to 2002, although only 9 started before 1998. 3GLs are used by 86% of projects; mainframes account for 40%, and multi-platform for 55%; these percentages for language and platform vary little from year to year. There is a trend over time towards more enhancement projects and fewer new developments. Enhancement projects tend to be smaller than new development, so there is a corresponding trend towards lower size and effort.

In this study we adopt the same range of window sizes as [2]. In [2], the smallest window size was based on the statistical significance of linear regression with windowed project data: the smallest window size with which all regression models were statistically significant was 12 months. The largest window size was based on the necessary number of testing projects for evaluation. As a result, we used window sizes from 12 to 84 months.

Table 2. Formulae of weighting functions

Name	Formula
Triangular	$W(x) = 1 - |x|, |x| < 1$
Epanechnikov	$W(x) = 1 - x^2, |x| < 1$
Gaussian	$W(x) = \exp(-(2.5x)^2/2)$
Rectangular (Uniform)	$W(x) = 1, |x| < 1$

3.2 Weighted Moving Windows with Linear Regression

Linear regression is one of the popular methods for effort estimation. A typical effort estimation model is as follows:

$$\text{Effort} = b_0 + b_1 \text{Size} + \epsilon. \tag{1}$$

Here, b_0 and b_1 are regression coefficients, and ϵ represents an error term following a normal distribution. The regression coefficients are inferred from a training set so as to minimize the following function:

$$\sum_{i=1}^{n} (\text{Effort}_i - b_0 - b_1 \text{Size}_i)^2. \tag{2}$$

Here, n denotes the sample size of the training set.

Equation 2 assumes that the errors of the training set are to be minimized equivalently. Weighted linear regression controls the importance of training projects via weighting. It minimizes the following function:

$$\sum_{i=1}^{n} w_i (\text{Effort}_i - b_0 - b_1 \text{Size}_i)^2. \tag{3}$$

Here, w_i represents case weights for the training set.

From this perspective, an unweighted moving window assigns zero weight to projects that are too old to fall within the window, and equal weights to projects in the window. Weights can be introduced, to take into account the chronological order of projects in the window. This study weights projects in the training set so that a more recent project has a heavier weight. Table 2 shows four weight functions that we examined. We determined x as follows:

$$x = \frac{s - s_i}{w}. \tag{4}$$

Here, s represents the start date of the target project. s_i represents the start date of training project i. w represents the duration of the window. $s - s_i$ is larger for older projects, giving them less weight.

Figure 1 shows the forms of weight functions. A rectangular function is equivalent to unweighted moving windows. Different curve functions affect estimation accuracy differently. This study adopted three typical curves: linear, concave, S-shape. These functions are common in local regression [9].

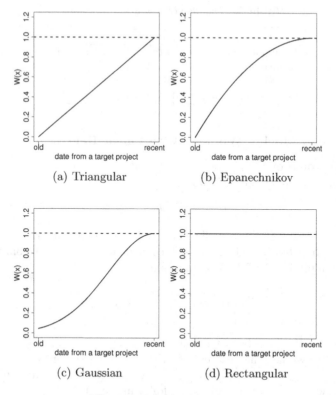

Fig. 1. weight function forms

3.3 Modeling Techniques

Weighted linear regression models were built using almost the same procedure as [1]:

1. The first step in building every regression model is to ensure numerical variables are normally distributed. We used the Shapiro-Wilk test on the training set to check if Effort and Size were normally distributed. Statistical significance was set at $\alpha = 0.05$. In every case, Size and Effort were not normally distributed. Therefore, we transformed them to a natural logarithmic scale.
2. Independent variables whose value is missing in a target project were not considered for inclusion in the estimation model.
3. Every model included $log(Size)$ as an independent variable. Beyond that, given a training set of N projects, no model was investigated if it involved more than $N/10$ independent variables (rounded to the nearest integer), assuming that at least 10 projects per independent variable is desirable [10].
4. Models were based on variables selected with Lasso[11] (the Lasso implementation we used is the "**glmnet**" function from **glmnet** package for R.)

5. To verify the stability of an effort model, we used the following approach: Calculate Cook's distance values for all projects to identify influential data points. Any projects with distances higher than $(3 \times 4/N)$, where N represents the total number of projects, were removed from the analysis [8].

This procedure performs variable selection, and thus all variables introduced in Section 3.1 are just candidates for independent variables. Models constructed in our experiment can be different for every project.

3.4 Effort Estimation on Chronologically-Ordered Projects

This study evaluated the effects of moving windows of several sizes along with a timeline of projects' history. The effects were measured by performance comparisons between moving windows and a growing portfolio. A growing portfolio uses all past projects as the training set: no project has a weight of zero.

For a window of w months, this evaluation was performed as follows:

1. Sort all projects by start date
2. Find the earliest project p_0 for which using that window size could make a difference to the training set: that is, at least one project that had finished by the start of p_0 was "too old" to be included in the window (it had started more than w months previously);
3. For every project p_i in chronological sequence (ordered by start date), starting from p_0, form four estimates using weighted and unweighted moving windows, and another estimate using a growing portfolio. For moving windows, the training set is the finished projects whose whole life cycle had fallen within w months prior to the start of p_i. For the growing portfolio, the training set is all of the projects that had finished before the start of p_i.
4. Evaluate estimation results.

3.5 Performance Measures

Performance measures for effort estimation models are based on the difference between estimated effort and actual effort. As in previous studies, this study used MMRE, PRED(25), and MMAE [12] for performance evaluation.

To test for statistically significant differences between accuracy measures, we used the Wilcoxon ranked sign test and set statistical significance level at $\alpha = 0.05$. `wilcoxsign_test` function of `coin` package for R was used.

4 Results

4.1 Accuracy with Different Window Sizes

We begin by comparing estimation accuracy with each of the weighting functions against a common baseline: not using a window at all, but instead retaining all past projects as training data.

Table 3. Mean absolute residuals with different window durations

Duration (months)	Testing Projects	Growing MAE	(a) MAE	p–val.	(b) MAE	p–val.	(c) MAE	p–val.	(d) MAE	p–val.
12	165	2541	2730	0.127	2772	0.114	2667	0.306	2560	0.981
18	193	2630	2565	0.445	2601	0.514	2580	0.822	2549	0.287
24	201	2638	2501	0.275	2466	0.085	2541	0.183	2610	0.984
30	202	2647	2428	0.013	2491	0.093	2571	0.116	2581	0.365
36	206	2645	2518	0.139	2585	0.378	2492	0.191	2526	0.001
42	206	2645	2594	0.084	2613	0.050	2597	0.140	2559	0.004
48	206	2645	2572	0.049	2596	0.068	2618	0.157	2599	0.003
54	206	2645	2572	0.035	2593	0.007	2541	0.042	2597	0.086
60	198	2642	2550	0.005	2574	0.000	2564	0.019	2655	0.254
66	184	2622	2570	0.001	2576	0.000	2465	0.004	2702	0.226
72	153	2527	2447	0.000	2498	0.000	2490	0.000	2554	0.016
78	126	2300	2232	0.000	2281	0.000	2237	0.000	2327	0.031
84	80	2211	2165	0.000	2204	0.000	2139	0.000	2238	0.022

(a) Triangular, (b) Epanechnikov, (c) Gaussian, (d) Rectangular

Table 4. Mean MRE with different window durations

Duration (months)	Testing Projects	Growing MRE	(a) MRE	p–val.	(b) MRE	p–val.	(c) MRE	p–val.	(d) MRE	p–val.
12	165	1.35	1.30	0.905	1.31	0.743	1.25	0.752	1.12	0.029
18	193	1.29	1.13	0.004	1.20	0.002	1.12	0.022	1.15	0.001
24	201	1.28	1.13	0.001	1.11	0.000	1.16	0.003	1.14	0.038
30	202	1.28	1.14	0.000	1.20	0.002	1.19	0.002	1.23	0.008
36	206	1.26	1.15	0.001	1.20	0.020	1.17	0.008	1.18	0.000
42	206	1.26	1.22	0.001	1.19	0.000	1.23	0.009	1.18	0.000
48	206	1.26	1.23	0.001	1.20	0.002	1.22	0.001	1.19	0.000
54	206	1.26	1.23	0.000	1.21	0.000	1.24	0.000	1.20	0.000
60	198	1.29	1.19	0.000	1.26	0.000	1.27	0.000	1.25	0.000
66	184	1.32	1.24	0.000	1.24	0.000	1.27	0.000	1.28	0.001
72	153	1.39	1.31	0.000	1.34	0.000	1.38	0.000	1.31	0.001
78	126	1.48	1.40	0.000	1.43	0.000	1.38	0.000	1.40	0.002
84	80	1.44	1.32	0.000	1.35	0.000	1.31	0.000	1.40	0.000

(a) Triangular, (b) Epanechnikov, (c) Gaussian, (d) Rectangular

Tables 3 and 4 show the effect of window durations on mean absolute residuals and mean MRE. The first column shows window durations. The 2nd column shows the total number of projects used as a target project with the corresponding window duration. The 3rd column shows accuracy measures with a growing portfolio. The 4th column shows accuracy measures when the Triangular function was used to weight projects within the window. The 5th column shows the p–value from statistical tests on accuracy measures between a growing portfolio and the Triangular function. The remaining columns show accuracy measures and p–values for the other weighting functions. The results were computed for

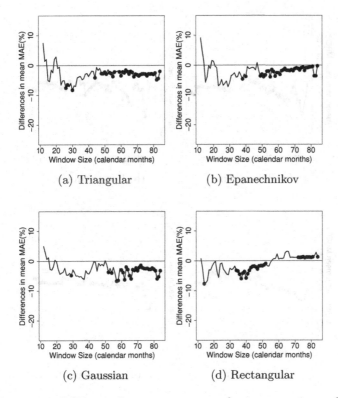

(a) Triangular   (b) Epanechnikov

(c) Gaussian   (d) Rectangular

Fig. 2. The percent difference of accuracy measures between growing and windowing (mean MAE)

every month; the tables only show every 6 months, due to space limitations. This is sufficient to show the essential trends.

Figures 2 and 3 show the difference in mean MAE and mean MRE between a growing portfolio and moving windows. The x-axis is the duration of the window, and the y-axis is the subtraction of the accuracy measure value with a growing portfolio from that with moving windows at the given x-value (expressed in relative percentage terms). Smaller values of MAE and MRE are better, so the window is advantageous where the line is below 0. Circle points mean a statistically significant difference, in favor of moving windows.

Figures and tables revealed characteristics of unweighted and weighted moving windows compared to a growing portfolio:

– With windows of up to 30 months, MAE rarely shows significant preference with any approach. The line starts above zero and quickly goes below zero (favoring windows), but the difference is seldom significant (and not at all in Fig. 2(b)). In contrast, as shown in Fig. 3, with MRE the difference was significant regardless of weighting functions.

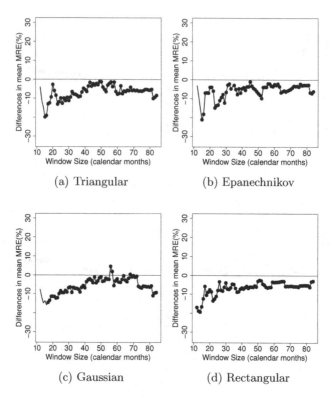

Fig. 3. The percent difference of accuracy measures between growing and windowing (mean MRE)

- For windows of 30 to 48 months, moving windows become advantageous in terms of MAE, but the effect varies for different weighting functions: Figure 2(c) has no significant difference through this range of durations. The preference for moving windows is still seen in terms of MRE, regardless of weighting functions. However, the difference looks smaller than at smaller window sizes.
- With larger windows, all measures are better using moving windows in Figs. 2(a), 2(b), 2(c) and Fig. 3. However, the improvements in mean MRE and MAE decrease compared to smaller windows, especially for Epanechnikov and Rectangular. Sometimes circle points in Figure 2 are found above zero. This is due to the use of a non-parametric statistical test.

In summary, in this data set, weighted and unweighted windows improve estimation accuracy significantly, particularly with larger windows. Different weighting functions affect accuracy in different ways.

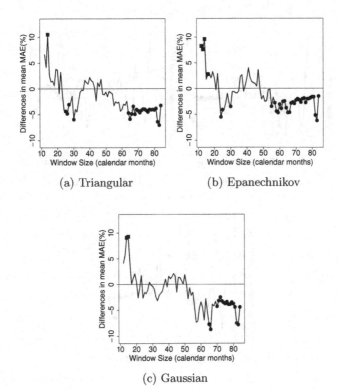

(a) Triangular   (b) Epanechnikov

(c) Gaussian

Fig. 4. The percent difference of accuracy measures between Rectangular and the other weight functions (Mean MAE)

4.2 Accuracy Comparisons among Different Weighting Functions

Figures 4 and 5 show the difference in mean MAE and mean MRE between Rectangular (unweighted) and the other functions (weighted). Weighted moving windows are advantageous where the line is below 0. Square points mean a statistically significant difference, with weighted moving windows being worse. The other notations are as same as Figs. 2 and 3.

Figures 4 and 5 reveal the following:

– With windows of up to 30 months, the advantage shifted from unweighted windows to weighted windows. Few differences are statistically significant.
– With windows of 30 to 54 months, weighted and unweighted moving windows are similar in terms of MAE. There is rarely clear preference between them. Statistical tests support weighted moving windows at some window sizes. The improvement by Gaussian function is small, and the circle points are rarely found, as shown in Fig. 4(c).
– With windows of more than 54 months, weighted moving windows are advantageous in terms of MAE and MRE. The Triangular and the Gaussian

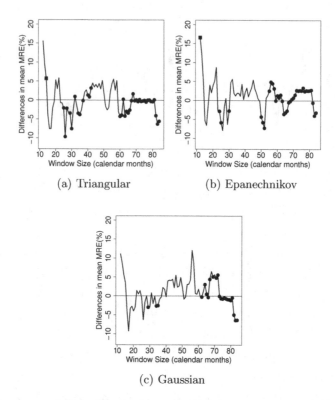

(a) Triangular   (b) Epanechnikov

(c) Gaussian

Fig. 5. The percent difference of accuracy measures between Rectangular and the other weight functions (Mean MRE)

functions make more difference than the Epanechnikov function. Most differences are small (plus or minus 2%).

5   Discussion

5.1   Answer to RQ1

First, the null hypothesis was rejected for the difference between weighted moving windows (with all weighting methods) and a growing portfolio. In this data set the use of both weighted and unweighted moving windows significantly improves estimation accuracy, compared to using a growing portfolio.

Next, statistical tests for differences in accuracy between unweighted and weighted moving windows also reject the null hypothesis at many window sizes. For the Epanechnikov function, for instance, the null hypothesis was rejected at durations around 30 months, and from 49 to 84 months, based on mean MAE. The difference based on mean MRE was significant at many window sizes.

We conclude that the use of weighted moving windows can improve estimation accuracy, compared to using unweighted moving windows, when fixed-duration windows are used.

5.2 Answer to RQ2

Even at small window durations, Figures 4 and 5 show some window sizes where weighted moving windows provide significantly better accuracy than unweighted windows. The difference in MAE becomes clear when using larger windows, of 54 months or more. Differences in MRE are significant at many window sizes, and the Gaussian and the Triangular functions showed better performance in larger windows as shown in Figures 4 and 5.

Results show that weighting is helpful, particularly at larger window sizes. However, it must be noted that the difference between accuracy with weighted and unweighted windows is small, mostly around 2%.

In [3], the effectiveness of weighting was reasoned to be due to an interaction between window sizes and the steepness of weight function curves. With small size windows, a weight function assigns steeply declining weights. With large window sizes, a weight function assigns gently declining weights. When the degree of steepness meshes with a window size, a weight function contributes to improvement of estimation accuracy.

Figure 1 depicts the difference of steepness among weight functions. Gaussian is the steepest function, and Epanechnikov is the most gentle function. The steepness of Triangular function is between them. Unweighted moving windows assigns equal weights and is more gentle than Epanechnikov function.

Figure 2 shows the gentlest Rectangular function meshed with window sizes earlier than steeper functions. The difference in larger windows is clear in steeper functions. For fixed-duration windows, steeper functions could appropriately reflect the importance of recent projects. Rectangular function eventually meshed with large window sizes again and improved estimation accuracy significantly. However, the range of significant durations was narrower than that of the other functions.

The results suggest that weighted moving windows can improve estimation accuracy when the steepness of its function is appropriately meshed. We conclude that all weight functions tend to mesh with large window sizes, as do unweighted windows, but their effectiveness differs depending on how well the steepness of the functions meshes with window sizes.

5.3 Answer to RQ3

In [2], the authors evaluated the difference between results with fixed-duration windows and fixed-size windows, and found:

- the preference of growing portfolio in smaller windows became smaller, and statistical significance almost diminished.
- the trend lines went upward as a window size increases.

- the significance range is narrower, around 40 months.
- the improvement in MAE and MRE was generally smaller with fixed-duration windows than with fixed-size windows.

Figure 2(d) supported these results, though there are additional significant window ranges because this study used another modeling approach. Fixed-duration windows allow a variable number of training projects, which may lead to improvement over unweighted moving windows, especially as short-duration windows might still contain numerous training projects. Figure 3(d) clearly reflected this effect. However, the trend lines still go upward, and window sizes around 40 months are still advantageous significantly. The range of significant durations varies with different weight functions, but the trends remain.

We conclude that the differences between fixed-duration and fixed-size windows found previously still apply when using weighted instead of unweighted moving windows.

6   Threats to Validity

This study shares the same threats to validity as the previous studies.

First, we used only one dataset. The dataset is a convenience sample and may not be representative of software projects in general. Thus, the results may not be generalized beyond this dataset; this is true of all studies based on convenience samples. We trust that numerous potential sources of variation can be removed from the dataset by the selection of a single-company dataset. Since the dataset is large and covers several years, we assume it is a fair representation of this organization's projects. The inclusion of the industry sector as an independent variable helps to allow for variations among sectors in the dataset.

Second, all the models employed in this study were built automatically. Automating the process necessarily involved making some assumptions, and the validity of our results depends on those assumptions being reasonable. For example, logarithmic transformation is assumed to be adequate to transform numeric data to an approximately normal distribution; residuals are assumed to be random and normally distributed without that being actually checked; multi-collinearity between independent variables is assumed to be handled automatically by the nature of Lasso. Based on our past experience building models manually, we believe that these assumptions are acceptable. One would not want to base important decisions on a single model built automatically, without at least doing some serious manual checking, but for calculations such as chronological estimation across a substantial data set we believe that the process here is reasonable.

Third, this study only used weighted linear regression. Many effort estimation models have been proposed, and each model can show better accuracy in particular situations. However, regression is a popular effort estimation approach. We thus think it is a reasonable choice.

7   Conclusion

This paper investigated the effect on effort estimation accuracy of using weighted moving windows, when fixed-duration windows are adopted. We have shown that it has a statistically significant effect; different weight functions affected estimation accuracy differently; with the steepness of the weight function being important; and weighted moving windows were particularly advantageous in larger windows. These findings reinforce previous results using fixed-size windows.

Compared to [2], the use of weight functions improves estimation accuracy significantly. Compared to [3], the percent improvements in MAE and MRE are smaller with fixed-duration windows than with fixed-size windows.

Our future work involves generalization with other settings: other companies' datasets and other effort estimation models. Furthermore, how to determine appropriate steepness is a crucial question for better estimation.

References

1. Lokan, C., Mendes, E.: Applying moving windows to software effort estimation. In: Proc. of ESEM 2009, pp. 111–122 (2009)
2. Lokan, C., Mendes, E.: Investigating the Use of Duration-Based Moving Windows to Improve Software Effort Prediction. In: Proc. of APSEC 2012, pp. 818–827 (2012)
3. Amasaki, S., Lokan, C.: The evaluation of weighted moving windows for software effort estimation. In: Heidrich, J., Oivo, M., Jedlitschka, A., Baldassarre, M.T. (eds.) PROFES 2013. LNCS, vol. 7983, pp. 214–228. Springer, Heidelberg (2013)
4. Auer, M., Biffl, S.: Increasing the accuracy and reliability of analogy-based cost estimation with extensive project feature dimension weighting. In: Proc. of ISESE 2004, pp. 147–155. IEEE (2004)
5. Mendes, E., Lokan, C.: Investigating the use of chronological splitting to compare software cross-company and single-company effort predictions: A replicated study. In: Proc. of EASE 2009 (2009)
6. Keung, J.W., Kitchenham, B.A., Jeffery, D.R.: Analogy-X: Providing Statistical Inference to Analogy-Based Software Cost Estimation. IEEE Trans. Softw. Eng. 34(4), 471–484 (2008)
7. Li, J., Ruhe, G.: Analysis of attribute weighting heuristics for analogy-based software effort estimation method AQUA+. Empir. Softw. Eng. 13(1), 63–96 (2007)
8. Maxwell, K.D.: Applied Statistics for Software Managers. Prentice Hall (2002)
9. Loader, C.: Local Regression and Likelihood. Statistics and Computing. Springer (1999)
10. Tabachnick, B.G., Fidell, L.S.: Using Multivariate Statistics. Harper-Collins (1996)
11. Tibshirani, R.: Regression shrinkage and selection via the lasso. J. Roy. Statist. Soc. Ser. B, 267–288 (1996)
12. Port, D., Korte, M.: Comparative studies of the model evaluation criterions mmre and pred in software cost estimation research. In: Proc. of ESEM 2008. ACM (2008)

Identifying Rationales of Strategies by Stakeholder Relationship Analysis to Refine and Maintain GQM+Strategies Models

Takanobu Kobori[1], Hironori Washizaki[1], Yoshiaki Fukazawa[1], Daisuke Hirabayashi[2], Katsutoshi Shintani[3], Yasuko Okazaki[4], and Yasuhiro Kikushima[5]

[1] Goal-oriented Quantitative Management Research Group (GQM-RG)
Waseda University 3-4-1, Okubo, Shinjuku, Tokyo, 169-8555 Japan
[2] T&D INFORMATION SYSTEM Ltd, Japan
[3] Software Engineering Center Information-technology Promotion Agency, Japan
[4] IBM, Japan
[5] National Personnel Authority, Japan
uranus-tk@ruri.waseda.jp, {washizaki,fukazawa}@waseda.jp
dieten10@yahoo.co.jp, katsu.shintani@k3.dion.ne.jp
yokazaki@jp.ibm.com, y-kiku@ark.ocn.ne.jp

Abstract. To achieve overall business goals, GQM+Strategies® is an approach that aligns the business goals at each level of an organization to strategies and assesses the achievement of goals. Strategies derived from business goals are based on rationales (contexts and assumptions). Because extracting all rationales is an important process in the GQM+Strategies approach, we propose Context-Assumption-Matrix (CAM), which refines the GQM+Strategies model by extracting rationales based on the analysis of the relationships between stakeholders, and the Context Assumption (C/A) definition template to unify the expressive style of contexts and assumptions. To demonstrate the effectiveness of CAM, we conducted an experiment involving 43 students majoring in information sciences at Shimane University in Japan. GQM+Strategies with CAM can extract rationales more efficiently and exhaustively than GQM+Strategies alone. Moreover, when the management policy or the business environment changes, GQM+Strategies with CAM can analyze the rationales and the GQM+Strategies model easily.

Keywords: stakeholder relationship, rationales (contexts and assumptions), business goal, organizational change.

1   Introduction

Because software is responsible for a lot business in corporate activities [1] and the complexity of software and IT systems in general has increased, linking business and system requirements is becoming increasingly difficult. Often it is unclear if IT/software related strategies and an organization's business goals are aligned. According to V. Mandi´c et al. [2], the success of measurement initiatives in software

A. Jedlitschka et al. (Eds.): PROFES 2014, LNCS 8892, pp. 78–92, 2014.

companies depends on the quality of the links between metrics programs and organizational business goals. One approach to resolve this issue is GQM+Strategies®[1] [3, 4], which aligns and assesses the business goals of each level to the overall strategies and goals of the organization. Many companies worldwide (e.g., the Japan Aerospace Exploration Agency [5], the global oil and gas industry [6], and non-software development domains such as the military training domain [7]) have applied GQM+Strategies for measurement-based IT-business alignment. GQM+Strategies is used to establish management strategies and plans, determine the value of a contribution, ensure the integrity of a goal between a purchaser and a contractor, and evaluate management based on quantitative data.

The GQM+Strategies approach have a hierarchy composed of business goals, strategies and metrics, which is called the GQM+Strategies grid. Strategies are determined from goals based on rationales (contexts and assumptions). To determine valid strategies, rationales must be identified exhaustively, but it is unclear whether the identified rationales cover all existing ones. Moreover, business environments are constantly changing. In order to win business, the GQM+Strategies grid must be adjusted, which may alter some contexts and assumptions. However, it is difficult to grasp exactly what has changed. Thus, GQM+Strategies needs a mechanism to identify exact changes and adapt the GQM+Strategies grid accordingly. Furthermore, rationales are often described ambiguously. It is important to unify them in an expressive style.

This paper proposes Context-Assumption-Matrix (CAM)[2] to refine business goals and strategies iteratively. To unify the expressive style of contexts and assumptions, the relationships of stakeholders are analyzed as a complement to GQM+Strategies and the Context Assumption (C/A) definition template. Herein three research questions are examined.

RQ1: Can CAM and the C/A definition template efficiently extract new rationales?

RQ2: Can CAM exhaustively extract rationales?

RQ3: When the management policy or business environment changes, can the rationales and the GQM+Strategies Grid be easily analyzed via CAM?

The contributions of this paper are two-fold. First, the proposed method may provide an efficient and exhaustive method to extract contexts and assumptions. Second, when the management or business environment changes, GQM+Strategies, contexts and assumptions can be easily analyzed.

The rest of the paper is structured as follows: in Section 2, an overview of the GQM+Strategies approach and motivating examples of our approach is given. In Section 3, our approach is explained. Section 4 presents the evaluation of our approach. Section 5 introduces related works. Finally, section 6 concludes conclusion and suggests future work.

---

[1] GQM+Strategies® is registered trademark No. 302008021763 at the German Patent and Trade Mark Office; international registration number IR992843.

[2] We have already submitted a short paper about idea of CAM to the APRES 2014 as a research previews [20]. This paper is added the result and evaluation of experiments to demonstrate the effectiveness of CAM.

2   Background

2.1   GQM+Strategies

GQM+Strategies was initially developed by the Fraunhofer Center for Empirical Software Engineering (CESE) [8] and Fraunhofer IESE [9]. The GQM+Strategies approach extends the goal/ question/metric paradigm to measure the success or failure of goals and strategies, while adding enterprise-wide support to determine actions on the basis of the measurement results [4, 10].

It is also difficult to understand the purpose of collecting such data if developers do not know that it is required [11]. GQM provides support for measurements by developing software-related goals and generating questions to refine goals and to specify measures that need to be considered in order to answer generated questions [6]. Although the GQM approach can measure whether a business goal is achieved in an organization, it lacks a mechanism to link higher- and lower-level business goals and cannot support and integrate goals at different levels of an organization.

On the other hand, GQM+Strategies creates maps between goal-related data at different levels, allowing insights gained relative to a goal at one level to satisfy goals at higher levels [12]. The major feature of GQM+Strategies is that the relationship between business goals and strategies is determined by rationales as "contexts" and "assumptions". Contexts are environmental characteristics, and assumptions are aspects of uncertain environments, including estimated ones. Although many strategies are considered for a goal, the best strategy is then selected based on the rationales. Because all of the selected strategies are detailed into lower level goals, it is possible to determine strategies that reflect the actual business environment. Figure 1 shows an overview of the concept of GQM+Strategies. The GQM+Strategies Grid visually confirms the link between a goal and a strategy, allowing the entire organization to communicate easily and work toward a common goal. Furthermore, through the GQM paradigm, it is possible to evaluate whether the goals at each level are achieved.

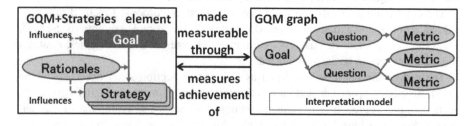

Fig. 1. GQM+Strategies components (based on Basili et al. [4])

Our approach uses the following terminology (based on Basili et al. [6]):

- **Organizational Goal:** Objective that the organization wants to accomplish within a given time frame that encompasses part of or the entire organization.

- **Strategies:** Possible approaches to achieve a goal within the environment of the organization. The number of strategies depends on the (internal) structure of an organization.
- **Rationales:** Relevant contexts and assumptions used to select goals and strategies.
- **Contexts:** External and internal organizational environment.
- **Assumptions:** Estimated unknowns.
- **GQM Graphs:** Definition of how to measure whether a goal is accomplished and a strategy is successful. Following the classical GQM approach, GQM goals are defined and broken down into concrete metrics. Interpretation models are used to objectively evaluate goals and strategies.

2.2 Motivating Examples

To successfully adapt GQM+Strategies, it is important to capture rationales. High-quality GQM+Strategies grids can guide an organization and help achieve business goals and strategies. However, this ability depends on the methods to "capture" relevant context (internal and external environment) [13].

As an example, we applied GQM+Strategies to the sales department of a stationary company, which sells stationary to corporations. The company receives orders from corporate customers and then ships based on the order form. Figure 2 overviews the corporate structure of the stationary company. The purpose of using GQM+Strategies is to improve the order acceptance process of the sales department and the shipping business. Figure 3 shows a level-3 business goal, strategy, and rationales.

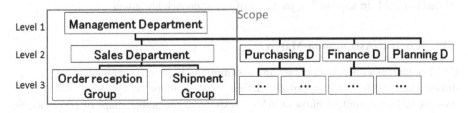

Fig. 2. Corporate structure of a stationary company

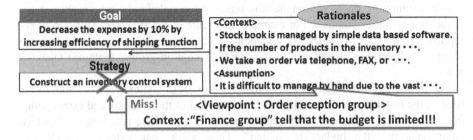

Fig. 3. Business goal, strategy, and rationales (excerpt)

In Figure 3, the strategy, which constructs an inventory control system, is determined from the goal to increases efficiency of the order reception business. Although the GQM+Strategies process derives business goals, strategies, contexts and assumptions, it is unclear whether contexts and assumptions have an impact on. For example, there may be a context that limits the budget, which may make the strategy determined in Figure 3 impossible to execute. The lack of contexts and assumptions tends to be misleading, which can result in deriving incorrect strategies. Therefore, a mechanism must be able to extract contexts and assumptions efficiently and exhaustively.

Moreover, rationales are often described ambiguously. In Figure 3, the context is "we take an order via telephone, FAX, or email". This context is unclear about "we", which may lead to a misunderstanding of the context or assumption even if it is extracted via CAM. Therefore, it is important to unify the expressive style of contexts and assumptions.

Business environments are constantly changing. For example, consider the management policy change when a company that began with individuals is sold to a corporation. The GQM+Strategies Grid must be adjusted, and some contexts and assumptions may change. Because the exact changes are difficult to understand, the mechanism must also be able to grasp exact changes and adapt GQM+Strategies.

3   Our Approach

In section 3.1, we propose the Context-Assumption-Matrix (CAM), which is a method to extract contexts and assumptions efficiently and exhaustively by analyzing the relationships between stakeholders. In section 3.2, we propose the Context Assumption definition template, which is an expressive style of contexts and assumptions related to CAM. In section 3.3, the steps of our approach are given.

3.1   Context-Assumption-Matrix

CAM organizes common contexts and assumptions between stakeholders into a two-dimensional table. Our approach defines stakeholders as people, systems, or processes. This definition allows CAM to respond to the actual shape of corporations. Figure 4 provides an example of applying CAM to a stationary company and GQM+Strategies Grid. Each row element denotes a stakeholder who views the context or assumption. Each column element represents a stakeholder who is the subject of the context or assumption. For example, in Figure 4, C3 (Context 3) is "order reception group takes an order via telephone, FAX, or email." This means that the "Corporate Customer" (row) views that "Order reception group" (column) takes an order.

The dotted circle in Figure 4 shows that this row lacks contexts or assumptions related to the order reception group. It is possible to omit the contexts and assumptions from the viewpoint of the order reception group. In fact, there is a context, "finance group says that the budget is limited". Thus, CAM can extract contexts and assumptions.

Moreover, CAM has a column labeled TBD, which stands for To Be Determined. In CAM, TBD represents that a stakeholder who is undecided or does not currently exist. For example, in Figure 4, C4 (Context 4) is "no one to integrate complaints from customers in customer service" indicates that currently this role is not assigned. The rationales in TBD may create new strategies. For example, they introduce CRM.

Who : the subject of the context or assumption

		Order reception Grp.	Shipment Grp.	Finance Grp.	...	Corporate Customer	TBD
Viewpoint: a stakeholder viewing the context or assumption	Order reception Grp.						C4:No one integrate···
	Shipment Grp.		C1:Twice a day, ··· C2:Based on ···			A1:It is easier for ···	
	...						
	Corporate Customer	C3:Order reception group takes an order via telephone, FAX or mail. A2:There are ···					
	TBD						

Fig. 4. An example of applying Context-Assumption-Matrix to a stationary company

Figure 5 shows the structure of CAM and a GQM+Strategies Grid for the stationary company. Similar to the GQM+Strategies grid, CAM has a hierarchy, which corresponds to the corporate structure.

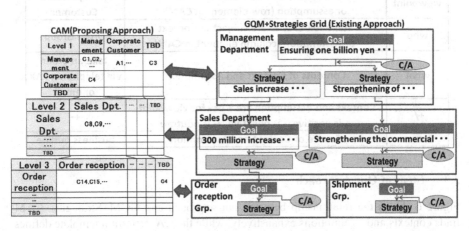

Fig. 5. Structure of CAM and the GQM+Strategies Grid of the stationary company (excerpt)

In this case, CAM has three levels because the example stationary company has three levels. The stakeholders of CAM have the same levels as the corporate structure. Initially, the stakeholders of CAM are determined based on the corporate structure (i.e., Management Department in level 1, Sales Department in level 2, and Order Reception Group and Shipment Group in level 3), but new stakeholders (e.g., for operations and maintenance) can be added if necessary.

The lower and upper levels are assumed to have the same rationales. In this case, rationales corresponding to their level are derived. Rationales at the higher level tend to be defined abstractly, while ones at the lower level tend to be defined concretely. Organizing the contexts, assumptions, and stakeholders two-dimensionally in CAM allows the contexts and assumptions to be visually reviewed.

3.2   Context Assumption (C/A) Definition Template

Contexts and assumptions are often described ambiguously. For example, consider the context, "We take an order via telephone, FAX, or email from a corporate company." This context does not clarify who "we" refers to, which may lead to a misunderstanding of the context or assumption even if it is extracted by CAM. Because it is important to unify the expressive style of the contexts and assumptions, we developed the C/A definition template. Table 1 shows the definitions and an example of a C/A definition template. This expressive style allows contexts and assumptions to be described exactly. Furthermore, the "viewpoint" in this template corresponds to the row elements, while "who" corresponds to the column elements in CAM.

Table 1. Definitions and an example C/A definition template

Item	Explanation	Example
Level	Level of corporate structure	Level 3
when	Period of Context and Assumption	until now
viewpoint	Stakeholder who views context or assumption (row element in CAM)	Corporate Customer
who	Stakeholder who are subject of Context or Assumption (column element in CAM)	Order Group
what	Contents of Context and Assumption	take an order via telephone, FAX or email
+/-	Context and Assumption are + or - for viewpoint. + is positive, - is negative, +- is neutral.	+-
Source	Source of Context and Assumption	business outline

3.3   Steps of Our Approach

Figure 6 shows the relationship between our approach and GQM+Strategies. CAM finds contexts and assumptions exhaustively, while the CA definition template defines contexts and assumptions clearly. Our approach uses the following steps:

1. Collect contexts and assumptions using the C/A definition template.
2. Extract stakeholders of CAM from departments and groups of the organizational structure at first.

3. Apply the collected contexts and assumptions to CAM.
4. Use CAM to extract missing contexts and assumptions.
5. Create a GQM+Strategies Grid based on contexts and assumptions.
6. Update CAM and the C/A definition template by referring to the related stakeholders when the management policy or business environment changes.
7. Update the GQM+Strategies Grid based on contexts and assumptions.
8. Repeat steps 6 and 7.

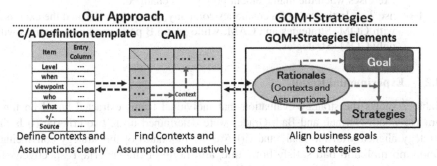

Fig. 6. Relationship between our approach and GQM+Strategies

4   Evaluation

4.1   Experimental Overview

To demonstrate the effectiveness of CAM, we conducted experiments involving 43 students majoring in information sciences at Shimane University in Japan. The experiments were conducted on the last day of the 4 days software engineering class by dividing students into seven teams of five or six people. Four teams were assigned to group A, and three were assigned to group B. Exercises 1 and 2 were cases of a stationary company and a cosmetic company, respectively (Figure 7).

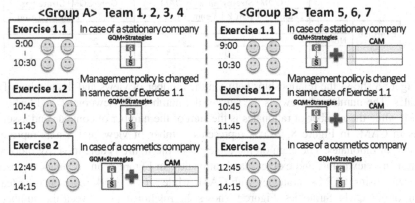

Fig. 7. Evaluation design

Teams were given a company profile and goals in a GQM+Strategies grid, and were instructed to derive contexts, assumptions, and strategies for the goals. These cases were created from examples adapted from GQM+Strategies.

Exercise 1.1   In the case of a stationary company, group A performed the exercises with only GQM+Strategies, while group B performed the exercises with GQM+Strategies and CAM.

Exercise 1.2   Under the same conditions as Exercise 1.1, students performed the exercises when the management policy was changed.

Exercise 2   In the case of a cosmetics company, group A performed the exercises with GQM+Strategies and CAM, while group B performed the exercises with only GQM+Strategies.

4.2   Experimental Result

Table 2 shows the strategy evaluation that individual teams extracted based on three grades: Good, Normal, and Bad. Grades were determined using two criteria: (i) Is the strategy aligned with the goal? and (ii) Are the rationales of the strategy convincing? Good, normal, and bad satisfy both, one, and none of the criteria, respectively. To compare the case of using only GQM+Strategies to that using GQM+Strategies with CAM, we mapped the rationales, which students extracted using only GQM+Strategies, to CAM.

Table 2. Evaluation of the strategies

		Only GQM+Strategies				GQM+Strategies with CAM		
		Team_1	Team_2	Team_3	Team_4	Team_5	Team_6	Team_7
Exercise 1.1	Good	1	1	2	2	4	1	2
	Normal	1	1	0	0	2	1	1
	Wrong	1	0	0	0	0	0	1
		Only GQM+Strategies				GQM+Strategies with CAM		
		Team_1	Team_2	Team_3	Team_4	Team_5	Team_6	Team_7
Exercise 1.2	Good	2	0	1	3	2	3	3
	Normal	1	2	2	0	2	1	1
	Wrong	0	0	0	1	0	0	2
		GQM+Strategies with CAM				Only GQM+Strategies		
		Team_1	Team_2	Team_3	Team_4	Team_5	Team_6	Team_7
Exercise 2	Good	1	3	5	2	2	1	3
	Normal	2	0	2	2	2	2	1
	Wrong	2	0	0	1	2	2	2

Figure 8 shows the relationships between the number of views and the number of rationales. The number of views is the sum of the number of "viewpoints" and "who" in CAM, while the number of rationales is the sum of the number of contexts and assumptions in CAM. In Figure 8, X-axis represents number of view, and Y-axis represents number of rationales. The team on the top right of the figure is able to verify rationales from many viewpoints and extract many rationales. In Figure 8, an "o" mark represents the teams using GQM+ Strategies with CAM, while an "x" mark represents the teams using only GQM+ Strategies. Figure 9 shows the relationships between the number of views and the number of strategies, where "o" and "x" marks are the same as in Figure 8.

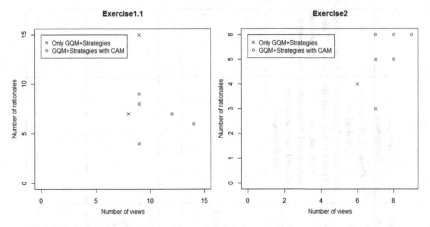

Fig. 8. Relationships between the number of views and the number of rationales

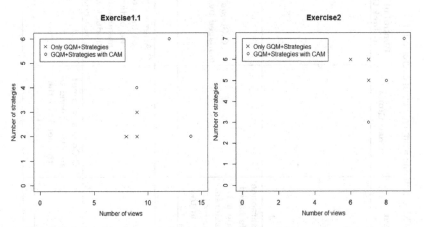

Fig. 9. Relationships between the number of views and the number of strategies

We conducted a questionnaire after experiments with CAM. Table 3 shows the results to the question: "When the management policy or business environment changes, are rationales and the GQM+Strategies Grid easily analyzed using CAM?" Table 4 shows an example of CAM which one team creates in exercise 1.1.

Table 3. Results of the questionnaire

Q: When the management policy or business environment changes, are rationales and the GQM+Strategies Grid easily analyzed using CAM?

	Strongly Agree	Agree	Neutral	Disagree	Strongly Disagree
ratio(%)	23	53	19	5	0

In addition, table 4 shows an example of CAM which one team creates in exercise 1.1. They extracted 5 contexts and 1 assumption (we provided some contexts and assumptions before the exercise).

Table 4. An example of CAM which one team creates in exercise 1.1

	Order reception Grp.	Shipment Grp.	Order Group	Control of goods in stock Group	Corporate Customer	TBD
Order reception Grp.	C:Order reception Grp manages catalog, customer ledger, stock ledger on simple database software. C:Because company have many goods, all products can not be posted in the catalog.				C: Claim information is not linked to customer information. C: There is a possiblity that we can't recommend products tailored to customer preferences.	A:Company doesn't sell to individual customers.
Shipment Grp.		C:Collection personnel assorts goods based on the pickup list. C: It is considered that the products will increase in the future.				
Order Group						
Control of goods in stock Group		C:Goods are managed by people.		C:After withdrawal of the stock, we order the manufacturer product which is not enough.		
Corporate Customer			C:Company is not able to respond to the needs of the market.			
TBD						

- C represents context, A represents assumption.

4.3   Discussion

RQ1: Can CAM and the C/A Definition Template Efficiently Extract New Rationales?

We conducted experiments to demonstrate the effectiveness of only CAM due to limited time in class. Teams using GQM+Strategies with CAM extracted average of 1.0 more rationales at exercise 1.1 (Team 4 is not included) and average of 1.75 more rationales at exercise 2 than the teams using only GQM+Strategies (Figure 8).

This is because CAM extracts new rationales based on "viewpoint" and "who". One team using only GQM+Strategies extracted 15 rationales in exercise 1.1. However, it appears that the team determined the rationales from the company profile, and although many rationales were extracted, the number of views is low.

RQ2: Can CAM Exhaustively Extract Rationales?

GQM+Strategies with CAM resulted in more numbers of views and rationales (Figure 8). In fact, an example of CAM is considered from many views (Table 3). This team should reconsider rationales from the viewpoint of order group later, because there are no rationales on the order group's row. GQM+Strategies with CAM can more exhaustively extract rationales than using only GQM+Strategies because CAM extracts rationales based on the relationships of stakeholders. In case of exercise 1.1 (Figure 9), teams using GQM+Strategies with CAM extracted more strategies than teams using only GQM+Strategies, but in exercise 2 (Figure 9), both methods extracted about the same number of strategies. However, the strategies extracted using GQM+Strategies with CAM tend to be more highly evaluated than those extracted using only GQM+Strategies (Table 2). By extracting rationales exhaustively, CAM helps to improve the quality of strategies.

RQ3: When the Management Policy or Business Environment Changes, Can the Rationales and the GQM+Strategies Grid Be Easily Analyzed via CAM?

The management policy changes from exercise 1.1 to exercise 1.2. In exercise 1.2 in Table 2, in addition to deriving more strategies, the teams using GQM+Strategies with CAM derived better strategies. In fact, one team added new stakeholders' views (e.g., individual customer, a character product company, etc.) to CAM. The teams of using only GQM+Strategies tended to extract strategies from the view of a few stakeholders, while the teams using GQM+Strategies with CAM tended to extract strategies from the view of many stakeholders. After the experiments, we asked students a question, "When the management policy or business environment changes, are rationales and the GQM+Strategies Grid easily analyzed using CAM?" Figure 10 shows that 76% people answered affirmatively. CAM can trace the changes easily, because its hierarchy corresponds to the same levels of the corporate structure.

We recognize that the final validation of CAM requires more empirical research. In this experiment, students derived contexts, assumptions, and strategies for goals in lower levels of an organizational structure (e.g., sales group, order reception group, and shipment group). For this reason, the derived strategies are limited, which may be why CAM did not have a large impact on determining strategies.

4.4   Limitations

One threat to the internal validity is the difference between the ability of students by team. To remove this, the group assignments were reversed between Exercise 1 and 2. That is, Group A used only GQM+Strategies in exercise 1, but used GQM+Strategies with CAM in exercise 2, and vice versa. The same results were obtained in the both case.

We conducted experiments involving students enrolled in a class on requirements engineering. Thus, the students had limited business knowledge. Our approach may not have much effect on a business person with experience. This is a threat to external validity. However, the possibility of overlooking unexpected requests is considered high for even a business person with experience. In the future, we would like to conduct experiments involving not only students but also business persons. Another threat to external validity is that the experiment was limited to two domains (a stationary company and a cosmetic company). Because CAM has a hierarchy corresponding to the corporate structure, it is possible that CAM also corresponds to other domains. In the future, we would like to verify the effectiveness of CAM for other organizations.

5   Related Work

The GQM+Strategies approach extends the goal/question/metric paradigm [4, 5], which is a goal oriented approach. In the past, various approaches have been proposed to execute a goal-oriented approach.

E. Yu has proposed the i* framework [14, 15], which describes the dependency relationships among various actors in an organizational context. These relationships are used to describe stakeholder interests and concerns, and how they might be addressed by various configurations of systems and environments [16]. Moreover, an actor relationship matrix analysis method (ARM) extends the i*framework. ARM enables requirements engineers to better ensure completeness of the requirements in a repeatable and systematic manner that does not currently exist in the i* framework [17]. We use the point of analyzing requirements from the relationships between stakeholders as a reference for our approach.

Another approach that combines GQM+Strategies and other methods is Utilizing GQM+Strategies for Business Value Analysis [12]. This method integrates these two approaches, coupling cost-benefit and risk analysis (value goals) with operationally measurable business goals, which helps evaluate business goal success and the effectiveness of the chosen strategies. However, in this case, how to extract rationales efficiently and exhaustively is unclear.

V. Basili et al. have applied the GQM+Strategies approach to ECOPETROL, a global player in the oil and gas industry, for measurement-based IT-business alignment [7]. ECOPETROL has continued to extend the model, collecting and analyzing data based upon questionnaires. Moreover, J. Munch et al. have applied the GQM+Strategies method to examine and align the strategic, tactical, and operational goals in software-intensive integrated product development [18].

Our approach has been applied to an example company, but we did not consider operation and maintenance. In the future, we should verify whether GQM+Strategies models using CAM can be used for refinement and maintenance.

6   Conclusion and Future Work

Often, insufficient requirements management is on top of the list of factors contributing to project failures [19]. GQM+Strategies is an effective approach to align business goals with the systemization of strategies. However, rationales may be ambiguous or omitted. In our approach, the rationales which are important in determining strategies are extracted by analyzing the relationships of stakeholders in an organization. Moreover, we propose a mechanism that can respond to changes in the management policy or business environment.

To demonstrate the effectiveness of CAM, we conducted an experiment involving 43 students at Shimane University in Japan. GQM+Strategies with CAM extracted rationales more efficiently and exhaustively than using only GQM+Strategies. Additionally, when the management policy or business environment changes, the rationales and the GQM+Strategies grid can be analyzed easily by GQM+Strategies with CAM.

In the future, we plan to conduct experiments to derive contexts, assumptions, and strategies for the goals at higher levels of the organizational structure or for multiple levels simultaneously. Moreover, we intend to develop a CAM tool to link to the GQM+Strategies grid and adapt CAM to other examples in order to validate the flexibility of CAM.

Acknowledgement. In addition to co-authors, we would like to thank other members of Goal-oriented Quantitative Management Research Group (GQM-RG) who provided carefully considered feedback and valuable comments.

References

1. Trendowicz, A., et al.: Aligning software projects with business objectives. In: Software Measurement, 2011 Joint Conference of the 21st Int'l Workshop on and 6th Int'l Conference on Software Process and Product Measurement (IWSM-MENSURA). IEEE (2011)
2. Mandić, V., Harjumaa, L., Markkula, J., Oivo, M.: Early empirical assessment of the practical value of GQM$^+$Strategies. In: Münch, J., Yang, Y., Schäfer, W., et al. (eds.) ICSP 2010. LNCS, vol. 6195, pp. 14–25. Springer, Heidelberg (2010)
3. Basili, V., et al.: Bridging the gap between business strategy and software development (2007)
4. Basili, V., et al.: Linking software development and business strategy through measurement. arXiv preprint arXiv: 1311.6224 (2013)
5. Kaneko, T., et al.: Application of GQM+Strategies in the Japanese Space Industry. In: Software Measurement, 2011 Joint Conference of the 21st Int'l Workshop on and 6th Int'l Conference on Software Process and Product Measurement (IWSM-MENSURA). IEEE (2011)

6. Basili, V., Lampasona, C., Ocampo Ramírez, A.E.: Aligning Corporate and IT Goals and Strategies in the Oil and Gas Industry. In: Heidrich, J., Oivo, M., Jedlitschka, A., Baldassarre, M.T. (eds.) PROFES 2013. LNCS, vol. 7983, pp. 184–198. Springer, Heidelberg (2013)
7. Sarcia, et al.: Is GQM+ Strategies really applicable as is to non-software development domains? In: Proceedings of the ACM-IEEE International Symposium on Empirical Software Engineering and Measurement. ACM (2010)
8. GQM+Strategies- the Fraunhofer CESE, Web site:
    `http://www.fc-md.umd.edu/` (retrieved October 1, 2014)
9. GQM+Strategies- Fraunhofer IESE Fraunhofer Gesellschaft, Web site:
    `http://www.iese.fraunhofer.de/de/produkte/gqm.html` (retrieved June 18, 2014)
10. Solingen, V., et al.: Goal question metric (gqm) approach. Encyclopedia of Software Engineering (2002)
11. Hall, T., et al.: Implementing effective software metrics programs. IEEE Software 14(2), 55–65 (1997)
12. Mandić, V., et al.: Utilizing GQM+ Strategies for business value analysis: An approach for evaluating business goals. In: Proceedings of the ACM-IEEE International Symposium on Empirical Software Engineering and Measurement. ACM (2010)
13. Mandić, V., Oivo, M.: SAS: A tool for the GQM$^+$Strategies grid derivation process. In: Ali Babar, M., Vierimaa, M., Oivo, M. (eds.) PROFES 2010. LNCS, vol. 6156, pp. 291–305. Springer, Heidelberg (2010)
14. i* Intentional STrategic Actor Relationships modelling – istar. from the Knowledge Management Lab, University of Toronto Web site:
    `http://www.cs.toronto.edu/km/istar/` (retrieved June 6, 2014)
15. Yu, E.S.: Social modeling and *i**. In: Borgida, A.T., Chaudhri, V.K., Giorgini, P., Yu, E.S. (eds.) Mylopoulos Festschrift 2009. LNCS, vol. 5600, pp. 99–121. Springer, Heidelberg (2009)
16. Yu, E.: Towards modelling and reasoning support for early-phase requirements engineering. In: Proceedings of the Third IEEE International Symposium on Requirements Engineering. IEEE (1997)
17. Yamamoto, S., Ibe, K., Verner, J., Cox, K., Bleistein, S.: Actor relationship analysis for the i* framework. In: Filipe, J., Cordeiro, J. (eds.) ICEIS 2009. LNBIP, vol. 24, pp. 491–500. Springer, Heidelberg (2009)
18. Münch, J., et al.: Experiences and Insights from Applying GQM+Strategies in a Systems Product Development Organization. In: 39th SEAA, p. 21 (2013)
19. Ebert, C.: Requirements before the requirements: Understanding the upstream impacts. Requirements Engineering. In: 13th IEEE International Conference on Proceedings. IEEE (2005)
20. Kobori, T., Washizaki, H., Fukazawa, Y., Hirabayashi, D., Shintani, K., Okazaki, Y., Kikushima, Y.: Efficient identification of rationales by stakeholder relationship analysis to refine and maintain gQM+Strategies models. In: Zowghi, D., Jin, Z., et al. (eds.) APRES 2014. CCIS, vol. 432, pp. 77–82. Springer, Heidelberg (2014)

The Sources and Approaches to Management of Technical Debt: A Case Study of Two Product Lines in a Middle-Size Finnish Software Company

Jesse Yli-Huumo, Andrey Maglyas, and Kari Smolander

Lappeenranta University of Technology, Finland
{jesse.yli-huumo,andrey.maglyas,kari.smolander}@lut.fi

Abstract. Fierce competition in the software market forces companies to release their product under tough time constraints. The competition makes companies reactive and they need to release new versions often. To achieve this need for speed, companies take shortcuts to reach deadlines. These shortcuts and resulting omitted quality are called technical debt. We investigated one middle-size Finnish software company with two independent product lines and interviewed 12 persons in different positions to understand the causes and effects of technical debt. We were also interested in specific strategies and practices for managing technical debt. The results showed that technical debt is mostly formed as a result of intentional decisions made during the project to reach deadlines. Customer satisfaction was identified as the main reason for taking technical debt in short-term but it turned to economic consequences and quality issues in the longer perspective. Interestingly, neither of the product lines had any specific management plan for reducing technical debt but several practices have been identified.

Keywords: technical debt, software project management, case study, software company, software quality.

1 Introduction

The increased competition in the software market forces companies to think about their time-to-market strategy. Balancing the choice of releasing poor-quality software early or high-quality software late is challenging [1]. This leads companies to an awkward situation w here they have to decide what quality is omitted and what shortcuts in the development process they have to take. These shortcuts and omitted quality are called "technical debt."

The term technical debt was first introduced by Ward Cunningham [2]. According to Seaman et al. [3] compromises in software development are the reason for technical debt and they should be paid back to avoid decreasing maintainability and health of the system. Technical debt might also cause economic consequences in a software project [4]. McConnell divides technical debt into two different basic types [5]. Type I occurs unintentionally where a design approach turned out to be bad or a junior coder writes bad code. Type II is intentional where a company makes a strategic decision

A. Jedlitschka et al. (Eds.): PROFES 2014, LNCS 8892, pp. 93–107, 2014.

to incur technical debt. The technical debt metaphor appeals to both project managers and software development teams [6]. The goal of a software development team is to create quality software and embrace tools and techniques for it [6]. People responsible for the management of the project and the company also care about quality but are more focused on cost and schedule factors [6].

In this paper we define technical debt as a shortcut in a software development project to reach certain deadlines. We firmly believe that technical debt is not only related to technical decisions but also to management and business decisions. Moreover, the decision to have some technical debt can be conscious to deliver the product to the market faster.

This case study is conducted in one middle-size Finnish software company with two independent product lines. The objective of this case study is to understand the sources of technical debt in software projects. Our secondary objective is in identification of strategies and practices for the management of technical debt.

The rest of the paper is organized as follows. Chapter 2 shows the related work of this topic. Chapter 3 provides the research method used in this study. In Chapter 4 we introduce the results analyzed from the gathered data. Then, in Chapter 5 we discuss about the results and conclude the paper.

2   Related Research

In this chapter we identify the related research conducted on causes and effects of technical debt. We are also focusing on strategies and practices used for managing and reducing technical debt.

2.1   The Causes and Effects of Technical Debt

The study conducted by Lim et al. [7] shows that technical debt is not always a result of bad coding. It can also include intentional decisions to trade off competing concerns during business pressures. The study also identified that technical debt can be used in short-term to capture a market share and even to collect early customer feedback. In the long-term technical debt effects tended to be negative. These effects included increased complexity, poor performance, low maintainability and fragile code. This furthermore led to bad customer satisfaction and extra working hours. However, the authors also mentioned that there were cases where short-term benefits of technical debt clearly outweighed the future costs.

Klinger et al. [8] studied the causes of technical debt by interviewing four software architects at IBM. The study revealed causes for technical debt including pressure from stakeholders, technical communication gap between stakeholders and project team, decision making without quantification of possible impacts, and unintentional debt occurring from acquisitions, change of requirements, and changes in the market ecosystem.

Siebra et al. [9] analyzed an industrial project that lasted six years by analyzing emails, documents, CVS logs, code files and interviews with developers and project managers. The analysis revealed that technical debt was taken mainly with strategic decisions. They also found that the use of a unique specialist could lead the development team to solutions that incur technical debt. The study also identified that the effects of technical debt can both increase and decrease the amount of working hours.

Zazworka et al. [10] studied the effects of god classes and design debt on software quality. God classes are examples of bad coding [11] and therefore include a possibility for refactoring. The results showed that god classes require more maintenance effort that include bug fixing and changes to software and are considered as a "cost" to software project.

Buschmann [12] explained three different cases of technical debt effects. In the first case technical debt in one platform started to grow so large that development, testing and maintenance costs started to increase dramatically. In the second case developers started to use technical debt to increase the development speed. This resulted to significant performance issues that turned later on to economic consequences. In the third case the software product had already incurred a huge amount of technical debt that led to increasing maintenance costs. However, management analyzed that reengineering the whole software would cost more than doing nothing. This resulted to situation where the management decided not to do anything for the technical debt because it was cheaper from the business point of view.

Guo et al. [13] studied the effects of technical debt by following one delayed maintenance task through a software project. The results showed that delaying the maintenance task would have almost tripled the costs if it had been done later.

Overall, the related research about the causes and effects show that technical debt is not always caused because of technical reasons. Studies [7][8][9] showed that technical debt can also be caused by intentional decisions that were related to business reasons.

The studies also show that taking technical debt may have short-term positive effects [7][9] such as the time-to-market benefit, but they will turn to economic consequences and quality issues in a long run if not paid back [7][9][10][12][13]. However, there are also situations where the short-term benefits overweigh the long-term costs [7][9].

We also noticed from the related research that technical debt is not just related to shortcuts in the coding phase. There are several different subcategories of technical debt mentioned in literature. We have gathered all of these technical debt subcategories in Figure 1.

Overall, the existing literature reveals large set of causes and effects incurring from technical debt, but lacks a clear mapping of relationships between different effects and causes.

2.2 Current Strategies and Practices of Technical Debt Management and Reduction

Lim et al. [7] found four different strategies for managing technical debt. The first strategy is to do nothing because technical debt might not be ever visible to the customer. The second strategy is the risk management approach to evaluate and prioritize technical debt's cost and value. The third strategy is to include different stakeholders

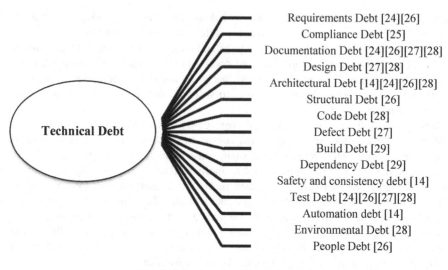

Requirements Debt [24][26]
Compliance Debt [25]
Documentation Debt [24][26][27][28]
Design Debt [27][28]
Architectural Debt [14][24][26][28]
Structural Debt [26]
Code Debt [28]
Defect Debt [27]
Build Debt [29]
Dependency Debt [29]
Safety and consistency debt [14]
Test Debt [24][26][27][28]
Automation debt [14]
Environmental Debt [28]
People Debt [26]

Fig. 1. Subcategories of technical debt

to technical debt decisions. The last strategy is to conduct audits with the development team to make technical debt visible.

Codabux & Williams [14] revealed practices such as refactoring, reengineering, and repackaging used for technical debt management.

The studies [15][16][17] propose the management of technical debt using the portfolio management. This approach is similar to the investment portfolio management. In the portfolio approach technical debt is collected to a "technical debt list" that is being used to pay the technical debt back based on its cost and value.

Krishna and Badu have also developed guides based on their own experience of technical debt management [18][19]. These guides are using different practices for minimizing technical debt. The practices include the basic steps that are focusing on improving refactoring, aspects of coding, continuous learning processes and teamwork. These practices were used in software projects and the results showed an improvement in the adaptation of new changes and better productivity in software project.

Overall, the existing literature is often concentrating on strategies and practices for reducing and preventing technical debt. As a result, the existing literature is lacking clear management approaches for controlling technical debt through the software development life cycle.

3   Research Methodology

Case study was selected as the research methodology for this study. Case studies have been around a long time and they account a large proportion of books and articles [20]. Case study is a method that involves an in-depth examination of a case [21]. Yin defines case study as an *empirical inquiry that investigates a contemporary phenomenon within its real-life context, especially when the boundaries between phenomenon and context are not clearly evident'* [22]. In this study, we focus on technical debt in software project. We focus more on technical debt causes and effects, rather than on the qualities of technical debt in source code and how to measure them. Therefore, we decided to use exploratory case study methodology with semi-structured interviews for data collection. The purpose of this study is to increase our knowledge of the relationship between technical debt causes, effects, and management. This case study consists of the following five steps [22]:

1. Designing the case study
2. Conducting case studies (stage 1): Preparing for data collection
3. Conducting case studies (stage 2): Collecting the evidence
4. Analyzing the case study evidence
5. Reporting the case study

3.1 Designing the Case Study

The strategy for this research was to find a suitable company to study technical debt and to arrange multiple interviews with people in different organizational positions (e.g. development, management, quality assurance). The reason for interviewing different organizational positions was to acquire information about technical debt from different viewpoints in software development projects. The research questions this study addresses are:

1. What are the causes and effects of technical debt?
2. What management and reduction strategies/practices are being used for technical debt?

3.2 Preparing for Data Collection

The selected company is a Finnish software company that offers SaaS business solutions for professional services automation and accounting. The company has three product lines that are managed and developed independently. This study includes two of the product lines that are referred to as Product Line A and Product Line B.

Table 1. The roles of the interviewees

ID	Product line	Role
A1	A	Software architect
A2	A	Software designer
A3	A	Project manager
A4	A	Software test engineer
A5	A	Production director
B1	B	Software architect
B2	B	Software developer
B3	B	Product line manager/Software test engineer
B4	B	Software architect
B5	B	Software developer
B6	B	UI designer

Product line A provides a financial management solution as a cloud service. The solution has more than 10 000 customers and it is currently the biggest financial management system provider in Finland. The product has been developed since 2004. The size of the development team in Product Line A is 18 persons. The development team is using agile methods and more specifically a Scrum-like approach.

Product line B is a SaaS-based project management solution for multi-organization projects. The solution is used by 1000 companies worldwide. Product Line B was founded 2004 and acquired by the parent company in 2010. The size of the development team in Product Line B is 13 persons. The development team is also using agile methodologies and a Scrum-like approach.

3.3   Collecting the Evidence

The interviews were conducted between February and March 2014. We had total of 11 interviews, of which five were from Product Line A and six from Product Line B. One of Product Line B interviews included an interview with two persons interviewed at the same time. The data collection started with a contact to the product line managers from both Product Line A & B. Both product managers agreed to have an interview and recommended persons from their own product line that might be suitable to interview about technical debt. We contacted all of the persons recommended and received positive response from each of them.

Table 1 presents the roles of the interviewees in this study. The interviewees were from different positions within the development team and we were able to discuss technical debt from various different viewpoints. We also tailored different questions depending on the role of an interviewee. For example if the interviewee was responsible for the management we focused our questions more on strategies and processes. All interviewees gave us a permission to record the session with a voice recorder. Seven interviews were conducted by one researcher in Finnish and the rest by two researchers in English. Later all interviews were transcribed and translated to English. Overall, the interviews lasted from 25 to 50 minutes, with the average of around 35 minutes.

3.4   Analyzing Case Study Evidence

The total amount of transcribed pages for analysis was 80. The collected data was analyzed with a tool designed for qualitative data analysis, Atlas.ti. The analysis of the transcribed data was performed with a similar method to open coding as in the grounded theory method [23].

4   Results

The main findings are presented in four subsections. The first subsection presents the causes related to technical debt. The second subsection examines strategies and practices for the management of technical debt. The third subsection focuses on the effects in short- and long term caused by technical debt. The final section presents improvements to product lines regarding technical debt.

4.1   Causes for Technical Debt

We asked from the interviewees what the causes for technical debt usually were. The most common cause mentioned was the lack of time given for the development. It was also added that the lack of time generates a lot of pressure to the development team, which ultimately leads to technical debt being taken.

"We have things that are almost well done but they are left undone properly because deadlines are coming and it is working like "ok" and we will just leave it like that." – B6.

We also identified that when the source code is getting more complex and bigger, it becomes also harder to change. This makes it easier and cheaper in the short run to just take technical debt and use patch code, instead of fixing the bigger problem. A software architect from Product Line A explained the situation where patch code was used to deal with the problem.

"We were working with our CRM product and our job was to refactor the data structure to this new type of data structure. This current data structure was used by almost every customer and it would have been really hard to change it. So we just made some script that syncs the data between these data structures and brings data to our CRM same way. This has generated a lot of problems, like in CRM the data is showing little bit differently even though it is the same data." – A1.

Another commonly mentioned reason for technical debt was the lack of knowledge. Sometimes it is just impossible to predict the future and some present decisions might incur technical debt later on. The interviewees also described different examples where lack of knowledge has caused technical debt to software product. One interviewee explained that lack of documentation in the source code causes technical debt because the code is then harder to understand and it takes more time to work with it. Also, if new coders do not have enough experience in coding with the company standards, they unintentionally incur technical debt because they produce different style of code compared to the company standards. The last example related to lack of knowledge described was about mistakes in specifications and requirements.

Another major aspect we were interested in at the causes of technical debt was the effect of the business decisions. We asked interviewees about the effects of business decisions to technical debt by causing pressures to the development team. A software architect in Product Line B thought that business decisions do have effect to the amount of technical debt.

"Previous years business decisions have affected us a lot. Reason for this that we have a release every two months and when we have a bigger release we just do not have enough time to do it. This means that we are in a hurry at the end of release and we have to just implement some faster solution. I think that problem is that management is not willing to see what people are actually doing during work day and how much time is doing something actually taking. This leads to problems in distribution of resources and I think that has been our problem these days." –B4.

A project manager of Product Line A also thought that business decisions are generating pressure to the development team, but he also added that it is not completely the decision of business managers to make deadlines for features.

"Well of course there is pressure coming, but what is the weight of it is case-by-case. At some point if we have promised something to our customer, we try to give deadlines so that there should not be any pressure coming. Of course deadlines are changing and there are situations where we have to reach fast and everything else is postponed, but if we were in a perfect world, this is how we would deliver." – A3.

We also asked about the communication between the development team and the business management related to decision making on technical debt. Interviewees from both product lines thought that they have a good communication structure where project managers act as good filters between business managers and development team for the decisions on technical debt. Some interviewees also added that they consider this communication structure to be much better compared to companies they have previously worked in. The reason for this was that the previous places were big companies, where getting an opinion about technical debt was more challenging due to more complex and larger communication structure.

We were also interested in whether business people usually listen to the technical opinions of the development team. Most of the interviewees thought that it is difficult to express technical opinions to business managers and to get more development time. However, a project manager of Product Line A expressed that the development team often mentions situations related to technical debt.

"Well we try internally say that if we don't have capacity for some feature to make it 100% solution, it will be told usually at most of the cases. We will picture it that we don't have time to make this and this feature completely. So they understand us quite well." – A3.

We asked could one of the causes for technical debt be the lack of technical knowledge of business managers that might drive not to do the best possible solution. The interviewees thought that it might be the case but did not see it as a problem because project managers usually can express their opinions to these kinds of situations, which limits the amount of bad decisions.

Also, one interesting fact we noticed during interviews was that the examples given by interviewees were not just related to the implementation phase. Interviewees also described how shortcuts were taken for example in testing, architecture and requirements phases of the software life cycle.

4.2   Management and Reduction Strategies for Technical Debt

The goal was to find out if the product lines A & B have any clear strategies for managing and reducing technical debt. Neither of the product lines had any specific approach for managing technical debt. However, we were able to identify some practices that were used to report technical debt.

"Well for bigger things we do keep a backlog. If some feature is dropped out we do have a backlog for it. If I am thinking myself at coding and I take some shortcut

somewhere, so do I mark-up it somewhere, not really. But if we are dropping some-
thing or finding some things to take, we write them up." – A1.

One interviewee from Product Line B mentioned that they are using a software
called JIRA to store their actions during development.

"Well there is that if we decide that we are going to make it better later, we have this
software called JIRA, where we have all the tickets about things we have done. So at
least it will be stored in there, other thing is that when it will be fixed." – B6.

Even though neither of the product lines used any specific approach to manage
technical debt we managed to identify practices that were being used to reduce and
prevent technical debt. Both of the product lines for example have a specific bug fixing day each week to reduce errors and bugs.

We identified that both product lines were using refactoring to reduce technical
debt. However, they did not have any specific refactoring schedule. Refactoring was
considered as a part of normal job and was done during the implementation.

Both product lines were using coding standards/guides to prevent and reduce technical debt coming from bad coding and to increase the consistency of the source code.

"We have guides, but they are still missing a lot of stuff. We are combining them all
the time and adding stuff. But at the moment they are mostly describing naming the
code, architectural stuff. We have different guides for different projects, like different
guides for APIs compared to normal software. But at least we have something." –B4.

For the situation where bad solutions or inconsistency still occurs even after coding
standards/guides, both companies had code reviews to check all produced code. This
served as the last checkpoint where technical debt can be seen before a release.

4.3   Short-Term and Long-Term Effects of Technical Debt

The analysis revealed several effects how technical debt can affect a software development project in a short-term. First, technical debt, or a shortcut, is used to save
development time and deliver a solution faster to the customer. The production director of Product Line A explained a situation from the early stages of the product where
taking technical debt saved the company.

"Well I think that the best example is when we started the company in 2001. We were
quite out of money, so we were leveraged with debt quite heavily and we were in a
hurry to get something done for the next presentation for pilot companies and inves-
tors. So we created a lot of stuff that looked it worked, but in reality it might not even
work. Time-to-market was so important for the existence of a company, so we did
everything we could just to get stuff out to convince that this is a viable solution." –
A5.

Second, the customer satisfaction can be increased by delivering the solution faster
but it also increases the technical debt. As customers are more interested in getting the
product on time rather than its technical details of implementation, they do not care

about technical debt as long as it does not directly affect the product quality. One interviewee also mentioned that taking technical debt doesn't feel good to take from developer's point of view because they know that the solution is not the best one and they might have to fix it later.

We were also able to identify long-term effects occurring from technical debt. The interviewees from both product lines explained that if technical debt is not being managed and reduced, it will have some serious effects in the long-term. A software architect from Product Line B explained a situation where technical debt effects have caused problems to the product line.

"We have things like calendar synchronization, which we have done years ago and there is a lot of bugs and errors in the functionality and problems in implementation. These kinds of things have generated us a lot of bugs in the long-term and lots of repairing. Repairing has been done by putting patches somewhere and not by creating a totally new base for it. For example we have had this calendar synchronization for two years and I believe we have used hundreds of hours for fixing bugs after its release. We should take plenty of time and look at the big picture." – B4.

The common effect mentioned by interviewees was more working hours spent for recoding and fixing errors/bugs of solutions made with technical debt. The interviewees felt that the solutions built on top of the already bad solutions were basically already implemented wrong and fixing with patch code is just postponing the issue. They explained that technical debt lowers the quality and performance of the product in the long run and it ultimately leads to a decrease in customer satisfaction.

4.4   Future Improvements for Dealing with Technical Debt

We were able to some identify possible improvements related to dealing with technical debt in both product lines. Neither of the product lines had any specific approach for dealing with technical debt management and reduction. Interestingly, majority of the interviewees thought that they would need improvement for that. We asked the interviewees about the backlog type management where technical debt is being managed and reduced through listing all the shortcuts to a backlog and starting the reduction from there.

"Well some feature control would be good, where you can see that what has been done in a short way and other stuff. So some kind of feature management system. Usually companies have these, but smaller the company less systems." – A2.

We were also able to identify practices related to refactoring, coding standards/guides and code reviews that were used to reduce technical debt. We noticed that the continuous delivery of new features is taking time away from refactoring. This might lead into a situation where technical debt stays in the software because the development team has to continuously implement new features. The risk is that if this debt is forgotten it might cause problems in the long-run. We think that having some refactoring time after every release to reduce the technical debt might be a good solution, instead of just moving to the new features of next release. Also one possible solution could be to assign for example two developers to do only refactoring. Project manager of Product Line A mentioned that they are trying to improve the estimation of deadlines and include also technical debt in this.

"Lately we have been trying to include, if we have some gap in some feature and if we have to do something to that feature and we know that there is something existing in that feature, that we make some time to fix it correctly." –A3.

We also identified practices in coding standards/guides and code reviews. We noticed that coding standards/guides are not used by everyone and they are also not updated. The lack of coding standards/guides has an effect on the consistency of the source code and especially junior coders are more exposed to write bad code that is considered as unintentional debt. Also, we identified that in the other product line the code reviews were not conducted on a regular basis, but only after a release. With code reviews it is possible to interrupt these bad solutions before they are included in the release of the software. However, we noticed that both product lines have acknowledged these problems and are currently improving them by updating the coding standards/guides and increasing code reviews. We think that improving these two aspects will have an impact on preventing unintentional technical debt.

4.5   Summary of the Findings

In Table 2 we summarize the results of this case study. We were able to identify several different causes for technical debt. These can be further divided into technical debt that is a caused with intentional decisions and technical debt is incurring unintentionally. We were also able to identify several short- and long-term effects of technical debt to a software project. As expected, the effects of technical debt seemed to be positive in a short-term, but turned negative in a long-term. Although we did not find any specific approach for managing technical debt, we were able to identify some practices for reducing technical debt.

5   Discussion and Conclusions

With this study we were able to identify empirical evidence from the relationship between technical debt causes, effects, and management. The results from both of the product lines are similar and clearly show that technical debt is appearing in both of them. McConnell [5] defined that technical debt can be divided into two different main types intentional and unintentional debt. The examples given by interviewees also show that technical debt is occurring in product either unintentionally or with intentional decisions. Based on these findings we agree with McConnell [5] that technical debt can be divided into these two main types. Moreover, based on our observations, technical debt does not seem to be only related to coding, where a coder takes a

Table 2. Summary of the findings

RQ1: What are the causes and effects of technical debt?	
Intentional causes of technical debt	<ul><li>Lack of time given for development</li><li>Pressure to the development team</li><li>Complexity of the source code</li><li>Business decisions<ul><li>- Lack of technical knowledge</li><li>- Communication challenges</li></ul></li></ul>
Unintentional causes of technical debt	<ul><li>Lack of coding standards and guides</li><li>Junior coders</li><li>Lack of knowledge about future changes</li><li>Lack of documentation</li></ul>
Short-term effects of technical debt	<ul><li>Time-to-market benefit</li><li>Increased customer satisfaction</li></ul>
Long-term effects of technical debt	<ul><li>Extra working hours</li><li>Errors and bugs</li><li>Customer unsatisfaction</li><li>Complexity of the source code</li></ul>
RQ2: What management and reduction strategies/practices are being used for technical debt?	
Practices for reducing and preventing technical debt	<ul><li>Refactoring</li><li>Bug fixing days</li><li>Code reviews</li><li>Coding standards and guides</li><li>Communication structure between business management and development team</li></ul>

shortcut in the source code. Instead, the results show that similar effects to take shortcuts were happening in different phases of the software development life cycle. Our observations suggest that similar phenomenon to take shortcuts can happen also in requirements, architecture and testing phases. We argue that technical debt should not be limited to shortcuts in source code only, but it should also include shortcuts in other phases of the software life cycle as well. Dividing technical debt into more specific subcategories may bring more clarity to the concept of technical debt over the whole software development life cycle.

The first research question was related to the causes of technical debt in the software development life cycle. The results suggest that technical debt is not necessarily caused by a single specific reason. The effect of the lack of time for the development was identified as the primary reason for technical debt in a software project. We also identified that common causes for the lack of time and pressure for the development team include business decisions. These findings are similar to other studies [7][8][9] where the researchers identified that taking technical debt is also caused by intentional decisions. We believe that the lack of time for development ultimately comes from business realities that set up the deadlines for project based on customer needs and current market situation. This makes the development team to take shortcuts to meet deadlines. However we also noticed that the both product lines had built a communication structure between the business and development departments that increased the capability of the development team to express their opinions on technical debt decisions. Klinger et al. [8] found in their study at IBM that the cause for technical debt is the technical communication gap between business managers and the development team. Based on these observations we think that in small and middle sized companies technical debt decisions might be easier to deal with when compared to large companies where the communication structure is more complex. Another thing we also observed in these cases was that unintentional debt was mainly caused by the lack of knowledge about future and lack of coding standards/guides that will especially affect junior coders.

The second part of the first research question was the short- and long term effects of technical debt in the software development life cycle. Other studies [7][9] argue that the good thing about technical debt is the short-term effect of time-to-market. We were able to identify similar situations, where technical debt was used to get the solution out faster. In the long-term technical debt tends to have more negative effects [7][9][10][12][13]. Our observations also revealed situations where technical debt in the long-term started to generate extra working hours and errors/bugs. The effects of technical debt are mostly positive the moment you take them but might turn into problems later if they are not paid back. This could be the reason why business people think that technical debt is something that is really easy to take to meet the deadlines and just fix it later.

The second research question focused on strategies of managing and reducing technical debt. Neither of the product lines had any specific management strategy for technical debt. However both product lines were using some practices to collect the technical debt items to a backlog, but they did not have any reduction strategy for them. A portfolio management strategy proposed in other studies [15][16][17], where technical debt is stored to backlog and the development team can use that for management and reduction, would be a good option to technical debt management. This kind of a backlog strategy might be beneficial to product lines in a long-run when older technical debt is traceable, instead of forgotten. Even though neither of the product lines had any clear strategy for managing technical debt we identified several practices used for reducing it. The practices included refactoring, coding standards and guides, code reviews, and specific bug fixing days. Similar practices have been proposed also in other studies [14][18][19]. We believe that all these practices can reduce and prevent the amount of technical debt and also increase the overall quality of the product.

In conclusion, technical debt is something that companies are unable to avoid during their software development projects. In this case study technical debt was formed as a result of different management level decisions that were made during the project to reach deadlines or unknowingly due to the lack of knowledge. However, technical debt is not always a bad thing to take. Companies can use technical debt as a powerful tool to reach their customers faster to gain an edge over the competition in the market. Nevertheless, if technical debt is not paid back in time, it might generate economic consequences and quality issues to the software. To use technical debt correctly companies need to create a management plan including practices that decrease technical debt.

Acknowledgement. The authors would like to thank the company and their employees for participating to this research. This research has been carried out in Digile Need for Speed program, and it has been partially funded by Tekes (the Finnish Funding Agency for Technology and Innovation).

References

1. Van de Laar, P., Punter, T. (eds.): Views on Evolvability of Embedded Systems. Springer, Dordrecht (2011)
2. Cunningham, W.: The WyCash Portfolio Management System. In: Addendum to the Proceedings on Object-Oriented Programming Systems, Languages, and Applications, OOPSLA 1992, pp. 29–30. ACM, New York (1992), http://dl.acm.org/citation.cfm?id=157715 (accessed: March 25, 2014)
3. Seaman, C., Guo, Y., Zazworka, N., Shull, F., Izurieta, C., Cai, Y., Vetro, A.: Using technical debt data in decision making: Potential decision approaches. In: 2012 Third International Workshop on Managing Technical Debt (MTD), pp. 45–48 (2012)
4. Zazworka, N., Vetro, A., Izurieta, C., Wong, S., Cai, Y., Seaman, C., Shull, F.: Comparing four approaches for technical debt identification. Software Quality Journal, 1–24 (2013)
5. McConnell, S.: Technical Debt-10x Software Development | Construx (November 01, 2007), http://www.construx.com/10x_Software_Development/Technical_Debt/ (accessed: March 25, 2014)
6. Eisenberg, R.J.: A Threshold Based Approach to Technical Debt. SIGSOFT Software Engineering Notes 37(2), 1–6 (2012)
7. Lim, E., Taksande, N., Seaman, C.: A Balancing Act: What Software Practitioners Have to Say about Technical Debt. IEEE Software 29(6), 22–27 (2012)
8. Klinger, T., Tarr, P., Wagstrom, P., Williams, C.: An Enterprise Perspective on Technical Debt. In: Proceedings of the 2nd Workshop on Managing Technical Debt, New York, NY, USA, pp. 35–38 (2011)
9. Siebra, C.S.A., Tonin, G.S., Silva, F.Q.B., Oliveira, R.G., Junior, A.L.O.C., Miranda, R.C.G., Santos, A.L.M.: Managing Technical Debt in Practice: An Industrial Report. In: Proceedings of the ACM-IEEE International Symposium on Empirical Software Engineering and Measurement, New York, NY, USA, pp. 247–250 (2012)
10. Zazworka, N., Shaw, M.A., Shull, F., Seaman, C.: Investigating the Impact of Design Debt on Software Quality. In: Proceedings of the 2nd Workshop on Managing Technical Debt, New York, NY, USA, pp. 17–23 (2011)
11. Vaucher, S., Khomh, F., Moha, N., Guéhéneuc, Y.: Tracking Design Smells: Lessons from a Study of God Classes. In: 16th Working Conference on Reverse Engineering, WCRE 2009, pp. 145–154 (2009)
12. Buschmann, F.: To Pay or Not to Pay Technical Debt. IEEE Software 28(6), 29–31 (2011)
13. Guo, Y., Seaman, C., Gomes, R., Cavalcanti, A., Tonin, G., da Silva, F.Q.B., Santos, A.L.M., Siebra, C.: Tracking technical debt - An exploratory case study. In: 2011 27th IEEE International Conference on Software Maintenance (ICSM), pp. 528–531 (2011)
14. Codabux, Z., Williams, B.: Managing technical debt: An industrial case study. In: 2013 4th International Workshop on Managing Technical Debt (MTD), pp. 8–15 (2013)
15. Power, K.: Understanding the impact of technical debt on the capacity and velocity of teams and organizations: Viewing team and organization capacity as a portfolio of real options. In: 2013 4th International Workshop on Managing Technical Debt (MTD), pp. 28–31 (2013)

16. Guo, Y., Seaman, C.: A Portfolio Approach to Technical Debt Management. In: Proceedings of the 2nd Workshop on Managing Technical Debt, New York, NY, USA, pp. 31–34 (2011)
17. Zazworka, N., Seaman, C., Shull, F.: Prioritizing Design Debt Investment Opportunities. In: Proceedings of the 2nd Workshop on Managing Technical Debt, New York, NY, USA, pp. 39–42 (2011)
18. Krishna, V., Basu, A.: Minimizing Technical Debt: Developer's viewpoint. In: International Conference on Software Engineering and Mobile Application Modelling and Development (ICSEMA 2012), pp. 1–5 (2012)
19. Krishna, V., Basu, A.: Software Engineering Practices for Minimizing Technical Debt. presented at the SERP 2013 The, International Conference on Software Engineering Research and Practice (2013)
20. Denzin, N.K., Lincoln, Y.S.: The SAGE Handbook of Qualitative Research, 4th edn. Sage Publications
21. Verner, J.M., Sampson, J., Tosic, V., Bakar, N.A.A., Kitchenham, B.A.: Guidelines for industrially-based multiple case studies in software engineering. In: Third International Conference on Research Challenges in Information Science, RCIS 2009, pp. 313–324 (2009)
22. Yin, R.K.: Case study research: design and methods. Sage Publications, Thousand Oaks (2003)
23. Strauss, A., Corbin, J.M.: Basics of Qualitative Research: Techniques and Procedures for Developing Grounded Theory. SAGE Publications (1998)
24. Ojameruaye, B., Bahsoon, R.: Systematic Elaboration of Compliance Requirements Using Compliance Debt and Portfolio Theory. In: Salinesi, C., van de Weerd, I. (eds.) REFSQ 2014. LNCS, vol. 8396, pp. 152–167. Springer, Heidelberg (2014)
25. Kruchten, P., Nord, R.L., Ozkaya, I.: Technical Debt: From Metaphor to Theory and Practice. IEEE Software 29(6), 18–21 (2012)
26. Zazworka, N., Spínola, R.O., Vetro', A., Shull, F., Seaman, C.: A Case Study on Effectively Identifying Technical Debt. In: Proceedings of the 17th International Conference on Evaluation and Assessment in Software Engineering, New York, NY, USA, pp. 42–47 (2013)
27. Tom, E., Aurum, A., Vidgen, R.: An exploration of technical debt. Journal of Systems and Software 86(6), 1498–1516 (2013)
28. Brown, N., Cai, Y., Guo, Y., Kazman, R., Kim, M., Kruchten, P., Lim, E., MacCormack, A., Nord, R., Ozkaya, I., Sangwan, R., Seaman, C., Sullivan, K., Zazworka, N.: Managing Technical Debt in Software-reliant Systems. In: Proceedings of the FSE/SDP Workshop on Future of Software Engineering Research, New York, NY, USA, pp. 47–52 (2010)
29. Morgenthaler, J.D., Gridnev, M., Sauciuc, R., Bhansali, S.: Searching for build debt: Experiences managing technical debt at Google. In: 2012 Third International Workshop on Managing Technical Debt (MTD), pp. 1–6 (2012)

Application of GQM+Strategies
in a Small Software Development Unit

Francisco Cocozza, Enrique Brenes, Gustavo López Herrera,
Marcelo Jenkins, and Alexandra Martínez

University of Costa Rica, San José, Costa Rica
{francisco.cocozzagarro,enrique.brenes,
gustavo.lopez_h}@ucr.ac.cr,
{marcelo.jenkins,alexandra.martinez}@ecci.ucr.ac.cr

Abstract. GQM+Strategies is an extension of the Goal-Question-Metric method that focuses on filling the vertical gaps in organizations in order to facilitate the alignment of levels. In this case study, we applied GQM+Strategies in small software organization to define its metric program. We describe how a set of metrics was devised using this methodology and show the implementation results.

Keywords: GQM+Strategies, software engineering, metrics.

1 Introduction

The alignment of software projects with business goals is critical for most software development organizations. Nevertheless, some organizations have serious vertical harmonization issues, making this alignment difficult to achieve [1]. In this paper, we describe the experience of an even worse scenario: a small software development unit in an academic environment that is in charge of some of the university's software needs. The situation is "worse" because the organization´s goals are usually not associated with software development, hence goal alignment is intricate.

GQM+Strategies is an extension of the Goal-Question-Metric method that focuses on filling the vertical gaps in organizations in order to facilitate the alignment of levels [2]. The purpose of GQM+Strategies is to help the software industry to create objectives and strategies that are aligned with high-level business goals by implementing a strategic measurement method that helps monitor either the fail or success of such strategies and organizational goals [3].

In this case study, we used the GQM+Strategies in small software organization that consists of 10 people. Through this paper, we show the results of definition of the GQM+Strategies elements, such as goals, strategies, interpretation models, metrics and classic GQM. Also, we expose some of the collected metrics results, defined following the GQM+Strategies methodology.

The rest of the paper is structured as follows: Section two describes the applied methodology, GQM+Strategies conceptual definitions, and the scope of this case

A. Jedlitschka et al. (Eds.): PROFES 2014, LNCS 8892, pp. 108–118, 2014.

study. Section three shows some related work. Section four gives an overview of the organization under study. Section five shows the actual results of applying the methodology. Section six incorporates some discussion on the results of the research. Finally, Section seven shows some conclusions and future work.

2   Methodology

We followed the GQM+Strategies methodology (version 2007) which consists of a series of predefined steps [4]: (1) Determine and define business goals, (2) Select the right strategic decisions set, (3) Select the software goals to implement the strategy, (4) Select the correct setting and define the steps to implement the software goals, (5) Select the adequate measurement goals, and (6) Derive questions and metrics using GQM.

First, an introduction to the organization background and context was needed. The presentation was led by the project manager of the organization, and it allowed us to understand the group's dynamics and its specific characteristics.

The next step involved an explanation of GQM+Strategies to the Project Manager and Software Architect, emphasizing on key concepts, value, and benefits of applying this methodology. Once they had a clear understanding of the methodology, the definition of the key elements began by specifying the assumptions, goals, metrics, and others. The definition process and information gathering was accomplished through several meetings and interviews.

From the interviews we identified that a critical point for this development unit is to deliver functionality according to the agreed schedule. Estimation precision and productivity are critical at the software level to achieve this organizational goal. In the next sections we will present the GQM+Strategies diagram using these objectives.

Then, we proposed the definition of the GQM+Strategies grid, which includes all the elements of the methodology. Also, to have an initial idea of the state of the organization, the defined metrics were collected and calculated. This helped us to evaluate the actual feasibility of collecting and calculating this set of metrics.

The definition of the GQM+Strategies grid is very important. As stated by Basili et al. [5], defining the grid is a major contribution per se. It provides the organization with the perspective goals, strategies, and measures that align the organization's approach for achieving its high-level goals. Basili et al. conclude their statement saying that "Even if an organization never collects a single piece of data, they have laid out a plan for all to see". It is worth mentioning that an evaluation of the effectiveness of the defined metric system will be performed as future work.

3   Related Work

The case study conducted in [3] proposed to analyze how much value does the GQM+ Strategies brings to the analysis of the business. The study found that its main advantage is that it ties together risk analysis with business objectives. It can identify branches within the resulting GQM tree that require further attention so they can be given priority in allocating effort for planning and monitoring. The authors concluded that the methodology helps in bringing into light certain blind spots of the managed process.

In [6] another interesting case study was conducted in which they analyzed how feasible is and what implications entail applying GQM+Strategies in domains unrelated to software development. They showed that it is possible to take advantage of the model in non-software development domains and that the model is more suitable in human-intensive domains, as they share many similarities with software development. The study also argues that for individuals outside the GQM paradigm is very difficult to understand and become familiar with the model, so it is necessary to apply intensive training in goal-oriented methodologies and GQM, which might result in a significant increase in the cost of introducing the model.

Another implementation case study was carried out at the Japanese Aerospace Exploration Agency [7]. In their report, they note that the application of the model benefited the organization in several ways, for example, it helped in clarifying relationships between different organizational units. As one criticism, they point out that the model needs to be extended with a mechanism to prioritize targets.

The model was also applied in the Japanese Information Technology Promotion Agency to determine the extent to which current projects are contributing to the high level objectives. The study identified five projects and strategic objectives were identified. Managers concluded that the application of the model helped them to achieve traceability from strategies towards the project-level objectives, in turn promoting project updates to align them with the strategy and high-level objectives [7].

4   Organization Context

In our case study, we applied the GQM+Strategies methodology to a small software organization with the aim of validating the features mentioned in the previous section. The Software Project Unit (SPU) is responsible for developing some of the software solutions for a large organization. Its main objective is to analyze, design, develop, and implement a variety of management information systems that seek to streamline and improve some of the main business processes of the organization. This software development unit was created in 2006 and it currently has a total of ten people arranged in the simple organizational structure shown in Figure 1.

As shown in the diagram, team size is small and given their recent inception the organization is in the process of maturation. Thus, some of the current processes are not documented or are not controlled at all. Aware of these shortcomings, the team leader has been focusing on improving process quality by implementing a variety of best practices and training his people on key topics such as software testing, among other activities.

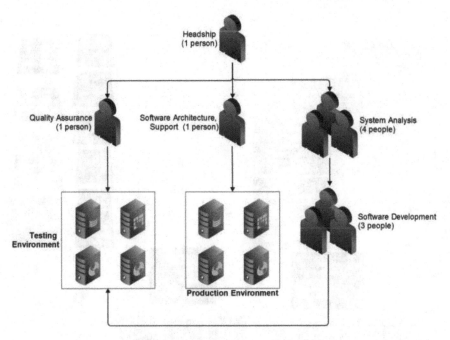

Fig. 1. The organizational structure

As far as software metrics is concerned, the organization keeps track of some process data, but data collection was not consistent across projects and therefore it was deemed not statistically usable, hence the importance of this work.

5   GQM+Strategies Application Results

In 2012, we conducted a CMMI-DEV 1.3 gap analysis [8]. CMMI models are collections of best practices that help organizations to improve their processes effectiveness, efficiency and quality. This maturity and capacity models are developed by teams composed by member of the industry, government and the SEI (Carnegie Mellon Software Engineering Institute) [9].

The evaluation evidenced a low capability level in Process Areas such as Project Planning and Project Monitoring and Control. Some of these issues are directly related to the lack of a software metrics program. Specifically, no metrics were being systematically and consistently collected, there was no analysis and decision making process based on data, and the unit did not know if its project portfolio was properly aligned with the organizational objectives.

We thus decided to apply GQM+Strategies in this unit to address these gaps. As shown in Figure 2, at the business level the main goal is to reduce time to market, and the proposed strategy is to improve productivity of the software development process. Two main constraints are imposed on the organization from the university high authorities: budget reduction and pressure to increase productivity. Hence, increasing staff is not feasible to improve time-to-market.

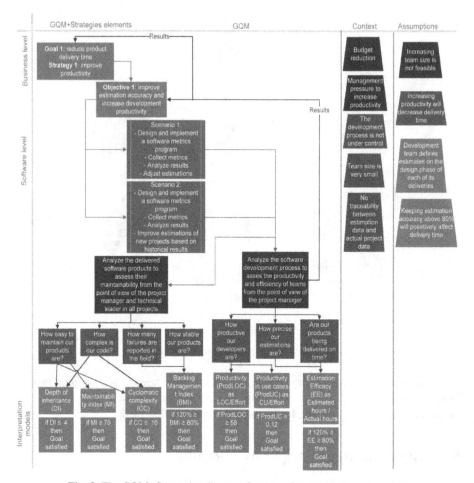

Fig. 2. The GQM+Strategies diagram for the software development unit

At software level the main goal is to improve project estimation accuracy and to improve team productivity. The main context for this level is that the team is very small and its members implement all project cycle activities. There is no traceability between time estimations and the actual duration of the development process. We assume that an improvement on productivity will reduce delivery time of software products, and that 80% accuracy on project estimations will have a positive effect on product delivery time as well.

Figure 3 shows a zoom in view of the GQM diagram that is part of the GQM+Strategies diagram (Figure 2). The project manager and the technical leader are mainly interested in increasing productivity because of budget reductions and the constant growth in the amount of software functionality to be delivered on time. Thus, they envision that the main objective is to deliver functionality according to the schedule agreed with the client. Both interviewees were repetitive in the importance of strengthening the estimation process and increasing productivity in the organization. They were also asked about the metrics collection process and the effort estimation process. After a review of the available data in their current process, this set of metrics was agreed upon.

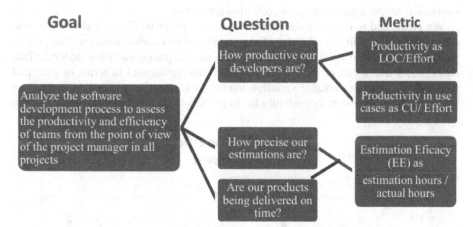

Fig. 3. The GQM diagram for the productivity goal

In a similar way, we derived a second GQM diagram related to a maintainability objective, as shown in Figure 4.

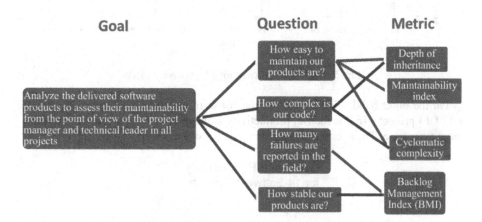

Fig. 4. The GQM diagram for the maintainability goal

In the definition of these metrics, we took into account the special interests of the project manager in assessing the quality of their products. In this case, maintainability is one of the aspects or attributes used to determine the quality of the software. The choice of these metrics also took into account the feasibility of obtaining the necessary data for their calculation. Thus, based on the set of development tools they currently use, metrics such as depth of inheritance, maintainability index, and cyclomatic complexity were chosen because their calculation can be done automatically. On the other hand, the organization is aware that in some particular projects it does not currently have sufficient data to calculate all of these metrics. However it should be noted that these metrics could be implemented in all software projects, once the organization adopts appropriate data collection procedures.

We proceeded to calculate the metrics in several projects. Figure 5 shows the time estimation efficacy in calendar days for a sample of 14 finished projects. The project manager defined the 80% to 120% range as an acceptable variation interval. This chart shows that 8 out of the 14 projects were underestimated in terms of time and they fall below the acceptable variation interval. Clearly, time estimation is an issue that presents an important opportunity for improvement in this software unit.

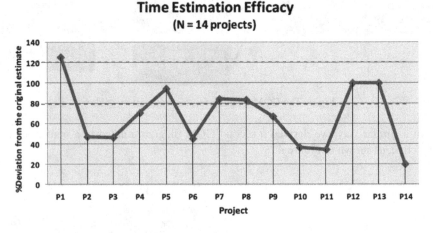

Fig. 5. Estimation efficacy for 14 software projects.

On the other hand, Figure 6 shows the software productivity metric for the same set of 14 projects. In this metric, productivity is measured in effort required to implement a use case. The average is 0.11 use cases per day of effort.

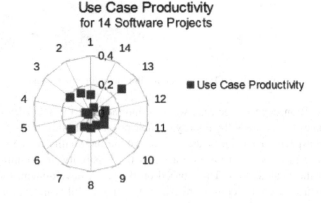

Fig. 6. Productivity in delivered use cases for 14 software projects

Figure 7 shows another productivity metric, LOC delivered per day of effort, in this case for five projects. The average productivity is 57 LOC per each day of effort invested in the project, with a large variation of up to 6 to 1 between projects. Sources of such a high variation need to be identified and removed from the process to make it more predictable.

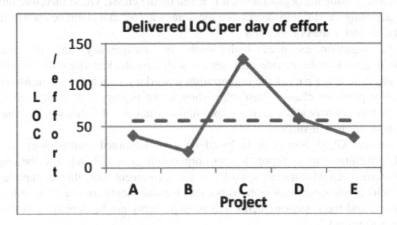

Fig. 7. Productivity in delivered LOC per day for 5 software projects

A maintainability index was also computed for some finished projects, as shown in Table 1. This metric can be automatically calculated from the source code once the project is delivered.

Table 1. Maintainability index for 2 software projects

Project	Maintainability Index (20-100 range is good)
X	72,6
Y	71

6   Discussion

Based on the application of GQM+Strategies in a small development unit we found some advantages and disadvantages of using it. The main disadvantage is that the method has not been tried extensively in small organizations or units. There is a lack of reports of case studies, compared with classic GQM. Its novelty generates this drawback. There is a lack of knowledge in organizations trying to apply GQM+Strategies method [2] [10]. The impact of this lack of trials increases on small companies with low maturity levels and can generate high risk consequences. Another disadvantage is that GQM+Strategies requires an extra effort because additional processes must be considered and this generates an overhead, therefore it is not normally used in small companies. In this scenario, using GQM+Strategies in a bottom-up perspective could be beneficial in order to align the software unit with the overall goals of the larger organization.

On the other hand, the main advantages of using GQM+Strategies in small units inside large organizations are: it facilitates alignment with the business, it increase transparency inside the organization, it is based on the classic GQM therefore inherits some advantages and finally works as a measurement tool that could be used in future inspections inside the organization.

Large organizations need high levels of transparency and the use of GQM+Strategies could provide management with a much clear vision of the business goals and how every part of the organization is working to achieve them. Moreover, businesses priorities change drastically when senior management change, therefore this transparency may allow laying responsibilities in case of failures or demonstrate good work in cases of success.

Given that GQM+Strategies is based on a well-adopted methodology such as GQM, it facilitates its incorporation into organizations that already use the original GQM method. GQM+Strategies works as a measurement tool, this is important in small units inside large organizations because measurements are crucial to determine efficiency, and these measurements will most probably not be performed if the method is not applied.

Even in small organizations it is important to use GQM+Strategies to make sure software projects and their respective measurement goals are properly aligned with the organizational strategy and goals.

In our experience with this software development unit, it was relatively easy for people to get familiar with the GQM+Strategies methodology. No special training was necessary beyond an introductory talk.

Given that the organization under study is a small and immature software unit, there are currently some weaknesses in the data collection and analysis processes. Somehow the metrics derived in this case study were driven by this constrain and the biased imposed by their current development tools. Nevertheless, we feel comfortable that the set of metrics that were implemented provides management hereon with a solid foundation for a data-driven decision making process.

7   Conclusions and Future Work

This research paper addressed the alignment of software projects with business goals. We developed a case study in which GQM+Strategies was applied in a small software development unit which is part of a larger organization whose business is not software development. A set of estimation and productivity metrics was first specified and then data were collected and analyzed for a sample of recent projects.

Our main motivation was a CMMI-DEV 1.3 gap analysis, because the results of such analysis showed weak metrics gathering processes and strategies. Therefore, we proposed the application of GQM+Strategies using the available data to align software and business goals.

We found several advantages of using GQM+Strategies in small development companies for instance: it increases transparency inside the organization, it inherits most of the advantages of classic GQM, and the process required for GQM + Strategies forces the collection of metrics which otherwise would hardly be addressed.

Also, we found some disadvantages: few case studies have addressed GQM+Strategies on small organizations; hence our findings require further validation, there is a lack of knowledge on the application of GQM+Strategies, the methodology requires an extra effort and this overhead can cause problems in small organizations.

The application of this methodology could help the development unit later on if the university as large organization changes its goals because the alignment would be easier. As further work, we are planning to assess the effectiveness of GQM+Strategies on this particular organization. We will measure the organization's alignment to proposed goals, and redefine objectives or metrics if necessary. Also, we are going to update the proposed GQM+Strategies grid using the latest version of the methodology as reference [5].

Acknowledgment. This work was supported by the Research Center on Information and Communication Technologies (CITIC) and Department of Computer and Information Sciences (ECCI) at University of Costa Rica, under grant No. 834-B2-A14.

References

1. Basili, V., Lindvall, M., Regardie, M., Seaman, C., Heidrich, J., Münch, J., Rombach, D., Trendowicz, A.: Linking Software Development and Business Strategy through Measurement. Computer, 57–65 (2010)
2. Münch, J., Heidrich, J., Mandić, V.: Business Alignment: Measurement-Based Alignment of Software Strategies and Business Goals. In: Bomarius, F., Oivo, M., Jaring, P., Abrahamsson, P. (eds.) PROFES 2009. LNBIP, vol. 32, pp. 435–436. Springer, Heidelberg (2009)
3. Mandic, V., Basili, V., Harjumaa, L., Oivo, M., Markkula, J.: Utilizing GQM+Strategies for Business Value Analysis: An Approach for Evaluating Business Goals. In: de ACM-IEEE International Symposium on Empirical Software Engineering and Measurement, Bolzano-Bozen, Italy (2010)
4. Basili, V., Heidrich, J., Lindvall, M., Münch, J., Regardie, M., Rombach, D., Seaman, C., Trendowicz, A.: Bridging the Gap between Business Strategy and Software Development. In: de International Conference on Information Systems, Québec, Canada (2007)
5. Basili, V., Trendowicz, A., Kowalczyk, M., Heidrich, J., Seaman, C., Münch, J., Rombach, D.: Aligning Organizations Through Measurement: The GQM+Strategies Approach. Springer International Publishing (2014)
6. Sarcia, S.A.: Is GQM+Strategies Really Applicable As is to Non-software Development Domains? In: de Proceedings of the 2010 ACM-IEEE International Symposium on Empirical Software Engineering and Measurement, New York, USA (2010)
7. Asghari, N.: Thesis: Evaluating GQM+ Strategies Framework for Planning Measurement System (2012)

8. Jenkins, M., Martínez, A., López, G.: A quality assurance experience in a Systems Unit. In: de Latin American Congress on Requirements Engineering & Software Testing, Medellín, Colombia (2012)
9. Chrissis, M.B., Konrad, M., Shrum, S.: CMMI for Development: Guidelines for Process Integration and Product Improvement, 3rd edn. Addison-Wesley (2011)
10. Basili, V., Heidrich, J., Lindvall, M., Münch, J., Seaman, C., Regardie, M., Trendowicz, A.: Determining the Impact Of Business Strategies Using Principles From Goal-Oriented Measurement. In: de Internationale Tagung Wirtschaftsinformatik, Vienna, Austria (2009)

Algorithmic Complexity of the Truck Factor Calculation

Christoph Hannebauer and Volker Gruhn

paluno – The Ruhr Institute for Software Technology, University of Duisburg-Essen, Germany
{christoph.hannebauer,volker.gruhn}@uni-due.de

Abstract. Software development projects differ in their sensitivity to losing developers. Some projects must stop already if they lose a few developers, while other projects can continue if the same number of developers leave the project. The Truck Factor (TF) quantifies these differences: It is the number of developers that would stop the project if they left the project. Multiple specific variants of the TF have been suggested in literature. This paper proves that some of these implementations are actually NP-hard to compute, including the promising worst-case metric $TF_{\min,c}$. NP-hardness prevents their use for large software development projects. For the TF variants not proved to be NP-hard, this paper provides efficient algorithms. However, this paper argues that these TF variants have less explanatory power.

Keywords: Truck Factor, Algorithmic Complexity, Project Survivability.

1 Introduction

The "Truck Factor" of a software project indicates "the number of people on your team who have to be hit with a truck before the project is in serious trouble" [2]. Projects with a high Truck Factor (TF) are less sensitive to developers leaving the project.

If a developer leaves a software development project, there is a direct and an indirect impact on the productivity of the project. As a direct consequence, the project has less raw programming work time at its disposal. But additionally, the project also loses expertise. The remaining developers may need more programming work time to solve some of the programming tasks than before, because they have less expertise with these tasks.

Spreading expertise in a software development project can prevent or at least soften the loss of expertise when developers leave the project. More specifically, projects are less sensitive to expertise loss if expertise is usually not exclusive to a few developers. After all, no expertise is lost to the project if others share the same expertise as the leaving developers. This corresponds to the "collective code ownership" principle known from Extreme Programming (XP) [1]. XP techniques like Pair Programming can therefore increase the TF [6].

The TF indirectly measures how broad the expertise is spread among the project members. The original phrasing [2] was qualitative and not an exact formula, probably intended as a thought-provoking impulse instead of a quantitative measurement. This may also be the reason for the gory backstory of the name Truck Factor. However, newer research used this impulse to calculate specific values for the TF [6]. The proposed

A. Jedlitschka et al. (Eds.): PROFES 2014, LNCS 8892, pp. 119–133, 2014.

algorithms to calculate the TF have a high algorithmic complexity that prevents their use on larger software development projects – calculation for 30 or more developers are impractical, calculation for more than about 50 or 60 developers are impossible using the available algorithms [5]. Efficient algorithms need to be found before the TF can also be calculated for larger projects.

This paper analyzes the algorithmic complexity of the TF calculations in general. For all proposed variants of the TF, the paper either presents an efficient algorithm or the proof that the calculation is NP-hard, and that therefore the existence of an efficient algorithm is unlikely. Section 2 describes existing research on TF calculation, including definitions of the variants $TF_{min,c}$, $TF_{max,c}$, and $TF_{avg,c}$. Section 3 contains some further definitions and a theorem important for the further analyses. The proof for NP-hardness of the TF variant $TF_{min,c}$ can be found in Sect. 4. This proof is of special importance, as Ricca et al. use $TF_{min,c}$ in their study [5]. Section 5 proves that the TF variant $TF_{max,c}$ is also NP-hard. Section 6 outlines an efficient algorithm calculating $TF_{avg,c}$. The paper concludes with a summary and open issues in Sect. 7.

2 Related Work

Zazworka et al. were the first to give a formal definition of the TF metric. They use the TF metric and other metrics to evaluate usage of XP techniques. They test their metrics on two development projects run by students of an XP class. Their definition of the TF involves a target coverage $c \in \left]0; 1\right]$, the fraction of code files for which developers should have expertise. The case $c = 0$ is not interesting, as it renders the concept of a target coverage useless. By definition, developers have expertise with a code file if they have edited the file at least once. Each function $cov_\alpha : \mathbb{N} \to [0; 1]$ ($\alpha \in \{min, avg, max\}$) assigns each number of lost developers to the fraction of code files that the remaining developers still have expertise with. More specifically, cov_{min}, cov_{avg}, cov_{max} are the minimum, arithmetic mean, and maximum coverages, respectively, among the coverages of all combinations of remaining developers. For each of the three coverage functions cov_α and for each target coverage c, there is one TF metric defined as $TF_{\alpha,c} := \max \{n | cov_\alpha (n) \geq c\}$. Thus, $TF_{\alpha,c}$ is the greatest number of developers a project may lose such that the remaining developers still have expertise with at least a fraction of c of all files. [6]

Note that the TF by Zazworka et al.'s definition is one below the original, prosaic definition: For example, $TF_{min,c} = 0$ means that there is at least one developer whose loss would be dangerous to the project. This corresponds to a TF of one in the original definition, where "the project is in serious trouble" if a truck hits one developer [2].

Ricca et al. [5] evaluated whether the TF metric can be used for real Free, Libre and Open Source Software (FLOSS) projects. They adopted Zazworka et al.'s definition of the TF, but they used only the coverage metric cov_{min}. They used 50%, 60%, and 70% as threshold c in their evaluation. Thus, they calculated the TF metrics $TF_{min,0.5}$, $TF_{min,0.6}$, and $TF_{min,0.7}$. They analyzed 37 FLOSS projects, most of which are small, i.e. have at most 10 developers. They considered a FLOSS project as large if it has more than 10 developers. The largest FLOSS project analyzed had 38 developers. They proposed an algorithm they dubbed "naive algorithm" to calculate the TF. They showed that the

Naive Algorithm has a worst case time complexity of $nm \cdot \sum_{i=1}^{n} \frac{n!}{i!(n-i)!}$, where n is the number of developers in the project and m is the number of files. They also tried to find out thresholds for the TF that no project should fall below. However, they find out that thresholds previously suggested are so high that all analyzed projects would be in danger. They concluded with four open issues:

1. A more precise expertise metric of code knowledge is necessary,
2. the algorithmic complexity of the Naive Algorithm for TF calculation is bad, as the TF calculation for their largest projects took days already,
3. the version control system (VCS) logs contain anomalies that have to be resolved manually, and
4. research should identify reasonable thresholds for the TF so practitioners can appraise the TF values they have calculated.

Their analysis shows that the proposed Naive Algorithm is unsuitable for larger software development projects: It took days already to compute the TF for the projects with 38 developers. Since the algorithm has an exponential time complexity, as will be shown in Sect. 4, even with cloud computing and advancements in computing performance, the Naive Algorithm cannot practically compute the TF for software development projects with more than about 50 or 60 developers.

3 Preliminary Remarks and Definitions

Before starting with the main proofs, a software development project as relevant for the TF will be defined, and as a result, coverage will be specified more precisely. Additionally, a lemma important for the later proofs will be proved.

The symbols $\lfloor$ and $\rfloor$ denote rounding to the floor, while $\lceil$ and $\rceil$ denote rounding to the ceiling. $\mathcal{P}(X)$ is the set of all subsets of the set X.

Definition 1. *A software development project (F, D, e) is a tuple of a finite set of files F, a finite set of developers D, and a function $e : D \to \mathcal{P}(F)$ that assigns each developer to the files that the developer has expertise with.*

The preceding definition allows a formal redefinition of the coverage functions:

Definition 2. *The function* avg $: \mathcal{P}(\mathbb{Q}) \to \mathbb{Q}$ *shall denote the arithmetic mean of a finite set. The functions* $cov_\alpha : \mathbb{N} \to [0; 1]$ *($\alpha \in \{\min, \mathrm{avg}, \max\}$) are defined as*

$$cov_\alpha : k \mapsto \alpha \left\{ \frac{\left| \bigcup_{d \in S} e(d) \right|}{|F|} \middle| S \subseteq D, |D \setminus S| = k \right\}$$

The following lemmata use the method of reducing one problem to another. A problem X is said to be reducible to Y if there is a polynomial-time-algorithm that maps each instance of X to an instance of Y such that the result of X equals the result of Y. If X is reducible to Y and X is NP-hard, then Y is also NP-hard. [4]

The resulting Theorem 1 implies that showing that if TF calculation is NP-hard for one target coverage c, or even if the target coverage c depends on the instance, then TF calculation is NP-hard for every target coverage c, except possibly $c = 1$.

Figure 1 illustrates the core idea of the proof for the first Lemma 1 in this section: Adding a set of dummy files N to a project lowers the relative target coverage from c_1 to c_2, but the absolute number of files that need to be covered stays the same. Therefore, an algorithm that calculates the TF for a specific target coverage c_2 can also be used to calculate the TF for the target coverage c_1.

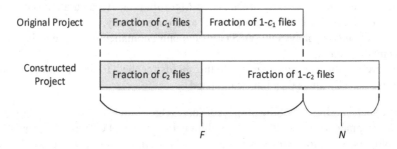

Fig. 1. Adding the set of files N to an original project constitutes a new project, in which the same absolute number of files within F need to be covered to reach the lower target coverage c_2

Lemma 1. *Let α be one of the functions* min, avg, max *and let $c_2 \in \,]0; 1[$ be constant. Deciding whether TF_{α,c_1}, with $c_1 \in [c_2; 1]$ as a parameter, is smaller than $k \in \mathbb{N}$ reduces to the problem of deciding whether TF_{α,c_2} is smaller than $k \in \mathbb{N}$.*

Proof. Assume there is a software development project (F, D, e) and a parameter $c_1 \in [c_2; 1]$. WLOG, assume that $c_1 |F|$ is integer, as only an integer number of files can be covered. Let there be a second software development project $(F \cup N, D, e)$, where N is chosen such that $N \cap F = \emptyset$ and $|N| = \left\lfloor \frac{c_1 - c_2}{c_2} |F| \right\rfloor$. Note that the developers in the second software development project have the same expertise as the developers in the first project, especially no developer has expertise with the files in N. Let ${}_i cov_\alpha$ and ${}_i TF_{\alpha,\gamma}$ ($\gamma \in \,]0; 1]$) denote coverage and TFs, respectively, for the i-th software development project ($i \in \{1, 2\}$).

The total number of files in the second software development project is therefore $|F \cup N| = |F| + \left\lfloor \frac{c_1 - c_2}{c_2} |F| \right\rfloor = \left\lfloor |F| + \frac{c_1 - c_2}{c_2} |F| \right\rfloor = \left\lfloor \frac{c_1}{c_2} |F| \right\rfloor$. Thus, there is a number $r \in [0; 1[$ such that $\left\lfloor \frac{c_1}{c_2} |F| \right\rfloor = \frac{c_1}{c_2} |F| - r$.

Since no developer has expertise with the files in N, after losing $k \in \mathbb{N}$ developers, the numbers of covered files are equal in both software development projects:

$$ {}_1 cov_\alpha (k) \cdot |F| = {}_2 cov_\alpha (k) \cdot (|F \cup N|) = {}_2 cov_\alpha (k) \cdot \left\lfloor \frac{c_1}{c_2} |F| \right\rfloor \tag{1} $$

As the next step, we prove the equivalence

$$ {}_1 cov_\alpha (k) \geq c_1 \Leftrightarrow {}_2 cov_\alpha (k) \geq c_2 \tag{2} $$

"⇒": Assume $_1cov_\alpha(k) \geq c_1$. Using Eq. 1, we see

$$_2cov_\alpha(k) \cdot \left\lfloor \frac{c_1}{c_2}|F| \right\rfloor = {}_1cov_\alpha(k) \cdot |F| \geq c_1|F|$$

$$\Rightarrow {}_2cov_\alpha(k) \geq \frac{c_1|F|}{\left\lfloor \frac{c_1}{c_2}|F| \right\rfloor} \geq \frac{c_1|F|}{\frac{c_1}{c_2}|F|} = c_2$$

"⇐": Assume $_2cov_\alpha(k) \geq c_2$. Since the number of covered files is always an integer number, this assumption implies the stricter condition

$$_2cov_\alpha(k)|F \cup N| \geq \lceil c_2|F \cup N| \rceil$$

$$\Leftrightarrow {}_2cov_\alpha(k) \geq \frac{\left\lceil c_2 \left\lfloor \frac{c_1}{c_2}|F| \right\rfloor \right\rceil}{\left\lfloor \frac{c_1}{c_2}|F| \right\rfloor}$$

Together with Eq. 1 and $\left\lfloor \frac{c_1}{c_2}|F| \right\rfloor = \frac{c_1}{c_2}|F| - r$, this shows

$$_1cov_\alpha(k) = {}_2cov_\alpha(k) \frac{\left\lfloor \frac{c_1}{c_2}|F| \right\rfloor}{|F|}$$

$$\geq \frac{\left\lceil c_2 \left\lfloor \frac{c_1}{c_2}|F| \right\rfloor \right\rceil \left\lfloor \frac{c_1}{c_2}|F| \right\rfloor}{\left\lfloor \frac{c_1}{c_2}|F| \right\rfloor |F|} = \frac{\left\lceil c_2 \left(\frac{c_1}{c_2}|F| - r \right) \right\rceil}{|F|} = \frac{\lceil c_1|F| - c_2 r \rceil}{|F|}$$

Because $0 \leq c_2 r < c_1 \leq 1$ and $c_1|F|$ is integer by assumption, the subtrahend $c_2 r$ has no effect after rounding to the ceiling and we see

$$_1cov_\alpha(k) \geq \frac{\lceil c_1|F| - c_2 r \rceil}{|F|} = \frac{c_1|F|}{|F|} = c_1$$

Equivalence 2 implies

$$_1TF_{\alpha,c_1} = \max\{n|_1cov_x(n) \geq c_1\} = \max\{n|_2cov_x(n) \geq c_2\} = {}_2TF_{\alpha,c_2}$$

Given the straightforward definition of N, there is a polynomial time algorithm that calculates the software development project $(F \cup N, D, e)$, to which $_2TF_{\alpha,c_2}$ applies, when given a software development project (F, D, e) and a parameter $c_1 \in [c_2; 1]$. $_2TF_{\alpha,c_2}$ is smaller than any $k \in \mathbb{N}$ iff $_1TF_{\alpha,c_1}$ is smaller than k.   □

The previous Lemma 1 stated that an algorithm that calculates the TF for a low target coverage c_2 can also be used to calculate the TF for any higher target coverage c_1. The following Lemma 2 states the complement: An algorithm that calculates the TF for a high target coverage c_2 may be used to calculate the TF for any lower target coverage c_1. The proof is very similar and the core idea is depicted in Fig. 2: A set of files C is added to the project, with which all developers have expertise with. The TF in both projects are identical and the target coverage is raised from c_1 to c_2.

Lemma 2. *Let α be one of the functions* min, avg, max *and let $c_2 \in {]}0; 1{[}$ be constant. Deciding whether TF_{α,c_1}, with $c_1 \in {]}0; c_2]$ as a parameter, is smaller than $k \in \mathbb{N}$ reduces to the problem of deciding whether TF_{α,c_2} is smaller than $k \in \mathbb{N}$.*

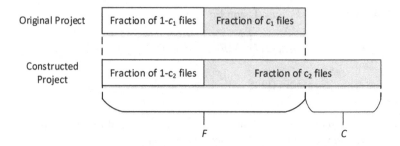

Fig. 2. Adding the set of files C to an original project constitutes a new project, in which the same absolute number of files within F can stay uncovered to reach the higher target coverage c_2

Proof. The proof is analogous to the proof for Lemma 1.

Assume there is a software development project (F, D, e) and a parameter $c_1 \in \;]0; c_2]$. WLOG, assume again that $c_1 |F|$ is integer. Let there be a second software development project $(F \cup C, D, \hat{e})$, where C is chosen such that $C \cap F = \emptyset$ and $|C| = \left\lceil \frac{c_2 - c_1}{1 - c_2} |F| \right\rceil$ and $\hat{e} : d \mapsto e\,(d) \cup C$. This time, all developers have expertise with the files in C. Obviously, $(F \cup C, D, \hat{e})$ can be calculated from any software development project (F, D, e) and any $c_1 \in \;]0; c_2]$ in polynomial time. Again, let $_icov_\alpha$ and $_iTF_{\alpha,\gamma}(\gamma \in \;]0; 1])$ denote coverage and TFs, respectively, for the i-th software development project ($i \in \{1, 2\}$).

This time, the number of *uncovered* files is the same in both software development projects, because of the definition of $\hat{e}$:

$$(1 - {_1cov_\alpha}\,(k)) \cdot |F| = (1 - {_2cov_\alpha}\,(k)) \cdot |F \cup C|$$

$$\Leftrightarrow 1 - {_1cov_\alpha}\,(k) = (1 - {_2cov_\alpha}\,(k)) \frac{|F| + \left\lceil \frac{c_2 - c_1}{1 - c_2} |F| \right\rceil}{|F|} = (1 - {_2cov_\alpha}\,(k)) \frac{\left\lceil \frac{1 - c_1}{1 - c_2} |F| \right\rceil}{|F|} \quad (3)$$

Analogously to the proof for Lemma 1, we prove the equivalence

$$1 - {_1cov_\alpha}\,(k) \leq 1 - c_1 \Leftrightarrow 1 - {_2cov_\alpha}\,(k) \leq 1 - c_2$$

"⇒": Assume $1 - {_1cov_\alpha}\,(k) \leq 1 - c_1$. Eq. 3 implies

$$1 - {_2cov_\alpha}\,(k) = (1 - {_1cov_\alpha}\,(k)) \frac{|F|}{\left\lceil \frac{1 - c_1}{1 - c_2} |F| \right\rceil} \leq (1 - c_1) \frac{|F|}{\frac{1 - c_1}{1 - c_2} |F|} = 1 - c_2$$

"⇐": Assume $1 - {_2cov_\alpha}\,(k) \leq 1 - c_2$. The number of uncovered files is integer, which implies $(1 - {_2cov_\alpha}\,(k)) |F \cup C| \leq \lfloor (1 - c_2) |F \cup C| \rfloor$. Let $r \in [0; 1[$ be chosen such that $\frac{1 - c_1}{1 - c_2} |F| + r$ is integer. Together with Eq. 3, this yields

$$1 - {_1cov_\alpha}\,(k) = (1 - {_2cov_\alpha}\,(k)) \frac{|F \cup C|}{|F|} \leq \frac{\lfloor (1 - c_2) |F \cup C| \rfloor}{|F|}$$

$$= \frac{\left\lfloor (1 - c_2) \left\lceil \frac{1 - c_1}{1 - c_2} |F| \right\rceil \right\rfloor}{|F|} = \frac{\left\lfloor (1 - c_2) \left(\frac{1 - c_1}{1 - c_2} |F| + r \right) \right\rfloor}{|F|}$$

$$= \frac{\lfloor (1 - c_1) |F| + (1 - c_2) r \rfloor}{|F|}$$

The last term equals $1 - c_1$, because $c_1 |F|$ and hence $(1 - c_1) |F|$ are integer and because $0 \leq (1 - c_2) r < 1$ and thus $(1 - c_2) r$ drops out when rounding to the ceiling.

$1 - {}_1 cov_\alpha (k) \leq 1 - c_1 \Leftrightarrow 1 - {}_2 cov_\alpha (k) \leq 1 - c_2$ is equivalent to ${}_1 cov_\alpha (k) \geq c_1 \Leftrightarrow {}_2 cov_\alpha (k) \geq c_2$ and thus ${}_1 TF_{\alpha,c_1} = {}_2 TF_{\alpha,c_2}$. □

The two Lemmata 1 and 2 together result in a more general reduction:

Theorem 1. *Let α be one of the functions* min, avg, max *and let $c_2 \in]0; 1[$ be constant. Deciding whether TF_{α,c_1}, with $c_1 \in]0; 1]$ as a parameter, is smaller than $k \in \mathbb{N}$ reduces to the problem of deciding whether TF_{α,c_2} is smaller than $k \in \mathbb{N}$.* □

Note that $c_2 = 1$ does not suffice for the preceding Theorem 1.

4   Calculating $TF_{\min,c}$

Ricca et al. [5] proposed an algorithm to calculate $TF_{\min,c}$. They call their algorithm the Naive Algorithm, as it basically tests all possible combinations of developers and calculates the resulting code coverage to find the value of $TF_{\min,c}$ for a project. Let n be the number of developers in the project and m be the number of files, then they show that their algorithm has a worst case time complexity of

$$T(n, m) := nm \cdot \sum_{i=1}^{n} \frac{n!}{i! (n - i)!} \tag{4}$$

This time complexity formula can be simplified using the Binomial Theorem shown in the following equation:

$$(a + b)^z = \sum_{k=0}^{z} \binom{z}{k} a^k b^{z-k} = \sum_{k=0}^{z} \frac{z!}{k! (z - k)!} a^k b^{z-k} \tag{5}$$

Setting $a := 1, b := 1$ and $z := n$ in Eq. 5, we get $2^n = \sum_{i=0}^{n} \frac{n!}{i!(n-i)!}$. Using this in Eq. 4 leads to the following reformulation of the time complexity $T(n, m)$:

$$T(n, m) = nm \cdot \sum_{i=1}^{n} \frac{n!}{i! (n - i)!} = nm \cdot (2^n - 1) \in O(nm2^n)$$

Ricca et al. tested that calculation of $TF_{\min,c}$ for projects with more than 30 developers takes multiple days on one of their computers. In a list of open issues, they call for an improvement of the Naive Algorithm to support larger projects. However, calculating $TF_{\min,c}$ is NP-complete, as will be shown in the following by reducing the CLIQUE problem to the $TF_{\min,c}$ calculation. First, the CLIQUE problem will be summarized. Second, the double-expert project is introduced as a special case of the general software development project. Third, CLIQUE is shown to reduce to $TF_{\min,c}$ calculation in double-expert projects. All graphs in this section refer to simple graphs, i.e. are undirected, have no loops, and there is at most one edge between any two given vertices.

Definition 3. *A set of vertices in a graph that are adjacent to each other is called a* **clique**.

Table 1. Example of a double-expert project

Developer	List of files with expertise
d_1	f_1, f_2
d_2	f_1, f_3
d_3	f_4, f_5
d_4	f_2, f_3, f_4
d_5	f_5
d_6	f_6
d_7	f_6, f_7
d_8	f_7

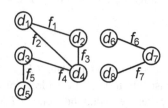

Fig. 3. Graph representation of the double-expert project example

Definition 4. *CLIQUE is the following decision problem: Given a graph G and $k \in \mathbb{N}$ as input, does G contain a clique with k vertices?*

CLIQUE is NP-complete, which means it is NP-hard and an element of NP, i.e. there is a non-deterministic, polynomial time algorithm for the problem. [4]

Definition 5. *A **double-expert project** is a software development project (F, D, e) where*

1. *for each file, exactly two different developers have expertise with the file, i.e. $\forall f \in F. |\{d \in D | f \in e(d)\}| = 2$, and*
2. *for any two developers, there is at most one file that they both have expertise with, i.e. $\forall d_1, d_2 \in D. d_1 = d_2 \vee |e(d_1) \cap e(d_2)| \leq 1$.*

Double-expert projects can be represented as graphs, where the vertices correspond to developers and edges correspond to files. Table 1 is an example for a double-expert project and Fig. 3 is its graph representation.

Remark 1. As an immediate result of its definition, in a double-expert project, for any number n of developers, there are at most $\sum_{i=1}^{n-1} i = \frac{n(n-1)}{2}$ files for which only those n developers have expertise with, i.e. $\forall \hat{D} \subset D. \left| \left(\bigcup_{d \in \hat{D}} e(d) \right) \setminus \left(\bigcup_{d \in D \setminus \hat{D}} e(d) \right) \right| \leq \sum_{i=1}^{|\hat{D}|-1} i.$

$\square$

Proposition 1. *CLIQUE can be reduced to the decision of whether $TF_{min,c}$ with variable $c \in]0; 1]$ is smaller than $k \in \mathbb{N} \setminus \{1\}$ in a double-expert project.*

Proof. Let $G = (V, E)$ be a graph and $k \in \mathbb{N}$, with V as the set of vertices and E be the set of edges. As CLIQUE is trivial for $k = 1$, we may assume $k > 1$. Note that in a clique with k vertices, there are exactly $\sum_{i=1}^{k-1} i = \frac{k(k-1)}{2}$ edges incident to two vertices of the clique. Therefore, WLOG, we assume $|E| \geq \frac{k(k-1)}{2}$.

Let there be a software development project (E, V, e) with $e : V \to \mathcal{P}(E)$ defined as $e(v) \mapsto \{f \in E | v \text{ and } f \text{ are incident in } G\}$. The transformation from G to (E, V, e) is obviously possible in polynomial time. As any edge is incident to exactly two different vertices, the software development project fulfills the first condition of Def. 5. As there is at most one edge between two vertices, the second condition of Def. 5 is also fulfilled. Thus, the software development project is a double-expert project. Let $\hat{c} := 1 - \frac{k(k-1)}{2|E|} \in \left[0; 1 - \frac{1}{|E|}\right]$ and let $c := \hat{c} + \frac{1}{2|E|} \in \,]0; 1[$.

We show in the following that there is a clique with k vertices in G iff $TF_{min,c} = k-1$:

"$\Rightarrow$": Assume that there is a clique with k vertices in G. Losing the k developers that correspond to the vertices in the clique results in the loss of all expertise with the files that correspond to the edges connecting the vertices in the clique. As noted above, there are $\frac{k(k-1)}{2}$ edges incident only to vertices in the clique. These edges correspond to files with no expertise after losing the developers. Thus, if these developers left the project, the remaining coverage would be the fraction between the number of files that the remaining developers still have expertise with and the total number of files. More precisely, the remaining coverage would be

$$\frac{|E| - \frac{k(k-1)}{2}}{|E|} = 1 - \frac{k(k-1)}{2|E|} = \hat{c}$$

Since $cov_{min}(k)$ is the lowest coverage possible among all combinations of k lost developers, this means

$$cov_{min}(k) \leq \hat{c} \qquad (6)$$

According to Remark 1, for any selection of k developers, there are at most $\frac{k(k-1)}{2}$ files that only those k developers have experience with. Hence, no choice of k developers results in a lower remaining coverage than $\hat{c}$. Therefore, Inequality 6 is in fact the equation $cov_{min}(k) = \hat{c}$. Because $\hat{c} < c$, $cov_{min}(0) = 1 > c$, and $cov_{min}(n) \geq cov_{min}(n+1)$ for all $n \in \mathbb{N}$, we conclude

$$TF_{min,c} = \max\{n \in \mathbb{N} | cov_{min}(n) \geq c\} < k \qquad (7)$$

For $k = 2$, this implies $TF_{min,c} = 1$ already. For $k > 2$, we see, again with Remark 1, that after losing any $k - 1$ developers, the remaining coverage $cov_{min}(k - 1)$ is at least $1 - \frac{(k-2)(k-1)}{2|E|} > 1 - \frac{k(k-1)-1}{2|E|} = c$. This implies $TF_{min,c} \geq k - 1$ and, together with Eq. 7, $TF_{min,c} = k - 1$.

"$\Leftarrow$": Assume $TF_{min,c} = k - 1$. This implies $cov_{min}(k) < c$. Accordingly, there is a set $\tilde{V} \subset V$ of k developers such that there are less than $|E| \cdot c$ files which the other developers in $V \setminus \tilde{V}$ have expertise with. Equivalently, there are at least $|E| \cdot (1 - c)$ files that only the developers in $\tilde{V}$ have expertise with. Thus, the number of edges that are incident only to the k vertices in $\tilde{V}$ is at least

$$|E| \cdot (1 - c) = |E| \cdot \left(1 - \left(1 - \frac{k(k-1)}{2|E|} + \frac{1}{2|E|}\right)\right) = \frac{k(k-1)-1}{2}$$

As the number of edges incident to the vertices in $\tilde{V}$ must be integer and k vertices can be incident to at most $\frac{k(k-1)}{2}$ edges, the vertices in $\tilde{V}$ are in fact incident to $\frac{k(k-1)}{2}$ edges. Therefore, $\tilde{V}$ is a clique.   □

Corollary 1. *Deciding whether $TF_{\min,c}$ in a double-expert project is smaller than $k \in \mathbb{N}$, with $c \in]0; 1]$ as a parameter, is NP-hard.*   □

Theorem 1 generalizes this result to the following corollary:

Corollary 2. *Let $c \in]0; 1[$ be constant. Deciding whether $TF_{\min,c}$ in a double-expert project is smaller than $k \in \mathbb{N}$ is NP-hard. Complementary, deciding whether $TF_{\min,c}$ in a double-expert project is greater or equal than $k \in \mathbb{N}$ is also NP-hard.*   □

It is obvious that there is a polynomial-time algorithm that calculates the remaining coverage after a given a set of k developers leaves a software development project. An example is the relevant part of Ricca et al.'s algorithm to calculate the TF [5]. Such an example set of k developers therefore gives an upper bound for the remaining coverage after losing k developers. This is also an upper bound for $cov_{\min}(k)$. If $cov_{\min}(k) < c \in]0; 1]$, then $TF_{\min,c}$ must be smaller than k. Thus, deciding whether $TF_{\min,c}$ is smaller than a given $k \in \mathbb{N}$ is a problem in NP. This yields the following corollary:

Corollary 3. *Given a constant $c \in]0; 1[$, deciding whether $TF_{\min,c}$ in a double-expert project is smaller than $k \in \mathbb{N}$ is NP-complete.*   □

Since the calculation of $TF_{\min,c}$ is NP-hard even in the special case of a double-expert project, it is also NP-hard in the general case for all software development projects, which leads to the main theorem of this section:

Theorem 2. *Calculating $TF_{\min,c}$ is NP-hard for any constant $c \in]0; 1[$.*   □

Interestingly, this performance restriction does not apply for the case $c = 1$:

Proposition 2. *Calculating $TF_{\min,1}$ can be calculated in polynomial time.*

Proof. In linear time, an algorithm can find the file that the least developers have expertise with. The number of developers that have expertise with the file is $TF_{\min,1}$: Losing these developers results in a coverage lower than 1, but after losing any lower number of developers, all files still have a developer that has expertise with the file.   □

However, a threshold of 1 is of little practical importance, and Ricca et al. also do not use this threshold [5]. If a single new developer added a single code file, $TF_{\min,1}$ would already be reduced to 0.

5   Calculating $TF_{\max,c}$

Ricca et al. adopted the metric $TF_{\min,c}$ for their approach, as it indicates the risk of a worst case scenario [5]. However, Zazworka et al. proposed two alternatives as TF values, namely $TF_{\max,c}$ and $TF_{\text{avg},c}$ [6]. This section proves that the calculation of $TF_{\max,c}$ is NP-hard as well.

Definition 6. *Set Covering Problem (SCP) is the following decision problem: The finite sets $S_1, \ldots, S_m$ with $m \in \mathbb{N}$ and a number $l \in \mathbb{N}$ are the inputs. Let $S := \bigcup_{j=1}^{m} S_j$ be the universe. Are there at most l sets S_j, $j \in C \subset \mathbb{N}_m$, $|C| \leq l$ such that the union of these chosen sets equals the union of all sets, i.e. $S = \bigcup_{j \in C} S_j$?*

Karp has shown that the SCP is NP-complete [4].

Proposition 3. *SCP can be reduced to the decision of whether $TF_{\max,1}$ is greater or equal than $k \in \mathbb{N}$ in a software development project.*

Proof. Assume we have an instance of the SCP with variable names as in Def. 6. We will construct a software project in polynomial time such that calculating $TF_{\max,1}$ solves the SCP.

Let there be a software development project $(S, \mathbb{N}_m, e)$, where S is the set of all files in the project, $\mathbb{N}_m = \{1, \ldots, m\}$, and $e : j \mapsto S_j$. Let $k := m - l$. This software development project can obviously be calculated in polynomial time.

Then there is a selection $C \subset \mathbb{N}_m$, $|C| \leq l$ of sets S_j, $j \in C$ such that $S = \bigcup_{j \in C} S_j$ iff $TF_{\max,1} \geq k = m - l$:

"$\Rightarrow$": Assume there is a selection $C \subset \mathbb{N}_m$, $|C| \leq l$ of sets S_j, $j \in C$ such that $S = \bigcup_{j \in C} S_j$. Then for every file, at least one developer in C has expertise with that file. Thus, it is possible to lose the at least $k = m - l$ developers in $\mathbb{N}_m \backslash C$ and still have a developer with expertise for each file. Thus, there is still maximum coverage and $cov_{\max}(k) = 1$. By the definition of the TF, this means $TF_{\max,1} = \max\{n | cov_{\max}(n) \geq 1\} \geq k$.

"$\Leftarrow$": Assume $TF_{\max,1} \geq k = m - l$. This implies $1 \geq cov_{\max}(k) \geq cov_{\max}(TF_{\max,1}) \geq 1$ and thus $cov_{\max}(k) = 1$. Hence, a selection $C \subset \mathbb{N}_m$, $|C| \leq m - k = l$ exists such that the developers in $\mathbb{N}_m \backslash C$ cover all files, i.e. for every file, there is a developer who has expertise with the file. By the definition of e, this implies that for every file $s \in S$, there is a developer $j \in C$ with $s \in e(j) = S_j$, or, in other words, $S = \bigcup_{j \in C} S_j$.   □

Proposition 3 and Theorem 1 show that, given a constant $c \in]0; 1]$, deciding whether $TF_{\max,c}$ is greater or equal than $k \in \mathbb{N}$ is NP-hard. As discussed in Sect. 4, given an set S of k developers, it is possible to check in polynomial time whether the remaining developers cover a fraction of c files with their experience. Such an example gives a lower bound for $cov_{\max}(k)$. This also implies a lower bound for $TF_{\max,c}$. It is therefore possible to decide whether $TF_{\max,c}$ is greater or equal than $k \in \mathbb{N}$ in NP. This leads to the following corollaries:

Corollary 4. *Given any constant $c \in]0; 1]$, deciding whether $TF_{\max,c}$ is greater or equal than $k \in \mathbb{N}$ is NP-complete.*   □

The preceding corollary directly implies the main theorem of this section. In contrast to Theorem 2 for $TF_{\min,c}$, the theorem for the best case metric $TF_{\max,c}$ also covers the case $c = 1$:

Theorem 3. *Calculating $TF_{\max,c}$ with any constant $c \in]0; 1]$ is NP-hard.*   □

6 Calculating $TF_{\mathrm{avg},c}$

The calculation of the two metrics $TF_{\mathrm{min},c}$ and $TF_{\mathrm{max},c}$ have been shown to be NP-hard with the exception of $TF_{\mathrm{min},1}$. This section analyzes the third metric $TF_{\mathrm{avg},c}$ defined by Zazworka et al. [6], which considers the arithmetic mean of all coverages resulting from losses of developers. In contrast to the others, $TF_{\mathrm{avg},c}$ can be computed efficiently:

Theorem 4. *Let (F, D, e) be a software development project with $m := |F|$ files and $n := |D|$ developers. Then the value of $TF_{\mathrm{avg},c}$ can be calculated in time $O\left(mn^2 \log^2(n)\right)$.*

Proof. Let $l := n - k$ be the number of developers that remain in the project after losing k developers. $cov_{\mathrm{avg}}(k)$ is the arithmetic mean of the coverages for all combinations of k lost developers, and can therefore be transformed in the following way:

$$
\begin{aligned}
cov_{\mathrm{avg}}(k) &= \mathrm{avg}\left\{ \frac{\left|\bigcup_{d \in S} e(d)\right|}{|F|} \,\middle|\, S \subset D, |D \setminus S| = k \right\} \\[2mm]
&= |F|^{-1} \binom{n}{l}^{-1} \sum_{\substack{S \subseteq D \\ |S|=l}} \left| \bigcup_{d \in S} e(d) \right| \\[2mm]
&= |F|^{-1} \binom{n}{l}^{-1} \sum_{\substack{S \subseteq D \\ |S|=l}} \sum_{f \in F} \left| \left\{ 1 \,\middle|\, f \in \bigcup_{d \in S} e(d) \right\} \right| \\[2mm]
&= |F|^{-1} \binom{n}{l}^{-1} \sum_{f \in F} \sum_{\substack{S \subseteq D \\ |S|=l}} \left| \left\{ 1 \,\middle|\, f \in \bigcup_{d \in S} e(d) \right\} \right| \\[2mm]
&= |F|^{-1} \binom{n}{l}^{-1} \sum_{f \in F} \left| \left\{ S \in \mathcal{P}(D) \,\middle|\, |S| = l \wedge f \in \bigcup_{d \in S} e(d) \right\} \right| \\[2mm]
&= |F|^{-1} \binom{n}{l}^{-1} \sum_{f \in F} \sum_{i=1}^{l} \left| \{ S \in \mathcal{P}(D) \big| |S| = l \wedge |\{ d \in S | f \in e(d) \}| = i \} \right|
\end{aligned}
\tag{8}
$$

For every file, the set S of remaining developers can be partitioned into two disjoint sets S_1, S_2 with $S_1 \cup S_2 = S$, $S_1 \cap S_2 = \emptyset$, such that S_1 contains only developers that have expertise with the file and S_2 contains no developers that have expertise with the file. Let $\gamma : F \to \mathbb{N}$ be the function that maps each file to the number of developers that have expertise with the file, i.e. $\gamma : f \mapsto |\{ d \in D | f \in e(d) \}|$. Using the sets S_1 and S_2 as well as the function γ, the following identity can be established for each file $f \in F$:

$$
\begin{aligned}
& \left| \{ S \in \mathcal{P}(D) \big| |S| = l \wedge |\{ d \in S | f \in e(d) \}| = i \} \right| \\
&= \left| \{ S_1 \in \mathcal{P}(\{ d \in D | f \in e(d) \}) \big| |S_1| = i \} \right| \cdot \left| \{ S_2 \in \mathcal{P}(\{ d \in D | f \notin e(d) \}) \big| |S_2| = l - i \} \right| \\
&= \binom{\gamma(f)}{i} \binom{n - \gamma(f)}{l - i}
\end{aligned}
\tag{9}
$$

Combining Eq. 8 and Eq. 9 results in the following equation, with the help of Vandermonde's identity:

$$cov_{\text{avg}}(k) = |F|^{-1} \binom{n}{l}^{-1} \sum_{f \in F} \sum_{i=1}^{l} \binom{\gamma(f)}{i} \binom{n - \gamma(f)}{l - i}$$

$$= |F|^{-1} \binom{n}{l}^{-1} \sum_{f \in F} \left(\binom{n}{l} - \binom{n - \gamma(f)}{l} \right)$$

$$= |F|^{-1} \binom{n}{k}^{-1} \sum_{f \in F} \left(\binom{n}{k} - \binom{n - \gamma(f)}{n - k} \right)$$

$$= 1 - |F|^{-1} \binom{n}{k}^{-1} \sum_{f \in F} \binom{n - \gamma(f)}{n - k}$$

Let $m := |F|$. As visible in the above notation for $cov_{\text{avg}}(k)$, a straightforward implementation calculates $cov_{\text{avg}}(k)$ using $O(m)$ calculations of binomial coefficients lower than $\binom{n}{k}$. Calculating a binomial coefficient $\binom{a}{b}$ is possible in time $O(b \log(a^a))$ using the formula $\binom{a}{b} = \prod_{i=1}^{b} \frac{a+1+i}{i}$. Considering $\binom{a}{b} = 0$ for $a < b$, the calculation is possible in time $O(a^2 \log(a))$. Other algorithms [3] may be faster, but the complexity of calculating binomial coefficients are not in the focus of this paper. Thus, the coverage for a given number of lost developers k can be calculated in time $O(mn^2 \log(n))$. For each $c \in \,]0;1]$, a binary search in $\mathbb{N}_n$ calculates $TF_{\text{avg},c} = \max\left\{ n \in \mathbb{N} \middle| cov_{\text{avg}}(k) \geq c \right\}$ in time $O(mn^2 \log^2(n))$. ☐

The above method allows calculation of $TF_{\text{avg},c}$ for larger projects than the calculation of $TF_{\text{min},c}$ and $TF_{\text{max},c}$. An average may also seem like a good metric of the real dangers on first sight, as compared to worst case and best case, i.e. $TF_{\text{min},c}$ and $TF_{\text{max},c}$: The influence of expertise on the chance of leaving the project may be small. However, there are cases where the explanatory power of $TF_{\text{avg},c}$ is low: Higher overall numbers of developers increase $TF_{\text{avg},c}$ if other parameters stay the same. As an extreme example, adding developers who do not write a single line of code also increases $TF_{\text{avg},c}$, while this obviously does not strengthen the project against losing developers. As another example, if an organization issued a policy that developers shall only cross the streets in groups of at most the size of the TF, the organization's projects would still be endangered by rampaging trucks if they used $TF_{\text{avg},c}$ as TF metric. When using $TF_{\text{avg},c}$, the overall number of developers in the project should hence always be taken into account.

7 Conclusion and Future Work

This paper analyzed the algorithmic complexity of calculating the TF for software development projects. For this analysis, the three definitions of Zazworka et al. [6] were regarded: $TF_{min,c}$, $TF_{avg,c}$, and $TF_{max,c}$ represent the worst, arithmetic mean, and best cases of losing developers, respectively. In Sect. 4 and 5, the paper proved that for every $c \in \,]0; 1]$, $TF_{min,c}$ and $TF_{max,c}$ are NP-hard to compute, with the exception of $TF_{min,1}$. Section 4 sketched an algorithm that computes $TF_{min,1}$ in polynomial time. $TF_{min,1}$ has only little practical importance, though.

Contrary to $TF_{min,c}$ and $TF_{max,c}$, the value of $TF_{avg,c}$ can be computed in polynomial time. Section 6 presents the core of an algorithm that computes $TF_{avg,c}$ in polynomial time. As a downside, Sect. 6 also illustrates caveats of the interpretation of $TF_{avg,c}$.

As a consequence of these findings, the "naive algorithm" to calculate $TF_{min,c}$, which Ricca et al. [5] have described and implemented as a tool, is despite its name unlikely to be outperformed by other algorithms. For small projects with up to 30 developers, this tool calculates $TF_{min,c}$ in less than a day with reasonable computing power. As a worst-case metric, $TF_{min,c}$ has high explanatory power. Low values of $TF_{min,c}$ indicate projects that rely on a small group of developers that have exclusive knowledge about major parts of the source code. These projects should spread their source code knowledge, for example through XP techniques.

Larger projects with more than 30 developers may calculate $TF_{avg,c}$, but have to take into account the lower explanatory power of $TF_{avg,c}$. In practice, managers of these larger project may have to rely mostly on their intuition until better tools are available. However, careful interpretation may counter the downsides of $TF_{avg,c}$. Future research should identify the constraints under which $TF_{avg,c}$ can be used.

As another direction, future research should develop alternatives to the TF These alternatives should be efficient to calculate and still have a higher explanatory power than $TF_{avg,c}$. This search for alternatives is important to software development projects with more than about 30 developers in particular, where computing $TF_{min,c}$ takes more than a day [5]. In addition to the algorithmic complexity, other techniques should also allow more qualitative conclusions as to which modules are in danger of becoming unfamiliar to the remaining developers in the team and which developers are especially important for the fate of the project.

Especially, three issues that Ricca et al. raised are still open: Capturing code knowledge more precisely, how to deal with anomalies in VCS logs, and getting more insight about which specific TF values indicate danger or safety for a project. [5]

Acknowledgements. We would like to thank Markus Kleffmann for his feedback on our work.

References

1. Beck, K., Andres, C.: Extreme Programming Explained: Embrace Change, 2nd edn. Addison-Wesley Professional (2004)
2. Bowler, M.: Truck factor (May 2005), http://www.agileadvice.com/2005/05/15/agilemanagement/truck-factor/ (accessed September 25, 2014)
3. Goetgheluck, P.: Computing binomial coefficients. The American Mathematical Monthly 94(4), 360–365 (1987), http://www.jstor.org/stable/2323099

4. Karp, R.M.: Reducibility among combinatorial problems. In: Miller, R.E., Thatcher, J.W., Bohlinger, J.D. (eds.) Complexity of Computer Computations. The IBM Research Symposia Series, pp. 85–103. Springer US (1972),
http://dx.doi.org/10.1007/978-1-4684-2001-2_9
5. Ricca, F., Marchetto, A., Torchiano, M.: On the difficulty of computing the truck factor. In: Caivano, D., Oivo, M., Baldassarre, M.T., Visaggio, G. (eds.) PROFES 2011. LNCS, vol. 6759, pp. 337–351. Springer, Heidelberg (2011),
http://dx.doi.org/10.1007/978-3-642-21843-9_26
6. Zazworka, N., Stapel, K., Knauss, E., Shull, F., Basili, V.R., Schneider, K.: Are Developers Complying with the Process: An XP Study. In: Proceedings of the 2010 ACM-IEEE International Symposium on Empirical Software Engineering and Measurement, ESEM 2010, pp. 14:1–14:10. ACM, New York (2010),
http://doi.acm.org/10.1145/1852786.1852805

Experiences in Applying Service Design to Digital Services

Stefanie Hofemann[1], Mikko Raatikainen[1], Varvana Myllärniemi[1], and Terho Norja[2]

[1]Aalto University, Finland
{firstname.lastname}@aalto.fi
[2]Steeri, Finland
terho.norja@steeri.fi

Abstract. An increasing number of services is mainly provided through digital channels and thus, implemented as software. Nevertheless, many companies struggle with developing digital services that are considered valuable by the users. Recently, service design has emerged as an approach to design better customer experience for services. We describe our experiences with a service design approach, and specifically prototyping, to explore user needs for a digital meeting scheduling service (MSS). We created an interactive prototype and paper prototypes and used them in a prototype test session with potential users to explore different design alternatives. The experiences include the peculiarities of service design for digital services as well as challenges in prototyping. The results indicate service design as a promising approach to develop digital services that better meet user needs. However, challenges exist on a practical level, such as operationalizing the value-in-use concept, applying service design for digital services, and lack of practical guidelines for prototyping.

Keywords: service design, prototyping, service-dominant logic, digital service.

1   Introduction

In today's fast changing economy, it has become increasingly important to develop software that meets users' and other stakeholders' needs. However, the development of software is often still technology-driven. This can lead to technically superior solutions that are not necessarily considered valuable by the customers [1]. In recent years, service design (SD) has evolved as a new discipline, and it is often described as the discipline that brings design thinking and designer's methods into services [2]. Design thinking has been increasingly acknowledged as beneficial for innovation and developing solutions to customers' problems [3]. Design thinking is characterized by first focusing on identifying the problem and exploring possible solutions; only after that on how to implement these solutions, instead of restricting one's thinking by implementation constraints in the beginning [4].

The most commonly used service design methods are prototyping and visualizations [5]. Prototypes have been used in various disciplines, but the understanding of what they

A. Jedlitschka et al. (Eds.): PROFES 2014, LNCS 8892, pp. 134–148, 2014.

are varies among them. While in software development prototypes are typically seen as a simplified version of the final software, in SD, most visualizations and other artifacts can be considered a prototype [6].

In the field of service design, few studies have focused on services that are mainly distributed through digital channels. Instead, most publications in service design literature focus on case examples from traditional service industries, such as airlines, restaurant, and public services.

This paper studies how to apply service design in general and prototyping in particular to the development of digital services to gain better understanding of users' needs. The study was carried out with an industrial partner to the case of a meeting scheduling service (MSS). Thus, we aim to investigate two key questions:

RQ1 How does the development of digital services benefit from service design?
RQ2 What are the challenges in applying service design to the development of digital services?

The remainder of this paper is organized as follows: Section 2 presents previous work on services, service design, and prototypes. Section 3 introduces the industry case. Section 4 describes the research method. Section 5 presents the results. Section 6 discusses the findings and Section 7 draws conclusions.

2   Previous Work

This section describes the paradigm shift to service dominant logic, followed by the concept of service design, and ends with providing an overview of prototyping.

2.1   Services: The Paradigm Shift to Service-Dominant Logic

Services have often been defined in relation to goods and described based on characteristics that differentiate them from goods. The most commonly cited characteristics are intangibility, heterogeneity, inseparability and perishability, also known as IHIP-characteristics [7]. In this goods-dominant logic (G-D logic), services are considered inferior to goods [8]. However, in current service management literature, the leading school of thoughts is service-dominant logic (S-D logic) [9], in which goods are merely considered as mechanisms for the distribution of services [10] Thus, a service offering might include tangible and intangible elements. This paradigm shift entails a turn in the view on value creation. One definition of value is as the trade-off between benefits and sacrifices [11]. In G-D logic, value is embedded in the goods and referred to as *value-in-exchange* [12]. In S-D logic, value is referred to as *value-in-use* and means the value as perceived by the customer, which arises and changes over time [10].

Software is challenging to categorize as a product or service based on the IHIP-characteristics. While software is intangible, the other three characteristics of service, heterogeneity, inseparability, and perishability, only apply partially [8], [13]. Degree of customization [14] and revenue models [15] are common approaches to categorize software as either product or service. Recently, Software-as-a-Service (SaaS) and cloud-based services have become popular business models. However, these models mainly refer to a change in the revenue model rather than a change in understanding of value as in S-D logic.

Digital services, such as online banking, have replaced some traditional services and new businesses have emerged, whose core offerings are digital [8]. In traditional services, the role of the front stage employees and their interaction with the customers is crucial for the service experience; in contrast, users of digital services might never get into personal contact with the service provider [16]. Moreover, many digital services, such as online social networks and online marketplaces, provide a platform for social interaction between their users [13]. The service experience of these services depends significantly on the behavior of other users instead of on the behavior of the front stage employees [17].

2.2   Service Design

Service Design originates in times, when services were defined based on the IHIP-characteristics. It was argued that not only products, but also services need design. The strong use of different designer's methods throughout the development process have been defined as the distinguishing characteristics of service design from other approaches to service development [18], [19]. The most common service design methods are prototyping and visualizations [5]. While most visualizations can be used as prototypes [6], not all prototypes are visualizations; for example, experience prototyping [20] and other enacting methods. Stickdorn [21] suggests five principles, which should guide the service design process: *user-centered*, *co-creative*, *sequencing*, *evidencing*, and *holistic*. Instead of user-centered, human-centered has also been suggested as one principle, in order to emphasize the inclusion of other stakeholders [22]. Co-creative refers to the active involvement of users and other stakeholders in the design process. Sequencing emphasizes the need to consider the whole customer journey. Evidencing refers to making the back stage process of the service visible to the customers. Holistic refers to considering also the context of use and thus, extending the principle of sequencing. Typically, a service design process is highly iterative and at each stage, it might be necessary to return to one of the previous stages [23].

Service design still seems to be dominated by the view that a service is different from a product rather than a higher-level concept, as in S-D logic [9]; however, it is seldom made explicit. Nevertheless, some authors have discussed the relation between service design and S-D logic [24]–[26]. Most principles of service design and S-D logic are overlapping and thus, service design is one approach to put the theoretic principles behind the S-D logic into practice [26]. Some authors refer to designing services driven by S-D logic as *design for service* instead of service design in order to make a clear distinction [13], [24]. However, there are different viewpoints concerning the relation of design for service and service design [24], [26]. One viewpoint is to consider design for service as the next step in the evolution of service design (Fig. 1). In this viewpoint product thinking equals G-D logic and service thinking equals S-D logic.

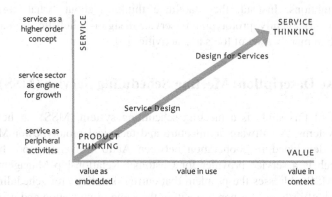

Fig. 1. The evolution from service design to design for service (Source: [25, p. 98])

Similarities exist between service design and other user-centered design disciplines, such as user-experience design. However, service design expands the focus to the long-term usage and across various channels [27].

2.3   Prototypes

Prototypes have been used in a variety of different disciplines; however, the purposes vary among different disciplines [6]. One way to refer to prototypes is as a "representation of a design idea" [28] and prototyping as "the activity of creating prototypes, or activities made possible by or with the prototype" [29]. In software development, and specifically user interfaces, prototyping has long been identified as one activity [30] that is performed before the final implementation [6] in order to evaluate hypotheses concerning the software to be build [31]. Recently, several incremental or iterative methods, such as agile software development, have evolved, in which the intermediate results can be considered a prototype representing a simplified, but almost ready version of the final system [32]. Technical prototypes are commonly used in software development to validate the technical feasibility of a solution; however, this is only one aspect of a whole solution – other aspects are role as well as look and feel [28]. Furthermore, prototypes have been used to evaluate the usability of a software.

In service design, prototypes are described as a learning tools [32], which can be used for various purposes with different levels of fidelity and at any stage of the process [28], [31] and thus, in a broader manner than traditionally in software development. Prototypes are not only used to evaluate a hypothesis or communication with different stakeholders [33], as typically in software development, but also for generation and exploration of ideas. In addition to prototypes that prototype different parts of the service, service prototypes can be used, which encompasses several service moments in order to prototype the holistic user experience [34].

Different frameworks exist to support prototyping [6], [31]. However, since there is not a single way to 'do it right' [33], the frameworks do not provide prototypes for specific situations. Instead, they facilitate thinking about 'what' and 'how' to prototype. Consequently, prototyping in service design is a holistic approach or mind-set rather than merely a set of tools and activities [6].

3   Case Description: Meeting Scheduling Service (MSS)

The object of this study is a meeting scheduling system (MSS) for heterogeneous calendar systems. A software architecture and technical prototype for MSS (Fig. 2) have been developed in cooperation between Aalto University and the company Steeri, which is a service provider for Customer Relationship Management (CRM) solutions. MSS addresses the problem that current solutions for scheduling meetings mainly work effortlessly for persons within the same organization and using the same calendar system, such as Microsoft Exchange. Across organizational borders and between different calendar systems, no solution seems to exist to automatically check availabilities for easier meeting scheduling.

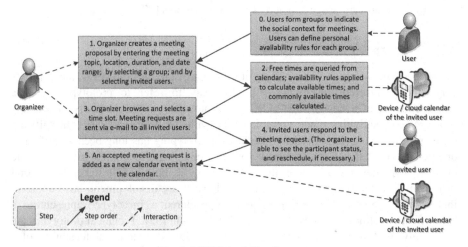

Fig. 2. MSS Scheduling Process

In contrast to existing solutions, MSS automatically retrieves free time slots from users' calendars and provides time slots that are free in the calendar of all meeting invitees to the meeting organizer as possible options for meeting times. Four basic assumptions were made regarding privacy concerns of the users and taken into consideration for the creation of the technical prototype and software architecture: First, users would not want to share free times with everybody. Thus, users first have to choose with whom they share their available time slots. Second, users will want to differentiate what times are shown as available based on so-called 'social context'. For each social context, e.g., a project team, users can set an availability rule to define what times are shown as available. For example, users can limit their availability for a certain project team to times in the afternoons. Third, users would not want information other than free time slots to leave their calendar system. Fourth, meeting organizers should only see time slots that are free for all meeting invitees and not the time slots that are free for each individual invitee. The technical prototype was developed to address and focus on technical feasibility of the solution.

4   Research Method

The research design adheres to the explorative design science research approach [35]. The phases include gaining understanding about meeting scheduling context, creating the interactive and paper prototypes, and a prototype test session with potential users. Finally, the experiences are elaborated.

In order to gain initial understanding, we conducted a case study [36] consisting of a study of the existing technical prototype and existing material, and a half-day workshop with Steeri. The objective of the workshop was to gain better common understanding of the practices and tools to schedule meetings. The participants were the chief executive officer (CEO), the sales & marketing director, a senior consultant, and a software developer. In particular, the three first frequently interact with external parties, but only the CEO was beforehand familiar with technical prototype. In the workshop, a short overview and demo of the prototype were given, different kinds of meetings and the meeting scheduling process were elaborated, and challenges and solutions were gathered on post-it notes, prioritized and discussed. We audio-recorded the workshop and took field notes, including photographs.

After the workshop, an interactive prototype was created with the prototyping tool Axure (Fig. 3). In order to focus the feedback on the service concept, rather than details of the user interface, the interactive prototype had an unfinished look. The interactive prototype demonstrates the whole process, i.e., from taking the service into use to scheduling a meeting. The focus was on the aspects of the service relevant to the users instead of the technical implementation of the back-end. In addition to the interactive prototype, seven different paper prototypes (Fig. 3) were created to present different design alternatives in order to explore factors that the researchers considered the most critical from users' perspective: Two alternatives for the amount of information available to the organizer when selecting a time slot; two alternatives on how to set the availability rules; two alternatives showing different alternatives if no common free time slot was found; and one showing alternatives for taking location information into consideration in order to determine the available time slots more accurately.

In a two-hour session, the prototypes were discussed with potential users. We expected the following outcomes of the session: first, feedback for the service concept based on the interactive prototype and the design alternatives presented as paper prototypes; second, better understanding of users' needs for meetings scheduling and attitudes towards sharing of calendar data in general. The participants of the prototype test session frequently have to schedule meetings with people in various locations and across company borders. There were four participants in the session: three of them are part of the IT department (one manager, two specialists); the fourth participant is a manager in the marketing department.

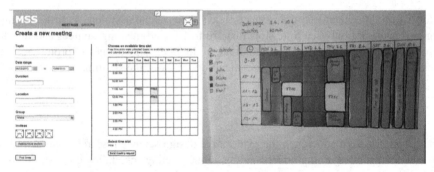

Fig. 3. Examples of the interactive prototype (left) and the paper prototype (right)

The session started by briefly introducing the goal of the session. Next, we showed the interactive prototype and asked the participants to evaluate the prototype. In order to spark discussion, different design alternatives were presented as paper prototypes. The researcher mostly asked questions to clarify certain statements and comment or to get feedback on specific topics. The session was audio recorded.

The data analysis started with extracting important points from the audio recordings and field notes from the initial workshop. Similarly after the prototype test sessions, we extracted the important statements and comments, resorting to the audio recording when necessary. The data analysis then interlaced with a re-analysis of the workshop data because we discovered differences between scheduling meeting behaviors, since different calendar access model were used in both companies. The later analysis focused on differences and similarities between the participants of the workshop and the participants of the prototype test session.

5   Results

The results include the observations and experiences from the workshop with Steeri as well as the prototype test session. This section describes the generalized findings based on the results.

5.1   Change in the Perception of Value

The perceived value varies from user to user and it can change over time, which implies that there is no value in a feature per-se. When applying the value-in-use concept, the user subjectively defines the value. There is rarely a 'one size fits all' solution in any complex service and thus, services need to support the individual customer journeys. For example, people at Steeri use an open calendar access model, i.e., they can see all calendar details of their colleagues, and they seem to use this information comprehensively for scheduling meetings. In contrast, the participants of the prototype test session, using a restricted calendar access model, mainly seemed to be interested in knowing free time slot in the calendar of their colleagues. Furthermore, there also seemed to be a difference depending on the position.

The specialists seemed to face more challenges that others do not prioritize the meetings that they schedule and thus, they seemed more interested in knowing more details concerning the schedule of others.

Value also depends on the sacrifices that a customer has to make. Surprisingly, for the participants of the prototype test session sharing information from their calendar did not constitute much privacy concerns. Rather, a reoccurring worry was the amount of meetings, and the risk that a service, such as MSS, could lead to having even more meetings. Consequently, the features focusing on privacy in the technical prototype cannot be considered generally valuable for all users.

5.2   Challenge to Consider the Whole Customer Journey

The focus of the technical prototype was on the functionality of scheduling meetings with people from different companies. Scheduling of internal meetings was left out of the scope. However, the results of the prototype test session indicate that people do not clearly distinguish between internal meetings and meetings with externals. Overall, they just wish to schedule meetings easily. Even though asked about scheduling meetings with people from other companies, in both, the workshop with Steeri and the prototype test session, a large amount of the discussion evolved around scheduling meetings with colleagues. Moreover, the participants of the prototype test session preferred not to have a separate service. While technical design sets borders clearly, these borders do not exist similarly in the users' mind. This can result in superior technical solution, but inadequate user experience, since the solution might not support the whole customer journey.

Similarly, the technical design focuses on features rather than the holistic customer journey. For example, easy adoption and how to connect with other users in order to share available time are crucial for the success of MSS; however, they had not been covered, when designing the technical prototype.

5.3   Applying Service Design to an Existing Technical Prototype

A SD process typically starts from the scratch to explore possibilities rather than from a technical prototype, as it was in the case of MSS. The technical prototype limited the exploration of different options and thus, the service concept is an incremental change rather than radically new compared to the existing technical prototype. The solution might have been different if the project had started with a service design approach to create the initial idea for the concept. However, discarding a technical prototype and software architecture denotes a significant change that is not necessarily wanted. This was also the case for MSS. Applying service design methods and principles, nevertheless, helped exploring and gaining deeper understanding of users' needs. Furthermore, the prototypes and visualizations facilitate better communication among the different stakeholders.

5.4   Service Design for Digital Services

Many service design methods focus on traditional services and thus, are not directly applicable when designing digital services. When designing traditional services, the interaction between the front stage employees and the customer is emphasized. Furthermore, they often take place in a specific physical space. In contrast in digital services, users interact with a software system. Moreover, the aim of many digital services, such as MSS, is to facilitate interaction between different users. This leads to less control of the service experience for the service provider, since the behavior of other users cannot be controlled in the same manner as the behavior of front stage employees. For example, the user experience of MSS depends significantly on how strict other users set the availability rules. Consequently, many characteristics of digital services are different from traditional services. Furthermore, some of the basic principles of service design do not apply in the same manner. For example, evidencing service takes a different form. Furthermore, the methods need consideration. For example, enacting techniques, which are common to prototype traditional services, would have not been suitable for MSS. Overall, SD provides little guidelines on methods for prototyping and implementing digital services.

5.5   Challenges in Choosing Prototyping Techniques

Due to the plethora of different techniques available for prototyping, it was challenging to choose suitable techniques for the given purpose. While there are some recommendations for which phase of the service design process some techniques are most suitable [37], [38], overall, the choice is left to the designer. While we were thinking prior to the prototype test session that it might be good to prototype the experience more holistically, we discovered during the session that prototyping only parts of MSS with the paper prototypes seems more suitable due to the early stage in the SD process and the focus on exploration. The holistic service experience can be prototyped at a later stage. In fact, it was challenging to achieve a service prototype for MSS: The technical prototype is only functioning on a specific device and thus, could not be easily used to retrieve actual data from the participants' calendars. Furthermore, it only covers parts of the service. The interactive prototype covers the whole process, but only simulates the service and does not retrieve actual calendar data. Thus, users could only imagine how it would work in practice, i.e., what kind of time suggestions they would get in real usage situations. However, as the participants are active users of electronic calendars, it seemed that they could imagine how the calendar data retrieval would work in practice.

The paper prototypes and the sketchy interactive prototype seemed to encourage open feedback, since they did not convey the notion of being close to the final version. We had a quick walkthrough of the interactive prototype, but then mainly focused on the paper prototypes, since they seemed to encourage more discussion than the interactive prototype. However, the chosen method did not seem to encourage proposing own ideas of the participants. The participants mostly focused on their preferences comparing the different design alternatives and possibly proposing to combine them. However, they did not make own suggestions. In order to encourage generation of own ideas, other prototyping methods might have been more beneficial. The interactive prototype could be more beneficial in a later stage of the process, when the concept is more finalized and the focus is on evaluation rather than a more open exploration.

5.6   Nature of Prototypes

On the basis of our experience, it seems that it was beneficial to have different design alternatives. The alternatives reduced the likelihood of receiving purely affirmative feedback for a proposed solution, since they forced the participants to take a stand on what they like and what they do not like. For example, it was discovered to be more intuitive to set the availability rules based on the organizer of the meeting rather than social context. Another example was the preference of showing less information in order to select free time slots. As one participant commented: "I only want to see common free time slots. I don't care about what others have before or after". However, some participants also preferred having more information available.

Besides new ideas and selection between alternatives, prototypes could exclude certain features. However, this did not occur. For example, although the participants were discussing about the availability rules during the prototype test session, none of the participants mentioned why or how they would want to use availability rules. This might indicate that the availability rules would not be used much. From service design perspective, the findings suggest that users might not exclude superfluous features if they do not disturb them. This can result in unnecessarily rich and complex services.

6   Discussion

This section discusses the findings related to the research problems, namely digital service design and prototyping.

6.1   Digital Service Design

It requires a change in the mindset to consider software as a service rather than as a product. In particular, it is more than a change in business or delivery model, as in the case of changing to SaaS. Essentially, the understanding of value is changed: from value-in-exchange to value-in-use. First, in contrast to traditional, technology-driven development, the focus is more on the holistic customer journey. It also covers the process on how the service is taken into use rather than just the usage. Second, services need to address various customer needs and different behavior and thus, the value of a certain feature varies between different users. In traditional services, this can be addressed through front stage employees of the service provider, but in digital services, there is not human intelligence to adapt to different customer needs. Third, technical design sets clear borders of the scope. However, these do not exist in the same manner in the customers' mind. Consequently, the user experience might be impacted negatively, since only parts of the customer journey are supported. While technical implementations will always have borders, it is important to understand the whole customer journey, in order to design the best possible solution.

Furthermore, introducing SD to software engineering requires a change in understanding of design and its role in the development process. User interface designers are often brought in late in the software engineering process. Their role is mostly the visual design and user experience of the user interface. Often, they are not involved in defining the problem that the software is solving. This was also the case of MSS – the project started off with a technical prototype, rather than starting with a user-centered perspective. However, the design of user interfaces requires a holistic understanding of the stakeholder needs, domain, and the problem [39]. Moreover, when starting with a technical prototype, as in the case of MSS, there is a risk that the existing technical prototype limits the possible solutions. For digital services, software plays a significant role and discarding a previously developed technical prototype and software architecture is often not a desired outcome. One risk of this technology-driven approach is that the wrong problem might be solved. While service design can nevertheless help to better understand users' needs and improve the overall user experience, the change is likely to be of incremental nature rather than radically new due to the constraints of the existing technical prototype.

Service design focuses on discovering and exploring the underlying problems of the customers first, before starting to think about solutions. A practical way to bring service design into the process is the usage of a variety design methods, such as explorative prototypes. In contrast to evaluative prototypes, traditionally used in software and usability engineering, their focus is on exploring the problem rather than evaluating the solution. Furthermore, design artifacts in software engineering often refer to the software specification and are mostly technical. Service design artifacts cover more holistically the customer experience over only specific requirements and can take a variety of forms. These can support better understanding of the problem and solution for different groups of stakeholders.

Service design originally focuses on traditional services, rather than digital services. Thus, SD does not have any methodology for the implementation of software and thus, it needs to be combined with models for software development, such as agile, to actually implement the service concepts. Moreover, SD visualizations and prototypes do not provide detailed specification to developers. Consequently, there is currently a gap in moving to the actual technical implementation. This issue could partially be overcome by including developers already in the development of the service concepts.

6.2   Prototyping in Digital Service Design

The technical prototype was built more closely to traditional software engineering approach [40], i.e. the requirements were documented in detail and the technical prototype was evaluated against these requirements. The purpose of the technical prototype was to evaluate the technical solution. In contrast, the service design prototypes were built without specified requirements. Furthermore, their purpose to explore user needs rather than evaluate a solution. This has also been referred to as a shift from 'specification-drive prototypes' to 'prototype-driven specification' [41].

Using prototypes in the session with the potential users proofed to be beneficial for gaining better understanding of users needs as well as discovering which aspects need to be explored further. In addition, presenting different design alternatives to the potential users, especially low-fi paper prototypes, facilitated an open mindset and open discussion with the users, which allowed proofing some assumptions to be wrong.

While prototyping is generally considered central to service design, there is little guidance on the choice of methods to use for a specific service. Existing frameworks for prototyping of services [6], [33] can guide the prototyping process. However, they do not provide any concrete methods for implementing prototypes depending on the type of service and purpose of the prototype. Thus, the success or failure of prototypes depends largely on the designers' choices. For MSS, paper prototypes were used in order to encourage more open feedback. Furthermore, different options were presented, in order to avoid solely affirmative feedback for the presented design. However, despite the presentation of design alternative, one challenge was to encourage the participants to create and share own ideas, and be critical. The participants seemed limited with the design alternatives. A possible approach to overcome this issue would be a workshop focusing on the creation of new ideas. The paper prototypes seemed more suitable than the interactive prototype. Thus, one success factor is to be clear about the purpose of the prototypes and choose the techniques most suitable [33].

Another challenge was prototyping the whole service experience. Enacting techniques are often suggested for traditional services, but they do not seem to be suitable for many digital services, such as MSS. However, as the purpose of the prototype test session was mainly exploration of design alternatives, the service experience can be prototyped in a more holistic manner at a later stage of the process. Nevertheless, with existing service design methods, it can be challenging to prototype the experience of digital services in a holistic manner.

7   Conclusion

This paper studies how to apply service design, and specifically prototyping, in the development of digital services to gain better understanding of users' needs. The development of digital services can benefit from service design in several ways. It supports gaining better understanding of the users' needs and developing a more holistic service experience. Furthermore, different service design artifacts facilitate the communication between different stakeholders. However, challenges exist on a practical level. These challenges include applying the value-in-use concept, adapting service design methods to digital service and practical guidelines for prototyping.

Thinking about software as a service rather than a product, mainly requires a change in the understanding of value: from value-in-exchange to value in use. This implies shifting from focusing on features to understanding the whole customer journey, even though the needs and behavior vary from customer to customer. One challenge in the design of digital services is that there is no human, as in traditional services, to adapt for different customer needs. Another challenge is that technical design sets clear borders of the scope. However, these borders do not exist in the same manner in the mind of the customer and thus, might impact the user experience. Using service design methods, such as explorative prototyping, facilitates understanding of underlying user needs and can help to avoid receiving just affirmative feedback. However, while the plethora of different service design methods offers many opportunities, challenges arise in choosing the right method for a given purpose and context.

The study was conducted in collaboration with an industrial partner and having a technical prototype is common practice in the industry. Thus, the results of this study are applicable to similar contexts.

The results of this study focus on the benefits and challenges of applying service design in the development of digital services. A few practices were given to address these challenges. However, this study revealed several areas for further research. For digital services, in which software engineering plays a crucial role, more research is needed on the integration of service design and software engineering. Furthermore, more work is needed in order to propose concrete guidelines for applying SD to digital services, and specifically to support the choice of prototyping and other service design methods most suitable for a given context. Furthermore, the special characteristics of digital services need further clarifications.

Acknowledgements. We acknowledge the financial support of TEKES as part of the Need for Speed (N4S) program of DIGILE.

References

1. Lindberg, T., Meinel, C., Wagner, R.: Design thinking: A fruitful concept for IT development? In: Meinel, C., Leifer, L., Plattner, H. (eds.) Design Thinking: Understand - Improve - Apply, pp. 3–18. Springer, Heidelberg (2011)
2. Ostrom, A.L., Bitner, M.J., Brown, S.W., Burkhard, K.A., Goul, M., Smith-Daniels, V., Demirkan, H., Rabinovich, E.: Moving forward and making a difference: Research priorities for the science of service. Journal of Service Research 13(1), 4–36 (2010)
3. Brown, T.: Design thinking. Harvard Business Review 86(6), 84–92 (2008)
4. Liedtka, J., Ogilvie, T.: Designing for growth: A design thinking toolkit for managers. Columbia University Press, New York (2011)
5. Wetter Edman, K.: Service Design – A conceptualization of an emerging practice, Licentiate thesis, University of Gothenburg, Sweden (2011)
6. Blomkvist, J.: Conceptualising prototypes in service design, Licentiate thesis, Linköping University, Sweden (2011)
7. Zeithaml, V., Parasuraman, A., Berry, L.: Problems and strategies in services marketing. The Journal of Marketing 49(2), 33–46 (1985)
8. Lovelock, C., Gummesson, E.: Whither services marketing? In search of a new paradigm and fresh perspectives. Journal of Service Research 7(1), 20–41 (2004)

9. Segelström, F.: Visualisations service design, Licentiate thesis, Linköping University, Sweden (2010)
10. Vargo, S.L., Lusch, R.F.: Service-dominant logic: continuing the evolution. Journal of the Academy of Marketing Science 36(1), 1–10 (2008)
11. Smith, J., Colgate, M.: Customer value creation: a practical framework. Journal of Marketing Theory and Practice 15(1), 7–23 (2007)
12. Vargo, S.L., Akaka, M.A.: Service-dominant logic as a foundation for service science: Clarifications. Service Science 1(1), 32–41 (2009)
13. Meroni, A., Sangiorgi, D.: Design for services. Gower Publishing Limited, Farnham (2011)
14. Lassila, A., Jokinen, J., Nylund, J.: Finnish software product business: Results of the national software industry survey 2006. Centre of Expertise for Software Product Business, Espoo (2006)
15. Cusumano, M.A.: The business of software: What every manager, programmer, and entrepreneur must know to thrive and survive in good times and bad. Free Press, New York (2004)
16. Williams, K., Chatterjee, S., Rossi, M.: Design of emerging digital services: A taxonomy. European Journal of Information Systems 17(5), 505–517 (2008)
17. Cho, E.: Interpersonal interaction for pleasurable service experience. In: Proceedings of the 2011 Conference on Designing Pleasurable Products and Interfaces. ACM (2011)
18. Holopainen, M.: Exploring service design in the context of architecture. The Service Industries Journal 30(4), 597–608 (2010)
19. Holmlid, S., Evenson, S.: Bringing service design to service sciences, management and engineering. In: Hefley, B., Murphy, W. (eds.) Service Science, Management and Engineering Education for the 21st Century, pp. 341–345. Springer, Berlin (2008)
20. Buchenau, M., Fulton Suri, J.: Experience prototyping. In: 3rd Conference on Designing Interactive Systems: Processes, Practices, Methods, and Techniques, pp. 424–433. ACM (2000)
21. Stickdorn, M.: 5 principles of service design thinking. In: Stickdorn, M., Schneider, J. (eds.) This is Service Design Thinking, pp. 34–45. BIS Publishers, Amsterdam (2011)
22. Mager, A.: Service design as an emerging field. In: Miettinen, S., Koivisto, M. (eds.) Designing Services with Innovative Methods, pp. 28–43. University of Art and Design, Helsinki (2009)
23. Miettinen, S.: Designing services with innovative methods. In: Miettinen, S., Koivisto, M. (eds.) Designing Services with Innovative Methods, pp. 10–25. University of Art and Design, Helsinki (2009)
24. Kimbell, L.: Designing for service as one way of designing services. International Journal of Design 5(2), 41–52 (2011)
25. Sangiorgi, D.: Value co-creation in design for services. In: Miettinen, S., Valtonen, A. (eds.) Service Design with Theory: Discussions on Change, Value and Methods, pp. 95–104. Lapland University Press, Rovaniemi (2012)
26. Wetter Edman, K.: Exploring overlaps and differences in service-dominant logic and design thinking. In: 1st Nordic Conference on Service Design and Service Innovation, pp. 201–212 (2009)
27. Holmlid, S.: From interaction to service. In: Miettinen, S., Koivisto, M. (eds.) Designing Services with Innovative Methods, pp. 78–97. University of Art and Design, Helsinki (2009)

28. Houde, S., Hill, C.: What do prototypes prototype. In: Helander, M., Landauer, T.K., Prabhu, P. (eds.) Handbook of Human-computer Interaction, 2nd edn., pp. 367–381. Elsevier Science B.V., Amsterdam (1997)

29. Blomkvist, J.: Conceptualisations of service prototyping: Service sketches, walkthroughs and live sERVICE prototypes. In: Miettinen, S., Valtonen, A. (eds.) Service Design with Theory: Discussions on Change, Value and Methods, pp. 177–188. Lapland University Press, Rovaniemi (2012)

30. Brocks Jr., F.P.: The mythical man-month: Essays on software engineering. Addison-Wesley, Reading (1995)

31. Lim, Y.-K., Stolterman, E., Tenenberg, J.: The anatomy of prototypes: Prototypes as filters, prototypes as manifestations of design ideas. ACM Transactions on Computer-Human Interaction 15(2) (2008)

32. Coughlan, P., Fulton Suri, J., Canales, K.: Prototypes as (design) tools for behavioral and organizational change: A design-based approach to help organizations change work behaviors. Journal of Applied Behavioral Science 43(1), 122–134 (2007)

33. Passera, S., Kärkkäinen, H., Maila, R.: When, how, why prototyping? A practical framework for service development. In: XXIII ISPIM Conference (2012)

34. Tassi, R.: Service prototype (2009),
    http://www.servicedesigntools.org/tools/24
    (accessed: October 07, 2014)

35. Peffers, K., Tuunanen, T., Rothenberger, M.A., Chatterjee, S.: A design science research methodology for information systems research. Journal of Management Information Systems 24(3), 45–77 (2007)

36. Yin, R.K.: Case study research, 2nd edn. Sage, Thousand Oaks (1994)

37. Stickdorn, M., Schneider, J.: This is service design thinking. BIS Publishers, Amsterdam (2011)

38. Tassi, R.: Service design tools, (2009), http://www.servicedesigntools.org/
    (accessed: October 07, 2014)

39. Heiskari, J., Kauppinen, M., Runonen, M., Männistö, T.: Bridging the gap between usability and requirements engineering. In: 17th IEEE International Requirements Engineering Conference, pp. 303–308. IEEE (2009)

40. Ramesh, B., Cao, L., Baskerville, R.: Agile requirements engineering practices and challenges: An empirical study. Information Systems Journal 20(5), 449–480 (2007)

41. Schrage, M.: Cultures of prototyping. In: Winograd, T. (ed.) Bringing Design to Software. ACM Press, New York (2006)

On Infrastructure for Facilitation
of Inner Source in Small Development Teams

Johan Linåker, Maria Krantz, and Martin Höst

Software Engineering Research Group, Computer Science,
Lund University, Lund, Sweden
{johan.linaker,martin.host}@cs.lth.se

Abstract. The phenomenon of adopting open source software development practices in a corporate environment is known by many names,
one being inner source. The objective of this study is to investigate how
an organization consisting of small development teams can benefit from
adopting inner source and assess the level of applicability. The research
has been conducted as a case study at a software development company.
Data collection was carried out through interviews and a series of focus
group meetings, and then analyzed by mapping it to an available framework. The analysis shows that the organization possesses potential, and
also identified a number of challenges and benefits of special importance
to the case company. To address these challenges, the case study synthesized the organizational and infrastructural needs of the organization
in a requirements specification describing a technical infrastructure, also
known as a software forge, with an adapted organizational context and
work process.

Keywords: Inner source, Open source software, Software development
practices, Software ecosystem, Life cycle, Programming teams, Software
process models, Software reuse, Software forge

1 Introduction

Many open source software products have been successful in recent years, which
have led to an increased interest from the industry to investigate how the development practices could be introduced in a corporate environment and take
advantage of the benefits seen in open source projects. Such practices include
e.g. universal access to project artefacts [8], early and frequent releases, and
"community" peer-review [2].

Mistrik et al. [11] address how closed development organizations could benefit
from open source practices as an area where further research is needed. Though
studies conducted so far are quite limited, several success stories [1, 2, 8, 13, 20]
can be found of large corporations adopting open source development.

The phenomenon of adopting these development practices in a corporate environment has in research been referred to by many names, e.g. *inner source* [17],
corporate open source [2, 3] and *progressive open source* [1]. In this report we
have chosen to use the term inner source, as described by Stol [17].

A. Jedlitschka et al. (Eds.): PROFES 2014, LNCS 8892, pp. 149–163, 2014.
© Springer International Publishing Switzerland 2014

The changes required when adopting inner source in a corporate environment led Gurbani et al. [3] to suggest two different methods to effectively manage inner source assets; an infrastructure-based model and a project-based model.

In the infrastructure-based model, the corporation provides the critical infrastructure that allows interested developers to host individual software projects on the infrastructure, much like SourceForge[1] or Github[2] does with open source projects. Platforms like these, also known as software forges [13], can be resembled as component libraries where each project represents a component of different abstractions, e.g. modules, frameworks or executables. Developers can browse between the components and use or contribute to those they wish. The reuse of software can be considered opportunistic or ad hoc and there is no limitation on the number of projects to be shared within the organization. Success stories include cases from SAP [13], IBM [16, 19], HP [1, 10] and Nokia [7, 8].

In the project-based approach the software is managed in a project, instead of as a long-term infrastructure. Gurbani et al. [3] describe how an advanced technology group, or a research group funded by other business divisions in a corporation takes over a critical resource and makes it available across the organization. This team is often referred to as the "core team" and is responsible for the project and the decision making. Philips Healthcare [20] and Alcatel-Lucent [3] are two documented cases where this variant has been adopted.

In order to assess the applicability of inner source on an organization, Stol [17] developed a framework. This framework is based on reviewed literature and a case study of a software company referred to as "newCorp". Though the framework focuses on project-based models, it is based on success factors and guidelines described in both project-based and infrastructure-based case studies.The framework consists of 17 elements divided into four categories; Software product, Development practices, Tools and infrastructure, and Organization and community. These categories were inspired and mapped to those proposed by Gurbani et al. [2]. The elements can be found in the left column of Table 1. In a later publication Stol et al. [18] present an updated version of the framework where it has been restructured, now consisting of nine elements divided into three groups; Software product, Practices and Tools, and Organization and Community. The elements are more generalized and covers all of those described in the initial framework [17].

Adopting inner source requires significant effort and change management, which is one reason why it may be of interest to start on a smaller scale before investing globally. However, this requires an understanding of how inner source can be implemented on smaller teams and what parts that can be implemented and evaluated. This study is focused towards the latter and aims to contribute theoretically by using a framework by Stol [17] to assess the applicability of inner source, and based on the identified challenges synthesize a solution that addresses the organizations needs.

---

[1] http://www.sourceforge.com/
[2] http://github.com

The outline of this paper is as follows. In Section 2 the research methodology is presented and the results are presented in Section 3 and 4. The results are discussed and further analyzed in Section 5. The validity of the conducted research is presented in Section 6 and the research results are summarized in Section 7.

2 Methodology

This research is of a problem-solving nature and conducted as a case study with an exploratory strategy approach [14, 15]. The case company is experiencing problems in regards to its reuse of code and overall efficiency. The hypothesis is that the concept of inner source, as described earlier, can help the organization manage these issues (e.g. [1, 2, 8, 16]).

The organization was observed in order to further define the problem during spring 2012. Then it needed to be assessed whether inner source would fit the organization or not, and what the challenges would be. Based on the findings, the parts of inner source suitable for the organizations needs were synthesized in a requirement specification describing a technical infrastructure together with an organizational context and work process.

This improving approach can be compared to that of action research. However, this study has focused on the initial parts and proposed a solution. This is yet to be implemented and evaluated. I.e. the complete change process is yet to be observed. Due to limitations in time for the researchers and organizational conditions of the case company, this is left for future research.

2.1 The Case Company

An international software development firm, hereby known as "the case company", has been chosen for this study. The case company has a division based in a local office in Sweden which specializes in rapid software development and deployment of projects where the customers seek a combination of high quality and a fast release.

The scope is limited to the local division, though a network of corresponding divisions is established globally. The division of interest is divided into two teams with similar set-up and structure. Each team consists of 20-25 engineers including developers, testers and project managers.

2.2 Case Study Steps

The data collection and analysis was carried out as outlined in Figure 1, and described below.

2.3 Situation Analysis

A situation analysis was conducted with the objective to describe and explain the current situation at the company. The main goal was to gain an understanding of how work is conducted within the organization and can be seen as an observational part of the research.

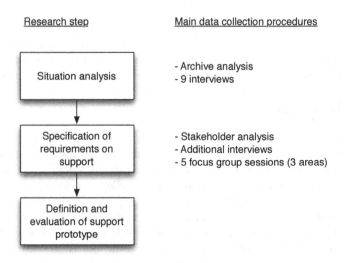

Fig. 1. Overview of data collection and analysis

Qualitative data was collected by studying documentation at the case company and by interviewing a sample group. The criteria for selecting people in this phase were that they should: be representatives from different areas, with different work tasks, to get a good variation of answers; have more than two years of work experience, within this or other companies; and be available for interviews.

In total 9 individuals were interviewed which included 4 project managers and senior back-end developers, 2 senior front-end developer, 1 junior front-end developer, 1 junior back-end developer, and 1 service manager.

The interviews were semi-structured with 20 questions prepared in advance. All interviews were recorded with both audio and supportive notes taken by the authors. The interview data was then analyzed using an editorial approach (e.g. [15]), meaning that the categories and statements for characterizing the reasoning in the interviews were not to a large extent predefined. The qualitative data was codified, commented and searched for patterns and themes in a first iteration. In a second step this was used to make generalizations and relate to the themes presented by Stol in his framework [17]. The mapping was then used to evaluate the compatibility of the company to adopt inner source, see Table 1. The framework was adapted with some modifications to suit the company, consisting of three additional factors located in the end of the Table 1.

2.4 Specification of Requirements on Technical and Practical Support

To define the technical infrastructure, related context and practices, a requirement specification was chosen because it is a natural approach within the software industry to describe a desired solution. The requirements specification is not presented here, although an overview of the domain can be found in Section 4, and more information is provided in [5].

Several methods were used in order to elicit requirements from all levels of interest, e.g. stakeholder analysis, additional interviews, and a series of focus groups.

Stakeholder Analysis. A stakeholder analysis (e.g. [6]) was used to map all of the stakeholders and elicit their different areas of interest. It is important that everyone with a stake in the product gets to contribute their view, goals and wishes concerning both functional and non-functional requirements in order for the final product to get a corporate wide approval.

Stakeholders were identified amongst developers, project- and service managers, team managers and corporate representatives. The analysis was based on material from the interviews held in the situation analysis, complemented by the focus group meetings and a longer interview with the case companys' former CTO.

Focus Groups. As it became clear early on in the case study that stakeholders had different opinions and priorities, this technique was considered appropriate. The incentive was to create an understanding between stakeholders in addition to identify problems and gather ideas and opinions in a structured manner [6]. The other objective of the focus groups [4] was to elicit requirements for a substantial part for the proposed solution. Three areas with different themes were therefore identified on which the focus groups were based upon: Reuse of code and knowledge; Tools and functionality; Time, sales strategy and incentives. With these themes the authors regarded to have covered all relevant aspects of the product. Several subtopics were then identified around which the discussions were held.

The focus groups were carried out in 1.5 hour sessions. Focus groups 1 and 2 were both split into two sessions, while focus group 3 was carried out in one single session. The sessions were moderated by one of the two first authors, whilst the other documented by audio recording and taking supporting notes.

Each session had a brief list of subtopics where participants were allowed to briefly describe bad experiences and focus more on the ideal usage and functions. Post-it notes were used by the participants to record their opinions, where considered appropriate by the authors. These were then collected by the moderator and presented for a joint discussion. The discussions also included different aspects of risk, cost and benefits of the proposals. Where different opinions were present, a collective prioritization of the ideas was conducted and motivation to the priorities encouraged by the moderator. The sessions concluded with a summary by the moderator.

Recordings, notes and post-its were analysed by the authors using the editorial approach as was for the interviews. Iterations with clarification and elaboration was performed with the participants when needed.

3   Results from Situation Analysis

The situation analysis is a product of applying Stol's framework [17] to the case company. A summarized version can be found in Table 1.

As recognized before, reuse today within the division is seen as insufficient. There is no overview documentation available on what software is available for reuse, causing knowledge of what has been developed and where it is located to be spread by a "mouth-to-mouth" manner. Certain modules and functions, which are commonly used, risk being re-developed. For example, one interviewee stated *"I use standard modules that are needed in projects that I sometimes know that someone else has done in another project or that I have done myself in another project and thereby I can use it. In other cases, we are not aware of it. Especially when a new developer enters [a project] who has not been around for so long and do not know what is available."*

It is recognized as possible to identify existing classes and functions for reuse which could constitute the initial foundation of shared assets, time is however viewed as a restricting factor. Also modularization of code is needed, which may require additional training for the developers. Another quote highlights the potential for a common framework that can be used as a standard template in many of the projects. *"We could benefit a lot from having our own demo site or basic platform, including common modules, that projects can be based on."*

An apparent need for a platform facilitating reuse and open access exist, since redundant work is conducted.

As each customer has his or her own specific requirements, potential shared assets used from project to project may have to be adapted. This allows the components to constantly evolve and mature with increased functionality, but also with the threat of increased complexity. Requirements are mainly set at the start of the project, but also constantly evolving incrementally in each sprint according to the agile scrum like process used by the teams. Releases are done frequently with each sprint. The quality assurance process with peer reviews does exist in an informal manner but needs structure and systematization.

Concerning standardized tools, one problem exists in regards with multiple version control systems with the effect of code being dispersed on multiple platforms. In general however a common set of collaborative tools are in place including an application lifecycle management tool (TeamForge[3]) which is under evaluation.

Two general and important aspects, tightly knit together, are time and budget. The time set for documentation is seldom used for its specific purpose. Transfer of knowledge in general is a subject that needs to be incorporated in the day-to-day work process in every project. There is little or no time between projects for project feedback and knowledge transfer. This would also be an issue in regards to maintenance of potential shared assets. Reason for this is to a high concern business oriented as time estimations are kept low in order to win customer deals and chargeable coverage is of high priority, leaving limited time for internal improvements.

---

[3] http://www.collab.net/products/teamforge

There is an open discussions ongoing in the case company, and a willingness to change exist, even if time is a restraining factor for internal improvements as noted.

Work coordination is maintained in each project in combination with project leads and the agile process in place. Developers felt that they had an influence and that there exists an open culture. The interviews specifically highlighted the need for evangelists to overcome the responsibility issue of inner source. Potential evangelists could be seen within the organization, if given enough encouragement and support to take on the responsibility. This can correlate to the evangelists described in Dinkelacker et al. [1].

One last aspect identified is about code ownership. If the customer has specific ownership of the code, then the question arises whether it is okay or not for the developers to turn the code into a shared asset and reuse it in other projects. Generally it is stated in the customer contract that the case company owns the code, whilst the customer has the rights to use it. However, this is sometimes negotiated to the customer owning the code, which means the case company has no rights to reuse the solutions.

4   Overview of Proposed Technical Infrastructure

The situation analysis showed both need and potential for the applicability of inner source. Infrastructure and defined processes are required in order to be able to create and organize shared assets, and to help facilitate inner source practices.

Based on the situation analysis, focus group meetings and additional elicitation techniques, an infrastructure comparable to that of a software forge [13] was defined and specified. The domain for the infrastructure, other than the forge, consists of the users of the forge, and the system administrator within the studied division of the case company. The systems for the developing and running customer projects, as well as the documentation of old projects, are outside

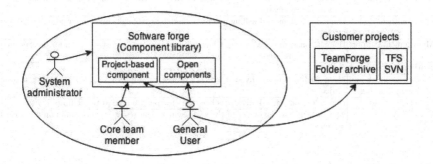

Fig. 2. Context diagram of the software forge domain and the outer domain of customer projects

the software forge domain, see Figure 2. The forge can be seen as a component library with a component project view for each shared asset, i.e. component. There are two types of components which is explained further below.

Table 1. Summary chart of findings from interviews in relation to inner source practices. Elements based on framework by Stol [17]

Element	Findings from interviews
Software product	
Runnable software	Classes and functions can be identified from previous projects, but the extraction may be very time consuming.
Needed by several project groups	There is potential for a common framework that can be used in several projects. An apparent need for a platform facilitating reuse exist, since redundant work is conducted.
Maturity state of the software	Constantly evolving techniques and modules for customer-specific solutions.
Utility vs simplicity	Some solutions may be too specific for the project in order to reuse.
Modularity	Modularization of code is needed, which may require training.
Development practices	
Requirement elicitation	Requirements are project-specific and are mainly set at the start of the project, but also constantly evolving in each sprint.
Implementation and quality control	Agile, sprint-driven development, planned per sprint. The level of competence in and knowledge of the process used varies. Senior developers review junior developers informally. Because of insufficient unit testing, quality can sometimes be an issue. Testing is to some extent "bazaar-like" and peer-testing is performed as much as possible.
Release management	Frequent releases, after each sprint. Customers are provided with prototypes.
Maintenance	Little or no time between projects. Development projects are generally transferred to maintenance projects after acceptance test.
Tools & Infrastructure	
Standardized tools	Common set of collaborative tools are in place, though older projects remain using older tools. Freedom to select tools locally.
Infrastructure for open access	Projects are archived in a traditional folder structure. A project platform for distributed development has been initiated and is under evaluation.
Organization & Community	
Work coordination	Developers are assigned tasks. In order to control that the correct tasks are prioritized, developers may switch between projects. Better overview desirable.
Communication	Developers sit closely together and are unlikely to benefit from "open" communication. Communication with customers is desired to be closer and steered away from e-mailing.
Leadership and decision making	Discussions are considered open and inputs appreciated. Evangelists and/or core team needed to take responsibility for a common framework.
Motivation and incentives	A lack of time is the biggest concern. Attractiveness of the tool also considered a critical success factor.
Open culture	Open discussions and willingness to change exist, though time a restraining factor for internal improvements.
Management support	Budget constraints a concern. Chargeable occupancy important. Plan for incorporating activities related to reuse in the sales strategy needed.
Additional factors	
Project feedback and knowledge sharing	More feedback on a division level desirable to improve knowledge sharing across projects.
Project initiation	Dependent on a few individuals because of expertise needed to set up projects.
Code ownership	The customer is the owner of the code, which may result in constraints on what can be reused.

4.1   Components

All components are stored in a component library (the software forge). A search function allows the user to find a component of interest. Clear visualization of ratings and issues as well as test- and review results for each components are available so that users early can determine the potential of the component. Components can be tagged by the users with self-defined names for easier search and categorization. There are two types of components that can be shared, project-based components and open components.

Project-based components require administration by a core team that is responsible for the maintenance and development of the component. All users can access the components but the core team may restrict the user's rights to make any changes. Different types of components that have been identified as project-based components are Product, Framework and Templates.

- **Product:** A basic solution that is ready to be sold to the customer, or to be customized. This type is a long term idea and though the forge provides the infrastructure to share this component, special requirements to support this type of component will not be further considered in this project.
- **Framework:** A framework for the most commonly used modules. The framework would be used to have an initial set of modules that are reusable and can easily be implemented in a new project. A core team decides what goes into the framework and makes sure the framework is up to date and of the required quality.
- **Templates:** Documentation templates developed by a core team in order to facilitate the documentation process.

Open components do not need any administration or anyone responsible for the development of the component. No quality or generalization requirements exist to share these components and the creator is not responsible for any maintenance or further development. Modules and Classes, and Knowledge Base are types of components identified as open components.

- **Modules and classes:** Modules and classes that have been used in projects. The size and complexity of these components may vary and may be more or less suitable to reuse.
- **Knowledge base:** User guides for commonly performed tasks, tutorials, lessons learned from previous projects, common errors etc. that could be helpful in future projects.

4.2   Users

The identified user types are all employees with access to the forge. They can be divided into three groups:

- **General user:** Developers reusing and contributing to components. The general users have full rights to open components and limited rights to project-based components.
- **Core team member:** Project-based components have at least one core team member. The core team members have full access to its components and are responsible for maintenance, support and further development of that component.

– **System administrator:** The system administrators is responsible for the technical support and maintenance of the forge.

Each user will have a recorded dataset of the users activity, e.g. number of contributed tests and reviews, number of contributed components, number of components applied in customer projects.

4.3   Component Project View

The components individual project views are unique and scalable, dependent of whether the component is open or project-based. Functionality as task management, issue tracking, version control, discussion areas, mailing lists and wikis are available and adapted according to each projects governance. Rating and review functionality is generically available.

5   Discussion

5.1   Infrastructure

The forge that was elicited and specified consists of two parts: The component library and component project view, which conforms to other cases e.g. SAP [13], Nokia [7, 8] and IBM [16, 19]. The former part is used for searching and finding projects, whilst the latter offers a project specific toolbox with common communication and development features where users and developers interact, also commonly identified the previously mentioned studies.

Riehle et al. [13] describes three critical design issues of a forge; finding, understanding, and contributing to projects. All three topics emerged and were heavily valued from the focus group meetings. The main feature requested for finding relevant projects was the possibility to assign self-defined tags to the projects. Concerning understandability, rating and reviews must be clearly presented to enable for a quick initial judgment. Discussion, wiki and mailing list functions described by Riehle et al [13]. was also requested to offer the user the possibility to get a more thorough understanding. Third point about the simplicity of contributing to projects regards usability and an intuitive design and integration of the different parts of the component project view.

The two types of components that were elicited, open and project-based components, offers two styles which conforms to Gurbanis [3] definitions of infrastructural and project-based inner source. Open components can be anything of general interest and the creator is not obligated to any support or maintenance of it. The main motivation for its existence is the request for simplicity to contribute and share knowledge, decrease dependency on individual developers and enable assets to be highly dynamic. Costs of creating modular and generic components need to be kept low as time is a scarce resource. For cases where more structure is needed, especially projects which are business critical and demands supervision, project-based components was introduced which are maintained and supervised by a core team. Depending on the complexity of the component, the amount of resources needed by the core team may vary. For a critical asset such as a framework, the core team members need to have deep technical knowledge as well as an understanding of the business- and delivery models.

The mixing of these two component types offers a broad scope of possibilities for the case company. A risk however is the possibility of confusion when to choose one or the other. Another risk is that the freedom offered by open components can result in the forge being cluttered with components no one will use. This could also result in troublesome searches for the right component. One solution, which is used in the case of IBM [19], could be having an approval process where an overall supervisor decides which components gets to be added. Similar governance to that of the forge described by this paper can be identified in the case of SAP, where *"Everyone who's interested can become a developer on the forge, and everyone can register a new project without going through a lengthy approval process"* [13].

5.2   Development Practices

As described in Section 4, the domain does not include the customer projects. Hence, the introduction of inner source, as proposed here, will have a low impact on the development practices used. Collaborative development is used to some extent and under improvement with the introduction of TeamForge (TF), which would benefit the implementation process of the forge.

It was revealed in the situation analysis, that the quality of the code is an issue from time to time. Hence, it is relevant to take advantage of the quality benefits associated with inner source [2,3,9,16]. With the use of ratings and peer reviews, quality can be improved both directly on the specific component and indirectly by allowing developers to gain skills through the identification of bugs and errors. A drawback of ratings, anticipated by the focus group meetings, is that it can be misleading. Users who have tested or reviewed the component may have done this to different extents why their conception of the component may vary. This is why additional information such as tagging, rating, comments and descriptions are considered important so that whole experiences are reflected and potential users can get a fair comprehension of the component. Uncertainty about the quality of a component will prohibit its use.

Alignment between the different projects is important to the team. A framework is considered to improve alignment of the development from project to project through a communal set of components, optimizing the initiation process, raising the general quality and facilitating for developers to enter a new project [1,9].

5.3   Organization and Community

Though the general organizational structure does not need to change, some effort on all levels is required to adapt to the new conditions and create business value from the initiative.

An incentive and motivational structure is essential for users to be attracted to the forge and to support the volunteer approach used, just as in any open source community [12]. From the case company managements perspective, there is a wish to acknowledge the competent developer and the platform could be used as a tool for doing so. However, it is required to put some thought into what is being measured to prevent that rewards, if any, are not misleading, nor cause negative implications for contributing. Statistics similar to what is described by Lindman et al. [8] was requested to serve as motivational data for the users directly, and also for management. This would include general measurements e.g. most popular project and more personal measures e.g. number of contributed components applied in customer projects.

The individual developer may be motivated to contribute by the rewards and acknowledgement of management, but motivation is also a highly cultural matter that needs to be incorporated in the working environment [13]. Developers as well as managers and technical leaders, need to encourage each other to contribute and to use the forge, foster awareness and integration of the solution in the day-to-day work. The need for an "evangelist" has been described in both literature [1,16] and the situation analysis, Section 3 as essential for the success of an inner source initiative. This important role is hence to be chosen carefully and early on in the initiation process in order to push the projects forward.

As described by Wesselius, [20], one of the limiting external factors of inner source development is overall profitability. That is, that the group should not optimize its own profits at the expense of the company's total profitability. By constantly keeping an awareness of what exists on the forge and the quality of it, which will be an increasing challenge as the content grows, individuals with responsibility for sales can adapt their estimates to presumptive customers and retain higher margins for tender processes [2,3,9,20]. This cross-divisional dependency calls for a communication and discussion between the different internal stakeholders. Planning and development of the assets on the forge is of communal interest since it benefits the whole company.

6   Validity

The interviews were analyzed with the compatibility framework developed by Stol [17]. The framework has to our knowledge not been evaluated before by others than the author. In a later publication Stol et al. [18] presents an updated version of the framework where it has been restructured and made more generalized, still covering the same elements described in original version [17] and now applied on three new cases by the author. By using a theoretical framework the assessment is more focused, and also framed to previous findings within the research of inner source.

The proposed solution on a forge to facilitate the inner source practices and reuse was an option that emerged in the situation analysis. This platform evolved during the focus groups and continued studies of the case company, together with a clear connection to the concept of a software forge and the similarity to

Gurbani et al.'s [3] concepts of infrastructure and project-based inner source. It was not a predefined solution and evolved due to a natural process, though as no other options were as thoroughly investigated, there is a risk that alternative solutions could have been ruled out unconsciously.

Since this is an individual case study, it cannot be established if the technical solution and recommendations are applicable to other case companies. Additionally, the solution proposed has yet not been implemented, nor evaluated. The authors consider the solution to be an option for similar size of development teams, being a small company or part of a larger company that want to experiment with the adoption of inner source on a smaller scale before making significant investments. Evaluation of the solution would be needed in order to investigate what challenges the solution truly impose as well as the benefits similar organizations can expect to gain.

The main measures taken to improve the validity (e.g. [15]) in the case study can be summarized as follows.

Prolonged involvement was achieved since the two first authors spend most of their working time at the premises of the case company during a time period of about 4 months.

Peer debriefing, meaning that fellow researchers comment on the results was achieved by having the third author reviewing the findings and research methodology during the research without being actively involved in the day-to-day data collection.

Member checking, in this case meaning that senior engineers at the case company reviewed findings around which discussions were held continuously.

Audit trails were achieved by recording all interviews and taking extensive notes during data collection phases.

7 Conclusion

Several potential benefits can be gained by the case company. The main motivation is the possibilities it offers for improved reuse of code and solutions to complex problems. Other benefits include improved quality of code and general level of knowledge amongst developers, creation of a framework to standardize and shorten initiation process of new projects, better visibility and spread of information and knowledge, and higher margins for tender processes.

During this research the framework of Stol [17] was used as a framework in the analysis. We conclude that this framework is useful for this purpose, and we believe that it includes the relevant factors. There is an updated version of this framework which is more generalized [18]. We believe that by the application of the older version, this paper can also support the validity of the new version as well.

In order to address the challenges seen in introducing inner source and to gain the benefits, this case study has proposed a technical infrastructure, also known as a software forge, presented in form of a requirement specification with an adapted organizational context and work process. The forge forms a collaborative platform where knowledge and code constitute shared assets, here known as components, and where people can interact according to the principles of inner source.

Two types of components were identified in order to address the types of data which the case company wishes to share internally. Project-based components which are, to some extent, to be seen as business critical and demands supervision by a core team. This can be related to the concepts of project-based inner source as identified by Gurbani et al. [3]. The other type, open components, relates in some parts to the concept of infrastructural inner source [3]. It can also be compared to a combination of a knowledge base and a code snippet library. This type of component can in general be anything of general interest and creator is not obligated to any support or maintenance of it.

With the specification and comprehensive description of a software forge, this paper has made a contribution as the studies available are limited and more focused on general challenges and practices. The forge presented is designed to practically handle the challenges identified and to facilitate the inner source practices of use to the studied organization. The process behind the analysis, elicitation and design of the forge can be seen as a reference for future implementations by other organizations. Focus has been from the small development team point of view, compared to global development and R&D organizations often depicted in other studies. By first understanding of how inner source can be implemented on smaller teams, the concept can be expanded with time more easily.

The division studied within the case company possesses potential for the application of inner source and if successfully applied, it can bring several rewards to the organization by optimizing its resources. An eventual future implementation is yet to be studied. Since this study has focused on one case, it cannot be generalized to other organization by default. Many of the findings though, can be of value to other cases where smaller teams and organizations are investigating the opportunities to introduce inner source, which is an area for future research.

Acknowledgments. This work was partly funded by the Industrial Excellence Center EASE - Embedded Applications Software Engineering.

References

1. Dinkelacker, J., Garg, P.K., Miller, R., Nelson, D.: Progressive open source. In: ICSE 2002: Proceedings of the 24th International Conference on Software Engineering, pp. 177–184. ACM Press, New York (2002)
2. Gurbani, V.K., Garvert, A., Herbsleb, J.D.: A case study of a corporate open source development model. In: ICSE 2006: Proceedings of the 28th International Conference on Software Engineering, Shanghai, China, pp. 472–481 (2006)
3. Gurbani, V.K., Garvert, A., Herbsleb, J.D.: Managing a corporate open source software asset. Communication of the ACM (Association for Computing Machinery) 53(2), 155–159 (2010)

4. Kontio, J., Lehtola, L., Bragge, J.: Using the focus group method in software engineering: Obtaining practitioner and user experiences. In: International Symposium on Empirical Software Engineering, Redondo Beach, CA, USA, pp. 271–280 (2004)
5. Krantz, M., Linåker, J.: Inner source: Application within small-sized development teams. Master's thesis, Lund University (2012)
6. Lauesen, S.: Software requirements: Styles and techniques. Addison-Wesley, Pearson Education Limited, Harlow (2002)
7. Lindman, J., Riepula, M., Rossi, M., Marttiin, P.: Open source technology in intraorganisational software development: Private markets or local libraries. In: Jenny, S.Z., Lundstrm, E., Wiberg, M., Hrastinski, S., Edenius, M., Ågerfalk, P.J. (eds.) Managing Open Innovation Technologies, pp. 107–121. Springer, Heidelberg (2013)
8. Lindman, J., Rossi, M., Marttiin, P.: Applying open source development practices inside a company. In: Russo, B., Damiani, E., Hissam, S., Lundell, B., Succi, G. (eds.) Open Source Development, Communities and Quality. IFIP, vol. 275, pp. 381–387. Springer, Boston (2008)
9. Martin, K., Hoffman, B.: An open source approach to developing software in a small organization. IEEE Software 24(1), 46–53 (2007)
10. Melian, C., Mahring, M.: Lost and gained in translation: Adoption of open source software development at hewlett-packard. In: Russo, B., Damiani, E., Hissam, S., Lundell, B., Succi, G. (eds.) Open Source Development, Communities and Quality. IFIP, vol. 275, pp. 93–104. Springer, Boston (2008)
11. Mistrík, I., Grundy, J., Hoek, A., Whitehead, J.: Collaborative software engineering: Challenges and prospects. In: Mistrík, I., Grundy, J., Hoek, A., Whitehead, J. (eds.) Collaborative Software Engineering, pp. 389–402. Springer, Heidelberg (2010)
12. Raymond, E.S.: The Cathedral and the Bazaar: Musings on Linux and Open Source by an Accidental Revolutionary. O'Reilly Media (2001)
13. Riehle, D., Ellenberger, J., Menahem, T., Mikhailovski, B., Natchetoi, Y., Naveh, B., Odenwald, T.: Open collaboration within corporations using software forges. IEEE Software 26(2), 52–58 (2009)
14. Robson, C.: Real World Research. Blackwell Publishers (2002)
15. Runeson, P., Höst, M., Rainer, A., Regnell, B.: Case Study Research in Software Engineering: Guidelines and Examples. John Wiley & Sons (2012)
16. Sabbah, D.: The open internet - open source, open standards and the effects on collaborative software developmen. In: 11th International workshop on High Performance Transaction Systems, Pacific Grove, CA, USA (2005)
17. Stol, K.-J.: Supporting Product Development with Software from the Bazaar. PhD thesis, University of Limerick (2011)
18. Stol, K.-J., Avgeriou, P., Babar, M.A., Lucas, Y., Fitzgerald, B.: Key factors for adopting inner source. ACM Trans. Softw. Eng. Methodol. 23(2), 18:1–18:35 (2014)
19. Vitharana, P., King, J., Chapman, H.: Impact of internal open source development on reuse: Participatory reuse in action. J. Manage. Inf. Syst. 27(2), 277–304 (2010)
20. Wesselius, J.H.: The bazaar inside the cathedral: Business models for internal markets. IEEE Software 25(3), 60–66 (2008)

Analysis and Improvement of Release Readiness – A Genetic Optimization Approach

S.M. Didar-Al-Alam[1], S.M. Shahnewaz[1], Dietmar Pfahl[2], and Guenther Ruhe[1]

[1] Software Engineering Decision Support Laboratory
University of Calgary, Calgary, AB, Canada
{smdalam,smshahne,ruhe}@ucalgary.ca
[2] Institue of Computer Science
University of Tartu, Tartu, Estonia
dietmar.pfahl@ut.ee

Abstract

Context: Release readiness (RR) quantifies the status of a product release by aggregating a portfolio of release related measures. Early identification of factors responsible in improving RR (i.e. RR improvement factors) can help project managers to (re)allocate resources to improve processes to achieve higher level of RR score.

Objective: This paper has two objectives: i) to identify time-dependent RR improvement (RRI) factor(s); and ii) to identify a budget allocation strategy for maximum improvement of RR score for the upcoming time interval.

Method: RELREA is an existing approach that determines RR from aggregating the degree of satisfaction of a portfolio of release process, product, deployment and support related measures. The proposed method DAICO enhances RELREA by performing dynamic instead of static analysis. For that purpose, the RRI factors identification problem is formulated and solved as a genetic optimization problem. Subsequently, recommendations are generated for cost-optimized RR improvement.

Results: We demonstrated the applicability of the DAICO method for release *Publify* 8.0 of an ongoing project *Publify*, hosted in GitHub OSS repository. Main contributions of this paper are: i) Formulating identification of RRI factors as an optimization problem, ii) Modeling and solving the problem using a GA, iii) Providing recommendations for cost-optimized RR improvement

Conclusions: DAICO is a part of an ongoing effort to detect, and analyze RRI factors when achieving RR. This method is intended to detect RRI factors earlier and to guide the effort spent on improving RR.

Keywords: Release readiness, Release readiness improvement factor, Cost optimization, Genetic algorithm.

1   Introduction

Failure in on-time delivery of software products may cause substantial loss in opportunity and revenue. Due to the complex nature of development, management

A. Jedlitschka et al. (Eds.): PROFES 2014, LNCS 8892, pp. 164–177, 2014.

faces difficulties in evaluating the software under development from the release perspective. In this context, release readiness (RR) is a time dependent attribute of the product release. It aggregates a portfolio of release process and product measures to quantify status of the release. The value (in terms of money) of knowing RR is studied in [1]. Continuous monitoring of RR keeps the management and development team aware of potential release problems. However, only knowing RR is not enough for achieving high RR score. It is equally important to identify the key factors responsible in improving RR score (i.e. RR improvement factors). Based on the available RR measures, identifying the RR improvement (RRI) factors and (re)allocating available budget to achieve higher RR is a challenging task. Therefore, our goal is to develop an analytical approach that allows i) identifying RRI factors at any point in time of the release cycle, and ii) (re)allocating available budget to achieve higher RR.

This paper is part of an ongoing effort to detect, and analyze RRI factors for achieving higher RR. In [2], we proposed an analytical approach called RELREA *(RELease REAdiness)* to evaluate RR which was partially based on the concept of fuzzy set theory [3]. RELREA aggregates the degree of satisfaction of a portfolio of release process and product measures to evaluate the readiness of a product for release. However, this approach was not designed to identify RRI factors. In this paper, we propose a comprehensive method called DAICO *(Dynamic Analysis of RR Improvement factors and Cost Optimized RR improvement)*. DAICO determines RRI factors and an optimized budget allocation strategy to increase RR by performing analysis based on genetic algorithms. We validated the applicability of the DAICO method with an illustrative case study using version *Publify* 8.0 of the OSS project *Publify* (hosted in GitHub). The main contributions of this paper are: i) Formulating RRI factor identification as an optimization problem, ii) Modeling and solving the problem using a GA, and iii) Providing recommendations for cost-optimized RR improvement.

The rest of the paper is organized as follows: Section 2 discusses related work. In Section 3, we present necessary background information including definitions of the key concepts. The problem is formulated in Section 4. Section 5 describes the proposed method DAICO. In Section 6, we present the empirical evaluation of the proposed method. Section 7 discusses the applicability and limitations of the proposed DAICO method. Finally, Section 8 presents a summary and outlines an agenda for future research.

2   Related Work

In the context of software development, release is a decision to deliver the developed product into the operational environment [1]. Though few attempts have been made to evaluate RR in academia and industry, RR is not yet well understood. Previous literature [4][5] evaluated RR with respect to defect tracking and test related metrics, e.g., number of defects, defect removal rate, test execution rate and test pass rate. Wild et al. [6] proposed to consider metrics from multiple dimensions (e.g., requirements, functionality, reliability etc.) in evaluating RR. Industry tools, e.g. *Borland TeamInspector*[1] and *PTC Integrity*[2], visualize and verify functionality, code and test related metrics before releasing a piece of software.

However, evaluating RR only at the end of the project is not sufficient to ensure project success. Continuous awareness of the status of the product release is required to identify release-related problems. Identification and analysis of the RRI factors is required to solve these problems and ensure project success. In our earlier research, we proposed an analytical approach RELREA [2] for evaluating RR score based on fuzzy set theory [3]. RELREA can evaluate RR at any point in time during the release cycle with respect to the degree of satisfaction of individual attributes. None of the existing approaches, including RELREA, attempted to identify the attributes that are responsible for improving RR (i.e., the RRI factors), or to optimally allocate resources to improve the RR score.

Some attempts were made in literature to identify key factors significantly influencing project success. Reyes et al. [7] applied GA based technique to identify these factors. Abe et al [8] collected 29 metrics to develop a prediction model for software project success. Hahn et al. [9] attempted to identify influencing factors of OSS success from project management perspectives. To the best of our knowledge, yet there is no uniform method to identify RRI factors of project success from the RR perspective. In addition, no previous literature proposed a cost optimization approach to improve the RR score. To mitigate this gap, we propose a sophisticated method to identify the RRI factors. Our new method, DAICO, also recommends how (re-) allocation of available resources can achieve a higher RR score.

3   Background

3.1   RR Attributes and Degree of Satisfaction

RR attributes are attributes of the candidate system that can define and judge the RR of the system. Satisfaction of *Defect find rate (DFR)*, and *Bug fix rate (BFR)* are two examples of RR attributes. We apply the Goal-Question-Metric (GQM) [10] paradigm to guide the selection of RR attributes.

In [2], the degree of satisfaction of the RR attributes is evaluated using the concept of membership function from fuzzy set theory [3]. A membership function $\mu_F(x)$ quantifies the degree of membership of element x in a fuzzy set F. The project manager select appropriate shapes and corresponding parameters of the membership function associated with each individual RR attributes to evaluate the degree of membership (i.e. the degree of satisfaction) based on its value. Further details regarding this is presented in [2].

---

[1] http://techpubs.borland.com/bms/TeamInspector2008
[2] http://www.ptc.com/solutions/application-lifecycle-management/

Definition 1 (Degree of Satisfaction): We assume that project P with duration $[0,T]$ at given week $t = t_0 \in [0,T]$ has

    i.   a given set of RR attributes $A = \{a_1, a_2, \ldots, a_n\}$;

    ii. for each RR attribute a corresponding membership function μ_i given by the set $\mu = \{\mu_1, \mu_2, \ldots, \mu_n\}$;

    iii. corresponding values of RR attributes given by the n-dimensional vector $x(t_0)$;

    iv. Then, $\mu_i(x(t_0)) \in [0,1]$ is the *degree of satisfaction* [3] of attribute a_i at week $t = t_0$. It is calculated based on the corresponding value in vector $x(t_0)$ and membership function μ_i.

3.2 Release Readiness

At any point in time during a release cycle $[0,T]$, the measurement of RR attributes helps project managers assess the status of the next release. RR is defined as the aggregation of various RR attributes that are considered to be essential to judge whether a product release is ready for shipping. Project managers based on successful legacy release and personal experience provide the relative weights of RR attributes. Details regarding RR measure is available in [2].

Definition 2 (Release Readiness): At given week $t = t_0 \in [0,T]$, we assume project P and consider (i) to (iv) from *Definition 1*. In addition, we define

    v. $w_1, w_2, \ldots, w_n$ are the attributes' weights, satisfying $w_i \in [0,1], \sum_{i=1}^{n} w_i = 1$;

Then *Release Readiness RR* is defined by the Weighted Arithmetic Mean (WAM) of degree of satisfaction of all RR attributes as follows:

$$RR(t) = WAM\big(\mu_1(x(t_0)), \mu_2(x(t_0)), \ldots, \mu_n(x(t_0))\big) = \sum_{i=1}^{n} w_i \times \mu_i(x(t_0)) \tag{1}$$

WAM considers the relative importance of RR attributes while aggregating them into one aggregated RR score.

3.3 Release Readiness Improvement Factor

Release Readiness Improvement (RRI) factors are defined as the factor(s) most influential to improve RR score of a project. For given project P with duration $[0,T]$ and given time $t = t_0 \in [0,T]$, $\Delta RR(a_i, c_i, t_0)$ denotes the increase in RR score achievable due to allocation of budget c_i towards RR attribute a_i. Project manager should allocate majority of available budget towards RRI factors to achieve maximum improvement in RR score.

Definition 3 (RRI Factor): At given time $t = t_0 \in [0,T]$, for a given project P the RR Improvement factor $RRI(t_0)$ is a RR attribute a_i that is determined by the highest value of $\Delta RR(a_i, c_i, t_0)$ among all RR attributes due to a budget allocation of c_i.

4   Problem Formulation

4.1   Illustrative Example

To better explain the problem dealt in this paper, we present an example for a hypothetical project P. We consider two releases called *version1* and *version2*. For each release, duration is $T = 20$ weeks and allocated total budget is $C = \$180,000$. Data are collected with respect to three RR attributes: *Bug fix rate (BFR), Feature completion rate (FCR) and Build success rate (BSR)*.

To evaluate the degree of satisfaction of RR attributes, we applied piecewise linear membership functions as presented in Eq. 2. This has proven sufficiently good in many applications [11]. For example, to evaluate satisfaction of *BFR* we collected the metric bugs_fixed/day. All values between 1 and 10 represent intermediate values for the degree of satisfaction. At week $t = 10$, for $BFR = 3$ bugs_fixed/day, the degree of satisfaction of *BFR* is 0.22 according to Eq. 2. Subsequently, for *FCR* and *BSR* we collected the metrics (closed features/total features) and (successful builds/total builds), respectively based on the last week observation. At week $t = 10$, respective satisfaction values are calculated as 0.64 and 0.75. Relative weights of *BFR, FCR* and *BSR* are 0.5, 0.3 and 0.2, respectively.

To aggregate the degree of satisfaction of individual RR attributes into an RR score, we applied operator as presented in Eq. 1. At week $t = 10$, RR score for project P was calculated 0.45. This is an aggregated measure that represents the perceived readiness of a release normalized to [0,1].

$$\mu_i(x) = \begin{cases} 0 & x < 1 \\ \dfrac{x-1}{10-1} & 1 \leq x \leq 10 \\ 1 & x > 10 \end{cases} \qquad (2)$$

For project P, the requested and actual RR scores for past 10 weeks are presented in Figure 1 using dotted and solid lines, respectively. Project manager defined the requested RR scores based on *version1*. *Version1* was a successful legacy release that achieved a RR score of 0.85. The gap between actual and requested RR score at week $t = 10$ is marked with the red circle.

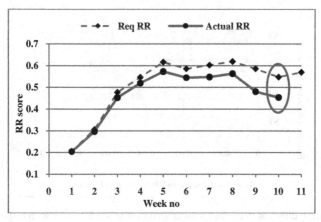

Fig. 1. Actual and requested RR scores and the gap in between for last 10 weeks from project P

We assume that the total budget is distributed equally among all weeks and all attributes. The project manager has a budget of $C(t) = \$9,000$ for week $t = 11$. $\Delta Sat(a_i, c_i)$, denotes the increase in degree of satisfaction of RR attribute a_i in one week, due to allocation of budget c_i. Based on *version1*, for *BFR, FCR* and *BSR* the value of $\Delta Sat(a_i, \$3000)$ are calculated 0.03, 0.06 and 0.06, respectively.

Project manager's goal is to i) identify RRI factor at week $t = 11$, and ii) propose a strategy for budget allocation for week $t = 11$, which ensures a maximum increase of the RR score and consequently, minimize the gap between actual (0.45) and the requested (0.57) RR score. We formulated this problem as an optimization problem and solved in our proposed solution approach. Details of the proposed method are described in Section 4.2 and in Section 5. Our solution identifies RR attribute *FCR* as the RRI factor and propose an optimized budget allocation for a maximum RR increase. The optimized solution allocated the entire budget of next week in *FCR*. The increased score for RR now is 0.51.

In week $t = 11$, allocation of an equal budget of $c_i = \$3000$ individually in *BFR*, *FCR* and *BSR* results in an increase of RR score of 0.015, 0.018, 0.012 respectively. It shows that *FCR* has higher influence on the RR improvement compared to *BFR or BSR*. The proposed solution allocated maximum budget to *FCR* and successfully identified *FCR* as the RRI factor. In Figure 2, we compare the increase in RR score at t=11 week due to four possible budget allocation strategies:

- *S1*: Actual *RR(t)* at $t = 11$ week.
- *S2*: The budget equally distributed among RR attributes,
- *S3*: The budget equally distributed among minimum satisfied RR attribute, and
- *S4*: Applying optimized budget allocation.

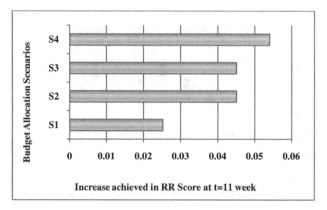

Fig. 2. Comparing different budget allocation scenarios at week $t = 11$ with respect to increase in RR scores

4.2   Problem Statement

4.2.1 Decision Variables

We consider a set of three (i.e. $n=3$) RR attributes $A = \{a_1, a_2, a_3\}$ for example *BFR*, *FCR*, *BSR*, respectively. For a project P with duration $[0, T]$ and a given time $t = t_0 \in [0, T]$, the actual degree of satisfaction of these attributes are defined as $\mu_1(x(t_0)), \mu_2(x(t_0)), \mu_3(x(t_0))$, respectively. RR (t_0) is the aggregation of degree of satisfaction of all RR attributes as presented in Eq. 1. The goal is to provide guidance on what need to be done next to increase the RR score in an optimal way. For that purpose, we consider the budget available $C(t_0)$ and being allocable among the different RR attributes at week t_0.

4.2.2 Constraints

Valid solutions of the optimization problem must satisfy all its constraints. In this problem, constraint is related to the budget. The allocation of budget c_1 for RR attribute a_1 at week $t = t_0 \in [0, T]$ is denoted as $budget(a_1, c_1, t_0)$. Total allocation of budget among all RR attributes must not exceed the available budget $C(t_0)$ at week t_0.

$$\sum_{i=1}^{3} budget(a_i, c_i, t_0) \leq C(t_0) \tag{3}$$

4.2.3 Objective

For project P, at given week $t = t_0 \in [0, T]$, three RR attributes are considered. The objective function $RR(t_0 + 1)$ is the aggregation of increased degree of satisfaction of RR attributes defined as follows:

$$RR(t_0 + 1) = \sum_{i=1}^{3} w_i \times \mu_i(x(t_0 + 1)) \tag{4}$$

In Eq. 4, w_i is the relative weight corresponding to RR attribute a_i defined by the project manager. $RR(t_0 + 1)$ is the increased RR score at time $(t_0 + 1)$. $\mu_i(x_i(t_0 + 1))$ is the increased degree of satisfaction of a_i due to budget allocation c_i defined as:

$$\mu_i(x(t_0 + 1)) = \mu_i(x(t_0)) + \Delta Sat(a_i, c_i) \tag{5}$$

In Eq. 5, $\mu_i(x(t_0))$ is the actual degree of satisfaction of attribute a_i. $\Delta Sat(a_i, c_i)$ is the average increase in the actual degree of satisfaction of RR attribute a_i due to budget allocation c_i.

4.2.4 Optimization Problem

The goal is to maximize RR by allocating limited budget $C(t_0)$ at week $t = t_0 \in [0, T]$ among RR attributes in an optimal way. Taking into account all the notations, constraints and concepts discussed above the optimization problem tackled in this paper is formulated below.

$$For\ given\ time\ t_0, Max\ \{RR(t_0 + 1)\ s.t.\ Eq.(3), (4), (5)\} \tag{6}$$

5   Proposed Solution Approach

5.1   Choice of Solution Approach

We analyze the optimization problem (formulated in Section 4) to determine a solution approach that finds an optimal solution. Subsequently, we present details of our proposed method DAICO. The number of RR attributes (n) is a key determinant of the size of the optimization problem. Another key determinant is the limit of budget allocation for individual RR attribute a_i at week $t = t_0 \in [0, T]$, denoted as $budget\_limit(a_i, t_0)$. Addition of new RR attribute will exponentially increase the problem size. Continuous range of $budget\_limit(a_i, t_0)$, theoretically allows infinite attempts to allocate budget while finding an optimal solution. Therefore, an exhaustive search is impractical to find the optimal budget allocation.

We applied a Genetic Algorithm (GA) to find near optimal budget allocation. GA was invented from natural process or biological evaluation [12] and has been successfully applied in various software engineering related problems, e.g. release planning [13]. Prior success in solving large optimization problems within reasonable duration and availability of empirically evaluated applications made GA a suitable choice for our solution approach to identify the RRI factors and recommend optimized budget allocation to achieve higher release readiness. Key steps of the proposed method DAICO are discussed in next section.

5.2   Steps of the Proposed Method DAICO

Step 1: Determine Requested RR Score: For any project P with duration $[0, T]$, project manager determines the requested RR score for week $t = T$ at the beginning of the project. Based on this, the requested RR score distribution over the period $[0, T]$ is determined. Successful legacy releases are used to guide this process.

Step 2: Define RR Attributes and RR Metrics: Project manager defines a set of context specific RR attributes and corrsponding RR metrics. Designing of this measurement program is guided by the Goal-Question-Metric (GQM) [10] paradigm. Questions correspond to processes (e.g., Implementation, Testing) related to RR attributes refine the goal "Evaluating overall RR". A set of RR attributes, corresponding questions and related RR metrics are presented in Table 1 below. The metrics represent 50% of the RR attributes found from comprehensive industry guidelines[3].

Step 3: Compute Actual RR Score: We evaluate the actual RR score by applying our former proposed approach RELREA. The degree of satisfaction of a set of individual RR attributes are determined by using the concept of membership function [3]. The shape of the membership function and corresponding parameters are determined by the project manager at week $t = 0$. Based on [2], we suggest applying heuristic membership function, e.g., piecewise linear functions. Applying Eq. 1, we calculate the RR score. We applied the Weighted Arithmetic Mean (WAM) operator to aggregate degree of satisfaction of individual RR criteria into an overall RR score. WAM considers relative weights of individual RR attributes which were defined at week $t = 0$ by the project manager.

Table 1. List of RR attributes, corresponding RR metric definitions and acronyms

RR Attributes	Questions	RR Metric Definitions	Acronyms
Satisfaction of feature completion	To what extend open features are closed?	# of closed features/ # of open features (per week)	FCR
Satisfaction of features implemented	To what extent requested features are completed?	# of closed features (per week)	FI
Satisfaction of build trends	To what extent the builds are successful?	# of successful builds/# of total builds (per week)	BSR
Satisfaction of implementation effort	To what extent the source code is becoming stable?	# of LOC last week / 7 (per day)	CCR
Satisfaction of change completion	To what extent requested changes are completed?	# of closed changes/ # of total changes (per week)	CR
Satisfaction of defect finding	To what extent the testing activity reducing the defects?	# of defects found /14 (per day)	DFR
Satisfaction of bug fixing	To what extent detected bugs are fixed?	# of closed bugs/ # of total bugs (per week)	BFR
Satisfaction of pull request completion	To what extent pull-requests are completed?	# of closed pull requests/ # of total pull requests (per week)	PCR

---

[3] http://www.softwareconsortium.com/software-release-readiness-criteria.html

Step 4: Optimal Allocation of Available Budget
Initialize GA: To maximize RR, the allocation of available budget applies a GA based optimization process. A set of initial population is generated to initiate GA. Each member of this population use a chromosome to abstractly represent a solution (i.e. budget allocation) of the problem. Genes represent individual RR attributes and allele (i.e. the value of the gene) represent corresponding $budget\ (a_i, c_i, t_0)$. $budget\ (a_i, c_i, t_0)$ denotes the allocation of budget c_i for a RR attribute a_i at time $t = t_0 \in [0, T]$. Initial population is generated by allocating random budget to RR attributes a_i within corresponding $budget\_limit(a_i, t_0)$.

The fitness function evaluates each chromosome of the population and assigns a fitness value. Fitness value indicates how good a member is in solving the problem. We apply the objective function (Eq. 4) as the fitness function such that the constraint (Eq. 3) is fulfilled. The fitness value of a solution is penalized with lower values if it violates the constraint.

Crossover and Mutation: Crossover generates new generation of chromosomes from selected parent chromosomes. We apply *Roulette-Wheel* method [14] to select the parent chromosomes. The probability of an individual chromosome to get selected as a parent is proportional to its fitness value. We apply a one-point crossover, which split parent chromosome at a single point and exchange the genes among themselves. The crossover rate limits the amount of genes parents can exchange. While giving privilege to the high fitness chromosomes in crossover, it is important to preserve the population diversity as well. Mutation randomly selects chromosomes and modifies random genes to introduce variance and avoid premature convergence. We apply a random bit-wise mutation [14] in DAICO. The mutation rate determines the probability of mutation of a chromosome.

Termination Criteria: After termination within a reasonable duration, GA offers the highest fitness member as the optimized solution. Two termination criteria are applied:

   i.   A pre-defined number of generations (e.g. 300 generations) are produced.
  ii. Improvement in best fitness value achieved within 0.5% deviation over 30 generations.

Step 5: RRI factor identification and optimized budget reallocation: Increase in degree of satisfaction of RRI factors will induce a higher increase of the overall RR score than the degree of satisfaction increase (by the same margin) of any of the other RR attributes. Consequently, *Assumption*1 is applied in RRI factor identification.

Assumption 1: To achieve maximum increase in RR score within a limited budget, majority of the budget should be allocated in increasing degree of satisfaction of RRI factor(s).

Based on *assumption*1, the RR attribute(s) with maximum allocated budget are identified as the RRI factor(s). The other objective was to recommend optimized budget allocation among RR attributes to achieve maximum increase in the RR score. The GA solution represents the optimized budget allocation and ensures maximum

RR increase. This guides (re)allocation of available budget among RR attributes to achieve maximum RR increase.

6   Empirical Evaluation

6.1   Case Study Context

We evaluated our proposed method DAICO in an illustrative case study with respect to project *Publify* hosted in GitHub repository. *Publify* is a powerful open source blogging engine and one of the oldest Ruby on Rails project started back in 2004. We selected the project by consulting with four propositions of case selection by Verner et al. [15]. We retrospectively collected data from two releases called *Publify* 8.0 and *Publify* 7.0 for a duration of 29 and 32 weeks, respectively. This study analyzes *Publify* 8.0. *Publify* 7.0 is considered as a successful legacy release, which aid in determining expected RR score and parameters for membership functions (MF) correspond to each RR attribute. Data are collected with respect to eight RR attributes as listed in Table 1. They are selected using the GQM paradigm. Selected RR attributes, corresponding relative weights, membership function parameters and satisfaction improvement per attributes are presented in Table 2 below.

Table 2. RR attributes along with their relative weights, MF parameters, and satisfaction improvement

RR Attributes	FCR	FI	BSR	CCR	CR	DFR	BFR	PCR
Max sat for MF	0.5	21	0.75	0	0.95	0	1	48
Min sat for MF	0	0	0.05	5000	0.15	1	0	0
Relative weights	0.09	0.14	0.12	0.18	0.11	0.13	0.12	0.11
$\Delta Sat\ (a_i, c_i)$	0.005	0.006	0.032	0.093	0.022	0.027	0.020	0.044

Case Study Goal: The goal of this empirical evaluation is to demonstrate the applicability of DAICO method in assisting the project manager and improving the development process. Two analyses conducted are i) How can identification of RRI factor aid project managers in improving RR score? and ii) How cost-optimized budget allocation in DAICO compare with other approaches with respect to RR improvement?

6.2   Implementation and Tuning of Parameters

We primarily implemented DAICO using the SAS[4] tool, a renowned statistical analysis tool developed by the SAS community. RR was evaluated by the RELREA approach. The optimization problem (formulated in section 4) is solved by applying a GA. While selecting the initial population size several values were experimented. For

---

[4] www.sas.com

example, initial population size: 100, 300 and 500 with crossover rate 0.9 and mutation rate 0.125 (i.e. $1/n$, with $n = 8$ being the number of RR attributes) were tested. No significant differences were found either in the RRI factors or in the achieved RR score. Therefore, we chose 300 as the population size to keep the computational time lower. Subsequently, this population size is checked with different crossover rate, e.g., 0.9, 0.8, 0.7 and varying mutation rate of 0.3, 0.5 and 0.2. We could not find any significant performance differences. Therefore, we decided to apply crossover rate = 0.9 and mutation rate = 0.125 along with an initial population size =300 to execute GA. We generated up to 300 generations for each week observations.

6.3   Case Study Results

To analyze *Publify* 8.0, we divided the duration of release $[0, T]$ in four quarters and applied DAICO in the last week of each quarter. At any given week $t = t_0 \in [0, T]$, budget allocation in RRI factors induces higher increase in RR score compared to the budget allocation (by the same margin) in any of the other RR attributes. Early identification of RRI factors aid project manager to take early action (e.g. re-allocation of budget) to achieve maximum improvement in RR score. In this study, PCR and BSR were identified as RRI factor in first and second two weeks of observation, respectively. None of these factors have highest relative weights or satisfaction improvement values (i.e. $\Delta Sat\,(a_i, c_i)$). Therefore, without analyzing different budget allocation strategies RRI identification is not possible. DAICO performs this analysis and successfully identifies the RRI factors. To achieve maximum improvement in RR score, the majority of the budget is allocated in the RRI factors. We further analyzed the influence of DAICO in RR improvement and compared with other approaches. Results of RR improvement are compared among three different approaches as listed below:

   i.   S1: Available budget equally distributed among all RR attributes.

   ii. S2: Available budget equally distributed among the least satisfied RR attributes.

  iii. S3: Optimized budget allocation from DAICO is applied

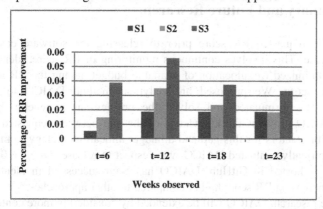

Fig. 3. Comparing three budget allocation scenarios with respect to increase in RR score

Figure 3, presents this comparison using a column chart. DAICO (S3) achieved highest improvement in RR score compared to S1 or S2 in all four observations. S3 applies an optimized budget allocation strategy and the increase in RR score is expected to outperform any random budget allocation. We found DAICO is capable of proposing optimized budget allocation that achieves maximum increase in RR score within a limited budget. However, due to optimizing towards next week, GA identifies local optimal solutions. Project manager should carefully choose the budget to be (re)allocated among the RR attributes.

7   Threats to Validity

DAICO applies GA in RRI factor identification and cost-optimized RR improvement. GA cannot guarantee optimality, which imposes a threat to the construct validity of the method. Empirical evaluations have shown that, GA produces reasonably near optimal solution within a realistic execution time. Therefore, this threat is partially mitigated. We have not yet incorporated subjective attributes (e.g. user experience) in our proposed approach. This imposes another threat to the construct validity. Considering subjective attributes requires more involvement of management staff and may create error prone results. For simplicity, we consider subjective attributes out of our scope. Representativeness of the selected project is a threat to the external validity of the case study. To mitigate this threat, we selected the project by consulting with four propositions of case selection by Verner et al. [15]. Due to unavailability of domain experts, the choice of RR attributes, their relative weights, corresponding membership function parameters are threats to the internal validity. To mitigate this threat, we applied GQM in RR attribute selection. Selected RR attributes represents RR attributes from comprehensive industry guidelines. Relative weights for RR attributes are selected by consulting with two senior industry developers. To avoid any further bias, membership function parameters are selected based on the past release data.

8   Summary and Future Research

Achieving the requested RR score prior to releasing the software ensures better software release. This involves continuous monitoring of RR score, identifying RRI factors and optimized (re)allocation of available budget among the RR attributes to improve RR score. We proposed an analytical method DAICO to fulfill this requirement. We formulated and solved the problem as a genetic optimization problem. DAICO provides the knowledge of the gap between requested and actual RR, responsible factors for this gap and a budget allocation strategy to minimize the gap. We empirically evaluated DAICO with respect to release *Publify* 8.0 of an OSS project *Publify* hosted in GitHub. DAICO has been successful in identifying RRI factors and increasing RR score higher compared to other approaches.

In future research, DAICO will be extended by considering more context specific parameters e.g. relation among the RR attributes, effort estimation etc. Broadening the project scope to proprietary projects and comparison of results with former observations from OSS projects can be an important step forward. Another major direction of future research is to analyze the robustness of the results in dependence on the varying weights of RR attributes and the defined membership functions.

Acknowledgement. This work was partially supported by the Natural Sciences and Engineering Research Council of Canada, NSERC Discovery Grant 250343-12, and by the institutional research grant IUT20-55 of the Estonian Research Council.

References

[1] Port, D., Wilf, J.: The Value of Certifying Software Release Readiness. In: ESEM, pp. 373–382 (2013)

[2] Shahnewaz, S., Ruhe, G.: RELREA - An Analytical Approch for Evaluating Release Readiness. In: SEKE (2014)

[3] Zadeh, L.A.: Fuzzy sets. Inf. Control 8, 338–353 (1965)

[4] Staron, M., Meding, W., Palm, K.: Release Readiness Indicator for Mature Agile and Lean Software Development Projects. Agil. Process. Softw. Eng. Extrem. Program., 93–107 (2012)

[5] Quah, J.T.S., Liew, S.W.: Gauging Software Readiness Using Metrics. In: SMCia, pp. 426–431 (2008)

[6] Wild, R., Brune, P.: Determining Software Product Release Readiness by the Change-Error Correlation Function: On the Importance of the Change-Error Time Lag. In: HICSS, pp. 5360–5367 (2012)

[7] Reyes, F., Cerpa, N., Candia-Véjar, A., Bardeen, M.: The optimization of success probability for software projects using genetic algorithms. J. Syst. Softw. 84(5), 775–785

[8] Abe, S., Mizuno, O., Kikuno, T., Kikuchi, N., Hirayama, M.: Estimation of project success using Bayesian classifier. In: ICSE, vol. 4, pp. 600–603 (2006)

[9] Hahn, J., Zhang, C.: An exploratory study of open source projects from a project management perspective. In: MIS Research Workshop. Purdue University, West Lafayette (2005)

[10] Basili, V.R., Caldiera, G., Rombach, H.D., Solingen, R.V.: The Goal Question Metric Approach. Encycl. Softw. Eng. 1(1), 578–583 (2000)

[11] Bilgiç, T., Türkşen, I.B.: Measurement of membership functions: Theoretical and empirical work. Fundam. Fuzzy Sets, 195–227 (2000)

[12] Holland, J.H.: Adaptation in Natural and Artificial Systems. University of Michigan Press (1975)

[13] Greer, D., Ruhe, G.: Software release planning: An evolutionary and iterative approach. Inf. Softw. Technol. 46(4), 243–253 (2004)

[14] Mitchell, M.: An Introduction to Genetic Algorithms. The MIT Press, Cambridge (1998)

[15] Verner, J.M., Sampson, J., Tosic, V., Bakar, N.A.A., Kitchenham, B.A.: Guidelines for industrially-based multiple case studies in software engineering. In: RCIS, pp. 313–324 (2009)

A Generative Development Method
with Multiple Domain-Specific Languages

Edmilson Campos[1,2], Uirá Kulesza[1], Marília Freire[1,2], and Eduardo Aranha[1]

[1] Federal University of Rio Grande do Norte, Natal-RN, Brazil
{edmilsoncampos,marilia.freire}@ppgsc.ufrn.br
{uira,eduardoaranha}@dimap.ufrn.br
[2] Federal Institute of Rio Grande do Norte, Natal-RN, Brazil

Abstract. This paper investigates approaches proposed in the literature to compose domain-specific languages (DSLs) and mechanisms to integrate DSLs with feature models (FMs) in product line engineering. We propose a method for the development of generative approaches based on existing related work, which provides guidelines for the systematic development of DSL composition integrated with FMs during domain and application engineering. The proposed method is evaluated through an exploratory study of development of a generative approach for the experimental software engineering domain.

1 Introduction

Over the last years, there is an increasing usage of domain-specific languages (DSLs) for the development of software systems. The adoption of DSLs raises the abstraction level and provides facilities for the generation of models or source code, especially used in generative approaches to specify and derive products, thus bringing the potential to increase the productivity of software development in various domains [1]. This development requires modeling product families, designing some means to derivative products, i.e. specifying products, providing the implementation components to assemble the products from generators that map the product specifications to concrete assemblies of implementation code assets [2,3]. In this context, DSLs play an important role because they are used to automatically derive products (instances) of a system family.

DSLs can also have different specialization levels. Complex projects require several and different DSLs to specify a complete application. Each DSL can provide a separate view or perspective of the software system modeling. However, the adoption of multiple DSLs brings some consequences that need to be addressed. The main concern is the increased risk of consistency loss among model elements, which requires greater concern with regard to this issue [4]. Consistency maintenance among models is a critical challenge involved on DSLs composition. In this way, new methods, techniques and tools must provide support to these problems.

The use of DSLs in generative development is already considered by some existing methods [5,6]. The generative development aims to specifying, modeling and

A. Jedlitschka et al. (Eds.): PROFES 2014, LNCS 8892, pp. 178–193, 2014.

implementing system families or software product lines so that a given system can be automatically generated from a features specification expressed in some high-level domain-specific language (DSL). Over the past few years, several methods for generative development [6,7,8,5] have been proposed. There is also research work exploring the integration between DSLs and feature models (FMs) [9]. However, most proposed methods for generative development do not explicitly address the issues of DSLs composition. On the other hand, some recent studies [8,9] discuss approaches for software development with multiple DSLs. In this context, this paper proposes a method for the development of generative approaches focused on the integration of FMs with multiple DSLs. The method is based on the investigation of existing research work. The proposed method is evaluated through an exploratory study of implementation of a generative approach for the automatic derivation of workflows for controlled experiments in software engineering.

The remainder of this paper is organized as follow. Section 2 describes our proposed method. Section 3 details the exploratory study of evaluation of the proposed method. Finally, Section 4 presents the conclusions and possible future works.

2   The Proposed Method

This section presents our method for generative development, which extends existing methods to deal with DSL composition. Existing research work already considers the usage of DSLs [5] and feature models [9]. However, existing generative development methods do not explicitly address the issues of development with multiple DSLs. Some recent research work [10,11] discusses approaches for development with multiple DSLs. Our proposed method focuses on the integration of FMs and composition of domain-specific languages.

2.1   Method Background

Our method is based on the approach proposed by Czarnecki and Eisenecker [5]. This approach is organized in two main phases from product line engineering (PLE): (i) *domain engineering* (DE) – which focuses on the identification of common and variable features/requirements, the definition of a flexible software product line architecture that addresses the implementation of reusable code assets, and the definition of DSLs that enable the customization of the architecture and code assets for generating specific products; and (ii) *application engineering* (AE) – that includes activities to derive specific products using the DSLs and code assets producing during DE. Our method focuses mainly in the domain design and implementation from DE, and in the product derivation from AE.

Voelter and Visser [7] investigate the application of DSLs in PLE as a middle ground between FM and code assets of the software product line (SPL). They analyze the limits of FM expressiveness and show that DSLs can be used as a complementary element in such cases. DSLs do not represent an alternative mutually exclusive to FMs, they can be used in combination with FMs in order to expand the possibilities of product derivation in SPLs. Since we are interested in investigating different strategies to combine FMs and DSLs in the DE and AE, their approach [7] contributed to the development of our method.

Regarding the adoption of multiple DSLs, several questions still need to be explored and investigated. Hessellund *et al.* [4] conducted a case study to investigate the kinds of existing constraints between DSLs. Four kinds of constraints were identified: (i) *well-formedness of individual artifacts*; (ii) *simple referential* integrity across artifacts; (iii) *references with additional constraints*; and (iv) *style constraints*. Moreover, constraints violation may be still classified according to the severity level, which can be errors or warnings [12]. Some of these issues are addressed by Hessellund [8], which proposes a method that provides activities for the identification, specification and application of composition between DSLs. This work played an important role in defining the development method of generative approaches proposed in this paper, specifically the activities to compose DSLs.

Fig. 1 presents an overview of our proposed method. The general structure of the method is based on the generative development approach proposed in [5] focusing on the steps that involve the use of DSLs (domain design/implementation and product derivation). There are several activities to identify and implement DSLs from input artifacts such as the domain requirements, FM, and the product line architecture. In addition, specific activities were included at each step to support the development and composition of DSLs as an alternative to the limits of FM expressiveness.

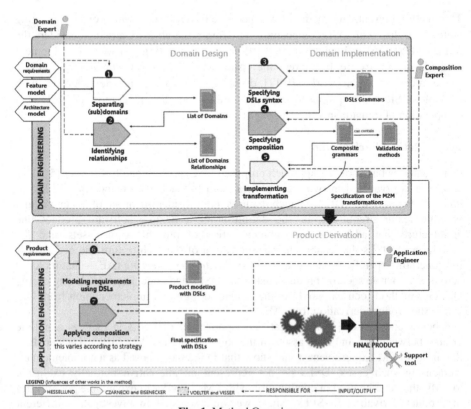

Fig. 1. Method Overview

2.2   Method Structure

The method is divided into three stages: (i) Domain Design, (ii) Domain Implementation; and (iii) Product Derivation. The first two are part of the domain engineering, and the last one of the application engineering. Each stage has activities that are performed by specific roles to produce or generate a set of artifacts. Some activities of our method are based or extend characteristics of other approaches (Section 2.1), which are represented in the legend of Fig. 1. The method also presents alternative strategies to integrate DSLs with FMs: (i) using only DSLs; or (ii) combining DSLs with FMs. The following sections provide an overview of each step.

2.2.1   Domain Design

The aim of this first stage is to identify the existence of different domains and their relationships. It receives as input a FM, the specification of the domain requirements, and an architectural model of the SPL (or system family). The input artifacts are then analyzed by a domain expert: (i) to identify which set of abstractions are more strongly connected to characterize a domain; and (ii) to identify the overlap between them. In summary, the activities of Domain Design are the following:

- *Separation of domains (Activity 1)*: It involves the identification and separation of the SPL scope elements into subdomains based on the input artifacts. The result of this activity will result in a list of domains, each one representing a specific aspect to be separately modeled and (possibly) reused;
- *Identification of relationships (Activity 2)*: After the organization into subdomains, it is necessary to verify the occurrence of references among subdomains and classify these overlaps based on the degree of entanglement of the subdomains. It results in a list of domains and their respective relationships.

This last activity brings consequences to the implementation of the DSLs composition. Once identified, the references must be classified according to the complexity and nature of the intertwining of the models. The classification task is part of the *Identification of relationships* activity and is fundamental to the approach. Based on the kind of reference, engineers can choose how to implement the DSL composition during the domain implementation stage. The references also imply the existence of some kinds of constraints that need to be maintained during the development of applications with multiple DSLs.

2.2.2   Domain Implementation

The goal of this stage is to implement specific solutions for each subdomain identified on previous stage. As a result, it must implement the reusable code assets of the SPL (or system family), as well as the DSLs and respective transformations, which are used to support the automatic product derivation during application engineering. The creation of DSLs, either graphical or textual, arises from the need to broaden the expressiveness of domain abstractions, limited by the representation of the FM [7]. The DSL implementation also involves the choice of technologies to implement its grammar and respective relationships. Moreover, the usage of modularly composable DSL has great advantages over monolithic DSL, including reusability and scalability [5].

The following three activities are accomplished in this stage:

- *Specification of DSLs syntax (Activity 3)*: It is necessary to choose the technology to implement a BNF (Backus-Naur Form) grammar that incorporates the variability of the SPL in each domain. The syntax of the DSL must allow specifying any product to be generated from the SPL reusable assets, including those that are not possible using only FM, but can be addressed using more expressive DSLs;
- *Specification of the composition (Activity 4)*: The purpose of this step is to implement the connections identified previously, according to the reference type. This activity will result in changes to the built grammar and, if necessary, the implementation of additional methods to validate restrictions of the DSLs;
- *Implementation of transformations (Activity 5)*: Finally, it is necessary to implement transformations that allow defining the mapping between the DSLs and the reusable code assets of the SPL. This activity will result in a specification of transformations ready to be executed in AE during the product derivation.

A complementary task to the activity of specification of the composition is the implementation of restrictions. Restrictions must be specified to validate primarily the consistency between the models of the DSLs. In some cases, such restrictions need to be implemented to complement the rules defined by the DSL grammar.

2.2.3 Product Derivation

The product derivation is the final stage of the method and belongs to the application engineering phase. The goal of this step is to generate products (systems) from the artifacts produced in the DE phase. The generation of products may occur in a manual or automated way. Generative development motivates automated product derivation using DSLs. The resultant product – software system – may be a partial or complete final product, according to the derivation strategy used. Our method provides two different strategies to product derivation. The first one adopts only DSLs, and the second one integrates DSLs and FMs. They represent distinct alternatives with different purposes for the same goal.

2.2.3.1 Product Derivation with DSLs

In this strategy, the developed DSLs in domain engineering are used to model products (systems) that we are interested to generate. As we are dealing with a composition approach, each DSL is used to specify a specific part of the final product. In this case, it is also necessary to manage the consistency between the DSLs and validate existing restrictions. Validations are only possible due to the implementation of restrictions tied to DSLs grammars. The modeling of the product using DSLs defines the features that will be part of it. The transformation models implemented in the Domain Implementation stage are used to generate the final product from product modeling using DSLs. The DSLs grammars must address all the variables elements of the SPL. This also allows for model validation before generating the final specification of the product, ensuring that the specified product can be transformed to generate the final product without violates any domain restriction.

2.2.3.2 Product Derivation with FMs and DSLs

This strategy is more appropriate when deriving products with similar characteristics to previous ones already generated in the same approach. In other words, the strategy is used when there is already existing DSL modeling containing fragments that can be reused to generate new and very similar products. Therefore, it is necessary to identify those reusable modeling fragments, and associate them to features in a FM. This initial effort will only occur on the first use of this strategy or during the SPL evolution. The first step in the product derivation for this strategy is to specify a selection of features in the FM. After that, it is generated a partial modeling of the desired product expressed in the DSLs. The application engineer can then edit and complement the specification of its product using the DSLs. Finally, this specification is automatically transformed to generate the code assets corresponding to the request product, similar to the previous strategy.

3 Exploratory Study

This section presents an exploratory study conducted aiming to evaluate the proposed method. Our study involves the composition of different DSLs to model controlled experiments in software engineering. Moreover, it has used both product derivation strategies of our method when generating specification of experiments.

3.1 Study Research Questions

The main aim of our exploratory study was to evaluate the proposed method at work, through the development of a generative approach that involves the composition of multiple DSLs. In particular, the exploratory study was developed in order to answer the following research questions:

RQ1. How the composition of DSLs can be specified and implemented during the domain engineering using our method, the xText framework and Ecore models?

RQ2. How to implement the product derivation strategies of our method that involve the DSLs and feature model composition in application engineering?

RQ3. Which kind of reuse can be accomplished with the DSLs in the domain and application engineering?

In order to answer these questions, the proposed method was applied to a real domain to investigate how to compose DSLs during the domain engineering and how to use derivation strategies during the application engineering with DSL composition.

3.2 Target Generative Approach

In our study, we have established the following prerequisites to be addressed by the generative approach to be modeled and implemented: (i) to belong to a real domain documented in the literature; (ii) to have a scope with enough complexity to be sectioned into smaller views, thus allowing reuse of parts and modeling of different

DSLs; and (iii) to have requirements and variabilities whose representation the FM was not able to express. We have chosen the domain of controlled experiments in Experimental Software Engineering (ESE). In particular, we apply the proposed method in the development of a model-driven generative approach to generate specialized workflows for each experiment subject according to the experiment design. The approach is under study and development in our research group [13,14,15,16].

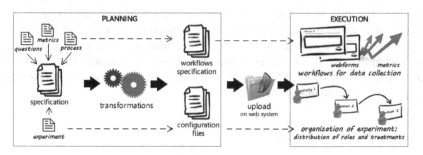

Fig. 2. Controlled experiment approach overview

Fig. 2 presents an overview of the model-driven approach for modeling of controlled experiments. It is presented from two perspectives: planning and execution. The planning perspective aggregates a series of elements used to specify experiments with their respective processes and metrics during the planning phase. This specification is then transformed with the aim of generating workflow specifications and configuration files. After this step, these generated files are deployed in a workflow engine web system in order to generate specialized workflows and web forms, which are responsible for the execution of the experiment and monitoring of the subjects' activities. Fig. 2 also presents this execution perspective. The mapping between the perspectives is implemented by means of model-driven transformations, which are not presented in this paper due to space limitation. In our study, we are more interested in the application of the method to the planning perspective.

3.3   Results Main Summary

This section presents a summary of the main results in terms of produced artifacts during the method application in our exploratory study. More details about these artifacts can be found at http://sites.google.com/site/generativedsl.

Initially, based on the know-how of our research group carrying out controlled experiments [13,15,16,17], we extracted the domain requirements and modeled commonalities and variabilities using a FM. Finally, we also specified the architectural models of the web system responsible for instantiating and executing workflows of the controlled experiment approach [13]. These artifacts – requirements, FM and architecture model – were then provided as input artifacts for our method. The method was applied following its activities in order to produce new artifacts at each stage. A summary of the artifacts produced in each activity is systematically presented below.

Activity 1: *Separating Subdomains*

In this first step, from the feature model and domain requirements specification received as input artifacts, we analyzed the features and grouped them into four subdomains, according to their relationships and reuse opportunity. Fig. 3 shows the FM of our experimental generative approach by highlighting the features from the different subdomains. Each identified subdomain represents a specific view or aspect of the controlled experiment domain that can be reused in other domains. The first one, (i) *Process*, involves the elements that define the procedures to be followed to collect the needed data from the subjects in a controlled experiment. The second, (ii) *Metric*, groups the features that allow specifying metrics related to some of the dependent variables of the specified experiment and that will be collected during its execution. The other, (iii) *Experiment*, is defined for the ESE context and it basically allows setting the treatments and the control variables that are required for the specified experiment. A treatment can be composed of the combination of one or more factors that can have different control levels. In addition, the last one subdomain, (iv) *Questionnaire*, allows specifying questionnaires with the aim of collecting feedback from the experimental subjects.

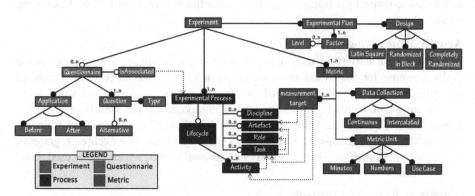

Fig. 3. FM of the experiment approach with subdomains

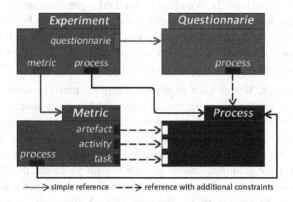

Fig. 4. Relationships between the subdomains

Activity 2: *Identifying Relationships*

After the separation of the subdomains, it was identified the existing overlaps between them, which were then classified in terms of the degree of complexity of the references. In this activity, the requirement specifications and constraints represented in the FM were used as input artifacts. This analysis resulted in the identification of eight reference points between the subdomains, which are illustrated in Fig. 4 and discussed below.

The *Process* subdomain is the only that does not reference another one. For this reason, it can be used to specify processes from distinct domains such as software development or experiment processes, or even a business process. The *Experiment* subdomain needs to reference the processes, metrics and questionnaires that are part of the experiment. A *Questionnaire* element is referenced in an experiment. Each questionnaire may reference one or more processes, because it defines specific questions to be accomplished during the process activities. Moreover, the *Metric* subdomain is always related to a process and must indicate the artifacts, activities or tasks of this process that have to be considered for measurement. Here we identified a typical reference case with additional constraint where the referenced element in the metric has to respect the restriction of being an artifact, activity or task in the existing related process.

Activity 3: *Specifying DSLs Syntax*

This is the first activity of the implementation stage, which aims to implement the DSLs grammar for each subdomain identified in the previous stage. It also requires selecting the technology to be used. Since one of the goals of this study is to investigate MDE technologies to implement composed DSLs, we chose a model-driven framework for the DSLs development based on Ecore metamodel from the Eclipse Modeling Framework (EMF) [18], known as xText (http://eclipse.org/xtext). Thus, each subdomain resulted in a DSL with its own syntax, which can be used alone or combined.

Activity 4: *Specifying Composition*

After specifying the DSLs grammar, we have specified and codified the references between the DSLs (Activity 2). We changed the DSLs grammar using special features from xText and wrote some additional validations in the Java language. The composition specification varies according to the reference type to be implemented. In our study, two reference types were identified in the investigated domain: (i) simple references and (ii) references with additional constraints.

a) *Simple references*: It was used explicit references, natively supported by xText. The framework offers the possibility that a metamodel imports another one in order to implement the explicit references among models. Since we are working with Ecore-based DSLs, xText has a model generator created for each grammar and responsible for the equivalent Ecore metamodel generation. To perform the importing, it is only needed to inform the grammar model generator path to create the reference. After that, each referenced metamodel can be recognized by an alias name making possible to explicitly refer to anyone of its elements. Fig. 5 illustrates an example of the *ExperimentDSL* grammar referencing the *ProcessDSL process element.*

```
ExperimentElement:
    'Experiment' name=STRING
    ('Process' process +=[processDsl::Process]*)?
```

Fig. 5. ExperimentDSL referencing ProcessDSL

b) *References with additional constraints*: In this case, we have also used explicit simple references, but it was needed to create extra validation routines. In Ecore-based grammars, the model generator also creates Java classes to each DSL model element beyond helper classes with specific function, such as formatting, validation, and so on. We used this xText support to encode additional restrictions required for a specific DSL. Java methods were implemented to validate this reference type.

Activity 5: *Implementing Transformations*
In this last activity of the domain engineering phase, model-to-model and model-to-text transformations were implemented to transform a ESE controlled experiment specification using the DSLs to workflows and configuration files that represent the experiment to be executed in the workflow engine web system [13]. The QVTo language (http://eclipse.org/mmt) and Acceleo language (http://eclipse.org/acceleo) was used to implement the transformations.

Activity 6: *Modeling the Requirements using DSLs*
The activity six and seven belong to the application engineering phase. They vary according to the chosen product derivation strategy. Aiming to assess the operation of these activities in both strategies, three controlled experiments were derived twice, one time for each strategy. The experiments were:

Experiment 1: *Programming Languages*, adapted from [19], the goal is to compare the development productivity using two programming languages.

Experiment 2: *Configuration Knowledge*, adapted from [20], the goal is to investigate the comprehension of configuration knowledge in three product derivation tools in the SPL.

Experiment 3: *Testing Techniques for SPL*, adapted from [21], the goal is to analyze the impact of two black-box testing techniques (hereby called treatments) for SPL products derived.

a) *Derivation using only DSLs*: Based on the definition of the scope of each experiment presented, we have used the four DSLs implemented in the domain engineering to model the features to be included in each derived experiment. In this strategy, the modelling was realized manually using the specific resources of the xText framework. Fig. 6 shows a specification example of a task using the *ProcessDSL*.

```
task {
    name DesignClassDiagram description "Design Class Diagram"
    roles { Subject primary }
    artifacts { UseCaseSpecfication input
                ClassDiagram output }
}
```

Fig. 6. Specification of a task using the *ProcessDSL*

Each part of the experiment was modeled using the correspondent DSL. The results of these modeling formed the final specification of each experiment to be derived.

b) *Derivation combining DSLs and FMs*: In this strategy, we initially identified reusable modeling fragments and then represented them in a FM. For this, it was used the *FeatureMapper* framework (featuremapper.org) to represent the features in a FM. This FM was used to choose the modeling fragments to be reused and after that a partial modeling of the experiment using the DSL was generated, which can be manually edited to conclude the specification of the experiment. Fig. 7 illustrates an example of this automatic reuse of modeling using the FM built with *FeatureMapper* framework.

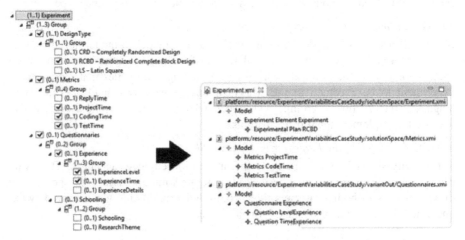

Fig. 7. Derivation using *FeatureMapper*

Activity 7: *Applying Composition*
After or during the modeling of the requirements of the experiment to be derived, it is need to compose the models applying the composition between them. This involves the inclusion of resources for (i) navigation between models, (ii) maintenance of the consistency, and (iii) presentation of guidance during the modeling activity. The maintenance checking is the method key-point because it allows examining whether the restrictions are maintained or violated. This consistency checking is consequence of the encoding performed on the specification step, and it becomes visible from the xText alert resources. The xText can provide warnings or errors guidance and also pop-ups with suggested values (Fig. 8) during the typing.

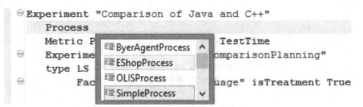

Fig. 8. Pop-up with reference suggestions

We also investigated the xText support for the four restrictions types listed in the case study performed in [4]. For the restriction related to the well-formed artefacts issue, the xText uses the DSL grammar to confront the syntax used in the modelling in order to check missing attributes or incorrect syntax. In case of failure, error alerts are displayed, e.g. when a task modelling using *ProcessDSL* does not inform the process name before the description attribute. Fig. 9 shows an example of an error message.

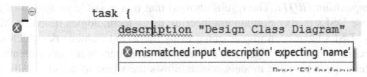

Fig. 9. Pop-up indicating not well-defined artefacts

The second restriction type, the simple referential integrity, is the constraint that is better supported by xText. The integrity validation among models only requires code implementation in the case of references with additional restrictions, such as presented in the next paragraph.

References with additional restrictions occurred in our study in the *MetricDSL* and *QuestionnaireDSL*. In this current stage, these restrictions result in similar effects to others, but with customized alerts messages presentation. The warnings and error messages are used to validate the constraints and are introduced through pop-ups conforming encoded in the specification step. Fig. 10 illustrates the metrics modelled using *MetricDSL* for the *Configuration Knowledge Experiment*. We can see that the *ReplyTimeOLIS* metric is related to the *OLISProcess* process but its attribute *activityBegin* refers to an activity (*Question 1*) that belongs to another process – *BuyerAgentProcess*. An error message was displayed as a result of the execution of the validation routine created in the specification step. The error is shown even whether the activity is a valid activity in other process. It does not make sense for this metric to refer to activities from different processes.

```
Metric "ReplyTimeOLIS" relates OLISProcess {
                    description "Time taken to answer a question correctly"
                    form intercalated unit minutes
 Invalid activity reference. activityBegin "ByerAgentProcess.Question1"
                    activityEnd "OLISProcess.Question10"
 }
```

Fig. 10. Metric modeling violating additional restriction

The last restriction type is the style constraint. The specification of this restriction also requires the implementation of validation methods. Our study has not identified any scenario to apply this kind of restriction. One possible situation to apply it in the experimental generative approach is to create a style that prevents processes to be typed with lowercase start letter. As this rule would not be an actual style, its violation would generate only a warning.

3.4   Discussions

After the usage of the method in our exploratory study, we can reflect about some preliminary results about its applicability. The study investigated the application of mechanisms for the integration of FMs and DSLs using current MDE technologies in order to answer the research questions of this study (Section 3.1).

DSL Composition (RQ1). The results showed that it is possible to apply our method to compose DSLs during domain engineering using technologies based on MDE. In our study, DSLs have been implemented using the xText framework, which is based on the Ecore meta-model. References between grammars were implemented using explicit references between models, which allows the xText to automatically manage the consistency between models during application engineering. Resources native of the xText, such as intelligent assistants, also enabled navigation assistance and models repairs during the modeling, and they were useful to validate the models built with DSLs. Also, the constraints among DSLs were specified and validated by only specifying the DSLs grammar. Just in the case of references with additional constraints and styles constrains that it was necessary to implement extra methods to validate the constraints of the domain using the Java language. Table 1 presents a summary of the implementation that was performed using xText to implement each constraint types.

Table 1. Summary of constraints implementation using xText

Constraint type	Implementation using xText
Well-formedness of individual artifacts	The grammar of the own DSL defines the format of the its element/attribute
Simple referential	Using only explicit references
References with additional constraints	Using explicit references among grammars and extra method to validate the constraint
Style constraints	Using method to validate the style

Derivation Strategies (RQ2). In our study, we derived products using both strategies provided by the method: (i) using only DSLs and (ii) combining DSLs with FMs. As a result, we observed that the first one seems more appropriate to derive new products from a SPL, when there is no reusable modeling fragments between the different products. For instance, when the research teams are still beginning to specify their controlled experiments using the generative approach. On the other hand, the strategy that integrates DSLs with FMs is more appropriate when there are already other similar products derived with model fragments that could be reused. We used the *FeatureMapper* framework to support the implementation of this second strategy. In our study, we have not quantified the spent effort in the application of each strategy. However, we noticed that the strategy combining DSLs and FMs requires additional effort in preparing the FMs. It is important to emphasize that such effort is necessary only in the first application of the strategy, in order to prepare the model fragments to be reused through of their mapping to the FM. Table 2 summarizes the main findings related to the use of each of the strategies in our exploratory study.

Table 2. Comparison of Derivation Strategies

Scenario/Strategy	Only DSLs	DSLs with FMs
Reuse of modeling fragments	Manual (copy-paste)	automatic (selection of features)
Derivation of new products (without fragments to be reused)	most indicated	less indicated
Derivation similar products (with fragments to be reused)	less indicated	most indicated
extra effort needed (in the first application)	none	Specifying the FM to represent variabilities

***Reuse with the DSLs* (RQ3).** The application of the method also allowed us to observe that the separation of domains into smaller views favors the reuse in the generative approach. In our study, we have applied the method on a specific scenario, but some of our DSLs could be reused in other contexts. The *ExperimentDSL*, for example, can be used to model experiments from other domains. On the other hand, the *MetricDSL* is always related to a process; whereas the *QuestionnaireDSL*, by definition, may or not be related to processes. Finally, the *ProcessDSL* is the only independent DSL in our approach that does not refer to any other. Because of that, it can be reused in different contexts, such as in the modelling of business or software processes. If we consider the reuse inside the same domain – in our case, reuse between ESE controlled experiments – we can notice that the processes, metrics and even questionnaires modeled for a given experiment using our DSLs can be completely or partially reused in the context of other experiments. Hence, despite reuse has not been explicitly investigated in this study, there is a great opportunity to explore the reuse of the specification of an experiment using our DSLs. We are currently conducting new studies to evaluate these issues.

4   Conclusions and Future Work

This paper presented a method for the development of generative approaches with multiple DSLs. Mechanisms to integrate DSLs and FMs, and specifying the DSLs composition were investigated through an exploratory study using the proposed method. Our study focused on the usage of current MDE technologies to provide support to the application of the method, resulting in the composition of Ecore-based DSLs implemented using the xText framework. The method was applied in the modeling and composition of DSLs that allow specifying and executing controlled experiments in software engineering. Our main contributions were: (i) to present a summary of existing approaches to deal with the DSLs composition and generative approaches; (ii) identification and implementation of different integration strategies that can occur between FMs and DSLs during generative development; (iii) proposal of a generative development method that supports multiple DSLs; (iv) evaluation of the proposed method through the design and implementation of a generative approach for the experimental software engineering domain.

We are currently conducting other studies to apply the method to other domains. The main purpose is to evaluate the proposed method considering different settings and contexts. Furthermore, we also intend to conduct more controlled studies with more participants to understand and analyze the method usability, as well as compare quantitatively the different derivation strategies regarding the reuse. Finally, we also plan to evaluate the usage of other MDE frameworks, which can be used to support the development with composition of multiple DSLs.

Acknowledgments. This work was partially supported by National Institute of Science and Technology for Software Engineering (INES) under grants CNPq 573964/2008-4 and 552645/2011-7.

References

1. Bräuer, M., Lochmann, H.: Towards Semantic Integration of Multiple Domain-Specific Languages Using Ontological Foundations. In: ATEM/MODELS (2007)
2. Clements, P., Northrop, L.: Software Product Lines: Practices and Patterns. Professional. Addison-Wesley (2011)
3. Weiss, D., Lai, C.T.: Software Product-Line Engineering: A Family-Based Software Development Process. Addison-Wesley Professional, EUA (1999)
4. Hessellund, A., Czarnecki, K., Wąsowski, A.: Guided Development with Multiple Domain-Specific Languages. In: Engels, G., Opdyke, B., Schmidt, D.C., Weil, F. (eds.) MODELS 2007. LNCS, vol. 4735, pp. 46–60. Springer, Heidelberg (2007)
5. Czarnecki, K., Eisenecker, U.: Generative Programming: Methods, Tools, and Applications. Addison-Wesley Professional, New York (2000)
6. Greenfield, J., Short, K., Cook, S., et al.: Software Factories: Assembling Applications with Patterns, Models, Frameworks, and Tools. Wiley, EUA (2004)
7. Voelter, M., Visser, E.: Product Line Engineering using Domain-Specific Languages. In: 15th SPLC, Washington, pp. 70–79 (2011)
8. Hessellund, A.: Domain-specific multimodeling. PhD Thesis, IT University of Copenhagen, Denmark (2009)
9. Lochmann, H., Hessellund, A.: An Integrated View on Modeling with Multiple Domain-Specific Languages. In: IASTED on ICSE, pp. 1–10 (2009)
10. Groher, I., Fiege, L., Elsner, C., Schwanninger, C., Völter, M.: Solution-driven software product line engineering. In: Aspect-Oriented Model-Driven Software Product Lines: The AMPLE WAY, pp. 316–344. Cambridge Univ. Press, NY (2011)
11. Zschaler, S., Sánchez, P., Nebrera, C., Fuentes, L., Gasiunas, V., Fiege, L.: Produt-driven software product line engineering. In: Aspect-Oriented Model-Driven Software Product Lines: The AMPLE Way, pp. 287–315. Cambridge University Press, New York (2011)
12. Bézivin, J.F.: Using ATL for Checking Models. In: GraMoT, pp. 69–81 (2005)
13. Freire, M., Accioly, P., Sizílio, G., Campos Neto, E., Kulesza, U., Aranha, E., Borba, P.: A Model-Driven Approach to Specifying and Monitoring Controlled Experiments in Software Engineering. In: Heidrich, J., Oivo, M., Jedlitschka, A., Baldassarre, M.T. (eds.) PROFES 2013. LNCS, vol. 7983, pp. 65–79. Springer, Heidelberg (2013)
14. Freire, M., Aleixo, F., Kulesza, U., Aranha, E., Coelho, R.: Automatic Deployment and Monitoring of Software Processes: A Model-Driven Approach. In: SEKE (2011)

15. Campos Neto, E., Freire, M., Kulesza, U., Aranha, E., Bezerra, A.: Composition of Domain Specific Modeling Languages: An Exploratory Study. In: 1st MODELSWARD, Barcelona, vol. 1, pp. 149–156 (2013)
16. Freire, M., Kulesza, U., Aranha, E., Jedlitschka, A., Campos Neto, E., et al.: An Empirical Study to Evaluate a Domain Specific Language for Formalizing Software Engineering Experiments. In: SEKE, Vancouver, pp. 250–255 (2014)
17. Campos Neto, E., Bezerra, A., Freire, M., Kulesza, U., Aranha, E.: Composição de Linguagens de Modelagem Específicas de Domínio: Um Estudo Exploratório. In: III WB-DSDM, Natal, vol. 8, pp. 41–48 (2012)
18. Steinberg, D., Budinsky, F., Paternostro, M., Merks, E.: EMF: Eclipse Modeling Framework, 2nd edn. Addison-Wesley Professional (2008)
19. Wohlin, C.: dRuneson, P., Höst, M., Ohlsson, M., Wesslén, A.: Experimentation in Software Engineering: An Intoduction. Kluwer Academic Publishers (2000)
20. Cirilo, E., Nunes, I., Garcia, A., Lucena, C.: Configuration Knowledge of Software Product Lines: A Comprehensibility Study. In: VariComp., New York, pp. 1–5 (2011)
21. Accioly, P., Borba, P., Bonifácio, R.: Comparing Two Black-box Testing Strategies for Software Product Lines. In: VI SBCARS (2012)

Role of Software Product Customer in the Bring Your Own Device (BYOD) Trend: Empirical Observations on Software Quality Construction

Frank Philip Seth, Ossi Taipale, and Kari Smolander

Department of Software Engineering and Information Management
Lappeenranta University of Technology, Lappeenranta, Finland
{frank.seth,ossi.taipale,kari.smolander}@lut.fi

Abstract. The Bring Your Own Device (BYOD) trend, allows employees to bring personal devices of their choice into the work environment. Since quality goals vary between employees and the organization where they work, it is difficult for software developers to deliver quality product that will satisfy both parties at the same time. This study presents seven findings: First, visible features of the software and functional requirements supersede nonfunctional (quality) characteristics when dealing with customer requirements; second, quality depends more on the market decision than standards' requirements; third, companies focus on 'just enough quality' and not on 'high quality' products; fourth, software quality has a dimension of cost; fifth, organizations try to alleviate threats brought by employees' device or software through policies (quality aspect of policy) ; sixth, simplicity and attractiveness of devices sell poor quality software; and seventh, the number of product features does not affect the sense of quality, but quality characteristics do. These findings identify the role of software customers in deciding about the quality of products and the impact in the BYOD. Software is developed according to end-user requirements, and the end-user has the freedom to choose devices, applications software, and place to use the devices including working environment, where the software may cause risk to the company.

Keywords: Consumerization, BYOD, Bring Your Own Device, software quality construction, functional requirements, nonfunctional requirements, attractiveness, software quality, quality characteristics.

1   Introduction

Software quality construction is a complex sociotechnical process (Hovenden et al. 1996) influenced by technical and nontechnical stakeholders, processes, organizational systems and tools (Park et al. 2012; Seth et al. 2014a; Seth et al. 2014b). It is difficult to define quality, there is no one ultimate definition of quality agreed upon all stakeholders (Garvin 1984; Seth et al. 2012; Smolander 2002), and either there is no specific approach to achieving software quality. For example, Kitchenham and Pfleeger (1996) describe quality as aiming an elusive target.

A. Jedlitschka et al. (Eds.): PROFES 2014, LNCS 8892, pp. 194–208, 2014.
© Springer International Publishing Switzerland 2014

This study adopts the ISO/IEC 25020 (2007) standard definition of software quality as: *internal quality* and *external quality*. The standard defines the *internal software quality* as the capability of a set of static attributes of a software product to satisfy stated and implied needs when the software product is used under specified conditions; and *external software quality* as the capability of a software product to enable the behavior of a system to satisfy stated and implied needs when the system is used under specified conditions.

Consumerization of IT, which is also termed as the *Bring Your Own Device* (BYOD) (Sangroha and Gupta, 2014; Scarfo, 2012), is a phenomenon where end-users bring their personal devices in the production environment, i.e. working places. BYOD phenomenon has increasingly gained popularity in the past decade (Scarfo, 2012). This phenomenon has also shaped the software and hardware industry; software and hardware companies try to reorient products and service designs around the individual end-users. For example, software development is focusing on the individual consumer as the primary driver of product and service design. There is also an increase use of smart phones, and tablets, which necessitates some companies and business to conform to delivering services into those platforms.

Several challenges surround software industry with regards to BYOD trend. One of the challenges is to develop quality software at reasonable cost and time (Osterweil, 1997), yet to meet quality requirements, such as security for achieving organizational goals in the company where the end-user works (Scarfo, 2012). BYOD phenomenon causes the software developers also to think about both the hardware i.e. devices, and the business environment where the end-user of the device is working. This means, although the software aims to meet end-user requirements, it should also meet some business requirements, which in this respect vary among the users depending on the type of business they are engaged.

This study considers the opinion that among the software engineering objectives is to reduce costs and improve product quality (Osterweil, 1997). However, the ultimate goal for software developing companies is not only to develop quality products, but also to win more customers for the purpose of acquiring economical gains and profit (Barney and Wohlin, 2009). Profit making aspects cannot be isolated from the aims of software development; otherwise the software companies will fail to operate. Barney and Wohlin (2009) argue that software quality construction should focus on achieving some common goals. In the BYOD trend, it is challenging to have a common goal between the software developing companies, individual end-users of software products, device manufacturing companies and the companies where the end-users work. So, in order to make profit, software-developing companies choose to optimize quality based on their customers and add value (Perner, 2008) that will also benefit companies where the software or devices will be used in other environments beyond personal use. Savolainen et al. (2007) discuss the importance of varying requirements; varying requirements that are adaptable in various situations provide key competitive advantages that allow economic success for the product line (Clarke and O'Connor, 2012).

This empirical study investigates practical experiences in software developing companies. The objective of the study is to understand the challenges to meet quality requirements of software products in the BYOD environment. A qualitative approach is adopted to increase understanding of how customer satisfaction and preferences influence the way software developing companies deal with software quality. Thus, the findings are expected to provide useful information that is applicable in the day-to-day software development activities. The scope of this study is confined to software development activities in the software companies. The research question studied is: *How does the role of a software product customer influence software quality construction in a BYOD environment?*

The rest of the paper is organized as follows: Section two presents the related literature; Section three presents research methodology and data analysis; Section four present results; Section five presents discussion and finally, Section six presents the conclusions of the study.

2   Related Literature

Software developing companies try various approaches to increase quality of software products. For example, Mäkinen and Münch (2014) elaborate test-driven development as one of many approaches. However, there is a different view of quality when the software is used in other environments, which were not included in the testing. Software is typically tested in a given set of parameters and scope. When the parameters and scope are changed, the quality of software also changes. This means, the quality of a software product is defined at given parameters. When any of the parameters is altered, the quality may be evaluated differently. For example, in the BYOD phenomenon, the software is not tested in various working environments where the end-user will use their devices, which imply that quality of the software may not meet the quality standards of the end-user's working place.

In the BYOD trend, customer-centered software development is the key success factor for both software development companies and hardware companies. In the quest to increase market share, software companies try to be innovative; in this way they attract more customers and boost sells. However, there is a risk involved. For example, Aslhford, (1985) report that detailed specification standards may discourage innovation. This means that some of the software development companies are flexible with some standards and regulations as long as their customers are satisfied with the products. Thus, quality is leaning to the customer and little emphasis is placed on other quality characteristics, which are not immediate end-user demands, hence imposing threat to the end-users' work place.

Software industry and technology at large have gained a pace that is ahead of standards and regulatory authorities (Kalyani, 2013). For example, business and services are migrating to clouds in the absence of the standards and regulations in that area, which contributes to the risk. While trying to innovate products, attend customer satisfaction and reduce costs (Osterweil, 1997), businesses are kept at risk especially when the employees of companies use their own devices, and also hook their devices to other online services which are not standardized or regulated, such as phishing sites, free apps and online downloadable software sites.

Types of devices such as smartphones, tablets and other handhelds, have influence on the type of software the end-user will use. In many cases, end-user will choose the device before choosing the platform or the software running in such devices, because he or she is attracted to the device. Eventually, the BYOD trend leads to end-users bringing their own software (BYOS) for their own devices, which means more difficulties in dealing with organizational software quality requirements and risk mitigation (Sophos 2014).

The end-user purchasing behavior suggests that decision is influenced by what they see or feel than what could be the actual value of the product. Savolainen et al. (2007) argue that customers do not care how the products are created; they value how well the product satisfies their needs. In this view, the quality of the software would also be judged and evaluated based on the visible or felt features of the software or device such as interfaces, graphics, camera, etc. For example, recently, some studies indicate that even size of the device contribute to customer satisfaction (Xue and Chen, 2011), and therefore influence the decision to buy a particular device. On the other hand, Hashmi et al. (2013) argue that cost has an influence to customer satisfaction. So, when we look into software quality in the light of BYOD trend, we should also consider the devices and software in terms of cost. According to Hashmi et al. (2013) we see that the users will buy what they are satisfied with, but considering the cost and not other quality characteristics in general. Thus, free software or low priced software and devices are likely to fall in user preferences and hence users use them in the working environment, which may result to security threats.

3   Research Methodology and the Sample

40 semi-structured interviews were used to collect information from testers, developers, managers, R&D personnel, marketing personnel and quality control specialists. The study involved 13 software-developing companies. We collected data during three interview rounds. The sample was identified using polar type criteria (Eisenhardt, 1989) to cover different types and sizes of companies in terms of mode of operation, business domains, etc. (Table 1). The sampling was theoretical (Eisenhardt, 1989). The goal of theoretical sampling is not to find a representative sample of all possible variations but to gain a deeper understanding of the analyzed cases and identify concepts and their relationships for the emerging theory (Eisenhardt, 1989).

The interview questions were sent to the companies beforehand so that the interviewees could prepare for interviews. The interviewees were let to answer the question without further guidance so that they could reveal new concepts beyond the questions. All interviews were recorded and transcribed by a specialized company. At the end of each interview, the data was analyzed and leads were identified. Every time a new lead was found, the interview questions were modified to follow the leads for the next interview session. We analyzed the data using the analysis tool Atlas.ti (2005). The study followed the grounded theory method (Strauss and Corbin, 1990).

The size of company is defined by the EU SME definition (EU, 2003). Themes and research questions are available at http://bit.ly/intquest.

Table 1. Business domain, data collection rounds, company size and role of interviewees

CASE	Business domain	1st Round interviews	2nd Round interviews	3rd Round interviews	Company size	Role of the interviewees
A	Inventory management systems.	1			Small	R&D and quality assurance manager (1).
B	Banking and insurance.	4	5		Large	Test analysts (1), test designer (2), Designer and developer (2).
C	Space satellite.	1	1	1	Small	Designer and developer (2) and Project manager (1).
D	Web applications.	1			Small	Tester and developer (1).
E	Embedded software.	4	4	2	Large	Tester (1), developer (2) and requirement management (1).
F	Quality and testing consultancy	1		2	Medium	Quality manager (1), developer (1) and consulting tester (1).
G	Various software developers.	1	1		Large	Quality manager (1) and tester (1).
H	Cloud computing Web applications.	1			Small	CEO, developer, tester and designer (1).
I	Fleet management systems.	2	1		Large	Test consultant (1) and test manager (1).
J	Cloud computing services and consultancy.	1			Small	CEO (1).
K	Banking, energy, health, etc.	1	1	1	Large	Quality assurance and tester (1).
L	Development and testing consultants.		2		Small	Consultant tester (1) and developer (1).
M	Various software developers.			1	Large	Project manager (1).
13		18	15	7	40	

4   Results

The purpose of our analysis was to understand how the role of a software product customer influences software quality construction in a BYOD environment. The analysis produced four major categories: *customer requirements, quality characteristics, software domain* and *goal of software development.*

4.1   Analysis and Categorizing

Following the grounded theory, the focus of the analysis was on the software development activities and particularly on how the companies dealt with customers during requirements prioritization, how they selected features and quality characteristics for software products. In the open coding concepts were identified from the data and coded. Concepts that were not aligned with the research goals were omitted.

The axial coding started by comparing and differentiating the concepts labeled in the open coding. Similar concepts were grouped into one category and labeled. So, we grouped the concepts into four major categories: *customer requirements, quality characteristics, software domain* and *goal of software development.*

The activities studied in the data indicated that companies solicited information from the customer in order to obtain important requirements for the products. However, some concepts indicated that some product features were developed not by using customer requirements but developers' creativity. Methods of requirements elicitation varied from company to company. All concept related to requirements were groped into the category named customer *requirements.*

Several concepts indicated that quality characteristics vary between customers depending on the purpose of the software. So, we grouped the concepts into in-house software and public software. The in-house software is the one that the company is building for its own internal use, and the public software is for outside customers. The two groups show that consideration for features and characteristics widely varied. Some concepts indicated that product features have an impact on quality but the number of features in the product does not affect much its quality because customers use only a few features of most interest. So we considered features as important subject, but to reduce the number of categories for analysis, all concepts describing product features were put into one category, which was named quality *characteristics.*

The domain in which the software was used seemed to decide the type of quality characteristics. For example, banking domain seemed to have special standards for security, despite of customer requirements. We grouped concepts depending of criticality of software and studied that criticality of software is also influenced by the domain. So, all concepts, which described domain, criticality and area of application, were assigned into one category named *software domain.*

Goal of software development varied from company to company. Some companies defined quality goals from the beginning of the development while other did not think about quality upfront. Some companies focused more on functional requirements and less on nonfunctional requirements. All concepts, which described the quality goals of development, were assigned into the category named *goal of software development.*

The last phase of grounded theory analysis is the selective coding. The goal of selective coding is to identify the core category. In this analysis none of the four categories was broad enough to describe all the other categories. So, we looked again into the categories and found that all categories contain concepts pertinent to product quality that indicated challenges in identifying or meeting those requirements, so we created a conceptual category and named it '*influence of software product customer on software quality construction*'.

4.2   Findings

We summarize seven findings based on the described categories, which explain the role of software product customer in the software quality construction process, hence the result is related to the current situation i.e. the BYOD trend.

Finding 1: Visible features of the software and functional requirements super-sede nonfunctional (quality) characteristics when dealing with customer requirements

In the data analysis we noted that some *quality characteristics* are not given as much attention as the functional characteristics. Generally, most of customers do not understand the internal details of the software and the backend side of the systems i.e. the *internal software quality* (ISO/IEC, 2007). Thus, customers evaluate software or systems in terms of the outer visible interfaces, usability, outputs, and efficiency in the production environment based on the behavior of software or systems i.e. *external software quality* (ISO/IEC, 2007). For this reason, software external characteristics are more likely to attract end-users than internal quality characteristics.

"More than 90% of the time and concentration go to the functionality. And sometimes it is quite interesting actually when we have not discussed about the security. Well, it is not so important, or not even the performance of the applications but how actually the product works." – **Tester, Case K.**

One of the important user acceptance tests is the functional suitability that indicates conformance to the requirements. When the software performs what the customer requires, the customer is satisfied and the software is termed as quality software.

Finding 2: Quality depends more on the market decision than standards' requirements

The *goal of software development* influences the development process. For example, it was observed that developers in most of the studied companies do not use the quality standards and frameworks such as the ISO/IEC 25020 (2007) standards. Good practices, rules and procedures seemed to be optional. For example, in company D the director says,

"In our company we have a set of best practices published in a book for use in software development projects, but this is totally up to the project manager to take those practices or not." – **Testing director, company D.**

This phenomenon was more evident in small companies than large companies. The questions raised from this observation were: If the development is not guided by some standards, or some best practices, how then the quality is achieved? What is so important in the software development? The development engineer in company E answers by saying,

"I don't need to care about the standards in my work. But I guess, probably the manager [cares]. At least we have some ISO 9000 but I don't see it in my own work." **- Development engineer, Case E.**

This observation suggests that quality depends on what the market decides rather than what standards require. People buy what they see other people buying. The companies are focusing to deliver what their customers need and not the best product described in the standards and books.

Finding 3: Companies focus on 'just enough quality' and not on 'high quality' products

When dealing with *quality characteristics* and features, developers' approach to quality prompts us in comparing 'high quality' and 'just enough quality' products. Winning the customers relies on "how the product *attracts* the customers" than "how the product is *too good*". In common circumstances, companies deliver *just enough quality* than *high quality* products as long as the customer is satisfied. From the observations in several companies including D and K above, we realized that *functionality* (ISO/IEC 25020, 2007) and *attractiveness* (ISO/IEC-25051, 2006) are the characteristics that push the market and customers to choose what to buy; what they find appealing to them in the unforeseeable future. The above two findings lead us to think that fictional characteristics of the product influence customers in buying decision. However, poor internal quality will render the product failure in the long run.

It is difficult to precisely distinguish between the "just enough quality" and the "high quality" products. The literature does not give the assurance of "high quality" products. Jørgensen (1999) argues that there is no universal measurement or scale for quality. He emphasizes that quality depends on the taste and preference of the user of the product. Therefore, the software developer may only try to produce relevant products with preferences of a specified domain or users. For example, the software developer in company E was asked, "*What kind of quality is important to you in software you develop?*" He responded by saying,

"*It's hard to say which quality is the most important, but I think quality in our case is much dependent on the fact that once we release a software to a customers, they might not be so willing to upgrade any firmware to their devices. So really whether the fact that the firmware is error-free, or has few errors, the functionality is what the customer expects. That's one of the key issues. We try to deliver what the customer wants in his situation.*" - **Software developer, Case E.**

The developer in company E tries to express the risk to deliver more quality than the customer required in the prevailing situations at customer's side, i.e. other software, platforms, firmware, etc. From this point of view, the "high quality" product may be defined in the customer's perspective and not from the developer of the software's perspective. What works best with the customers is the "high quality" product for them.

Finding 4: Software Quality has a Dimension of Cost

Looking into *customer requirements* category, we noted that there is a cost dimension that limits customer demands when comes to requirements. Customer satisfaction includes being satisfied with the cost of a product.

"*If you think about the total quality. If the product has a higher cost to the customer, then you can see that the total quality is getting lower; because total quality is how your customer is happy and satisfied with the product.*" - **Quality advisor, Case F.**

Two important questions to answer before software development projects are: First, *what is the important quality to build for a particular customer?* Second, *how to build such quality into a product at reasonable cost and time*? The first question targets the customer and the second targets the developer (companies). Dromey and McGettrick (1992) suggest that the quality of software product is about features, quality characteristics and satisfaction of customers. So the stakeholders of the software decide what to include or exclude, and how to implement these features and characteristics in the software. The efforts of the developers to understand the customers have positive effect on quality. On the other hand, Boehm (1984) argues that since we work in limited resource environments, there is never enough time or capital, monetary and intellectual, to consider all the good features we would like to put into a software product. Thus, the balance between the "just enough quality" and the "high quality" products should be carefully observed. For example, development engineer in company E was asked, *"What are the indicators that the quality you aimed at has been reached?"* and he responded,

"We have a department that is testing the products. They test the product in the way that it works as the previous product has worked. So it is merely just test that we haven't broken anything. That is the main testing." - **Development engineer, Case E.**

Thus, companies try to deliver what the customers need according to their budget and time frame. Customer satisfaction is also affected by cost involved, which means a customer weighs between the product quality and the cost to determine the total quality of the software.

Finding 5: Quality Aspect of Policy in the Software

Since the software in various devices is focusing on satisfying an individual, but it may be used in other undetermined environments such as end-user's working place, the policies may be considered as an important aspect of software quality. For example, Sangroha and Gupta (2014) gave an example of an end-user of a device, which has vulnerable software. This end-user connects to the office network and exposes the threats to the entire network through his infected device. Since it is difficult to deal with individual user's devices, the companies need to enforce some policies that will determine the allowable standard of devices and software, which could be used in the office network.

"The security is a problem and must be taken care seriously. Also if we think about an industry or big factories using LAN networks, they use own networks but almost every sensor can be connected to LAN, therefore raising security and safety concerns. However, security is not a problem for stand-alone servers." - **Senior consultant, Case B.**

It was also noted that software developers, intentionally put less attention to some quality characteristics because they assume that the system where the software is going to be applied will take care of some of those characteristics, for example, security.

"I am aware of security but we do not really consider security in the normal work. We do not spend time on that in every day's work because the security is integrated into the system so we do not have to think about it" - **Developer engineer, Case A.**

Thus, some of the quality characteristics may exist as policies to those systems where the software will be applied. For example, if the end-user software does not have some security features, but the developers explain how the system should deal with that software, then the software is of good quality.

Finding 6: Simplicity and Attractiveness of Devices Sell Poor Quality Software

Usability has proven to be key item for software acceptance or rejection (Chao, 2009). In the BYOD trend, it is the user of device who choses what he is comfortable with. So the choice may be based on the simplicity of the software interfaces.

"The key thing is that we implement applications that user should be able to use the application without any user guides. If software application needs a user guide then it is too complex to use, no enough usability. That is the reason why iPhone is so successful because of the usability. You don't need any kind of instructions to use it." - **Senior consultant, Case B.**

According to Cisco annual security report (Stewart, 2014) of January 2014, ninety nine percent (99%) of all mobile malware targeted Android devices in 2013. However, Truong et al. (2014) report that infection rates in Android devices are at around zero point two five per cent (0.25%), significantly higher than the previous independent estimate.

Android is a one of the large provider of platform and applications for handheld devices. The finding 4.1.1 suggests those users are more attracted with what they see than what they don't, which means the external quality is important in the buying decision. The blooming number of Android users suggests that the stake is higher in the BYOD trend because users chose devices based on the attractiveness and simplicity overlooking some important internal characteristics. Arthur, (2013) suggest that some mobile phone companies have lost their market share because their products are not simple to use and do not have attractive interfaces, although they might be superior in the internal quality.

Finding 7: The number of Product 'features' Does not Affect the Sense of Quality, but Quality Characteristics Do

In the analysis we noted that quality of the product is not much affected by the number of features, but functionality, and usability. Users chose only a few of features and use them while forgetting about the rest. Form this observation we can also argue that product features have impact on product quality in similar manner as quality characteristics.

"Usually a lot of customers are still satisfied because they normally use only few of the product's features. The experience shows that when we release software with some few problems only 10 to 15 percent of the customers will complain." The senior consultant in company B claims that *"we put too much focus on functionality and there should be more focus on usability and reliability particularly for web applications. It's better to have fewer features. The less features you have, the better the software."* - **Development engineer, Case E.**

When looking closer at this observation, we can also cement the above finding 4.1.1 that visible features of the device or software have a remarkable impact on the way user judge product quality. In most of the devices features are conspicuous and could be counted, or easily compared among devices at the layman's point of views, but characteristics are difficult to see and evaluate. Therefore, devices with attractive features are likely to cause more threat in the BYOD environment because users are likely to buy them despite of internal weak characteristics.

5   Discussion

This study consist of seven major findings that describe software development activities, and challenges involved in quality construction in the light of BYOD trend. According to the results of this study, the risks involved in the BYOD including security risk, are potentially caused by the buying behavior of the end-users of the software and devices. Although some end-users may understand security risks, they are still satisfied with the software or device they use because of cost. Similar finding is discussed by (Chang and Lee 2013; Hashmi et al. 2013; Savolainen et al. 2007). For example, Savolainen et al. (2007) argue that the customers do not care how the products are created; they value how well the product satisfies their needs. On the other hand, Chang and Lee (2013) discuss the impact of the free apps. Results show that end-users are satisfied while they put their personal data at risk and in the BYOD, the companies' data is also at risk.

Devices attract end-users and they prefer device to software. This observation suggests that visible features of the device or software, and functional requirements supersede nonfunctional (quality) characteristics when customers judge software quality. Furthermore, the finding of this study suggests that the number of product 'features' does not affect the customer sense of quality. Software development companies pay more attention on functional requirements than quality requirements. This result suggests that, customers are more satisfied when they have working software with great observable features such as interfaces, graphics, etc. Similar findings are disuse by Savolainen et al. (2007).

Software companies are not strict with quality standards such as ISO and IEEE in the development of generic software. This behavior enables the companies to innovate products and cater better for their customers' requirements without limitations. However, some companies were strict with some specific standards for mission critical software, such as banking software, space satellite, and software for nuclear rectors. Quality for generic software seemed to depend more on the market decision than standards' requirements. Similar finding is reported by (Aslhford, 1985; Kalyani, 2013).

Software quality has a dimension of cost (Savolainen et al. 2007). Companies focus on delivering 'just enough quality' and not on 'high quality' products as to optimize the cost of production. Companies deliver 'just enough' quality to avoid problems caused by over-spec products. It was observed that the over-spec products lead to incompatibility with the existing systems at the customer side. Osterweil, (1997) discusses the goals of software development as to meet high quality products at low cost. On the other hand, Savolainen et al. (2007) points out that cost is part of the customer satisfaction. The finding of this study suggest that since customers are willing to pay less, and the companies are willing to deliver what the customers are satisfied (just enough quality), the problem of poor quality products persist and increase threat on the BYOD environment.

This study has several theoretical and practical implications. First it establishes that software quality is more customer dependent than developer dependent. What satisfies the customers is high quality to them. Second, customer satisfaction as the indicator of quality is influenced by cost and value of the products. There is a dimension of cost in measuring customer satisfaction in relation to quality. Third, customer prefer device to software, which implies that physical appearance, such as graphics, interfaces, etc., have a large impact on customer satisfaction. Fourths, the risks associated to BYOD are manageable, but at the company side, by enforcing security policies.

Threats to validity inherent in qualitative studies have been discussed in several studies. For example, some of the phenomena were observed in only one or a few companies. However, since the study is qualitative and not quantitative, the value of the findings is not affected by the frequency of occurrence but by its relevance and the grounding in the data (Klein and Myers 1999; Van Manen 1990). Strauss and Corbin (1990) emphasize on theory emergent from the data analysis. However, the theory created is rather dynamic than static, and can be extended by adding new data. This study involved 13 companies and 40 interviews were conducted. The process of data collection continued until saturation point where there were no new concepts emerged. So we believe that the observed phenomena are relevant and applicable in other situations. To minimize the threat of bias, this study involved a team of four researchers, who collectively prepared the interview questions and collected the data. The interviews were tape-recorded and transcribed by a specialized company. However, there could be some expressions of the interview, which could not be captured and transcribed.

Future study may focus on establishing standard requirements for devices allowable to be used in corporate environment, which will be enforced by organizational security policies.

6   Conclusions

This study concludes that end-user of devices in the environment where the BYOD is allowed, is a threat factor. Software and device companies deliver quality products at the level of their customers' satisfaction. The customers' preferences on quality and cost are the source of the threat. However, BYOD phenomenon comes with many advantages. Companies exploit its employees' resources to achieve their mission and goals. Despite of threats, the BOYD adds value to business because the company extends services beyond office premises and working hours.

Since the goal of software development is to make profit, at the same time compete in the market, software companies focus on delivering 'just enough' quality as per customer requirements. In this view, software-developing companies focus on catering for the requirements of the immediate customer, and not other environments where the software or devices can be used. Therefore, this study suggests that companies may include policies to alleviate security risks caused by employees' devices or employees' behavior.

References

1. Scarfo, A: New Security Perspectives around BYOD. In: 7th International Conference on Broadband, Wireless Computing, Communication and Applications (BWCCA), Victoria, BC, pp. 446 – 451 (2012).
2. ISO/IEC-25020: Software Engineering — Software quality requirements and evaluation (SQuaRE) —Quality measurement, Geneva, Switzerland, International Organization for Standardization (2007)
3. Aslhford, N.A., Ayer, C., Stone, R.F.: Using Regulation to Change the Market for Innovation (1985),
   http://dspace.mit.edu/bitstream/handle/1721.1/1555/%252319.PDF?sequence=1 (accessed on May 7, 2014)
4. Kalyani, M.: Setting Standards for the Murky Cloud Market (2013),
   https://spideroak.com/privacypost/business-the-cloud/cloud-computing-regulations-on-the-rise/ (accessed on May 7, 2014)
5. Osterweil, L.J.: Software processes are software too. In: The 19th International Conference on Software Engineering, Boston, pp. 343–344 (1997)
6. Strauss, A.L., Corbin, J.: Basics of Qualitative Research: Grounded Theory Procedures and Applications. Sage Publication, Newbury Park (1990)
7. ISO/IEC-25051: Software engineering — Software product Quality Requirements and Evaluation (SQuaRE) — Requirements for quality of Commercial Off-The-Self (COTS) software product and instructions for testing, Geneva, Switzerland, International Organization for Standardization (2006)
8. Dromey, R.G., McGettrick, A.D.: On Specifying Software Quality. Software Quality Journal 1(1), 45–74 (1992)
9. Boehm, B.W.: Software engineering economics. IEEE Transactions on Software Engineering Se-10(1), 4–21 (1984)
10. Jørgensen, M.: Software Quality Measurement. Advances in Engineering Software 30(2), 907–912 (1999)
11. Chao, G.: The usability test methods and design principles in the human-computer interface design. In: 2nd IEEE International Conference on Human-computer Interaction: Computer Science and Information Technology, ICCSIT, Beijing, pp. 283–285 (2009)
12. Sophos.: BYOD Risks & Rewards, http://www.sophos.com/en-us/security-news-trends/security-trends/byod-risks-rewards/what-is-byos.aspx (accesses on September 26, 2014)
13. Stewart, J.N.: Cisco Annual Security Report Documents Unprecedented Growth of Advanced Attacks and Malicious Traffic (2014),
   http://newsroom.cisco.com/release/1310011/Cisco-Annual-Security-Report-Documents-Unprecedented-Growth-of-Advanced-Attacks-and-Malicious-Traffic

14. Truong, H.T.T., Lagerspetz, E., Nurmi, P., Oliner, A.J., Tarkoma, S., Asokan, N., Bhatta-charya, S.: The Company You Keep: Mobile Malware Infection Rates and Inexpensive Risk Indicators. In: The International World Wide Web Conference (WWW 2014), Seoul, Korea (2014)
15. Park, C., Pattipati, K.R., An, W., Kleinman, D.L.: Quantifying the Im-pact of Information and Organizational Structures via Distributed Auction Algorithm: Point-to-Point Communication Structure. IEEE Transactions on Systems, Man and Cybernetics, Part A: Systems and Humans 42(1), 68–86 (2012)
16. Seth, F.P., Taipale, O., Smolander, K.: Organizational and Customer re-lated Challenges of Software Testing: An Empirical Study in 11 Software Companies. In: IEEE-RCIS 2014 Conference, Marrakech (2014a)
17. Seth, F.P., Mustonen-Ollila, E., Taipale, O.: The Influence of Management on Software Product Quality: An Empirical Study in Software Developing Companies. In: Barafort, B., O'Connor, R.V., Poth, A., Messnarz, R. (eds.) EuroSPI 2014. CCIS, vol. 425, pp. 147–158. Springer, Heidelberg (2014)
18. Hovenden, F.M., Walker, S.D., Sharp, H.C., Woodman, M.: Building quality into scientific software. Software Quality Journal 5(1), 25–32 (1996)
19. Seth, F.P., Mustonen-Ollila, E., Taipale, O., Smolander, K.: Software Quality Construction: Empirical Study on the Role of Requirements, Stake-holders and Resources. In: Asia Pacific Software Engineering Conference APSEC 2012, Hong Kong, pp. 17–26 (2012)
20. Smolander, K.: Four metaphors of architecture in software organizations: Finding out the meaning of architecture in practice. In: International Symposium on Empirical Software Engineering (ISESE 2002), Nara, Japan (2002)
21. Garvin, D.A.: What Does "Product Quality" Really Mean? Sloan Management Review (4), 25–43 (1984)
22. Kitchenham, B., Pfleeger, S.L.: Software Quality: The Elusive Target. IEEE Software 13(1), 12–21 (1996)
23. Clarke, P., O'Connor, R.V.: Business Success in Software SMEs: Recommendations for Future SPI Studies. In: Winkler, D., O'Connor, R.V., Messnarz, R. (eds.) EuroSPI 2012. CCIS, vol. 301, pp. 1–12. Springer, Heidelberg (2012)
24. Barney, S., Wohlin, C.: Software Product Quality: Ensuring a Common Goal. In: Wang, Q., Garousi, V., Madachy, R., Pfahl, D. (eds.) ICSP 2009. LNCS, vol. 5543, pp. 256–267. Springer, Heidelberg (2009)
25. Mäkinen, S., Münch, J.: Effects of test-driven development: A comparative analysis of empirical studies. In: Winkler, D., Biffl, S., Bergsmann, J. (eds.) SWQD 2014. LNBIP, vol. 166, pp. 155–169. Springer, Heidelberg (2014)
26. Sangroha, D., Gupta, V.: Exploring Security Theory Approach in BYOD Environment, Wireless Networks and Security. In: Proceedings of the Second International Conference on Advanced Computing, Networking and Informatics (ICACNI 2014), Kolkata, India, pp. 259–266 (2014)
27. Eisenhardt, K.M.: Building Theories from Case Study Research. Academy of Management Review 14, 532–550 (1989)
28. Perner, L.: (2008),
http://www.consumerpsychologist.com/
marketing_introduction.html (accessed on June 17, 2014)
29. Savolainen, J., Kauppinen, M., Mannisto, T.: Identifying Key Requirements for a New Product Line. In: 14th Asia-Pacific Software Engineering Conference (IEEE-APSEC 2007), Aichi, pp. 478–485 (2007)

30. Xue, J., Chen, C.W.: 2011 IEEE International Conference on Multimedia and Expo (ICME), Barcelona, pp. 1–6 (2011)
31. Hashimi, U.S., Anjum, N., Israr, A.: Impact of Software Quality Standards on Commercial Product Development and Customer Satisfaction for Software Industry in Pakistan. In: Fifth International Conference on Computaional Intelligence, Modelling and Simulation (CIMSim), Seoul, pp. 269–274 (2013)
32. Chang, S.E., Lee, P.-F.: Leveraging Social Network APIs for Enhancing Smartphone Apps. In: IEEE International Conference on and IEEE Cyber, Physical and Social Computing, Beijing, pp. 1219–1224 (2013)
33. Van Manen, M.: Researching lived Experience: Human Science for an Action Sensitivity Pedagogy. Althouse Press, London (1990)
34. Klein, H.K., Myers, M.D.: A set of principles for conducting and evaluating interpretive field studies in information systems. MIS Quarterly 23(1), 67–94 (1999)
35. Arthur, C.: Why BlackBerry failed (2013), http://www.theguardian.com/commentisfree/2013/nov/05/why-blackberry-failed (accessed on May 23, 2014)

Envisioning a Requirements Specification Template for Medical Device Software

Hao Wang[1,*], Yihai Chen[2,**], Ridha Khedri[3,***], and Alan Wassyng[4,†]

[1] Faculty of Engineering and Science, Aalesund University College, Norway
[2] School of Computer Engineering and Science, Shanghai University, China
[3] Department of Computing and Software, McMaster University, Canada
[4] McMaster Centre for Software Certification (McSCert), McMaster University, Canada

Abstract. In many health jurisdictions, software is considered to be *medical device software* (MDS), when it is used to analyze patient data in order to render a diagnosis or monitor the patient's health; when it is to be used by a patient to diagnose an ailment; or when it is used to deliver functionality for a medical device. Flaws in MDS can result in patient harm, including death. Legislators and regulatory agencies publish guidelines and regulatory standards that are aimed at ensuring the safety, security and dependability of MDS. These guidelines and standards universally agree that a complete and consistent requirement specification is vital to the success of medical device software. Moreover, we observe that regulators are shifting from being *process focused* to being *product focused* in their approval guidance. In this paper, we review challenges associated with requirements used in the development of MDS, current standards and guidelines relevant to MDS, and existing templates for requirement specifications. We then propose a set of design objectives for a 'good' MDS requirements template and propose a template structure for MDS requirement specification fulfilling all the design objectives. Our template is, by design, tailored to facilitate the gathering and documenting of high quality requirements for MDS.

1 Introduction and Motivation

Many medical devices nowadays rely heavily on software. In 2006, over half the medical devices on the U.S. market involved software [10]. The *European Medical Device Directive* MDD 93/42/EEC [26], one of the foundational Council Directives in medical devices, includes software as one type of medical device. The guidance on *Medical Device Directives* [8] explicitly lists the following circumstances under which software is regarded as a medical device: (a) The software is for a purpose explicitly mentioned in a Medical Device Directive; (b) The software is intended to control or influence the

---

* Supported by IBM Canada R&D Centre, McSCert, and Southern Ontario Smart Computing Innovation Platform (SOSCIP) while he conducted this research in Canada.
** Supported by Natural Science Foundation of China (NSFC) through the grant No. 61170044.
*** Supported by SOSCIP, and the Natural Sciences and Engineering Research Council of Canada (NSERC) through the grant RGPIN 2014-06115.
† Supported by SOSCIP, Ontario Research Fund - Research Excellence, and NSERC.

A. Jedlitschka et al. (Eds.): PROFES 2014, LNCS 8892, pp. 209–223, 2014.

functioning of a medical device; (c) The software is intended for the analysis of patient data generated by a medical device with a view to diagnosis and monitoring; (d) The software is intended for use for/by patients to diagnose or treat a physical or mental condition or disease. In addition, the *International Electrotechnical Commission* (IEC) and the U.S. *Food and Drug Administration* (FDA) have included software as a category of medical devices and presented standards and guidelines regulating them. Software regarded as a medical device is called *Medical Device Software* (MDS).

The literature abounds with data that clearly show that any shortcoming in defining the requirements for computer-based systems in general imperils the deliverables of all the subsequent stages of their development [35]. The importance that ought to be given to documenting system requirements is undeniable when dealing with medical devices due to their significant role in altering human biological function or structure. Even slightly erroneous behavior by such a device could lead to a grave incident. The FDA *Manufacturer and User Facility Device Experience* (MAUDE) database [28] contains a large number of reports on such incidents: nearly 17,000 insulin pump-related adverse-event reports from October 1, 2006, through September 30, 2009. Among the 310 death reports, 41 were associated with blood-sugar levels being too high or too low, suggesting the device may not have been working properly [6]. As to security, experts showed that a popular wireless-enabled pump could be hacked [24]. In 2002-2010, there were more than 537 recalls of devices that used software, which affected over 1.5 million devices being used in the U.S. [16]. Until recently, regulatory approval of MDSs was dependent on *process based* guidance, e.g., IEC 62304 regulates the development processes of medical device software. The large number of adverse-event reports has proven that this practice is inadequate. The FDA recently changed its approval process to be more *product focused* for infusion pumps, so that the production of an *assurance case* that demonstrates that the device is safe and effective is now a *recommended* regulatory requirement in the U.S. [5].

In fields such as manufacturing [2] or aerospace [27], engineers are expected to develop and use requirements templates that are designed to put more emphasis on documenting key requirements of their systems. However, in the field of MDS, the almost complete lack of regard for the specification of requirements [22] is striking. Moreover, we cannot directly use existing templates as they do not properly help address some of the requirements that are specific to MDS (see Section 2.2). Medical devices are a class of systems that have stringent safety and security requirements that ought to be documented and updated regularly at every newly reported incident. A precondition for ensuring the safety and reliability of MDS is having a complete and consistent requirements document. A MDS specific template for eliciting and documenting requirements is an important step toward achieving this precondition. Medical devices are subject to government and international laws and regulations. Therefore, a MDS specific template to guide capturing all the requirements from these standards and regulations would be invaluable. Safety and security requirements for MDS ought to be given sufficient attention so that the devices may be shown to be safe, secure and dependable. A requirements template has to provide adequate means for ensuring the completeness of the requirements, especially regarding safety, security, and other aspects of system dependability.

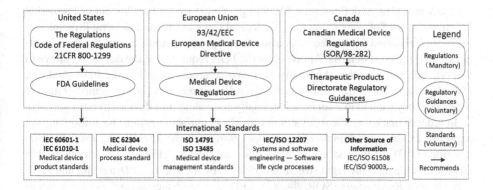

Fig. 1. Regulations and Standards related to MDS

In this paper we discuss the main design objectives for a MDS requirements template. Based on these objectives, we present the highlights of a template that is intended to guide the eliciting and documenting of the requirements for MDSs. We have also assessed the proposed template versus the outlined design objectives.

The remainder of this paper is organized as follows: Section 2 introduces the standards and guidelines related to MDS, and reviews existing requirement templates. Section 3 proposes a set of objectives for a 'good' MDS requirements template. Section 4 gives the main characteristics of the proposed MDS requirements template and assesses it based on the design objectives set in Section 3. Then, we conclude and point to our future work in Section 5.

2   Background

2.1   Standards and Guidelines on Software Medical Devices

We briefly review European and North American current regulations and guidelines as well as ISO/IEC standards. Figure 1 shows the hierarchy of regulations and related international standards relevant to the development of medical device software. Governments publish laws and regulations to control medical device industries, which are expected to abide by them. Governments also provide guidelines and a list of harmonized standards for medical device manufacturers for reference and voluntary adoption. Usually, compliance with guidelines and harmonized standards is deemed to satisfy the applicable regulations. This has necessarily resulted in regulatory regimes that are primarily process focused, rather than a more modern product focus.

U.S. regulation requires that medical devices go through premarket approval or a premarket notification process [33, Page 15]. The FDA defines the regulations in Title 21 of the U.S. Code of Federal Regulations, which is commonly referred to as 21 CFR. The articles 800 to 1299 of the regulations cover responsibilities of the medical device manufacturer [33, Page 17]. To help manufacturers through the premarket processes, the FDA provides guidelines w.r.t. MDS (e.g., Guidance for the Content of Premarket Submissions for Software Contained in Medical Devices [32] and General Principles of Software Validation [31]). The FDA also encourages the manufacturers to take advantage of recognized standards. Approval by the FDA requires that the device be shown to be both *safe* and *effective*. Alternatively, manufacturers can follow the FDA guidance *Use of Standards in Substantial Equivalence Determinations* [30] to demonstrate that the device they want to market is 'substantially equivalent' to a device already approved.

In order to market medical devices in Canada, manufacturers must be authorized and approved by the *Canadian Medical Devices Bureau* of the *Therapeutic Products Directorate* (TPD) for their safety, effectiveness and quality. TPD is a Directorate within *Health Canada*, and the legal structure is defined by the *Food and Drugs Act* and *Medical Devices Regulations* (SOR/98-282). TPD also publishes several guidance documents to assist in the interpretation of policies and governing statutes and regulations. For example, the TPD *Guidance Document on Recognition and Use of Standards* under the Medical Devices Regulation lists recognized standards for MDS.

In Europe, the Medical Device Directive (MDD) 93/42/EEC and its latest amendment MDD 2007/47/EC regulate the implementation of MDS. Some ISO/IEC standards cover the development process and quality aspects of MDS. They are all recognized by regulatory agencies depicted in Figure 1.

2.2   Review of Existing Requirements Templates

There are several published requirements templates [15,23,9,27,4,2,20] in the literature. However, as commented in [11], "the needs of organisations working on different projects can, and do, vary", and unfortunately none of these templates can fully satisfy the needs of quality requirements documents for MDS. For example, the above templates fall short in helping to guide the requirements analyst in documenting safety requirements or making sure that the requirements specification contains all the elements needed to comply with the applicable regulations and standards. Unlike other industries, the agencies that regulate medical devices mentioned above have not provided documentation templates for requirements or any other software life cycle processes.

IEEE Standard 830-1998 [15] provides a template along with detailed recommended practice for software requirements specification. It has been one of the most important references for software industrial and academic projects. One important feature of the IEEE template is that the specific (functional) requirements can be structured in several ways (e.g., using system modes or use-cases). The Volere template [23] is a general purpose requirements template It emphasizes project requirements. Three sections, project drivers, project constraints, and project issues, give detailed coverage on issues related to contractual matters and understanding between different stakeholders, which makes it unique among templates in this respect. The shortcoming of the Volere template compared with the IEEE one is that the functional requirements part is general without clear guidance on organization. More importantly, there is a common problem with the two templates that they are short on means to support hazard identification and safety requirements, which are vital in the development of MDS.

The European Space Agency provides a set of Software Engineering Standards, PSS-05-0. A requirements specification that is compliant with this standard ought to include a *user requirement document* (URD), targeted at non-technical audiences such as users and project managers. It should also include a *software requirements document* (SRD) that is intended for use by designers and developers. In an effort to pursue homogeneity across space organizations in Europe, the *European Cooperation for Space Standardisation* (ECSS) replaced the PSS standard family with a new set of standards. ECSS-E-40C [9] is the ECSS standard for software engineering and is based on ISO/IEC 12207 for general software life cycle processes. To be compliant with ECSS-E-40, an *interface requirements document* (IRD) and a *software requirements specification* (SRS) are needed. The new standard is closely related to its ancestor, the PSS standard in the following ways: 1) the division of the requirements specification into IRD and SRS is similar to the division into URD and SRD in PSS-05-0; 2) the prescribed content could be traced back to the PSS standards; 3) the shortcomings are common: a) the SRS template requires that functional requirements shall be organized by subject and links to system states and modes shall be provided. Other than that, there is no further guidance; b) explanations of content to be filled into each sub-sections are still too general (high level) and could cause confusion.

We have found several other requirements templates and requirements guidelines that we now describe briefly. The U.S. Federal Aviation Administration provides a set of recommended practices on how to collect, write, validate, and organize requirements in its *Requirements Engineering Management Handbook* [27], targeted at real-time, embedded systems and, specifically, the avionics industry. The A-7E software requirements document [4] was a result of a joint project of the Naval Research Laboratory and the Naval Weapons Center to re-engineer the A-7 *operational flight program*. The software was rebuilt by applying numerous software engineering techniques such as modularity and information hiding, formal specification and abstract interfaces, to mention a few. In addition, Ahmadi [2] and Lai [20] proposed respectively, requirements templates for manufacturing systems and scientific computation. These references, though specific to a particular industry, provide useful guidance for our proposed template.

In summary, the existing templates are typically used in non-medical applications domains. We need to tailor the existing templates to medical devices, taking into account medical device specifics and the regulatory requirements.

3 Objectives for a Robust MDS Requirements Template

Similar to designing systems, designing a requirements template for MDS starts with a list of design objectives. Their purpose is to specify which characteristics of the template are to be achieved. In this section, we present and discuss the list of objectives that we think are necessary for the sought template.

Compliance with the Regulations and Standards

MDS regulatory systems consist of regulations adopted into law through whatever legislative or administrative procedures are appropriate to the legal system in place.

The public expectations and the dependability and safety of MDSs are embodied in the regulations to ensure that they perform as expected. For instance, the FDA regulation *21 CFR* (discussed in Section 2.1) describes the responsibilities of medical device manufacturer. Also, the FDA proposes guidelines on how developers should present the software content of premarket submissions for approval and clearance. Submissions are made to FDA to demonstrate that the device to be marketed is safe and effective.

Regulations cannot include details of technical methods and evaluation criteria. Therefore, standards are proposed to provide this level of details. They are more technical documents that rely on significant input from technical experts and participants on standards committees are often from the industry to be regulated, and who may have financial interests in the items covered. There are several standards for the requirements of medical devices. However, while they contain recommendations on the general approach to produce MDSs, they do not prescribe the explicit content of the requirements document. The decision on how to package the requirements is left to the user of the standard. For example, we read in IEC62304 [13, Page 14], "The MANUFACTURER of MEDICAL DEVICE SOFTWARE shall demonstrate the ability to provide MEDICAL DEVICE SOFTWARE that consistently meets customer requirements and applicable regulatory requirements."

In summary, the template has to satisfy the following objectives:

Objective 1. *The template should guide the elicitation of the requirements governed by the relevant regulations and standards.*

Sections in the template should help capture and document requirements coming from the regulations and the standards, and list all the regulations that apply to the targeted markets. The template should provide means to trace the regulations and the standards to sections in the template. The structure should enable requirements engineers or analysts to locate what information must be collected in order to comply with the applicable regulations and standards.

System Approach to the Elicitation of the Requirements

In fields such as aeronautics it has been observed [21,34] that system factors for accidents result from dysfunctional interactions among components, not from individual component failure. This kind of accident is referred to as a *system accident*. Each of the components operates according to its specification, but the combined behaviours leads to a dysfunctional system. A quick look at the FDA MAUDE database shows that the situation is similar for medical devices. It has been reported [34] that accidents involving software often occur within an engineering culture that has unrealistic expectations about software and the use of computers. Providing a structured way to document the requirements can help overcome some aspects of this culture. It would help engineers establish the safety and effectiveness of the medical device that contains software components. Moreover, all the standards for the development of medical devices that we consulted [29] clearly indicate a system approach to the elicitation and documentation of the requirements of medical devices. For instance, we read in IEC62304 [13, Page 18] "For each SOFTWARE SYSTEM of the MEDICAL DEVICE, the MANUFACTURER shall define and document SOFTWARE SYSTEM requirements from the

SYSTEM level requirements." Hence, any proposed template should be structured to facilitate the system approach to the requirements elicitation and documentation. The system approach is one of the objectives that a template suitable for documenting the requirements for medical devices has to satisfy.

Objective 2. *The template should guide the elicitation of the requirements from several system perspectives. Each perspective should be the viewpoint of one of the system's environment actor, or partner applications or systems.*

The observed behaviour of an open system is governed by the stimuli it gets from its environment [19]. The actors in a system environment interact with the system and affect its behaviour. The system responds to the stimuli from these actors. There are some stimuli that are particular as they are not a response to a previous stimulus. They are without apparent cause and initiate a sequence of action and reaction between the system and the actors of its environment. These special stimuli are commonly referred to as *business events* and we call each of them an *initiator-event* (IE). A technique for requirements elicitation is to identify both the actors (or at least the most relevant ones) of the system's environment and the major initiator-events that affect the system. A template that guides the elicitation of the requirements from several system perspectives ought to be structured to capture the requirements from each influential actor in the system environment and that with regard to each IE that is relevant to the system. This approach helps to conquer the complexity and largeness of systems; any system is looked at from the perspectives of its environment actors and with regard to an IE. A perspective of requirements would constitute a use-case or a scenario that give the actor-system interactions to fulfill the set of behaviours demanded by the considered IE.

Each Section Should Encapsulate Only One Concern

This objective is about the application of the principle of separation of concerns, which is a means to achieving information hiding. Each section in the template should address a separate concern. A concern in the functional requirements could be an IE or a mode as perceived by one of the actors or stakeholder in the system's environment. The application of this principle enhances modularity, where each module (i.e., section in the template) has a set of cohesive requirements that are lowly coupled to the rest of the requirements in the document. Therefore, the obtained document will exhibit desirable properties such as modifiability, non-redundancy, verifiability, and ease of validation.

Objective 3. *The decomposition of the template should be based on the principle of separation of concerns.*

For the functional requirements, if we adopt the decomposition of the requirements based on initiator-events, we are going to have a decomposition that satisfies the above objective. Any change in the environment is relative to an actor and that with regard to an IE. To ensure this principle in the nonfunctional requirements, we ought to have a fine grained decomposition of each of the expected overall qualities of the system. For instance, the security requirements, should be decomposed into access requirements, integrity requirements, privacy requirements, audit requirements, and immunity (prevention) requirements. Each of these sub-classes of security requirements can be decomposed further, which helps to better separate the several security concerns.

Capturing Safety Requirements

This objective aims at ensuring that we document all the known and foreseen hazards and their mitigating measures. A hazard is the potential source of harm, which is a physical injury or a damage to property or the environment [18]. IEC 62304 [13, Sec 4.2] states that "the MANUFACTURER shall apply a RISK MANAGEMENT PROCESS complying with ISO 14971". The term risk refers to the combination of the probability of occurrence of harm and the severity of that harm [18]. Usually in risk management an emphasis is put on the most likely risks. Analysts prioritize risks to be prevented based on their probabilities of occurrence. However, we are cautious to propose prioritization based on probabilities for the following reasons. Estimating the probability of occurrence of a harm is quite difficult and often inaccurate when dealing with critical systems in general and medical software in particular. The other reason is that unlikely to happen harm can have extremely damaging and irreversible consequences. Therefore, we think that the only criterion on whether to consider a risk or not is based on whether we can technically come up with the appropriate mitigating measures. Hence, we should consider all risks regardless of their probabilities. The *deviations* of European harmonized ISO 14971 from the original international standard support our recommendation. Indeed, Deviation 1 indicates that manufacturers should not discard negligible risks, and Deviation 2 disallows manufacturers to decide the acceptability of risks. The risks left without control measures due to technical infeasibility of the measures are called *residual risks*. The user should be clearly notified that the medical device does not cope with them. Indeed, Derivation 7 of ISO 14971 [17, Page 7] states "users shall be informed about the residual risks" and that "manufacturers shall not attribute any additional risk reduction to the information given to the users." We need to keep in mind that economic considerations of mitigating measures are inappropriate in considering risks with MDS. European harmonized ISO 14971 in Deviation 3 [17, Page 7] requires reducing risks as far as possible as opposed to as low as reasonably practicable.

We call an IE that leads to a risk a *Risk Initiator-Event* (RIE). The common sources for gathering RIEs are accident and incident reports documented for previous version of the medical device or for similar medical devices. For instance, FDA *Manufacturer and User Facility Device Experience* (MAUDE) database [28] contains a large number of reports that can be used for gathering RIEs. In identifying these events, one needs to keep in mind their root cause. For instance, if the RIE is "Patient is having blurred vision" the requirement for the mitigation mechanisms would be ineffective and vague: prescribe new set of glasses, or see the doctor, or have a blood test, etc. Whereas, if the root cause is "Patient is having blurred vision due to low level of glucose in the blood", then the requirements for mitigating actions would be easily articulated. Ideally, the analysts should reach a one-to-one mapping between the RIEs and the risks for which a specific functional requirement is documented.

Analysts should hold RIE workshops where different stakeholders brainstorm and discuss possible RIEs. Then, they should refine them to relate them to relevant root causes, and document requirements for the appropriate responses to handle or at least mitigate their affects. The literature abounds with techniques for analyzing and discovering safety related hazards [7] that can be attributed to safety risks. ISO 14971 recommends traditional techniques like *Fault Tree Analysis* (FTA), *Failure Mode and*

Effects Analysis (FMEA). The more recent *System-Theoretic Process Analysis* (STPA), proposed by Leveson [21], considers new causal factors, which are not handled by the traditional techniques, including design errors like software flaws, component interaction accidents, and human decision-making errors.

Ranking risks eases the management and documenting the requirements of a portfolio of complex risks. For this purpose we need to carefully breakdown risks into simple (not too long) risk scenarios. For this purpose, the requirements analyst and the stakeholders need to identify a set of RIEs and evaluation criteria. The ranking is done by combining the evaluations of RIEs against set criteria into a single risk score. This approach helps in dealing with systems with a high degree of complexity. It is flexible for any type of risk and may be used with a variety of quantitative and qualitative evaluation criteria. However, it has several disadvantages such as requiring significant effort in establishing RIEs and evaluation criteria. It requires significant effort in breaking down risk events into many elementary RIEs related to their root causes as described above.

Once we have a list of RIEs, we need to assess the severity of the risk that can be reached from each risk initiator-even. A class is assigned to each level of severity. For instance, IEC 62304 [13] requires "The MANUFACTURER shall assign to each SOFTWARE SYSTEM a software safety class (A, B, or C) according to the possible effects on the patient, operator, or other people", Class A, B, and C are based on the severity of the effects: for a system of Class A, "No injury or damage to health is possible", while for Class C, "Death or SERIOUS INJURY is possible".

The risks of a system are dependent on its scope. It is extremely important that the scope of the system be carefully defined as well as its components, users, and partner applications. All of them can trigger RIEs , and the requirements must document the reaction of the medical device to each RIE .

Objective 4. *The template should guide documenting the safety RIEs that are handled by the device and support their ranking. As well, it should support articulating the device/environment interactions in response to these safety RIEs.*

Capturing Security Requirements

It is commonly believed that the most secure system is a closed system. The sources of the most serious security threats to a system come from its environment. Figure 2 illustrates the environment of a medical device. It includes several kind of actors: the legitimate users of the device, the partner application and systems, and other actors that might exist in the device environment such as hackers or illegal users. To ensure device security, we need to make sure that all the device environment actors do not misuse common assets of the device such as data stores (e.g., registers, files), and channels of communication that it uses for internal or external communication. Explicit access policies ought to be articulated in the requirements to clearly assign each of the legitimate users to a security class that enables her to have specified access rights to the device common assets. Also, we need to make sure that no environmental actor can change the prescribed behaviour of the device or affect its overall qualities (nonfunctional requirements). To achieve this goal, we need to require that all the functional requirements of the software and hardware comprising the device are space complete; we have explicit prescribed behaviour for every possible device state-space.

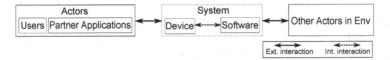

Fig. 2. Software Intensive Medical Device and its Environment

To ensure the secure use of the device data stores, the template needs to guide the analyst to document the requirements on the confidentiality policies, the measures for the prevention of unauthorized data leakage, the detection of unauthorized usage of data, and for the recovery of any data lost or corruptions by malice or unintended error, such as transmission errors. Mechanisms for recovery or detection could necessitate the requirements of their corresponding auditing mechanisms.

To secure the device's overall properties, the template ought to help identify all the system-environment shared resources such as communication channels, or any shared hardware or software elements. The template should help document the fair and legitimate sharing of these common resources. In other terms, the analyst ought to document the liveness properties regarding the access to these resources. Any request from authorized users ought to be granted within a reasonable time or the device needs to be put in a safe and secure space-state. The time period prescribed for a reasonable access to a shared resource needs to be clearly specified. These requirements will help avoid denial of service for a user or a partner application that might put the patient health in danger.

We call the data stores and the shared resources *threat targets*; they are targeted by the security threats. The template as explained above ought to help document the security requirements for a secure access and use of each of these threat targets. For each one of them, it should allocate a section that encompasses the requirements for prevention of, detection of, and recovery from security threats targeting it.

Objective 5. *The template should guide documenting the device's threat targets and specify the reasonable time for accessing the resources it shares with the environment. It should provide the needed requirements for a thorough security assessment according to Common Criteria for Information Technology Security Evaluation Models (e.g., [1, Fig 5, Page 60]).*

Capturing Privacy Requirements

Privacy essentially deals with the question how to preserve and protect all information that can be used to identify the user. It is related to the security aspects specially to the confidentiality aspect. However, when we discuss the privacy issue, we are focusing on *personally identifiable information*. It includes all information that is connected directly or indirectly to the user personally. When dealing with MDS, especially in the case of the Implantable Medical Devices (IMD), the following concerns rise [12]:

1. Whether a patient has a Medical Device (MD) or not should remain protected from unauthorized users. These users should not be able to determine that a patient is using a MD. This requirement prevents patients using medical devices from being targeted either by curious parties or by criminals that could harm them by interfering with their devices.

2. Unauthorized parties should not be able to link a specific-device identifying feature (e.g., device Identification Number) to the user. This requirement is to prevent compromising the user identity and might lead to compromising other Personally identifiable information such as the user's location.

3. All the standards and regulations regarding of the privacy of medical data should be taken into account, e.g., IEC 62443 [14] is recognized by FDA for medical devices [29]. These standards are about any data gathered about patients and about all the measurements taken regarding their health. Usually, a MD generates patient data intended for diagnosis and monitoring of the state of the patient. This data could be in many instances considered as private data that can be used to identify the user as individual or to reveal information about her health.

Some of the above issues are already covered by the security objective as they deal with the authorised access to the data in the device and its partner applications data stores. However, due to technical or performance reasons, we might not be able to ensure strict control on all the common assets of the device (e.g., registers, files, communication channels). This privacy objective puts emphasis on the importance of securing some information that might lead to breach of the privacy of the user.

Objective 6. *The template should guide documenting the privacy requirements that ensure the protection of the user's personally identifiable information.*

Template Provides Several Presentation Views

The requirements content that a template helps document is intended for diverse stakeholders. For instance, some users and project managers would need non-technical requirements giving a very general presentation of the device. While, designers and other technical stakeholders would require very technical content. The template needs to help get requirements that can be presented at several technical levels. For instance, a requirements specification that is compliant with the PSS-05-0 standard should include a *user requirements document* that targets non-technical audiences and a *software requirements document* that is intended for technical stakeholders. A template for documenting MDS ought to capture the material relevant for different presentation views.

The functional requirements part of a requirements template can be organised in several ways. For instance, the requirements could be organised by (IE, Viewpoint, Use-case) or by (Viewpoint, IE, Use-case). These ways of organizing this part of the requirements are isomorphic, and therefore one organization can be obtained from another. In practice, we notice that one representation could lead to a sparse document where some sections are empty. On the other hand, an isomorphic representation to the sparse document gives a more compact document.

Objective 7. *The template should help formally document the functional requirements, while at the same time help document requirements intended for non-technical users. The formalism should at least support formal and automated verification of the space completeness, and the dictionary (i.e., naming) and behaviour consistency of the functional requirements.*

Supporting a Family Approach to Document the Requirements

One important dilemma faced by developers of MDSs is the following. On the one hand, we seek systems that are simple, and carry the needed functionality, no more no less. This minimality objective is sought in all critical systems. A module or element that is not essentially needed could interfere with the rest of the system and lead to a failure. On the other hand, we have several classes of users of a MDS. For instance, an insulin pump for children should have common features with one for adults, but could have other features relevant only to children. One can think about having one pump that includes all the features possible for an insulin pump but configurable for each specific patient. However, it is against the minimality condition in building critical and dependable systems. Therefore, we should adopt a family approach to the development of MDSs. Software product family engineering proposes techniques and processes that enable us to focus on the commonality and variability among the members of a MDS family. The template should at least provide the feature model of the MDS family and clearly capture the characteristics of each member of a product family or subfamily. It is widely reported in the literature that a family approach to software development in general helps to deal with unexpected changes to the requirements. The MDS industry is heavily regulated, which leads to unexpected changes in the requirements of MDS due to changes in the regulations. Hence, we should have the following objective.

Objective 8. *The template should support a family approach to document software medical devices.*

4   A Structure for a Template Satisfying the Objectives

Based on the objectives given in the previous section, we propose a template that has the structure given in appendix A. In the proposed template we adopted the features of the surveyed templates that are appropriate for MDS. We started from the template proposed in [2]. Then, we amended it to satisfy the objectives presented above to remedy the limitations of the other templates found in the literature [15,23,9,27,4,2,20]. Table 1 traces the sections of the proposed template structure to the design objectives.

Table 1. Tracing Sections in the template to the design objectives

Obj. 1	Obj. 2	Obj. 3	Obj. 4	Obj. 5	Obj. 6	Obj. 7	Obj. 8
Sec. 2.6 & 7	Sec. 5 & 6	Sec. 5 & 6	Sec. 6	Sec. 8	Sec. 9	Sec. 5 & 6	Sec. 2 & 3

An open source tool called *SMART II* [3] that supports the proposed template structure has been developed. It is an amended version of the tool *SMART* [2]. This Java-based user-friendly tool stores requirements in XML with access control mechanisms, and it can generate a full requirements specification in RTF and PDF formats and enables math formulae and tabular expressions written in LATEX. This tool provides mechanisms to control the access and the modification of the requirements, audit the changes to all the sections of the requirements document, and makes it easy to document and retrieve requirements. In summary, the proposed template, supported by a user-friendly tool, helps capture requirements and reduce errors in the development of MDS.

5   Conclusions and Future Work

Documenting the requirements for MDSs is a very challenging task due to the nature of the systems to be built and the stringent regulatory rules that need to be followed. These systems ought to exhibit the highest dependability qualities such as safety, security, and availability. A systematic approach to tackle the gathering and documentation of the requirements of the system in general is usually very desirable. However, we think that it is a must for MDS . In this paper we presented the objectives for designing a suitable requirements template for MDS . We do not claim that the list of proposed objectives is complete. They are in our view the essential and the most pressing objectives for a suitable template for MDS . We perceive that the proposed template is a work in progress. It can be taken as an initial scheme for formatting a requirements document and for guiding analysts in their quest of getting the information needed to build a dependable MDS. We provide as well a software system that can be used to automate the production of the MDS requirements document based on the proposed template.

The tool that we developed requires other supporting tools to automate the formal verification of the requirements. They will be needed to discover all the implicit requirements in order to document them properly and make sure that our requirements are complete and consistent. Other partner tools and techniques [25] will be needed to help trace the requirements to the regulations. We are working on building these tools.

References

1. Common Criteria for Information Technology Security Evaluation, Part 1: Introduction and General Model (September 2012),
   http://www.commoncriteriaportal.org/cc/
2. Ahmadi, M.: Requirements Documentation for Manufacturing Systems: Template and Management Tool. Master's thesis, McMaster University (September 2006)
3. Ahmadi, M., Tounsi, N., Khedri, R., Chen, Y., Wang, H., Huang, M.: SMART II. A Tool for the Documentation of Software Requirements Specification (August 2014), (Available for download under the GNU General Public License)
   http://www.cas.mcmaster.ca/~khedri/?page_id=460
4. Alspaugh, T.A., Faulk, S.R., Britton, K.H., Parker, R.A., Parnas, D.L.: Software Requirements for the A-7E Aircraft. Tech. rep., Naval Research Lab (1992)
5. Chen, Y., Lawford, M., Wang, H., Wassyng, A.: Insulin Pump Software Certification. In: Gibbons, J., MacCaull, W. (eds.) FHIES 2013. LNCS, vol. 8315, pp. 87–106. Springer, Heidelberg (2014)
6. Dooren, J.C.: FDA Sees Increasing Number Of Insulin Pump Problems. Wall Street Journal (March 2010),
   http://online.wsj.com/article/
   SB10001424052748703862704575099961829258070.html
7. Ericson, C.A.: Hazard Analysis Techniques for System Safety. Wiley-Interscience (2005)
8. European Co-ordination of Notified Bodies Medical Devices: European NB-MED Recommendation 2.2 on Council Directives 90/385/EEC, 93/42/EEC and 98/79/EC (June 2001)
9. European Cooperation for Space Standardisation: ECSS-E-ST-40C: Standard on Space Engineering – Software general requirements (2009)
10. Faris, T.H.: Safe and Sound Software: Creating an Efficient and Effective Quality System for Software Medical Device Organizations. ASQ Quality Press (2006)

11. Giakoumakis, E., Xylomenos, G.: Evaluation and Selection Criteria for Software Requirements Specification Standards. Software Engineering Journal 11(5), 307–319 (1996)
12. Halperin, D., Kohno, T., Heydt-Benjamin, T.S., Fu, K., Maisel, W.H.: Security and Privacy for Implantable Medical Devices. IEEE Pervasive Computing 7(1), 30–39 (2008)
13. IEC 62304: Medical Device Software – Software Life Cycle Processes (May 2006)
14. IEC 62443: Industrial communication networks–Network and system security
15. IEEE Standard: IEEE Recommended Practice for Software Requirements Specifications. IEEE Std 830-1998 (June 1998)
16. Institute of Medicine: Medical Devices and the Public's Health: The FDA 510(k) Clearance Process at 35 Years. The National Academies Press (2011)
17. ISO 14971:2007: Medical devices – Application of Risk Management to Medical Devices (2007)
18. ISO/IEC Guide 51:1999: Safety aspects – Guidelines for their inclusion in standards (1999)
19. Jaskolka, J., Khedri, R., Zhang, Q.: Endowing Concurrent Kleene Algebra with Communication Actions. In: Höfner, P., Jipsen, P., Kahl, W., Müller, M.E. (eds.) RAMiCS 2014. LNCS, vol. 8428, pp. 19–36. Springer, Heidelberg (2014)
20. Lai, L.: Requirements Documentation for Engineering Mechanics Software. Master's thesis, McMaster University (2004)
21. Leveson, N.: Engineering a Safer World: Applying Systems Thinking to Safety. MIT Press (2012)
22. Networking and Information Technology Research and Development Program (NITRD): High-Confidence Medical Devices: Cyber-Physical Systems for 21st Century Health Care. Tech. rep. (2009)
23. Robertson, J., Robertson, S.: Volere Requirements Specification Template (August 2007)
24. Robertson, J.: The trials of a diabetic hacker. Bloomberg Businessweek (February 2012),
    http://www.businessweek.com/articles/2012-02-23/
    the-trials-of-a-diabetic-hacker
25. Singh, N.K., Wang, H., Lawford, M., Maibaum, T.S.E., Wassyng, A.: Formalizing the Glucose Homeostasis Mechanism. In: Duffy, V.G. (ed.) DHM 2014. LNCS, vol. 8529, pp. 460–471. Springer, Heidelberg (2014)
26. The Council Of The European Communities: Council Directive 93/42/EEC concerning medical devices (June 1993)
27. U.S. Federal Aviation Administration: DOT/FAA/AR-08/32. Requirements Engineering Management Handbook (June 2009)
28. U.S. Food and Drug Administration: Manufacturer and User Facility Device Experience Database, http://www.accessdata.fda.gov/scripts/cdrh/cfdocs/
    cfmaude/search.cfm
29. U.S. Food and Drug Administration: Recognized Consensus Standards Database,
    http://www.accessdata.fda.gov/scripts/cdrh/cfdocs/
    cfStandards/search.cfm
30. U.S. Food and Drug Administration: Guidance for Industry and for FDA Staff: Use of Standards in Substantial Equivalence Determinations (March 2000)
31. U.S. Food and Drug Administration: General Principles of Software Validation; Final Guidance for Industry and FDA Staff (January 2002)
32. U.S. Food and Drug Administration: Guidance for the Content of Premarket Submissions for Software Contained in Medical Devices (May 2005)
33. Vogel, D.A.: Medical Device Software Verification, Validation, and Compliance. Artech House (2011)
34. Weiss, K., Leveson, N., Lundqvist, K., Farid, N., Stringfellow, M.: An Analysis of Causation in Aerospace Accidents. In: DASC 2001: The 20th Conference on Digital Avionics Systems, vol. 1, pp. 4A3/1–4A3/12 (2001)
35. Wiegers, K.E., Beatty, J.: Software Requirements, 3rd edn. (August 2013)

A SRS Template for Product Family

Revision history
1. Introduction
  1.1 Document Purpose
  1.2 Abbreviations and Acronyms
  1.3 References
  1.4 Document Organization
2. General Family Description
  2.1 Medical Condition (Pathology)
  2.2 Family Purpose
  2.3 Family Scope
  2.4 Family Context
  2.5 User Characteristics
  2.6 Standards and Regulations to Comply with
3. Family Model
  3.1 Feature Models
  3.2 Constraints on Family Views
  3.3 Constraints and Assumptions on Ext. Entities
4. Non-functional Requirements
  4.1 Accuracy Requirements
  4.2 Performance Requirements
  4.3 Maintainability Requirements
  4.4 Look and Feel Requirements
  4.5 Usability Requirements
  4.6 Portability Requirements
  4.7 Life cycle Requirements
  4.8 Others
5. Functional Requirements (device main purpose)
  5.1 Normal Event 1
    5.1.1 Viewpoint 1
      5.1.1.1 Use Case
  ...
6. Safety Functional Requirements
  6.1 Risk Events
    6.1.1 Class C

      6.1.1.1 Risk Event 1
        6.1.1.1.1 Viewpoint 1
        6.1.1.1.2 Use Case
    6.1.2 Class B
  ...
  6.2 Residual Risks
    6.2.1 Class C
      6.2.1.1 Risk 1
        6.2.1.1.1 Description
        6.2.1.1.2 Tech constraints
  ...
7. Security and Privacy Regulations
8. Security Requirements
  8.1 Data Stores
    8.1.1 ST for Data Store 1
      8.1.1.1 ST Introduction
      8.1.1.2 Conformance Claims
      8.1.1.3 Security Problem Def
      8.1.1.4 Security Objectives
      8.1.1.5 Security Requirements
      8.1.1.6 TOE Summary Spec
  ...
  8.2 Shared Resources
    8.2.1 ST for Shared Resource 1
  ...
9. Privacy Requirements
  9.1 Mechanisms for anonymizing users
  9.2 Mechanisms for protecting users from attacks
10. Traceability Matrices
  10.1 Traceability to Regulations and Standards
11. Open Issues
12. Waiting Room
13. Expected Possible Changes
  13.1 Fundamental Assumptions

Combining Static and Dynamic Impact Analysis for Large-Scale Enterprise Systems

Wen Chen, Alan Wassyng, and Tom Maibaum

McMaster Centre for Software Certification,
McMaster University, Hamilton, Ontario, Canada
{chenw36,wassyng}@mcmaster.ca, tom@maibaum.org

Abstract. Software changes and their impact on large-scale enterprise systems are critical, hard to identify and calculate. A typical enterprise system may consist of hundreds of thousands of classes and methods. Thus it is extremely costly and difficult to apply conventional testing techniques to such a system. In our previous work [1], a conservative static analysis with the capability of dealing with inheritance was conducted on an enterprise system and associated changes to obtain all the potential impacts. However, since static analysis takes into account all the possible system behaviours, the analysis often results in a good number of *false-positives* and thus *over-estimation* of the impact on other methods in the system. This work focuses on extending our previous static approach by an *aspect-based* dynamic analysis, to instrument the system and collect a set of dynamic impacts at run-time. The new approach is still *safe*, but more *precise* than the static analysis. Safety is preserved since the static analysis serves as the input source to the dynamic analysis, and we are careful not to discard impacts unless we can show that they are definitely not impacted by the change. It is more precise since dynamic analysis examines behaviours that do definitely occur at run-time and hence is able to reflect the real impacts. Additionally, our analysis is able to handle the *scalability* issue. The targeted system is orders of magnitude larger than the system other existing approaches can deal with. A case study was conducted to illustrate that specific objectives can be attained.

Keywords: Large-scale Enterprise Systems, Impact Analysis, Static Analysis, Dependency Graph, Dynamic Analysis, Instrumentation, Aspect-oriented Programming, AspectJ, Regression Testing.

1 Introduction

Enterprise systems are commercial software packages that enable the integration of transaction-oriented data and business processes throughout an organization. They are gaining popularity in organizations all over the world. Take ERP (Enterprise Resource Planning) systems as an example. By 1998, approximately 40% of companies with annual revenues of more than $1 billion had implemented

A. Jedlitschka et al. (Eds.): PROFES 2014, LNCS 8892, pp. 224–238, 2014.

ERP systems [2]. One of the largest enterprise vendors, SAP, had 2012 revenue of 16.22 billion Euros [3]. Among SAP product lines, SAP Business One Operation, Financials and Human Resources has over 40,000 customers. Enterprise systems are clearly a common phenomenon in the IT marketplace, with fast growing needs.

Some crucial characteristics of enterprise systems are:

1. Scalable. The size of typical enterprise systems is extremely large. For instance, Oracle Corporation's *E-Business Suite* consists of a collection of ERP, CRM, SCM computer applications either developed or acquired by Oracle. The total number of classes in release 11.5 is around 200 thousand, and the total number of methods is over 4.6 million.
2. Complex. Since the richness of functionalities in enterprise systems, it's not trivial to fully understand how the components within the system communicate.
3. Critical. In spite of scalability, complication, enterprise system plays a critical role in organizations, they can reflect the actual business process, information flows, reporting, data analytic, etc. It's critical to implement all the modules correctly and maintain it in a safe and efficient way.
4. Costly. It is estimated that "Large companies can also spend $50 million to $100 million on software upgrades. Full implementation of all modules can take years" [4].

As a consequence of these characteristics, these systems can also often be classified as *legacy systems* and are poorly understood and difficult to maintain.

Software changes are inevitable and *change impact analysis* is a key approach in analyzing software changes or potential changes and in identifying the software objects the changes might affect [5]. Organizations need a change impact analysis tool to identify the impacts of a change after or even before making a change. If the impacts can be obtained even before applying the change, it enables the organization to make test plans or to run tests in advance, saving the lag between system deployment and release. By using the identified impacts, organizations can know what to test, instead of having to run all their existing tests, and can augment the test suite to cover software entities that are affected but not covered in the existing test suite.

Static analysis examines program code and reasons over all possible behaviours that might arise at run-time. Typically, static analysis is conservative and sound. Soundness guarantees that analysis results are an accurate description of the program's behaviour, no matter what inputs or in what environment the program is run. Conservatism means reporting weaker properties that are guaranteed to be true, preserving soundness, but may not be strong enough to be useful [6]. For example, in our case, the static analysis reports all impacts possible, which includes the complete set of inherited sub-classes, even though many of those sub-classes will not be affected in a particular case.

Dynamic analysis operates by executing a program and observing the executions. The dynamic information consists of execution data for a specific set of program executions, such as executions in the *field*, executions based on an *operational profile*, or executions of *test cases*. Apiwattanapong *et al.* [7] defines the dynamic impact set to be the subset of program entities that are affected by the changes during at least one of the considered program executions. It is precise because no approximation or abstraction needs to be performed. The analysis examines the actual run-time behaviour of the program, and so the control-flow paths that were taken during those executions are known. Another benefit over static analysis in the context of object-oriented software is the exposure of object identities and the actual resolution of late binding. A drawback is that in dynamic analysis the results obtained are valid only for the scenarios that were exercised during the analysis.

Our contributions in this work are: (1) We have developed a multi-tasking, aspect-oriented instrumentor to adequately instrument large-scale systems and collect traces at bytecode level; (2) We have successfully combined static analysis and dynamic analysis, providing both safety and improved precision; (3) We have empirically demonstrated the practical applicability of the improved approach on a very large enterprise system involving hundreds of thousands of classes.

2   Related Work

Apiwattanapong *et al.* [7] pointed out that static impact analysis algorithms often come up with impact sets that are too large to be useful, due to their over conservative assumptions. For example, regression testing techniques that use impact analysis to identify which parts of the program to retest after a change would have to retest most of the program. Therefore, recently, researchers have investigated and defined impact analysis techniques that rely on dynamic, rather than static, information about program behaviour [8,9].

The dynamic information consists of execution data for a specific set of program executions, such as executions in the field, executions based on an operational profile, or executions of test suites. `CoverageImpact` [9] and `PathImpact` [8] are two well known dynamic impact analysis approaches that use this information. `PathImpact` works at the method level and uses compressed execution traces to compute impact sets. `CoverageImpact` also works at the method level but it uses coverage, rather than trace, information to compute impact sets. However they are not suitable for enterprise systems. For instance, the coverage-based instrumentation that collects dynamic data from either field execution or test case execution, is not suitable because:

- Field execution requires the collection of users' executions of methods in the set of changes, and this is often not available, since methods may have been newly added to introduce new functionalities. After changes have been applied to the system, there is no way to collect the information concerning executions of the new methods. In addition, the coverage information in the collection will be inaccurate.
- Due to the size of enterprise systems, it is extremely unrealistic to collect users' executions in a continuous way. Orso *et al.* [9], with the aid of 12 users,

spent 12 weeks to collect 1,100 executions on a program JABA which consists of 550 classes and 2,800 methods. For enterprise systems, the number of classes can easily exceed 100,000, which is nearly 200 times the size reported in JABA. To collect user information on such systems is very time consuming, and may be even longer than rerunning the entire regression test suite.

In all these dynamic approaches, one of the most important tasks is to instrument the program in an appropriate way. We can divide the instrumentation into two categories: (1) those which simulate, emulate, or translate the application code, and (2) those which instrument the application code. SPIM [10], Shade [11] and more recently Pin [12], Soot [13] fall into the first type in which the original code was simulated or transformed to some *intermediate representation* to be processed. On the other hand, tools like ATUM [14] and more recently BCEL [15], AspectJ [16] and InsECTJ [17] fall into the other type, where the application code is executed and in the meantime runtime information is collected.

Instrumentation tools in the first category requires extra computing time and space resources to accomplish the simulation, emulation or translation. For instance, Soot provides four intermediate representations for code: Baf, Jimple, Shimple and Grimp [13]. The representations provide different levels of abstraction on the represented code and are targeted at different uses. This tool works perfectly for small or medium programs, but when it comes to systems of the size of enterprise systems, it runs out of memory quickly since an intermediate representation is required for each class. Instrumentation tools in the first category are not a viable choice in solving our problem.

3   Research Motivation

The complexity and large-scale of an enterprise system make it impossible for a tester to adequately comprehend the impact of changes, and often results in high costs, over-estimation and/or under-estimation. The majority of testing work is dependent on the tester's domain knowledge, which makes the testing results very risky to rely on. There has been extensive research work on conventional impact analysis approaches, but they do not deal adequately with the scale of enterprise systems or provide a good solution in terms of both safety and precision. We observed that there is great potential in combining static and dynamic approaches in analyzing change impacts. Static analysis considers all possible software behaviours which may result in imprecision, but it provides a conservative way to assess the impacts that lead to soundness and safety. Also, as software impact analysis often works for regression testing and test selection, it can be used to jointly determine whether changes made on the system have been fully covered by a user's test suite. It is important that no necessary impacts are omitted. Starting with an abstract model of the state of the program, dynamic analysis can be used to make the analysis more precise. Thus our research motivation is to investigate the possibility of combining static and dynamic analysis to achieve: (1) the preservation of both safety and precision; and (2) the capability of dealing with extremely large enterprise systems.

4   Static Analysis

In our previous work [1], a static impact analysis was conducted on a large-scale enterprise system. In particular, we built a *access dependency graph* to abstract a static graph representation of the system. Both calling dependencies and field dependencies were taken into account, and it was able to handle object-oriented features like inheritance and dynamic binding.

Most modern enterprise systems were written in an object-oriented language to encapsulate fields and methods, provide information hiding, etc. However, in analyzing the impacts of a change, object-oriented features can make the analysis more complex. We observed that many of the over-estimated impacts in the static analysis are caused by inheritance and dynamic binding. Surprisingly, vendors prefer to add or modify a feature by simply inheriting a parent method and then adding the new/changed functionality to the inherited method. For the sake of safety, one has to include all the possible superclasses in determining the dependencies. The method we use to construct an access dependency graph looks into each method invocation and only includes methods that have actually implemented parents' methods. Effectively it reduces the amount of dependencies we used to include.

However, even with the ability of dealing with inheritance and dynamic binding, the analysis may still contain a good number of false-positive for two resons: (1) many of the methods identified as impacted by the static analysis cannot be executed in real time; or (2) "impacted" methods may be possible, but cannot be affected. To make the results more precise, dynamic instrumentation of the system is needed.

5   Dynamic Analysis

Dynamic analysis is more efficient than static analysis, with respect to running time and precision in finding impacts, locating defects, etc. It requires run-time executions of the program to collect information such as field data, coverage, event traces, etc. Then software developers/testers can compute dynamic impacts of a change by identifying affected entities in the program. Even though a dynamic approach is more efficient, one cannot instrument the program to cover all feasible executions, so dynamic analysis often leads to under-estimation, and thus violates our quest for safety.

As mentioned earlier, coverage-based dynamic approaches are not suitable for us, while path-based approaches seems more practical and effective. However current path-based approaches [7,8] have a number of limitations that can lead to long running time and low precision, and one has to to have particular domain knowledge such as a full understanding of the application logic to conduct the instrumentation. Certain functions require certain inputs and a certain order of executions to make the instrumentation meaningful, which dramatically increases the difficulty and complexity. Long execution time is mainly caused by duplicate traces, even though compression algorithm or finer analysis (*e.g.*

execute-after) can be employed, it still requires a large amount of time that may almost equal running the entire regression suite.

Considering the pros and cons of static and dynamic analysis, and limits of current approaches, there exists a good potential of combining the two approaches to achieve a hybrid approach which is safe, precise but requires a smaller running time. Since our target systems are typically very critical, the first and most important consideration is *safety*. Hence an access dependency graph G can be used to capture all the potential impacts S and serves as the input source of dynamic analysis. Then we could run *aspect-oriented instrumentation* on each method in S. The major reason is, aspect-oriented instrumentation doesn't require any domain knowledge, nor test data. In the aspect we created, we define a *pointcut* for each method execution, as well as *advice* in collecting event traces from the method. In this way, we compute a set of dynamic impacts D which is essentially a subset of S, as well as a set of *potential over-estimated impacts* (PO): impacts that were not traversed by the instrumentation.

In the next section we briefly introduce the background of aspect-oriented programming and its popular implementation AspectJ, and then details of why and how we use it in instrumenting enterprise systems.

5.1 Aspect-Oriented Programming and AspectJ

Aspect-oriented programming. (AOP) [18] has been proposed as a technique for improving separation of concerns in software. AOP builds on previous technologies, including procedural programming and object-oriented programming, which have already made significant improvements in software modularity. Kiczales *et al.* [19] pointed out the central idea in AOP is that while the hierarchical modularity mechanisms of object-oriented languages are extremely useful, they are inherently unable to modularize all concerns of interest in complex systems. Instead, we believe that in the implementation of any complex system, there will be concerns that one would like to modularize, but for which the implementation will instead be diffused over a number of modules. This happens because the natural modularity of these concerns crosscuts the natural modularity of the rest of the implementation.

AOP does for concerns that are naturally crosscutting what OOP does for concerns that are naturally hierarchical. It provides language mechanisms that explicitly capture crosscutting structure. This makes it possible to program crosscutting concerns in a modular way, and thereby achieve the usual benefits of modularity: simpler code, that is easier to develop and maintain, and that has greater potential for reuse [16].

AspectJ, originally developed at Xerox Parc, is an implementation of the aspect-oriented programming paradigm for the Java language. It adds to Java just one new concept, a *join point* and a few new constructs: *pointcuts*, *advice*, *inter-type declarations* and *aspects* [20].

- *Pointcuts* pick out certain joint points in the program flow.
- After pointcuts pick out join points, we use *advice* to implement crosscutting behaviour. Advice brings together a pointcut (to pick out join points) and a body of code (to run at each of those join points).
- *Inter-type declarations* in AspectJ are declarations that cut across classes and their hierarchies. They may declare members that cut across multiple classes, or change the inheritance relationship between classes.
- The definition of *aspects* is very similar to classes, which wrap up point-cuts, advice, and inter-type declarations in a a modular unit of crosscutting implementation.

5.2   Aspect-Oriented Instrumentation

Unlike many other tools, AspectJ works at bytecode level, which is powerful since organizations usually only have the running version from the vendors. Moreover, it doesn't require any modifications of the existing code. The instrumentation code is encapsulated as an aspect which may be developed by a different developer/tester who is familiar with the instrumentation environment, not necessarily with the application logic. The application code is simply recompiled using a special compiler, the *aspect weaver*, which connects the aspect code with the application code. Thus, the instrumentation can easily be integrated into an existing application.

The idea is to define a pointcut on every method execution, as well as some advice to run when they turn up before the code is executed. Below is an aspect we use to trace system executions:

Listing 1.1. Aspect Trace

```
1   aspect Trace{
2       pointcut traceMethods() : (execution(* *(..))&& !cflow(within(Trace)));
3       before(): traceMethods(){
4           Signature sig = thisJoinPointStaticPart.getSignature();
5           String line =""+ thisJoinPointStaticPart.getSourceLocation().getLine();
6           String sourceName = thisJoinPointStaticPart.getSourceLocation().
                getWithinType().getCanonicalName();
7           Logger.getLogger("Tracing").log(
8               Level.INFO,
9               "Call from "
10                  + sourceName
11                  +" line " +
12                  line
13                  +" to " +sig.getDeclaringTypeName() + "." + sig.getName()
                    );
14      }
15  }
```

In the aspect **Trace**, we define a pointcut *traceMethods()* (Line 2) to pick out executions of every method in every class, as long as the control flow is not in the current class, such that we can identify all the other methods being called in each particular execution. Then we define an advice immediately before executing the method (Line 3). In the advice we log information of caller and callee when the pointcut is hit, including names and line numbers of the calling sites. AspectJ provides a special reference variable, *thisJointPointStaticPart*, that contains reflective information about the current join point for the advice to use.

To use this aspect, we need to compile it using AspectJ's compiler **ajc**:

```
ajc -outxml -outjar aspects.jar Trace.java
```

ajc is AspectJ's compiler and bytecode weaver for the Java language. The ajc command compiles and weaves AspectJ code together with Java source or .class files, producing .class files compliant with any Java VM. Now we can use this compiled Jar file aspects.jar to run the instrumentation process:

```
java -javaagent:<path to aspectjweaver.jar> -cp <path to aspects.jar>:
<path to target jar/folder> <name of main class to run>
```

A sample output of running this Jar on a class `MGPApp.class` from Oracle E-Business Suite is listed below:

Listing 1.2. Output Sample for MGPApp.class

```
1    \$ java −javaagent:/ebs/orahome/
2    aspectj1.7/lib/aspectjweaver.jar −cp /ebs/orahome/aspects.jar:/ebs/oracle/
         prodcomn/java/ MGPApp
3    INFO: Call from oracle.lite.sync.ConsNls line 37 to oracle.lite.sync.ConsNls.
         initialize
4    INFO: Call from MGPApp line 106 to MGPApp.main
5    INFO: Call from oracle.lite.web.util.JupMGPDebug line 134 to oracle.lite.web.util.
         JupMGPDebug.init
6    INFO: Call from oracle.lite.web.util.JupMGPDebug line 27 to oracle.lite.web.util.
         JupMGPDebug.load
7    INFO: Call from oracle.lite.common.Profile line 153 to oracle.lite.common.Profile.
         getBinDirectory
8    ....
```

We can then extract the dynamic event traces from this output. It is worth pointing out, our instrumentation does not alter system behaviour in any ways. It is used only to log necessary information from the code being executed and does not pass any arguments to the execution. We already discussed the alternative aspect-oriented instrumentation approach implemented in AspectJ, which allows us to conduct a fully dynamic instrumentation on the bytecode level of programs. Aspect-oriented instrumentation "weaves" together the program code/bytecode and the aspects, and encapsulates advice (insertion code) to monitor and collect dynamic information, without modifying the program. Developers/testers can focus on the instrumentation and data collection, saving effort in learning the application logic. Additionally, space and running time is quite reasonable: it requires hundreds of kilobytes per class, and running time of seconds per class. Details will be discussed in the case study.

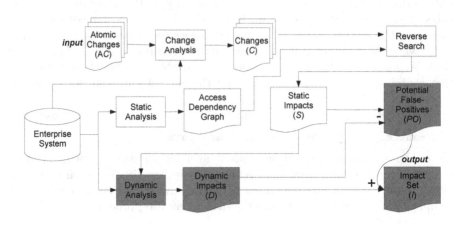

Fig. 1. System Flow Chart. In this chart, greyed modules were newly introduced to our previous static approach [1]. The input to the analysis was a set of atomic changes, such as *patches*; and the output was calculated by adding the potential false-positives and the dynamic impacts (see below).

6   Impact Analysis Overall

We extended the static approach in [1] using dynamic analysis, to form the new process depicted in Figure 1. In this overall process, an aspect-based dynamic instrumentation and data collection is conducted to collect event traces for functions $f \in S$ identified in the static impact set. The traversing information obtained in this process includes names of invoked functions; where they come from and where they will go. Then a dynamic impact set D is computed to gather that traversing information for each f. Essentially D is a subset of S, that is, functions and thus associated dependencies are proved to exist in real time. In the meantime, a set of potential over-estimated impacts PO can be obtained by a subtraction: $PO = S - D$.

7   Case Study

Our goal in the case study is to empirically investigate whether our motivations of (1) safety and precision, and (2) capability of dealing with the size of enterprise systems, can be met in practice. We now present the variables and measures, experiment setup and design, threats to validity and final results with analyses.

There is only one independent variable in this study: the extended impact analysis tool. Dependent variables in this study include *precision* and *time overhead*. To retain consistency with existing literature, our measure of precision remains the conventional one at the moment (Equation 1), where M represents

Table 1. Oracle E-Business Suite Release 11i and Some Facts

Release			Facts		
Application	Database	Classes	Entities (functions and fields)	LOC (approx.)	
11.5.10.2 (11i)	10.2.0.2.0 (10g)	195,999	3,157,947	8.7 Million	

Table 2. Patches for Oracle E-Business Suite 11i

Patches	Release	Facts	
		Size	Description
# 5565583	11.5.10.2	212MB	Fusion Intelligence for E-Business Suite Family Pack 11I.BIS PF.H.
# 10107418		10KB	This patch has fix for bug 9086631 and bug 9190120 (CPU bugs).
# 14321241		99MB	ORACLE Applications With 11i.ATG_PF.H RUP6: CPU ConsolidatedPatch For OCT 2012.

the total number of methods and fields in the program [21].

$$Precision = \frac{|I|}{|M|} \qquad (1)$$

To evaluate the execution cost of the new approach, we measured the time overhead of each major step in the overall process.

7.1 Experiment Setup

The experiment was set up on a desktop server with a Quad core 3.2GHz CPU, 32G RAM and the operating system was Red Hat Enterprise Linux Server release 5.10 (Tikanga) 64 bit. We used Oracle E-Business Suite 11.5.10.2 (Table 1) as the object of the analysis, and for source of atomic changes we used multiple patches (Table 2) that can be obtained either from Oracle E-Business Suite *Patch Wizard* or manually downloaded from Oracle Metalink. The patches were selected by an industrial user of the software, who had tried to analyze those patches and could then see whether our analysis added value - it did.

Vendor patches can range from a couple of KBs to hundreds of MBs, depending on what the purposes are for applying them. The smallest patch in this study is a patch (# 10107418) that was developed to fix responses to some CPU bugs – presumably this would not affect any system's behaviour, in terms of functionality, but certainly we cannot make any conclusion before conducting the impact analysis.

7.2 Experimental Design

We want to empirically examine if our approach is safe and scalable. At first, we intended to conduct only static analysis. In particular, the experiment was

Table 3. Execution Time for Patch #5565583, where G is the access dependency graph, S and D represents the set of static impacts and the set of dynamic impacts, respectively.

Build G	Extract Changes	Reverse Search	Compute S	Instrumentation	Compute D	Total
9.5 Hrs	2 Hrs	3.8 Hrs	1 Hr	48 Hrs	2 Hrs	~50 Hrs

conducted on the system and the above three patches respectively. Details of performing the static analysis are omitted, since they are exactly the same as described in [1].

After the static analysis, we ran dynamic instrumentation on the system via the aspect-oriented instrumentor `Trace`. The instrumentation was *only* executed on methods in the static impact set, since the whole point of dynamic analysis in our approach is to investigate which paths in the static impact set are valid in runtime. Instrumenting the entire system is not necessary and very expensive. The result to be gathered in this experiment is essentially the remaining and the "verified" dependencies. With those impacts we could then calculate the precision.

7.3   Results and Analysis

The entire system contains 195,999 classes. We determined that there are 3,157,947 entities (both functions and fields) in the system. The process of building the access dependency graph added over 18.4 million dependencies and took over 9.5 hours (Table 3) to complete, which is large but quite manageable, especially as this process is independent of any patch or proposed change, and thus can be prepared in advance. Reverse searching this dependency graph takes only a few seconds for each starting point method or field. By patch analysis[1], we found 16,787 direct database changes, and 25,613 direct library changes for patch #5565583; 610 direct database changes, and 3,374 library changes for patch #14321241; no direct database changes, and no library changes for patch #10107418. Apparently patch #5565583 is the largest patch among the three and hence it is intended to change quite a number of functions in the system. Patch #10107418 is a pretty small one and only intended to fix some CPU issues, just as we expected, it doesn't contain any functional changes.

The computed static impacts for each patch are listed in Table 4. As we can observe from Table 4, the static impacts can reach up to 22.2% of functions in the system, including the "top functions". We had almost one out of ten top callers identified as impacted. It is quite a large portion of the system, and if testers were given this set of impacts, a large amount of testing work still

---

[1] Patch analysis is to analyze patch files (bytecode, xml, database procedures, etc.) to extract direct changes to either the library application or the database. Those direct changes are then used to serve as atomic changes in the impact analysis.

Table 4. Static Impacts of the Patches

Patch	Direct Changes	Affected Functions (% of total functions)	Affected Top Functions (% of total top functions)
# 5565583	42,400	699,534 (22.2%)	160,800 (9.6%)
# 14321241	3,984	230,209 (7.3%)	69,971 (4.2%)
# 10107418	0	0	0

Table 5. Results after Instrumentation for Patch # 5565583

Patch	Total Function	Total Top Function	Static Impacts	Dynamic Impacts	Potential False-Positives
# 5565583	3,157,947	1,673,132	699,534	4,806	694,728

has to be conducted. This is mainly caused by false-positives. In other words, we may have included many over-estimated impacts that come from infeasible executions, invalid calling paths, etc.

We ran AspectJ to instrument the identified static impacts, for each "affected function". In the experiment this was accomplished by looking into the production directory, executing predefined "aspects" for each class when a `main` function was found. The instrumentation was extremely time consuming, since our target system is very large. Initially this process took over one week. On one hand, many executions were simply long - may take up to hours for a single run. On the other hand, many of them prompted the user for inputs to continue. We split the instrumentation into sub-tasks, each one of them focused on instrumenting just one component in the system and for the latter problem, we conservatively collected all the calling relations no matter what the user inputs were. With this approach we tried to maximize the usage of CPU and memory, and in the end, the instrumentation was reduced to around 48 hours.

After the instrumentation, dynamic information was collected (Table 5): among the total static dependencies, only 8,357 were covered in the executions, that is, 0.45‰; and 4,806 functions, that is, 0.26% of all top callers (of 1,673,132) were covered. From the numbers, it seems the instrumentation touched only a tiny portion of the system. However, the fact is, for that tiny portion of the system, these paths were executed in total 159,367 times. In other words, certain executions pointed to certain top callers, which did not vary much with respect to the number of executions. By actually running the system, we observed that only a small portion of the system can be impacted – however, this does not mean other impacts in the static impact set are not valid. Those 4,806 functions were kept in the final impact set, as they were "confirmed" in run time.

The entire process currently requires considerable time to complete. Considering the sizes of the system and patch, it is still much more manageable than rerunning everything in the regression suite. More crucially, it provides testers confidence in which parts in the system are affected. The most time-consuming task is the instrumentation, which occupies around 56.8% of the total execution time. Just as the static dependency graph, the instrumentation forms a substantial corporate asset for future analysis, and can be easily and quickly updated as needed.

7.4   Threats to Validity

Like most of other empirical studies, our study also has limitations that we should be aware of while interpreting the results. At the moment of this study, a user's application and test cases are not accessible to us. Hence our case study currently focuses on identifying impacts within the system, though it's not hard to extend our study to cover customized code since the underlying techniques remain the same. Also, while interpreting the results, the way of calculating precision can vary. Since the validity of computing the size of actual impacts by extracting from program logs the direct modifications [22] is quite complicated, and in practice not available most of the time, Maia's definition [23] is accurate but not useful. We intend to use Orso's definition [21], which is straightforward but less accurate, and sometimes even dangerous when the approach is not safe. However, since our approach of impact analysis computes a complete static dependency, Orso's definition would not be risky for our case study.

8   Conclusion

8.1   Achievement

In this work, we investigated how to conduct an impact analysis that combines static analysis and dynamic analysis on large-scale enterprise systems, to achieve safety and precision. The achievements reported on are:

- We have developed a multi-tasking, aspect-oriented instrumentor to adequately instrument large-scale systems and collect traces at bytecode level. The instrumentor does not require testers to fully understand the application logic or prepare any test data. This is extremely useful when the size of the program is large, given that existing tools are too expensive and require extra information such as test coverage and operational profiles, which are usually hard to access.
- We have successfully combined static analysis and dynamic analysis. The hybrid approach retains the safety of the static approach, but is more precise since the dynamic analysis removes some of the false positives. Safety is retained since the static analysis was used as the input to the dynamic analysis, and our techniques were carefully designed not to remove impacted methods from the impact set unless we could prove that they were false positives. Instead of instrumenting the entire program, our instrumentor only instruments those methods of interest – functions or fields that have been already identified as static impacts.

– We have empirically demonstrated the practical applicability of the improved approach on a very large enterprise system involving hundreds of thousands of classes. Such systems are perhaps 2 orders of magnitude larger than the systems analyzed by other approaches.

Our approach is *safe*, more *precise* than the static analysis and *scalable*. Additionally, it is able to compute the impact result before applying the changes, since the access dependency graph in static analysis was augmented to include the original changes. The final impact set obtained from our approach can be used in regression test selection, focused testing, and planning enhancements to applications, etc.

8.2   Future Work

As we can observe from the case study, the instrumentation took approximately 2 days to finish, even with taking into account dividing the task into smaller ones. This amount of run time is reasonable, with respect to the size of the system. However, from a software tester's point of view, it may still need to be reduced to improve the efficiency.

Results of the case study also indicate that dynamic analysis only found a small portion of the static impacts are real impacts. It might be the case that runtime use of a large software system may only access a small part of the software. However, we may also not have filtered out enough false-positives. For instance, if we break down the static analysis to include control-flow information, we might be able to identify infeasible paths with mis-matched calls and returns. And then, mapping those infeasible paths to dependencies, we could cut off further false-positives in the static impact set. Also, even for feasible paths, there is some chance that they are not affected. If we are able to look into changes and identify what they really intend to change, *e.g.* changing a field's name, modifying a function's signature, we can further find out whether functions that have access to them can be affected.

References

1. Chen, W., Iqbal, A., Abdrakhmanov, A., Parlar, J., George, C., Lawford, M., Maibaum, T., Wassyng, A.: Large-scale enterprise systems: Changes and impacts. In: Cordeiro, J., Maciaszek, L.A., Filipe, J. (eds.) ICEIS 2012. LNBIP, vol. 141, pp. 274–290. Springer, Heidelberg (2013)
2. Caldwell, B., Stein, T., Beyond, E.: New it agenda. Information Week 711, 30–34 (1998)
3. AG, S.: Annual report 2012, financial highlights (2012)
4. Monk, E.F., Wagner, B.J.: Concepts in enterprise resource planning. CengageBrain. com (2008)
5. Bohner, S.A.: Software Change Impact Analysis. In: Proceedings of the 27th Annual NASA Goddard/IEEE Software Engineering Workshop (SEW-27'02) (1996)
6. Ernst, M.D.: Static and dynamic analysis: Synergy and duality. In: WODA 2003: ICSE Workshop on Dynamic Analysis, Portland, OR, pp. 24–27 (May 9, 2003)

7. Apiwattanapong, T.: Efficient and precise dynamic impact analysis using execute-after sequences. In: Proceedings of the 27th International Conference on Software Engineering (2005)
8. Law, J., Rothermel, G.: Whole program path-based dynamic impact analysis. In: Proceedings of the 25th International Conference on Software Engineering (2003)
9. Orso, A., Apiwattanapong, T., Harrold, M.J.: Leveraging field data for impact analysis and regression testing. In: Proceedings of the 9th European Software Engineering Conference held Jointly with 11th ACM SIGSOFT International Symposium on Foundations of Software Engineering, vol. 28(5) (September 2003)
10. Patterson, D.A., Hennessy, J.L.: Computer organization and design: The hardware/software interface. Morgan Kaufmann (2008)
11. Cmelik, B., Keppel, D.: Shade: A fast instruction-set simulator for execution profiling. Springer (1995)
12. Luk, C.K., Cohn, R., Muth, R., Patil, H., Klauser, A., Lowney, G., Wallace, S., Reddi, V.J., Hazelwood, K.: Pin: Building customized program analysis tools with dynamic instrumentation. In: Proceedings of the 2005 ACM SIGPLAN Conference on Programming Language Design and Implementation, PLDI 2005, pp. 190–200. ACM, New York (2005)
13. Lam, P., Bodden, E., Lhotak, O., Lhotak, J., Qian, F., Hendren, L.: Soot: A Java Optimization Framework. Sable Research Group, McGill University, Montreal, Canada (March 2010), Electronically available at http://www.sable.mcgill.ca/soot/
14. Agarwal, A., Sites, R.L., Horowitz, M.: ATUM: A new technique for capturing address traces using microcode, vol. 14. IEEE Computer Society Press (1986)
15. Sosnoski, D.: Java programming dynamics, part 7: Bytecode engineering with bcel (April 2004)
16. AspectJ: Aspectj main page (2014)
17. Seesing, A., Orso, A.: Insectj: A generic instrumentation framework for collecting dynamic information within eclipse. In: Proceedings of the 2005 OOPSLA Workshop on Eclipse Technology eXchange, Eclipse 2005, pp. 45–49. ACM, New York (2005)
18. Kiczales, G., Lamping, J., Mendhekar, A., Maeda, C., Lopes, C., Loingtier, J.M., Irwin, J.: Aspect-oriented programming. Springer (1997)
19. Kiczales, G., Hilsdale, E., Hugunin, J., Kersten, M., Palm, J., Griswold, W.G.: An overview of aspectJ. In: Lindskov Knudsen, J. (ed.) ECOOP 2001. LNCS, vol. 2072, pp. 327–354. Springer, Heidelberg (2001)
20. Project, E.A.: Introduction to aspectj (February 2014)
21. Orso, A., Apiwattanapong, T., Law, J., Rothermel, G., Harrold, M.J.: An empirical comparison of dynamic impact analysis algorithms. In: Proceedings of the 26th International Conference on Software Engineering, ICSE 2004, pp. 491–500. IEEE Computer Society, Washington, DC (2004)
22. Hattori, L., Guerrero, D., Figueiredo, J., Brunet, J., Damasio, J.: On the precision and accuracy of impact analysis techniques. In: Seventh IEEE/ACIS International Conference on Computer and Information Science, ICIS 2008, pp. 513–518 (May 2008)
23. Maia, M.C.O., Bittencourt, R.A., de Figueiredo, J.C.A., Guerrero, D.D.S.: The hybrid technique for object-oriented software change impact analysis. In: European Conference on Software Maintenance and Reengineering, pp. 252–255 (2010)

Towards Adaptation and Evolution of Domain-Specific Knowledge for Maintaining Secure Systems*

Thomas Ruhroth[1], Stefan Gärtner[2], Jens Bürger[1],
Jan Jürjens[3], and Kurt Schneider[2]

[1] TU Dortmund, Germany
{thomas.ruhroth,jens.buerger}@cs.tu-dortmund.de
[2] Leibniz Universität Hannover, Germany
{stefan.gaertner,kurt.schneider}@inf.uni-hannover.de
[3] TU Dortmund and Fraunhofer ISST, Germany
http://jan.jurjens.de

Abstract. Creating and maintaining secure software require a good understanding of the system and its environment. Knowledge management is therefore one of the key factors to maintain secure software successfully. However, acquiring and modeling knowledge is a labor-intensive and time-consuming task. Thus, knowledge ought to be shared among different projects and must be adapted to their specific needs. In this paper, we present an approach allowing the stepwise adaptation from domain- to project-specific knowledge based on OWL ontologies. For this purpose, we define a basic set of adaptation operators which allows effective and frugal changes. Moreover, we discuss how our approach can be integrated into common software process models in order to adapt knowledge required for maintenance. Since domain- and project-specific knowledge changes over time, we show how our approach copes with changes efficiently, so that the affected knowledge remains consistent. The shared use of knowledge significantly reduces the complexity and effort to model required knowledge in various projects. Our case study and tool implementation shows the benefits for maintaining secure systems.

Keywords: ontology adaptation, domain-specific adaptation, maintaining secure systems, (co-)evolution.

1 Introduction

Knowledge is part of a software development process at many points. While it often seems easy to take knowledge about security and compliance into account in the design phase of a project, it becomes more difficult during later maintenance phase. Overall, maintaining software is a knowledge-intensive activity [28]. Thus, it is important to have access to the knowledge that has already been used

---

* Funded by the DFG project SecVolution (JU 2734/2-1, SCHN 1072/4-1), part of the priority programe SPP 1593 "Design For Future - Managed Software Evolution".

A. Jedlitschka et al. (Eds.): PROFES 2014, LNCS 8892, pp. 239–253, 2014.

for security analysis as well as additional knowledge gained while the development took place. Regarding security and compliance, required knowledge differs according to the domain and system context and also includes domain-specific knowledge as well as assumptions about the environment. Thus, some issues are common to a wide range of systems (e.g. encryption, privacy) and others need only to be considered for a specific domain or system (e.g. biometric, malware). Moreover, most required knowledge is nowadays documented in natural language and contains references to further natural language documents. Typical examples are regulations, laws, and best practices.

To support knowledge intensive tasks in an at least semiautomatic manner [6], a formal representation of knowledge is inevitable. Since collecting, formalizing, and maintaining required knowledge is a laborious task, a formal representation of knowledge should be shared among various projects and adapted to the specific needs and requirements. For example, privacy should be fulfilled by an organization according to given security standards and regulations. Therefore, the European Union defines privacy rules [5] which have to be refined by each member state (compare Germany: *Bundesdatenschutzgesetz* BDSG [2], France: *Data Protection Act* DPA98 [1]). Additionally, each organization has its own privacy guidelines extending and re-defining the respective country regulation.

To model such knowledge, ontologies are a commonly used technique [9,20]. They represent knowledge in a formal manner by using a set of types, properties, relationships, individuals, and axioms.

In this paper, we present a knowledge management approach based on ontologies which allows sharing common knowledge between projects for the integration in the maintenance process of the development cycle. The idea is to provide a simple and straight set of adaptation operators to support maintenance of domain- and project-specific knowledge. Moreover, knowledge management activities (e.g. use of ontologies) need to fit into the developers' workflow since rigid integration typically results in retarding instead of supporting the development as well as the maintenance process [17]. On this account, our approach is designed to fit well in existing development process models.

As knowledge evolves regularly, the corresponding links between domain- as well as project-specific knowledge must be re-adapted. This task, however, is laborious and error-prone and should be supported to cope with knowledge changes efficiently. Since the proposed set of adaptation operators is simple and straight, we show that our approach is suitable for this task.

The remainder of this paper is structured as follows: In Sec. 2 we sketch our approach and define the scope of our research as well as relevant research questions. The set of adaptation operators is proposed in Sec. 3 and it is shown in Sec. 4 that our approach is suitable to cope with knowledge changes efficiently. Afterwards, in Sec. 5 we introduce the case study and evaluate our approach. In Sec. 6, we discuss how to integrate our approach with common process models. Related research in the field of knowledge adaptation and evolution is listed in Sec. 7. Finally, in Sec. 8 our results and insights are discussed and future research is outlined.

2   Proposed Approach and Research Objective

In this paper, we focus on the distribution of domain-specific knowledge between different software projects. The aim of our research is to provide knowledge for evaluating the compliance and security of a software product. Thus, it is important to be compatible with different development process models and various domains.

We explain our research objective using the running case study of the paper that addresses privacy in software and its legal foundation. The European Union (EU) passed a privacy directive (Directive 95/46/EC [5]) which had to be refined into a local law of all EU member states. In Germany, the *Bundesdatenschutzgesetz* (BDSG) [2] resembles the local refinement of this directive. Some parts of Directive 95/46/EC are optional to implement and the BDSG does not implement all optional parts (e.g. regulations about safety of privacy data). In contrast to the EU directive, the BDSG was amended several times during the past years. In Fig. 1, the adaptation of the above-mentioned directives is shown. As Directive 95/46/EC is implemented differently in the member states, the first adaptation is required to refine EU privacy rules. The second adaptation reflects modifications necessary to fit the development process and different compliance analysis techniques. The resulting structure builds a hierarchy upon the privacy knowledge. However, adaptation of ontologies is not supported sufficiently by existing ontology frameworks at this moment.

Regarding our case study, we identified following research questions in software maintenance and knowledge management. The first question is **RQ1**: How can common or domain-specific knowledge efficiently be shared among different projects? Here, we assume that among different projects the domain-specific

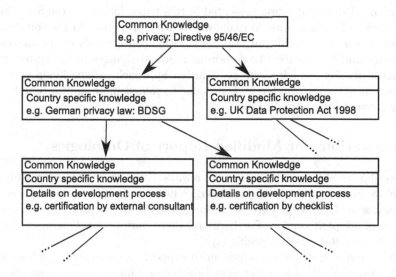

Fig. 1. Adaptation of knowledge

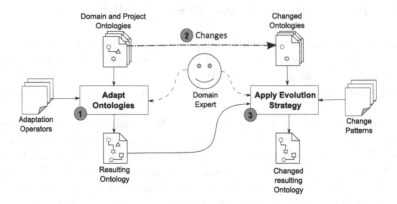

Fig. 2. Workflow of our proposed ontology adaptation approach

knowledge only differs in details. This leads to the second research question **RQ2**: Which operations can adapt the common or domain-specific knowledge to fit the needs of different projects in a straight and sound manner?

To answer the given research questions, we propose an approach as illustrated in Fig. 2. Our approach consists of two activities: *Adapt Ontologies* (see 1) and *Apply Evolution Strategy* (see 3). To adapt ontologies to certain projects as well as process-specific needs, we establish a straight set of adaptation operators which are used by domain experts. To cope with changes (depicted as 2) of the original ontologies, we combine these operators with pre-defined knowledge changes. They are used to determine co-evolution strategies for the adapted ontologies semiautomatically. For ambiguous cases, the domain expert must decide which strategy fits best.

The knowledge adaptation presented in this paper facilitates the SecVolution [22,3] approach, which aims to maintain security properties in the software development process. For this purpose, SecVolution continuously monitors security knowledge and its evolution to determine required changes to the system semiautomatically. By applying our SecVolution approach, a long-living system is wrapped into a layer of relevant knowledge to maintain an appropriate level of security over a long period of time.

3   Operations for Modified Import of Ontologies

As described in Sec. 2, ontologies do not always match their intended use exactly. Hence, we must be able to *adapt* ontologies because during creation of a refined ontology, some knowledge may be missing, needs to be adapted or parts are not used in an adapted version. Furthermore, there may be *local* changes that are unique to an ontology of a specific layer.

OWL already features a mechanism to support the integration of knowledge called *import*. With this it becomes possible to simply insert elements from another ontology without any constraint. However, the import mechanism is

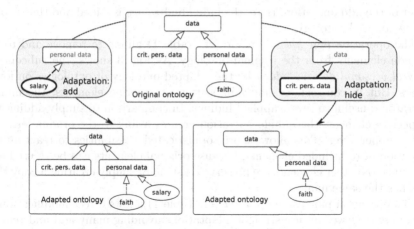

Fig. 3. Example depicting the hide and implicit add operation

insufficient because importing an element of an ontology may enforce a cascade of element additions. They may become necessary if a change needs to be applied to an element that has been imported beforehand. For example, regarding the EU directive for privacy of 2001, a number of classes have to be redefined when creating a refined ontology to reflect its German implementation. The standard import mechanism does not support redefinition of elements, so new concepts ought to be created. Hence, every role restriction and concept depending on these concepts needs to be changed as well so that the new (redefined) concept can use it.

In summary, it can be stated that not only the replaced parts of an ontology need to be changed but also every element that is directly or indirectly related to the elements that have been changed in the first place, needs to be altered as well.

To overcome the above-mentioned limitations, we propose a set of ontology modification operators extending OWL's import mechanism. The extension consists of two pairs of operators: *hide / unhide* and *change / reset*. These operators are used to realize the activity *Adapt Ontologies* (1) of our workflow presented in Fig. 2. By this means, it becomes possible to organize (i.e. *layer*) ontologies hierarchically in order to adapt them to project-specific needs. Table 1 gives an overview about the operators and their relation to each other.

Since there is currently no common graphical notation for ontologies, we use the representation as depicted in Fig. 3 throughout this paper. Individuals (rectangles) are the basic elements of ontologies and represent the actual knowledge. Individuals can share properties and are assigned to concepts (or classes) which are depicted as ovals. Axioms and properties are omitted in our representation due to simplicity and clearness of the example. Fig. 3 sketches an exemplary ontology that is adapted in two ways using two different adaptation operators.

The operator *add* (cf. Table 1) is implicitly defined by the existing import mechanism of OWL. It is easy to import a small ontology by featuring the elements that need to be added from the original ontology. Fig. 3 depicts the effect of the add operation. Here, the individual *salary* is added and thus is part of the adapted ontology.

The operation pair *hide / unhide* (cf. Table 1) allows to remove and to re-include elements from the original ontology. As Fig. 3 shows, the subconcept *critical personal data* is *hidden* by the adapted ontology or ontologies on lower layers. But in contrast to simply importing or ignoring elements, the unhide operator is useful to revert applied hidings. In comparison to simply adding the respective element, the unhide operation creates a link to the original element of the upper layer. This allows more sophisticated possibilities to react on the evolution of re-included elements, because original elements can be re-used and relations to further elements are preserved instead of simply creating a copy that just has the same name.

The operation pair *change / reset* (cf. Table 1) allows direct modification of elements, thus we can use straight adaptations avoiding many add and remove adaptations (straightness). For the reset operation the same arguments as for the unhide operator apply here.

As shown in Table 1, every adaptation operation is guarded by a precondition to ensure that the resulting ontology is syntactically and semantically sound. For example, a concept should only be hidden if it is not used by elements that are still visible. To ensure this, a concept can only be hidden if there is no unhidden reference pointing at it in the ontology. We assume that all adaptation operations between two ontologies take place in an atomic step and therefore avoid a problem with cyclic hide and unhide operations.

The adaptation operators are chosen in a way that they can build a set of simple, straight and revertable adaptation operations of ontologies. *Simple* means that the goal is to have a small set of basic operations that is sufficient to describe all possible modifications. The *straight*ness property describes that we can use the operations without having to resort to complex sequences which include pathological states. For example, the operators *add* and *remove* are as basic operations to describe all possible modifications, but the only use of them leads to complex adaptations. In the worst case, nearly or even all elements of an ontology have to be deleted until it contains only a few (or even no) elements and the whole ontology has to be rebuild in the modified structure from scratch. The

Table 1. Adaptation operators for include operations

Operation	Description	Reverted by	Precondition
add	Addition of new OWL 2 elements. The add operation is defined by the usual means of the import.	hide	
hide	Removal of OWL 2 element.	unhide	There are only hidden references to this element
unhide	Reinclude a previously hidden element	(hide)	The element is not referencing any hidden element and the hide is in scope.
change	Change a property of an element	reset	
reset	Revert a change	(change)	

third property *revertable* is used in import chains of ontologies when a former state should be reinstated. Regarding the running case study, reverting can be necessary if a system is implemented in Germany but is also involved in international (i.e. *EU-wide*) relationships. Therefore, the system inherently is related to the German adaptations of the privacy regulations but needs to revert some of them to get parts of the EU directive hold directly.

4 Application to Evolving Domain-Specific Knowledge

In Sec. 3 we explained the first part of our approach (see Fig. 2) that enables ontologies to import knowledge from one another. In this section, we show the second part dealing with changes of the ontology (evolution) and the needed modifications of adapted ontologies (co-evolution). Based on a formalism that describes possible patterns of ontology changes, we apply our approach exemplary and show how to determine strategies to solve co-evolution problems semi-automatically.

Figure 4 shows a typical adaptation as well as evolution process, featuring two ontologies on different layers. The boxes shows two states of the adaption where the left one is an evolved version of the right one. The question mark reflects an issue coming from the German privacy law BDSG as described in our running case study. In a former version of the BDSG, data is distinguished in two subcategories: anonymized data and personal data. During the adaptation process it was decided that, considering the specific system, data is needed to be distinguished into three categories: anonymized data, data of 1st / 2nd party and 3rd party data. As an evolution of the domain knowledge, we consider a change of the BDSG so that a new category is introduced to represent critical personal data. Thus, the domain ontology evolves and all adapted ontologies need to inherit these changes. Therefore, the changes that are unique to

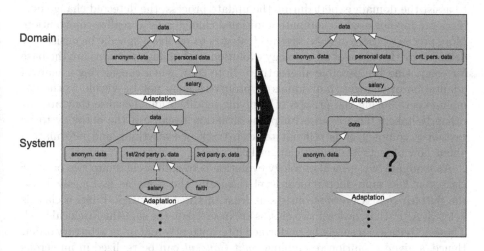

Fig. 4. Example of layered ontologies and the reaction to knowledge evolution

Table 2. Examples for occurring change patterns (compare [12])

Change Pattern Parameters	Description	Constraint
Split Concept $(X,(Y_1,\ldots,Y_n))$	A class X is split into two or more classes $Y_1,\ldots,Y_n$	Concept X deleted $\land$ Concept $Y_1,\ldots,Y_n$ created $\land\ \forall i$ superclass(X) = superclass(Y_i)
Merge Concepts $((Y_1,\ldots,Y_n), X)$	One ore more classes $Y_1,\ldots,Y_n$ are merged into one class X	Concept $Y_1,\ldots,Y_n$ deleted $\land$ Concept X created $\land\ \forall i$ superclass(Y_i) = superclass(X)
Pull up Concept (X, Y)	Concept X is pulled up to class Y	before: superclass(X) = Y, after: superclass(X) = superclass(Y)
Pull down Concept (X, Y)	Concept X is pulled down to class Y	before: superclass(X) = superclass(Y) after: superclass(X) = Y

the system layer and the changes of the domain ontology have to be combined to update the whole ontology and to preserve consistency between the layers. Ontologies may become complex very fast, so avoiding inconsistencies is an important and non-trivial problem. Firstly, syntactic or structural inconsistencies arise when constraints are violated or entities cannot be referenced. Secondly, semantic inconsistencies arise when the meaning of an entity changes or gets ambiguous. Thirdly, adaptations themselves need to be evolved if the adapted elements evolve. Hence, the evolution process requires a detailed analysis of side effects as consequence of change operations [26].

For avoiding inconsistencies, it is important to perceive the ontology changes and their actual meaning. To keep track of what changes on a syntactic level mean on a semantic level, we use the concept of *change patterns* as proposed by Javed et al. [13,12]. These change patterns are used to provide the semantic part of the ontology evolution process. To resolve occurring inconsistencies and to assist the domain expert during the update process, the detected change patterns are further used to compute additional change sets to realize co-evolution. More precisely, there may be several strategies to resolve a specific inconsistency detected by the cause of an ontology evolution, and change patterns are the base for computing the possible alternatives. Note that, when considering a manual adaptation of changes, individuals or properties may not be visible to the domain expert during the process of applying modifications because they are not properly linked. This is an error-prone situation because if the ontology to be revised is complex, it is difficult to keep track of everything and information about how objects are linked can get lost.

An example of a typical ontology evolution is to split a class into two or more classes at the same hierarchical level (basically the same as in Fig. 4) Thus, the pattern *Split Concept* consists at least of three activities. First, a class is deleted. After that, at least two classes are inserted on the same hierarchical level. These activities can surely be performed intermittently and in an arbitrary order. Hence, a given evolution resembling *Split Concept* can be realized in numerous ways. The discovery of relevant change patterns as well as finding a complete set of change patterns is a key task to make our approach able to react on evolution. It can be achieved by mining frequent patterns from change logs or by simply defining them as done in [13]. Some change patterns related to our running case study are shown in Table 2 according to [12]. Every pattern is defined by a function with a parameter set and a description. A list of constraints for each pattern shows which detected actions in the course of ontology evolution indicate that a given change pattern is present.

After all occurred changes are characterized by instances of change patterns, the consecutive step is to determine appropriate evolution strategies. Since every evolution has its own precondition, not all possible strategies are applicable in certain cases [23]. For example, if a class is split into two classes that are disjoint, it is not possible to re-attach the individuals to all new classes. If more than one evolution strategy is enabled for a given change pattern occurrence, different evolution strategies can also be combined arbitrarily.

In the following, we give an example how adaptation operators can be combined with change patterns and co-evolution strategies to realize the integration ontology evolution and co-evolution. Fig. 5 shows an evolution of a simple ontology with the split concept pattern and a possible evolution strategy following and extending the example of Fig. 4. On the left, the ontology in its unmodified state is shown. Now, the domain expert decides to refine the structure of the ontology such that normal and critical personal data can be distinguished. Thus, the *Split Concept* pattern occurs: The class *personal data* is deleted and two new classes are introduced, both also being subclasses of *data*. The resulting ontology is shown in the middle. The problem to be solved is how the individuals *salary* and *faith* should be linked now. To react upon the change pattern, a possible evolution strategy is to involve the domain expert who decides how every individual is re-attached to one of the new classes. More precisely, the *salary* individual will be re-attached to the *personal data* class and *faith* to the *crit. personal data* class. By applying this strategy of re-attaching to the two individuals, the ontology is now in a consistent state again.

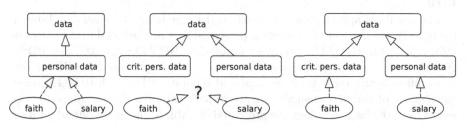

Fig. 5. Split Concept Pattern

5 Case Study and Implementation

To evaluate the feasibility of our approach, we implemented the adaptation stage in Java and OWL. To be compatible with standard OWL tools such as Protégé [25], we include the adaptation operators as annotations in the OWL files.

We use our prototype for our case study to show that our approach is capable of adapting knowledge in real world scenarios. Therefore, we use the BDSG to define the privacy properties in an extended version of the CoCoME case study [11]. CoCoME represents a trading system as it can be found in most supermarkets. The system consists of a number of cash desk PCs connected to a store server. A number of store servers again is connected to a central enterprise server. As the communication paths between these systems are used to transmit business as well as personal data (e.g. when processing electronic cash (EC) transactions), communication between the systems has to satisfy given security requirements. Moreover, a lot of additional hardware is plugged into the cash desk PC providing various entry points to the whole trading system.

In this case study, which is also part of a larger scenario of the SecVolution project, we describe the privacy regulations using three layers of ontologies: The global layer is defined by the EU directive (directive 95/46/EC), the domain is reflected by the German law (BDSG) and the system layer contains information specific to the CoCoME system and its development process model. In the global and domain layer, some concepts resembling regulations from the laws are defined. Moreover, various objects and subjects are introduced, e.g. different stakeholders like data subject or processor. Roles are defined so that they can be used in the system layer to define the relationship of different individuals. For example, we need to know if an operation requires the *the data subject's consent* (technically also called OptIn) before it is performed. The system layer includes information that is specific to the CoCoME, e.g. which data is to be considered as personal data. Using reasoning techniques, we can derive a number of concepts that allow to determine easily if the system is compliant to the laws.

An interesting point of this case study is that the BDSG failed to be a rigorous implementation of EU directive in the beginning, and thus needed some adaptations regarding concepts and roles. Later on, Germany was forced to change the BDSG to fully implement the directive and so raised the need for adaptation. In this case study, we therefore consider two significantly different versions of the BDSG.

The results of applying our approach to the case study are shown in Table 3. On the left, the number of elements is presented that are included in the basic ontology (EU Directive). The two other ontologies (BDSG before 2003 and BDSG 2009) are examples of adaptations of the basic ontology. Since both BDSG versions differ significantly, they are analyzed separately. For each BDSG version, the number of ontology elements are given that have been used to adapt the elements from the basic ontology. As presented in Table 3, the use of our adaptation operators in contrast to the standard OWL features reduces the number of elements up to 34%. Thus, the OWL import feature is not sufficient to build up an ontology hierarchy because the BDSG extends the meaning of derived concepts that cannot be expressed without redefining parts of the ontology structure. For example, the EU directive does not incorporate the notion of anonymization which is only part of the BDSG. Anonymization means that if data is changed in a way that it cannot be associated with the subject anymore, the data can

Table 3. Sizes of privacy ontologies with/without using adaptation operators. (*) Not fully compliant with EU Directive.

EU Directive		BDSG (before 2003)(*)				BDSG (actual - 2009)			
	Size	Size without | with Adaptation		Difference # diffs | reduction		Size without | with Adaptation		Difference # diffs | reduction	
Concepts	31	52	40	12	**23%**	46	39	7	**15%**
Individuals	4	4	4	0	**0%**	4	4	0	**0%**
Axioms	20	44	29	15	**34%**	41	29	12	**29%**
Roles	6	12	8	4	**33%**	12	8	4	**33%**
Assertions	0	0	0	0	**0%**	0	0	0	**0%**

be used without the consent of the subject. Thus, the derived concepts needs to be redefined to include the new regulations. In summary, the use of adaptation operators reduces the number of newly defined elements in the ontologies due to the reuse of existing (changed) elements in contrast to additionally defined specializations.

6   Process Model Integration

In this section, we discuss how our approach as presented in Fig. 2 can be integrated with existing development and maintenance processes. To identify reasonable connection points, we therefore reviewed common development process models in software engineering. They reviewed models are: Waterfall Model (with iterations), Rapid Prototyping, iterative development, agile development, incremental development, and Boehm's spiral model (cmp. [18]). Moreover, the adapted knowledge must be used, re-adapted, co-evolved, and extended in the maintenance process. Here, we considered following models: Quick-Fix Model, Boehm's Model, Osborne's Model, and Iterative Enhancement Model (cmp. [7]).

During initial development, the required knowledge is adapted to the domain and project requirements as described above for activity *Adapt Ontologies* (see Fig. 2). For this purpose, the domain expert or requirements engineer chooses an appropriate knowledge base in the system analysis or requirements engineering phase that is provided by all abovementioned process models (part of the planning stage). The knowledge is adapted to the actual development project based on the corresponding project management, assumptions about the environment, and system as well as software requirements. In the development stages (e.g. design, coding, testing), the adapted knowledge can then be utilized by various assessment techniques to analyze software artifacts (cmp. [6]). Feedback cycles and iterations can be used to re-adapt and extend the knowledge during development. This is important because domain experts or requirements engineers are not able to adapt the knowledge at once, as they usually have to deal with vague requirements and constraints. Thus, process models which contain feedback cycles and iterations (e.g. Rapid Prototyping, agile development) increase the efficiency of our approach.

Compared with new development, maintenance process models have similar stages. But in software maintenance more effort is required in the early stages in order to understand the system at hand as well as to analyze and classify incoming change request [7]. Moreover, documentation is of particular importance in software maintenance to discover dependencies between development artifacts and to avoid ripple effects. Thus, knowledge that has been adapted during the initial development can be used to support these tasks. To incorporate knowledge changes properly, the analysis, re-design, or documentation stage and their corresponding feedback cycles of the maintenance process can be used. This includes to re-adapt, co-evolve, and extend the knowledge as required for activity *Apply Evolution Strategy* (see Fig. 2).

7   Related Research

Ontology reuse is an important issue in many areas such as knowledge management and software engineering. For this purpose, global ontologies must be adapted to a specific domain or system which is known as adaptation, integration, or matching. The fundamental problem is to specify the mapping between the global ontology and the local ontologies. To cope with this problem, Calvanese et al. [4] proposed a framework for ontology integration. Another approach addressing ontology integration based on integration operations is given by Pinto et al. [21]. Integration operators specify how elements from a global ontology are included and combined with elements in the local ontology. They comprise composing, combining, modifying, and assembling operators. Additionally, ontology integration is closely related to ontology alignment. There, relationships between two ontologies must be determined based on a pre-defined similarity measure. Udera et al. [29] proposed an approach leveraging the data and structure contained in ontologies. Alignment of ontologies can be used to identify knowledge elements which need to be added in an adaptation.

To cope with changes, Ruhroth et al. [23,24] described a basic set of evolutions and co-evolutions. It represents a formal foundation of (co-)evolutions which can be utilized in a wide scope of applications. Heflin et al. [10] pointed out the problem of changing ontologies in distributed environments. They argue that a changed ontology can be used without any problems if it is backwards compatible to the original ontology. An ontology is backwards compatible if only concepts and relations have been added. Otherwise, the ontology or query needs to be modified manually to reflect changes. Ontology evolution allows access to the elements through the most recent ontology, while ontology versioning allows access through different versions. For that reason, ontology evolution can be treated as part of ontology versioning [16]. Noy et al. [19] emphasized that existing versioning systems are not able to compare and represent structural changes. Thus, they present an ontology versioning environment to address the problem of maintaining versions of ontologies. Based on this approach, the domain expert is able to analyze changes in order to accept or reject them. They extended their approach in [20] and proposed a framework for ontology evolution in collaborative environments based on their own experiences. Stojanovic et al. [27] proposed a well-structured ontology evolution process which provides the domain expert capabilities to control it. Therefore, the domain expert can select one of the proposed co-evolution strategies. Moreover, Stojanovic [26] also presented an approach to solve inconsistencies by using co-evolution strategies. For this purpose, they used a model for the semantic of changes in OWL ontologies as well as resolution strategies to ensure consistency [8]. Javed et al. [13,12] presented a graph based approach of pattern matching and the discovery of frequent changes in ontologies.

In summary, most approaches propose a rather large number of adaptation operators which makes adaptation of ontologies complex and error-prone. Thus, to support maintenance of knowledge more efficiently we presented a simple and straight set of operators. Hence, our operators are more suitable to cope with evolution and co-evolution of knowledge. In contrast, approaches regarding ontology changes in response to certain needs do not cope with integrated ontologies sufficiently or even address co-evolution strategies.

8   Discussion and Conclusion

We introduced a set of adaptation operators that allow one to modify an ontology on special needs of different projects. Thus, we can share common knowledge between projects without ignoring the different needs and also reducing the workload for the elicitation and maintenance of knowledge. The case study as introduced in Sec. 5 shows that the use of adaptation operators can reduce the size of modifications significantly. The effect can be explained by the straightness property. Since modifications can be made locally, the changes are smaller compared to the case where only a minimal set of operations (add/remove) are used.

We discuss the achieved results with our research questions: *RQ1: How can common or domain-specific knowledge efficiently be shared among different projects?* Knowledge given by an ontology can be shared among projects by using stepwise adaptation to different domains and in the last step to the system itself. As presented in Fig. 1, knowledge is therefore hierarchically structured. This means that the most common knowledge is stored on top of the hierarchy. Thus, a maximal amount of the knowledge can be reused. Additionally, maintaining widespread knowledge becomes more straightforward.

RQ2: Which operations can adapt the common or domain-specific knowledge to fit the needs of different projects in a straight and sound manner? The defined adaptation operators (add, hide/unhide, change/reset) give an answer to RQ2. Adaptation operators can be used to add, change or remove knowledge. They are complete in the sense that they can be used to adapt an ontology to any other ontology. To show this, we can use the sometimes used argument by destructing the ontology by removing (here hiding) all elements, such that we get an empty ontology. Afterwards we can build any new ontology. The strength of our adaptation set is to be compatible with evolution, such that the evolution of common knowledge can be co-evolved in the adapted versions. Since many co-evolutions need a manual interaction, the straightness and the reversibility reduces the amount of manual interaction. This is also a result of the small adaptations between ontologies.

The presented approach is a foundation of the central part of the approach developed in the project SecVolution, namely the Security Maintenance Model. The sharing of global knowledge as well as the adaptation and evolution of the Security Maintenance Model is used to trigger semiautomatic evolutions of the software itself and thus forms an important base for a security aware evolution approach of long-living software systems. The advantages of the presented approach are used to integrate our project work with other projects in the joint case study CoCoME of the SPP "Design for Future - Managed Software Evolution". In future work, we furthermore plan to use the results presented here in the context of model-based development of secure software [15,14].

In summary, software maintenance of long-living software can benefit from domain-specific knowledge which is gathered and adapted during development. Our approach aims to decrease the effort to adapt required knowledge and thus increases the return of investment.

References

1. British Parliament: Data Protection Act (1998)
2. Bundesministerium des Inneren: Bundesdatenschutzgesetz. Bundesgesetzblatt
3. Bürger, J., Jürjens, J., Ruhroth, T., Gärtner, S., Schneider, K.: Model-based security engineering: Managed co-evolution of security knowledge and software models. In: Aldini, A., Lopez, J., Martinelli, F. (eds.) FOSAD VII. LNCS, vol. 8604, pp. 34–53. Springer, Heidelberg (2014)
4. Calvanese, D., De Giacomo, G., Lenzerini, M.: A Framework for Ontology Integration. In: The Emerging Semantic Web. IOS Press (2002)
5. EU Parliament: Directive 95/46/EC of the european parliament and of the council of 24 october 1995. Official Journal of the European Union L 281, 0031–0050 (1995)
6. Gärtner, S., Ruhroth, T., Bürger, J., Schneider, K., Jürjens, J.: Maintaining Requirements for Long-Living Software Systems by Incorporating Security Knowledge. In: 22nd IEEE International Requirements Engineering Conference, pp. 103–112. IEEE (2014)
7. Grubb, P., Takang, A.: Software Maintenance: Concepts and Practice. World Scientific (2003)
8. Haase, P., Stojanovic, L.: Consistent evolution of OWL ontologies. In: Gómez-Pérez, A., Euzenat, J. (eds.) ESWC 2005. LNCS, vol. 3532, pp. 182–197. Springer, Heidelberg (2005)
9. Happel, H., Seedorf, S.: Applications of ontologies in software engineering. In: Proc. of Workshop on Sematic Web Enabled Software Engineering (SWESE) (2006)
10. Heflin, J., Hendler, J., Luke, S.: Coping with changing ontologies in a distributed environment. In: AAAI 1999 Workshop on Ontology Management (1999)
11. Herold, S., et al.: CoCoME - The common component modeling example. In: Rausch, A., Reussner, R., Mirandola, R., Plášil, F. (eds.) The Common Component Modeling Example. LNCS, vol. 5153, pp. 16–53. Springer, Heidelberg (2008)
12. Javed, M.: Operational Change Management and Change Pattern Identification for Ontology Evolution. PhD thesis, Dublin City University (May 2013)

13. Javed, M., Abgaz, Y.M., Pahl, C.: Ontology change management and identification of change patterns. J. Data Semantics 2(2-3), 119–143 (2013)
14. Jürjens, J.: Secure Systems Development with UML. Springer (2005)
15. Jürjens, J., Wimmel, G.: Security modelling for electronic commerce: The Common Electronic Purse Specifications. In: Schmid, B., Stanoevska-Slabeva, K., Tscham-mer, V. (eds.) Towards the E-Society. IFIP, vol. 74, pp. 489–506. Springer, Boston (2001)
16. Klein, M., Fensel, D.: Ontology versioning on the Semantic Web. In: SWWS, pp. 75–91 (2001)
17. Meyer, S., Averbakh, A., Ronneberger, T., Schneider, K.: Experiences from Es-tablishing Knowledge Management in a Joint Research Project. In: Dieste, O., Jedlitschka, A., Juristo, N. (eds.) PROFES 2012. LNCS, vol. 7343, pp. 233–247. Springer, Heidelberg (2012)
18. Münch, J., Armbrust, O., Kowalczyk, M., Soto, M.: Software Process Definition and Management. Springer (2012)
19. Noy, N.F., Kunnatur, S., Klein, M., Musen, M.A.: Tracking changes during ontol-ogy evolution. In: McIlraith, S.A., Plexousakis, D., van Harmelen, F. (eds.) ISWC 2004. LNCS, vol. 3298, pp. 259–273. Springer, Heidelberg (2004)
20. Noy, N.F., Chugh, A., Liu, W., Musen, M.A.: A framework for ontology evolu-tion in collaborative environments. In: Cruz, I., Decker, S., Allemang, D., Preist, C., Schwabe, D., Mika, P., Uschold, M., Aroyo, L.M. (eds.) ISWC 2006. LNCS, vol. 4273, pp. 544–558. Springer, Heidelberg (2006)
21. Pinto, H.S., Martins, J.P.: A methodology for ontology integration. In: Proc. of K-CAP, pp. 131–138. ACM (2001)
22. Ruhroth, T., Gärtner, S., Bürger, J., Jürjens, J., Schneider, K.: Versioning and evo-lution requirements for model-based system development. In: International Work-shop on Comparison and Versioning of Software Models (CVSM) (2014)
23. Ruhroth, T., Wehrheim, H.: Refinement-preserving co-evolution. In: Breitman, K., Cavalcanti, A. (eds.) ICFEM 2009. LNCS, vol. 5885, pp. 620–638. Springer, Hei-delberg (2009)
24. Ruhroth, T., Wehrheim, H.: Model evolution and refinement. Science of Computer Programming 77(3), 270–289 (2012)
25. Stanford Center for Biomedical Informatics Research (BMIR): Protege - homepage, http://protege.stanford.edu
26. Stojanovic, L.: Methods and tools for ontology evolution. PhD thesis, Karlsruhe Institute of Technology (2004)
27. Stojanovic, L., Maedche, A., Motik, B., Stojanovic, N.: User-driven ontology evo-lution management. In: Gómez-Pérez, A., Benjamins, V.R. (eds.) EKAW 2002. LNCS (LNAI), vol. 2473, pp. 285–300. Springer, Heidelberg (2002)
28. Tiwana, A.: An empirical study of the effect of knowledge integration on software development performance. Information and Software Technology 46(13), 899–906 (2004)
29. Udrea, O., Getoor, L., Miller, R.J.: Leveraging data and structure in ontology integration. In: Proc. of SIGMOD, pp. 449–460. ACM (2007)

Metrics to Measure the Change Impact in ATL Model Transformations

Andreza Vieira and Franklin Ramalho

Department of Computer and Systems,
Federal University of Campina Grande
Campina Grande, Paraíba, Brazil
andreza@copin.ufcg.edu.br,
franklin@computacao.ufcg.edu.br

Abstract. The Model-Driven Development (MDD) shifts the focus on code to models in the software development process. In MDD, model transformations are elements that play important role. In the software process, MDD projects evolve as changes in their transformations are frequent. Before applying changes it is important to measure their impacts in the transformation. However, currently no technique helps practitioners in this direction. In this work, we conducted an exploratory study to identify the criteria used by practitioners to measure the impact of changes in model transformations. As a result, we propose a set of metrics to measure such impacts. By measuring the change impact, practitioners can (i) save effort and development time for estimating costs to apply changes; and (ii) better schedule and prioritize changes according to the impact.

Keywords: MDD, model transformation, ATL, change impact, metrics.

1   Introduction and Motivation

An approach that works to provide greater automation and higher productivity within the software development process is the MDD (Model-Driven Development) [1]. It separates the specification of a system from its implementation details. The main objective of this approach is to shift the focus on code to models in the software development process. Within the MDD, transformation definitions are transformation rules describing how input models can be transformed into output models. ATL (ATLAS Transformation Language) [2] is an example of transformation languages.

During the software process, projects evolve and their requirements constantly change for several reasons, such as to satisfy the user expectations or to reach software design improvements. In the same way, MDD-based projects evolve and their transformation definitions constantly change. Before applying changes to a transformation it is important: (i) to understand the whole transformation, *i.e.* the dependencies and relationships between its elements; and (ii) to know the consequences of the change in advance, *i.e.* the whole impact caused by the change. An approach that can be used to achieve such information is the change impact

A. Jedlitschka et al. (Eds.): PROFES 2014, LNCS 8892, pp. 254–268, 2014.

analysis: the process to find potential consequences of a change and estimate what needs to be modified to accomplish a change.

In the MDD context there is a lack of techniques for helping practitioners during the MDD-based software process. Nowadays, when practitioners have to apply changes to their model transformations they adopt a manual process to analyze and measure the impacts, which is a hard, labor-intensive and error-prone activity. In MDD, [3] proposes a catalogue of refactorings for model transformations. On the other hand, some works [4, 5, 6, 7, 8, 9] propose approaches to help practitioners adapting their transformations and models according to changes performed in the metamodels referenced by them. However, these works allow neither the analysis nor the measurement of the impact caused by a change in the transformation. In the general context of software change, there are some works that use change impact analysis techniques to guide changes. For instance, [10] applies data mining to version histories in order to identify related changes from files changed in the past.

Within the software process most of the time is spent during maintenance tasks, such as correcting bugs and improving functionalities. Therefore, the metrics to measure the change impact could improve the software process.

In this paper, we conducted an exploratory case study to investigate how the practitioners manually measure the change impact within ATL model transformations before a change is applied. As the nature of the changes, we consider bug correction, transformation evolution, transformation maintenance and transformation refinement. We analyzed all answers of the participants and the results of this study pointed to significant criteria. The objective of this work was to identify such criteria and define a set of metrics to help practitioners measuring such impact automatically. With the proposed metrics the practitioners can: (i) save effort and development time for estimating costs to apply changes; and (ii) better schedule and prioritize changes according to the impact. By knowing the impact of a change, project managers can more easily realize the costs and time required to accomplish a change and thus they can better optimize the development process.

This paper is organized as follows. In Section 2, we introduce concepts on MDD and ATL transformation language, as well as change impact. In Section 3, we explain the exploratory study we conducted to obtain some criteria that practitioners use to measure the change impact. In Section 4, we show the metrics we defined. In Section 5, we give an overview concerning related work on change impact measure. Finally, Section 6 summarizes our conclusions and gives some pointers to future work.

2   Background

2.1   MDD and ATL Transformations

The MDD approach recognizes the need of having several kinds of models to represent the software, such as business processes, system requirements, architecture, design and tests. In MDD, the effort and time spent during the tests and implementation tasks of the software development lifecycle are shifted to modeling, metamodeling and transformations tasks. The elements specified in a given model are defined by its metamodel, which is a model that describes another model. Metamodels are MDD artifacts that define the abstract syntax of languages and domains. An example of a metamodel is the UML (Unified Modeling Language) metamodel introduced by the UML specification [11]. For instance, modelers can design classes, attributes, associations and other elements in a UML class diagram because these elements are defined by the UML metamodel.

In MDD, source models can automatically be transformed into target models by means of transformation definitions that are model transformation rules that describe how source models must automatically generate target models. Transformation languages, such as ATL, are used to express the transformation definitions, which are executed by a tool called transformation engine.

ATL is one of the most popular transformation languages. It allows developers to define ATL *modules*, which specifies the way that source models will automatically generate target models. Within *modules* developers can specify helpers and rules. ATL supports two kinds of helpers: *functional* and *attribute*, which can be viewed as methods and constants, respectively. Both can be referenced from different points of an ATL transformation. On the other hand, ATL supports three kinds of rules: matched rules, lazy matched rules and called rules. A matched rule is a declarative rule that specifies for which kinds of source elements the target elements must be generated. It is automatically executed when the ATL transformation is executed. A lazy matched rule is a kind of matched rule that must explicitly be invoked by another rule to be executed. A called rule is an imperative rule that can optionally generate target model elements and must be invoked by another rule to be executed.

Fig. 1 presents an excerpt of the UML2JAVA transformation [12] that generates a Java model from a UML model. The Java model to be generated holds information for creating Java classes, as well as their attributes and methods. Line 1 specifies the module name, whereas line 2 specifies the input and output model names, both followed by their metamodel names. Lines 3-4 specify a functional helper that verifies if a UML model element has public visibility or not. The matched rule *AttributeToField* is specified at lines 5-10. It enables to match an attribute of a UML model and generate a field of a Java model in the way that the field's properties assume the same values as the attribute's properties: *name*, *isPublic* and *type*.

```
1   module UML2JAVA;
2   create OUT : JAVA from IN : UML;
3   helper context UML!ModelElement def: isPublic() :
4           Boolean = self.visibility = #vk_public;
5   rule AttributeToField {
6       from e : UML!Attribute
7       to out : JAVA!Field (
8               name <- e.name,
9               isPublic <- e.isPublic(),
10              type <- e.type ) }
```

Fig. 1. Excerpt of the UML2Java transformation module

2.2   Change Impact

Software changes within the software development process must carefully be managed given that changes to requirements may lead to massive software changes and unpredictable consequences that often delay their implementation. It is important to understand the software to be changed and the consequences of the change in advance. The change impact analysis is a way to accomplish such information.

According to [13], the change impact analysis is the process in which it is possible to identify the potential consequences of a change and estimate what needs to be modified to accomplish it. The change impact analysis can be used by means of: (i) static analysis to detect the impacts of a change before it is applied based on the source code (or bytecode) inspection; and (ii) dynamic analysis to detect the impacts of a change after it is applied based on the software execution traces.

3   An Exploratory Case Study

This section describes an exploratory case study we conducted as a preliminary research to define some metrics with the intent to measure the change impact in model transformations. All the study material is available online[1].

3.1   Study Definition

The main objective of this case study was to *identify which criteria the participants adopt to previously analyze and measure change impacts in model transformations before applying them*. Thus, we asked them to manually analyze some changes to measure the impact of applying them and report to us the criteria they adopted. After, we analyzed all criteria and defined a set of metrics to measure the change impacts.

In this context, we elaborated a research question for the study: *Which criteria the participants adopt to measure the impact of changes in model transformations?*

3.2   Study Planning

To gather a group of participants for this study we sent a message inviting ATL communities and ATL experts. As a result, we gathered 12 persons available to engage in this case study, which: (i) were from different universities and research groups; (ii) were undergraduate and postgraduate (PhD or MSc) students in Computer Science; (iii) were experts[2] in ATL transformations; and (iv) had different level of expertise since some of them worked with ATL for years in their projects. We also invited the professional community to engage in this study, but nobody was available. Even considering only students in this study, it is important to emphasize that we

---

[1] http://goo.gl/T22wKG

[2] As criteria we consider *experts* the participants with at least one year of experience with ATL. Therefore, all participants of this study were experts.

selected only students with wide experience in using and that adopted ATL to implement their real projects during their researches.

We adopted ATL in this work as a proof of concept because: (i) it is a popular transformation language; (ii) there is a rich documentation available for users and developers; (iii) there are many repositories with transformations available for use, becoming possible the evaluation of this work; and (iv) our research group has large experience in constructing ATL transformations.

We selected ATL transformations as the cases used in this study. To select them we investigated several changes from repositories with real ATL projects developed by different research groups. We choose four ATL projects and, for each of them, we selected one transformation module: (i) *PITM2PSTM* [3] (project Mobit); (ii) *BPMN para Atividades* [4] (project Transformacao-bpm) (BPMN to Activities, project Transformation BPM); (iii) *emig2EMFTVM* [5] (project Emf Migrate); and (iv) *SimpleGTtoEMFTVM* [6] (project SimpleGT).

For each transformation module we choose three changes to be analyzed, which we extracted from different versions of their repositories. Therefore, a set of 12 changes were analyzed. To select these modules we followed the criteria: (i) they should not be very large (up to 1.400 LOC[7]) because the participants had to manually analyze each change and this task would be time-consuming for very large transformation modules; and (ii) the changes should not be the same. We selected four ATL model transformations and three changes for each one to be analyzed due to the time the participants would spend to perform the study. If we have selected many cases, the results of the study would have been damaged due to the fatigue of the participants.

To allow the execution of this study we provided all instrumentation for the participants. It includes: (i) a presentation on the case study, where the study's conductor presented to the participants the study context, objectives, material to be used, changes to be analyzed and tasks to be accomplished; and (ii) an execution guide, where the participants followed a set of instructions to execute the study.

To collect all data for this case study we applied the execution guide to the participants, where they followed the instructions to analyze each change and then answered a questionnaire related to the change being analyzed.

3.3 Study Execution

We executed a pilot study to revel deficiencies in the design of this case study before conducting a larger study. After, we did some adjustments in the execution guide and we started the execution of the case study. As the participants were located in different places, we conducted the study through videoconferences where the study's conductor: (i) presented the study to be executed; and (ii) assigned to each participant an execution guide with a different order of the changes to be analyzed, which were

---

[3] https://sites.google.com/a/computacao.ufcg.edu.br/mobit
[4] https://code.google.com/p/transformacao-bpm
[5] https://code.google.com/a/eclipselabs.org/p/emfmigrate
[6] http://soft.vub.ac.be/soft/research/mdd/simplegt
[7] To count the LOC (Lines Of Code) we consider the lines of code, the empty lines and the comments of the code.

randomly defined to avoid that the analysis of the latter changes be affected due to the fatigue of the participants. Then, the participants executed the analysis of each change and after they answered a questionnaire about the impact of the changes and criteria they should adopt to measure such impacts. Each participant spent about three hours to execute the case study.

3.4   Study Analysis and Interpretation

With the case study we could observe that the participants do not have a common consensus about all the criteria adopted to measure the impact of changes to be applied to model transformations. In general, the majority of the participants measured the change impacts according to the parts of the transformation affected with the change, which we call as *impacted elements*[8].

To answer *the research question* for this case study, we present as follows a compilation of all criteria the participants adopted to measure the change impacts as well as the respective metrics we defined to them.

- *Characteristic of the element* - each element has its own characteristics. For instance, a matched rule can be an abstract rule and extend other rule. On the other hand, a helper can be invoked by other elements and accept parameters. Therefore, the more relevant characteristics are, the higher the change impact. The associated metric we defined to this criteria is the *RTEC* (section 4.1);

- *Types of relationships* - within a model transformation there are several relationships between the elements. For instance, a matched rule R1 can have a relationship called *extends* with another matched rule R2, which indicates that R1 extends R2. Therefore, as the element has more relationships and the more important they are, the higher the impact is. The associated metric we defined to this criteria is the *RTERT* (section 4.2);

- *Number of impacted elements* - for each change to be applied, the participants identified the element to be changed within the transformation and they looked for possible dependencies of this element. For instance, if a helper that is invoked by two rules will be removed from the transformation, then such rules will be impacted with the change. Therefore, the more elements affected with the change, the higher the change impact. The associated metric we defined to this criteria is the *RITE* (section 4.3);

- *Change type* - the impact in a transformation module depends on the change type to be applied. Some change types can impact it more than others. For instance, the change *removeHelper* usually causes an impact higher than the change *changeHelperName* since the elements invoking the helper to be changed can become inconsistent if they are not adapted to the change. Therefore, the more complex is the change type, the higher the impact. The associated metric we defined to this criteria is the *RCTAE* (section 4.4);

---

[8] In this paper, *element* is a term we use to represent: helpers, attributes, called rules, matched rules and lazy matched rules of a model transformation.

- *Impact in the output model* - some changes can affect the output model generated by the transformation. For instance, if a matched rule will be removed, then the output model generated by this rule will be affected. Therefore, the more the output model is affected, the higher the impact. The associated metric we defined to this criteria is the *RCITOM*.

3.5 Threats to Validity

We enumerate as follows the threats to the validity that we identified in this study as well as how we tried to control or mitigate their effects on the observations.

Internal Validity: The participants had to analyze 12 different changes and answer a questionnaire for each one, which took to them about three hours. We believe that the analysis of the latter changes would be affected by the fatigue of the participants or by the hurry to finish the study. To address this threat, we developed different versions of the execution guide and for each one we randomized the order of the changes to be analyzed. Also, the execution guides were randomly assigned to the participants.

External Validity: As we have conducted a case study, a condition limits the generalization of our results: they were obtained from the analysis of only 12 participants. In addition, even though the transformation modules used in this study are real and non-trivial, a few number of changes were analyzed (only 12).

4   Definition of the Metrics

This section presents the metrics we defined based on criteria reported by the participants of the study to measure the impact of changes in model transformations. As a starting point, we defined five metrics: *RTEC, RTERT, RITE, RCTAE* and *RCITOM*. Due to limit of space the metric *RCITOM (Relevance of the Change Impact in the Transformation Output Model)* is neither described nor considered in this paper. Table 1 shows a summary of the metrics to be described in the next subsections.

The result calculated by each metric can assume values in a range between *0* and *1*. The closer to 0 is the value the lower is the impact and the closer to 1 the higher is the impact. Let $E = \{e_1,..., e_n\}$ be the set of elements specified in a transformation, where n is the number of elements specified within the transformation under analysis. Each ATL transformation has a given number of elements that can be helpers, attributes, called rules, matched rules and lazy matched rules. Therefore, the proposed approach obtains (automatically) this number from the transformation to calculate the metrics.

Table 1. Summary of the proposed (and described in this work) metrics

Set of Metrics
RTEC (Relevance of the Transformation Element Characteristics)
RTERT (Relevance of the Transformation Element Relation Types)
RITE (Relevance of the Impacted Transformation Elements)
RCTAE (Relevance of the Change Type Applied to an Element)

4.1   RTEC

The *RTEC (Relevance of the Transformation Element Characteristics)* metric states the relevance of a transformation element in terms of the characteristics it can assume in the transformation. They give a different meaning and relevance for the element since their occurrence (or not) may become the element more or less complex. We analyzed each element of several ATL transformations to find characteristics they can assume.

Table 2. Classification of the transformation elements characteristics

Characteristic	ATL Transf. Element	Relevance Index
isAbstract	Matched or Lazy Matched Rule	0.16
isEntrypoint	Called Rule	0.15
hasUsingBlock	Matched or Lazy Matched Rule	0.16
	Called Rule	0.13
hasNotPrimitiveContextType	Helper	0.17
	Attribute	0.22
hasNotPrimitiveReturnType	Helper	0.17
hasNotPrimitiveType	Attribute	0.18
hasFilter	Matched or Lazy Matched Rule	0.18
hasParameter	Called Rule	0.15
	Helper	0.19
hasImperativeBlock	Matched or Lazy Matched Rule	0.16
	Called Rule	0.13
hasToBlock	Called Rule	0.16
hasIfExpression	Helper	0.16
	Attribute	0.20
	Matched or Lazy Matched Rule	0.16
	Called Rule	0.13
hasLetExpression	Helper	0.12
	Attribute	0.16
hasCollectionExpression	Helper	0.19
	Attribute	0.24
	Matched or Lazy Matched Rule	0.18
	Called Rule	0.15

Table 2 details the characteristics (*Column 1*) as follows: (i) *Column 2* shows the elements that can assume the characteristics. For instance, a *matched rule* can assume the characteristics *isAbstract* and *hasUsingBlock*, *i.e.* it can be abstract and comprise a block responsible for declaring and initiating variables; and (ii) *Column 3* shows the relevance index we defined for each characteristic. It captures the level of influence that a characteristic can reach in the whole transformation in a way that its presence (or not) can become the maintenance of the transformation easier (or not). For instance, a rule that comprises an imperative block is commonly more complex than another one without any characteristic, since it enables users to specify imperative code, in which one can invoke others elements as well as specify statements. Therefore, the bigger is the number of characteristics an element assumes, more relevant we consider it is.

To define the relevance indexes we conducted a new study with the objective of obtaining a number to represent the relevance of each characteristic. To engage in this study we selected 09 expert ATL users from the 12 ones engaged in the previous study. We elaborated a form[9] where the participants had to assign for each characteristic a value in a range between 0 and 5, where 0 means *no relevance* and 5 means *extreme relevance*. They had to consider the relevance they think the characteristics represent to a transformation as well as to observe what and how the characteristics can influence the impact of changing an element. We collected the results and, for each characteristic, we calculated the average of the values assigned by the participants. After, we normalized each calculated average in the way that the sum of the values normalized (relevance indexes) for each characteristic should be 1.

The metric *RTEC* is calculated through the function *calcRelevOfCharac(e$_i$)*, where e_i represents the element to be changed. As presented in (1), this function sums the relevance indexes for the characteristics that e_i assumes. Let $C = \{c_1,...,c_s\}$ be the set of relevance indexes for the characteristics c_k $(k = 1,...,s)$ that e_i assumes, where s is the number of characteristics that e_i assumes.

$$calcRelevOfCharac(e_i) = \sum_{k=1}^{s} c_k \qquad (1)$$

To illustrate this metric we present in Fig. 2 an excerpt of the called rule TDFile (the element to be changed) from the transformation PITM2PSTM[10] (project Mobit) that assumes the characteristics *hasToBlock* and *hasImperativeBlock*. Considering their relevance indexes, after calculating the *RTEC* we obtain the result *0.29*.

```
1   rule TDFile() {
2       to db: C!DeclarationsBlock(
3           name <- 'includes'),
4       stH: C!CompilationDirectiveDeclaration(
5           name <- '<stdio.h>',
6           kind <- #include)
7       do {
8           self.createvStartTestFunction();
9           self.createvTestConfigurationFunction();
10          self.createScheduler();
11      }
12  }
```

Fig. 2. Called rule TDFile

---

[9] http://goo.gl/1KAGYn
[10] http://goo.gl/aEpyqM

4.2   RTERT

The *RTERT (Relevance of the Transformation Element Relation Types)* metric states the relevance of an element in terms of the relation types it assumes. By observing the dependencies between the elements of many transformations, we found four relation types: (i) *invokes*, when an element invokes another one; (ii) *isInvoked*, when an element is invoked by another one; (iii) *extends*, when a rule extends another one; and (iv) *isExtended*, when a rule is extended by another one. Each element can simultaneously assume several relations and optionally it can assumes neither of them.

It is important to consider the relation types when measuring the change impact because they indicate the relevance of the element to be changed through its dependencies: the bigger is the number of relations it assumes, more elements in the transformation are related to and potentially depend on it. For instance, a lazy matched rule that assumes the relation types *isExtended*, *invokes* and *isInvoked* has more dependencies in the transformation than another one that assumes only the relation *isInvoked*, since the former assumes more relations.

Similarly to the metric *RTEC*, we defined a relevance index for each relation type to represent the level of influence a relation can reach in the transformation in a way that its presence (or not) can become the maintenance of the transformation easier (or not). We believe that each relation type can cause a different impact in the element, therefore, it must have a different relevance index.

The relevance indexes were defined through the same study conducted to obtain the relevance of the characteristics, as previously discussed in the metric *RTEC*. Table 3 shows the relation types and the relevance indexes we obtained from the study.

Table 3. Classification of the relation types

Relation Type	ATL Transf. Element	Relevance Index
Invokes	Helper, Attribute or Called Rule	0.49
	Matched Rule	0.34
	Lazy Matched Rule	0.25
isInvoked	Helper or Attribute	0.51
	Lazy Matched Rule	0.27
	Called Rule	0.51
Extends	Matched Rule	0.30
	Lazy Matched Rule	0.22
isExtended	Matched Rule	0.36
	Lazy Matched Rule	0.26

The metric *RTERT* is calculated through the *calcRelevOfRelType(e_i)* function, where e_i represents the element to be changed. As presented in (2), this function sums the relevance indexes for the relations that e_i assumes. Let $R = \{r_1,...,r_m\}$ be the set of relevance indexes for the relation r_k $(k = 1,...,m)$ that an element e_i assumes, where m is the number of relations that e_i assumes, considering all relation types.

$$calcRelevOfRelType(e_i) = \sum_{k=1}^{m} r_k \qquad (2)$$

To illustrate this metric we suppose that a change will be applied to the called rule previously presented in Fig. 2, which assumes relations of the types *invokes* and *isInvoked*, whose relevance indexes are 0.49 and 0.51, respectively. After calculating the metric *RTERT* we obtain the result *1*.

4.3   RITE

The *RITE (Relevance of the Impacted Transformation Elements)* metric states the relevance of a transformation element e_i in terms of the elements impacted when a given change is applied to e_i. As our approach adopted static analysis, it considers as impacted all elements that invoke or extend e_i, even if they do no invoke e_i in execution time. In addition, it only considers the impacted elements specified in the same transformation definition of the element to be changed.

It is important to consider the impacted elements when measuring the change impact because they indicate the parts of the transformation that must be adapted after the change is applied: the bigger is the number of impacted elements, the bigger is the effort to adapt them after the change. For instance, it is easier to apply a change to a rule that impacts two elements than to another rule that impacts seven elements.

The metric *RITE* is calculated through the function *calcRelevOfImpactedElem(e_i)*, where e_i represents the element to be changed. As presented in (3), this function calculates the ration between the number of elements impacted with the change (t) and the total number of elements of the transformation (n). Let $E' = \{e'_1,...,e'_t\}$; $t < n$; $E' \subseteq E$ be the subset of elements impacted $e'_i (i = 1,...,t)$ when a change is applied to e_i, where t is number of impacted elements.

$$calcRelevOfImpactedElem(e_i) = \frac{t}{n} \qquad (3)$$

To illustrate this metric we suppose that a change will be applied to the called rule previously presented in Fig. 2. As the *TDFile* rule is invoked by only one rule within the transformation, the change has only one impacted element. The transformation is composed by a total of 26 elements, resulting in the value *0.04* for the RITE metric.

4.4   RCTAE

The *RCTAE (Relevance of the Change Type Applied to an Element)* metric states the relevance of a change type according to the difficulty to apply it to an element of the transformation module. Such difficulty is measured through the number of actions required to apply the change as well as the relevance of the element to be changed. If this metric was not considered, change types as *removeRule* and *changeRuleName* would have the same impact. However, the impact of removing a rule is usually higher. The table comprising all possible actions that must be performed to apply each change type we defined is available online (see http://goo.gl/kcZ3sJ).

It is important to emphasize that the number of actions required to apply a given change type to an element is automatically obtained by the tool support according to the actions actually required for it, instead of all possible actions. For instance, to apply the change type *removeHelper* to a helper *H1* a number of four actions are possible: (i) to verify if any element of the transformation invokes *H1*; (ii) if it is invoked, to remove the invocations from the elements that invoke it; (iii) if it is invoked, to adapt the elements that invoke it after the removal; and (iv) to remove *H1* of the transformation. However, only two actions (the first and the last one) are actually required to remove this helper since it is not invoked.

Besides the difficulty to apply the change type, *RCTAE* also considers the relevance of the element to be changed. Therefore, we defined a different value for each transformation element, *i.e.* a different relevance index.

In the same study that we conducted to obtain the relevance indexes used in the metrics *RTEC* and *RTERT*, we obtained the relevance indexes used in the metric *RCTAE*. Table 4 shows the transformation elements and the relevance indexes we obtained from the study.

Table 4. Classification of the transformation elements

ATL Transformation Element	Relevance Index
Called Rule	0.62
Attribute	0.69
Lazy Matched Rule	0.72
Helper	0.76
Matched Rule	0.87

The metric *RCTAE* is calculated by means of the *calcRelevOfChangeType(e_i, ch)* function, where the parameter e_i represents the element to be changed and *ch* represents the change type. As presented in (4), this function calculates the ration between the number of actions required to apply the change *ch* and the maximum number of possible actions required to apply a change (considering all change types we defined). Then, it calculates the average between this result and the relevance index of the element to be changed. Let:

- $A = \{a_1,...,a_p\}$ be the set of required actions $a_i(i = 1,...,p)$ that must be performed to apply a given change type *ch* to an element e_i of the transformation, where *p* is the number of required actions;

- *d* be the maximum number of possible actions required to apply a change, considering all change types we defined. To obtain this number we enumerated the actions for each change type and among them the maximum number of possible actions is 08 (for the change type *removeRule*);

- *b* be the relevance index of the element to be changed.

$$calcRelevOfChangeType(e_i, ch) = \frac{p/d + b}{2} \tag{4}$$

To illustrate this metric we suppose that the change type *AddRuleParameter* will be applied to the called rule previously presented in Fig. 2. To add a parameter to this called rule it is required to perform 03 actions. According to the results obtained from the study, the relevance index for a *called rule* is 0.62. Given that the maximum number of possible actions required to apply a change (considering all change types we defined) is 08, after calculating the metric *RCTAE* we obtain the result 0.50.

4.5   Measuring the Impact Value

To automatically measure the impact value based on the four metrics previously presented we defined the function *calcChangeImpactValue(e_i)* presented in (5), where e_i is the element to be changed. Let: $M = \{m_1,...,m_y\}$ be the set of metrics m_k ($k = 1,...,4$) defined by (1), (2), (3) and (4) where y is the number of metrics to be calculated.

$$calcChangeImpactValue(e_i) = \frac{\sum_{k=1}^{y} m_k}{y} \tag{5}$$

Practitioners that specify their transformations in ATL can use the proposed metrics given that the information required for calculating them can be retrieved from any ATL transformation through a static analyzer. For instance, to calculate the metric *RTERT* for an element e_i it is required to: (i) identify number of relations that e_i assumes considering all relation types; and (ii) define a relevance index for each relation type. All these information are available in ATL transformations. Thus, a static analyzer for ATL is important to help practitioners extracting such information.

In addition, the metrics can also be adopted to calculate the change impact of programs specified in general purpose languages, such as Java. However, they must be adapted according to the semantics of Java constructors. For instance, before removing a given Java method the metric *RTERT* would be reused to calculate the relevance of this method in terms of its relation types.

Practitioners can customize the function named *calcChangeImpactValue(e_i)* by considering just the metrics they are interested. For instance, they can remove the metric *RTEC* if they do not wish to consider the properties assumed by the element to be changed. Additionally, practitioners can add new metrics.

5   Related Works

To the best of our knowledge, within the MDD context few works are focused on change impact measure. [3] proposes a catalogue of refactorings to improve the performance and quality attributes of model transformations. However, [3] does not measure the impact on the transformation caused by the change (refactoring).

[4] proposes an approach to help developers adapting their model transformations according to changes performed in the source metamodel. It uses HOTs (Higher-Order Transformations) [14] to generate *annotated transformations* that include suggestions about how metamodel changes have impacted the rules.

[5] and [6] propose a methodology to adapt transformations after the metamodels referenced by them are evolved. The former is composed by three phases (impact detection, impact analysis and transformation adaptation) to reestablish consistency after metamodel evolution, while the latter proposes to adapt transformations by means of external transformation composition.

[7] addresses the identification, prediction and evaluation concerning the significance of the metamodel change impact over the artifacts. It proposes an approach that allows developers to define relationships between the metamodel and its related artifacts, as well as to detect such elements within the artifacts affected by the metamodel changes. In addition, there are some works that propose to automate the migration of existing models according to the evolved metamodel [8, 9].

Although [4, 5, 6, 7, 8, 9] are pretty related to our work on impact analysis, they are focused on metamodel evolution and they allow developers neither to analyze nor to measure the impact on the transformation caused by a change applied to any element of the transformation itself.

Software metrics are widely used to assess the quality of software in general. Within the MDD context, such issue has also been addressed. Both [15] and [16] propose a set of metrics to measure model transformations and to enable assessing their quality. However, the former is applied to transformations defined using the ASF+SDF term rewriting system, while the latter is applied to ATL modules and libraries (but the metrics are not focused on change impact measurement).

In the context of software process and MDA, [17] proposes a conceptual framework with a metrics suite to evaluate maintainability of MDA process models, *i.e.* software process. However, the metrics proposed in [17] are related to MDA process models and not to change impact analysis.

6   Conclusions and Future Works

In this work, we have conducted an exploratory case study to identify criteria that practitioners adopt to analyze and measure the change impact in ATL model transformations. We found five criteria: (i) the characteristic of the element to be changed; (ii) the relationship types of the element to be changed; (iii) the number of elements impacted with the change; (iv) the change type to be applied; and (v) the impact caused in the output model generated by the transformation. Based on these criteria, we defined a set of metrics to measure the change impact.

The metrics are very important for the MDD-based software process because they aid practitioners with their maintenance tasks. When the change impact is measured by using the proposed metrics, then project managers can use the impact value as support to make project decisions, as well as to better schedule and prioritize changes according to the impact. By knowing the impact of a change, project managers can more easily realize the costs and time required to accomplish a change and thus they can better optimize the development process. In addition, the risk of costly change (re-work) and the potential for errors in planning estimates are reduced.

To complement the metrics proposed in this work, it would be useful to define metrics in the context of dynamic analysis to consider the impact in the logic and behavior of the transformation elements. For instance, the metric would detect if the removal of a helper affects the behavior of the rule that invokes.

As ongoing work, we are: (i) elaborating a study to evaluate the effectiveness of the metrics; (ii) developing a tool support to automatically measure the change impact based on the proposed metrics; (iii) elaborating more metrics to be incorporated in the tool support; (iv) defining a generic change impact measure approach for any model transformation language; and (v) defining new metrics based on dynamic analysis.

Acknowledgments. We would like to acknowledge the CAPES for the financial support as well as the participants engaged in the study we conducted in this work.

References

1. Selic, B.: The Pragmatics of Model-Driven Development. IEEE Softw. 20(5), 19–25 (2003)
2. Jouault, F., Kurtev, I.: Transforming Models with ATL. In: Bruel, J.-M. (ed.) MoDELS 2005 Workshops. LNCS, vol. 3844, pp. 128–138. Springer, Heidelberg (2006)
3. Wimmer, M., Martínez, S., Jouault, F., Cabot, J.: A Catalogue of Refactorings for Model-to-Model Transformations. Journal of Object Technology (JOT) 11(2), 1–40 (2012)
4. Garcia, J., Díaz, O.: Adaptation of Transformations to Metamodel Changes. Library 2, 1–9 (2010)
5. Mendez, D., Etien, A., Muller, A., Casallas, R.: Towards Transformation Migration After Metamodel Evolution. In: Model and Evolution Workshop, Olso, Norway (2010)
6. Garcés, K., Vara, J., Jouault, F., Marcos, E.: Adapting Transformations to Meta-Model Changes via External Transformation Composition. Software and Systems Modeling (2012)
7. Iovino, L., Pierantonio, A., Malavolta, O.: On the Impact Significance of Metamodel Evolution in MDE. Journal of Object Technology 11(3), 1–33 (2012)
8. Garcés, K., Jouault, F., Cointe, P., Bézivin, J.: Managing Model Adaptation by Precise Detection of Metamodel Changes. In: Paige, R.F., Hartman, A., Rensink, A. (eds.) ECMDA-FA 2009. LNCS, vol. 5562, pp. 34–49. Springer, Heidelberg (2009)
9. Herrmannsdoerfer, M., Benz, S., Juergens, E.: COPE - Automating Coupled Evolution of Metamodels and Models. In: Drossopoulou, S. (ed.) ECOOP 2009. LNCS, vol. 5653, pp. 52–76. Springer, Heidelberg (2009)
10. Zimmermann, T., Zeller, A., Weissgerber, P., Diehl, S.: Mining Version Histories to Guide Software Changes. IEEE Transactions on Software Engineering 31(6), 429–445 (2005)
11. Object Management Group. Unified Modeling Language (UML) Infrastructure 2.4.1 (2011), http://goo.gl/9W81lu
12. INRIA, UML to Java Example (2005), http://goo.gl/2yPY2O
13. Bohner, S., Arnold, R.: Software Change Impact Analysis. IEEE Computer Society Press, Los Alamitos (1996)
14. Tisi, M., Cabot, J., Jouault, F.: Improving higher-order transformations support in ATL. In: Tratt, L., Gogolla, M. (eds.) ICMT 2010. LNCS, vol. 6142, pp. 215–229. Springer, Heidelberg (2010)
15. Vignaga, A.: Metrics for Measuring ATL Model Ttransformations, Tech. Report, University of Chile (2009)
16. Amstel, M.F., Lange, C.F.J., Brand, M.G.J.: Metrics for Analyzing the Quality of Model Transformations (2008)
17. da Silva, B.C., Maciel, R.S.P., Ramalho, F.: Evaluating Maintainability of MDA Software Process Models. In: Heidrich, J., Oivo, M., Jedlitschka, A., Baldassarre, M.T. (eds.) PROFES 2013. LNCS, vol. 7983, pp. 199–213. Springer, Heidelberg (2013)

Initial Data Triangulation of Agile Practices Usage: Comparing Mapping Study and Survey Results

Philipp Diebold

Fraunhofer IESE, Fraunhofer-Platz 1,
67663 Kaiserslautern, Germany
philipp.diebold@iese.fraunhofer.de

Abstract. *Background:* Agile software development methods are commonly customized to a specific need, such as usage or adaptation of agile practices. In order to identify which agile practices organizations are using, we performed a systematic mapping study. *Objective:* In this paper, our goal is to present the generalizable state of the practice in agile practices usage. *Method:* We used triangulation of these study data and the data of the state of agile development survey related to agile practices usage. *Results:* This comparison shows similar results; obvious deviations and contradictions are discussed. *Conclusion:* The results of the triangulation of the two studies can be considered as an initial generalizable state of the practice for the usage of agile practices.

Keywords: software processes, agile software development, agile practices.

1   Introduction

Today software companies are commonly using agile methods, e.g. Scrum, by adopting a subset of the related agile practices that are appropriate for their development context [2]. Therefore, it is important to know which agile practices are used to which extend in industry.

In the mapping study [1] we identified a preliminary set of the *most frequently used agile practices in industry* and the domains and lifecycle processes in which they are being used. However, the results of this mapping study can only be generalized in terms of the published literature results.

In order to get a better understanding of the state of the practice of agile practices, we triangulated the results of the mapping study with the largest available survey on agile software development, namely the state of agile development survey [4].

After providing some background information about the two data sources and sets, we will present the data triangulation and its results, including threats to validity. Based on the results, we will conclude the paper, answer the question of representativeness, and sketch some future work.

A. Jedlitschka et al. (Eds.): PROFES 2014, LNCS 8892, pp. 269–272, 2014.
© Springer International Publishing Switzerland 2014

2   Background

From the meagre amount of literature reporting about agile practices, we selected the first mapping study [1] about this aspect and the state of agile development survey [4], as this is the best known and most frequently referenced survey dealing with agile development.

Mapping Study [1]: At the end of 2013, we performed a mapping study to determine *which agile practices are used in industry*. This study included 24 studies from the years 2010-2013 with 68 different projects. We identified 18 agile practices and characterized their usage as full, partial, or none. This study gave us an overview of the usage of agile practices as reported in the literature, especially regarding domains.

State of Agile Development Survey [4]: VersionOne performed a yearly survey on agile software development aimed at representing the state of the practice in agile development [4]. The survey sample included 3500 participants, most of them practitioners. The question regarding agile practices was "Agile techniques employed" [4, p. 4]. For each of their 26 agile techniques, a Boolean question was asked as to whether it is used.

3   Data Triangulation

Triangulation Method [3]: We first mapped the agile practices reported in our mapping study and the agile techniques from the survey (Table 1):

Table 1. Mapping of Agile Practices

Mapping Study	Agile Development Survey (Agile Techniques)
Time boxing	
Learning loop	retrospectives, velocity
Planning meeting	iteration planning, release planning
Specification	story mapping
Daily discussion	daily standup
Product vision	
Continuous integration/deployment	continuous integration, continuous deployment, automated builds
Specification analysis	
Customer involvement	dedicated product owner
Validation practice	automated acceptance testing, unit testing
Frequent releases	
Outcome review	
Progress monitoring	burndown, digital task board, Kanban, analog task board
Quality check	pair programming, unit testing, TDD, integrated Dev/QA
Common knowledge	collective code ownership
Refactoring	refactoring
Unattached com. teams	open work area
Small cross-func. teams	

Out of the 18 agile practices identified in our mapping study, six practices were not covered by the survey (see Table 1). In addition, four agile techniques reported in the survey – *agile games, cycle time, coding standards,* and *BDD* – could not be mapped to the agile practices identified in our mapping study because the first one was not known and the others were not agile practices.

Next, we calculated the percentage values of the usage for each agile practice. For the mapping study, we based our calculation on the absolute numbers of projects (k) reported in [1]: $\frac{p_i}{k}$. We only used the overall agile practices usage and combined the full and partial usage values into one. For the survey, we recalculated the values for each practice mapped to $j > 1$ techniques as the average: $\frac{\sum_1^j t_i}{j}$ and as the minimum: $\min_{1 \le x \le j} t_i$. We needed both statistical measures, as some techniques were orthogonal to the respective practice, while others were not.

Results: The overall results of the comparison are shown in Fig. 1. They contain all 18 agile practice categories of the mapping study [1]. The left side presents the percentage values from the mapping study; the gray bars and practices are those not covered by the agile techniques in the survey [4]. In contrast, the right side contains the resulting values from the survey (average black; minimum white). The agile practices are listed in descending order, based on their occurrence in [1]. Since our focus is on the mapping study's results, we did not consider the results for practices in the survey that do not fit into our categorization.

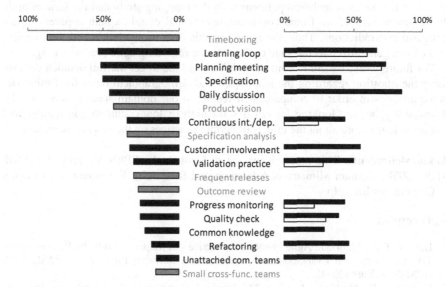

Fig. 1. Comparison of occurrence for mapping study [1] (left; gray = not in survey) and survey [4] (right; black = average; white = minimum) expressed in percentage

At first glance, the results of the different studies do not seem to be very similar to each other. But in general the right side of the figure also shows that the more frequently used practices are at the top, e.g., *learning loop, planning meeting,* and *daily discussions.* The only exception is *specification practice*, which makes sense because the survey only asked about story mapping and not about any further possible specification practices, such as user stories, which are also covered by the mapping study. Thus, we assume that *specification* is also used very similarly in both studies.

The remaining practices are all close together and most are also ordered similar to those on the left side. Only the position of *continuous integration and deployment* as well as *common knowledge* is a little bit too low. The reason for the position of *common knowledge* is similar to that for *specification* because only *collective code ownership* is mapped to it. In contrast, *continuous integration and deployment* is mapped to three different practices, which are rated very differently in the survey: *automated builds* with 56%, *continuous integration* with 50%, and *continuous deployment* with 25%, which results in an aggregated value that is lower than some others.

Threats to Validity: We did not have access to the raw data of the survey. We could check overlapping between the survey sample and the authors of the studies identified in the mapping study by analyzing the countries where the participants and authors were working. Whereas the survey participants are mainly from North America (66%) and Europe (20%), the authors of the studies identified in the mapping study were mainly working in South America (19%), Asia (31%), and Australia (18%).

4   Summary and Conclusions

Based on the data triangulation performed on the mapping study and the state of agile development survey, we found consistent results and could explain apparent deviations and contradictions. Thus, the results of this data triangulation and the two studies can be generalized as the state of the practice regarding agile practices usage.

For future work, we are in contact with VersionOne to get the full detailed data set (only the question regarding the techniques and demographical data) for further detailed analysis in order to compare their results to our domain-specific usage in [1]. Additionally, we are looking for reasons for high or low occurrence in the original studies to learn more about the effects of certain practices on the respective context.

Acknowledgments. This research was carried out in the SPES-XT project (BMBF 01IS12005E, German Ministry of Education and Research). We would like to thank L. Guzmán for her help.

References

1. Diebold, P., Dahlem, M.: Agile Practices in Practice – A Mapping Study. In: Proceedings of 18th Conference on Evaluation and Assessment in Software Engineering, EASE 2014. ACM, New York (2014)
2. Rodriguez, P., Markkula, J., Oivo, M., Turula, K.: Survey on Agile and Lean Usage in Finish Software Industry. In: Proceedings of 6th International Symposium on Empirical Software Engineering and Measurement, ESEM 2012, pp. 139–148. ACM, New York (2012)
3. Rothbauer, P.: Triangulation. In: The SAGE Encyclopedia of Qualitative Research Methods, pp. 892–894. Sage Publications (2008)
4. VersionOne: 8th Annual State of Agile Development Survey. VersionOne Inc. (2014)

What Is Large in Large-Scale?
A Taxonomy of Scale for Agile Software Development

Torgeir Dingsøyr[1,2], Tor Erlend Fægri[1], and Juha Itkonen[3]

[1] SINTEF,
NO-7465 Trondheim, Norway
{torgeird,toref}@sintef.no
[2] Department of Computer and Information Science,
Norwegian University of Science and Technology
[3] Aalto University, Department of Computer Science and Engineering
FI-00076 Aalto, Finland
juha.itkonen@aalto.fi

Abstract. Positive experience of agile development methods in smaller projects has created interest in the applicability of such methods in larger scale projects. However, there is a lack of conceptual clarity regarding what large-scale agile software development is. This inhibits effective collaboration and progress in the research area. In this paper, we suggest a taxonomy of scale for agile software development projects that has the potential to clarify what topics researchers are studying and ease discussion of research priorities.

Keywords: Large-scale agile software development, portfolio management, project management, coordination, software engineering, agile methods.

1   Introduction

In the introduction to the special issue on agile methods in IEEE Computer in 2003, Williams and Cockburn stated that "agile value set and practices best suit co-located teams of about 50 people or fewer who have easy access to user and business experts and are developing projects that are not life-critical" [19]. Since then, agile methods have received significant attention from practitioners and academia [6], and have increasingly been applied in new settings, such as global, distributed development [16] and large-scale development [13].

The rise of agile methods has also brought out critics, e.g. related to lack of focus on architectural decisions and that the methods are suitable only for small teams. Large projects are likely to have high societal impact and thus justify a serious consideration of critique. It is very important to understand if, when, and how agile methods can be suitable 'in the large.' Adaptions of agile principles may be necessary when scaling along dimensions of project size, project complexity and distribution of personnel.

The continued interest in this research area is exemplified by the practitioners at the XP2010 conference voting "agile in the large" to be "the top burning research question" [8]. Boehm and Turner discussed how risk exposure can be used to balance

A. Jedlitschka et al. (Eds.): PROFES 2014, LNCS 8892, pp. 273–276, 2014.

agile and plan-driven methods [2]. Lindvall et al. reported from meetings and a workshop amongst large companies and their experience with agile in the large [10].

However, there is little agreement on what large-scale agile development is [5]. Webster´s define 'large-scale' as "very extensive; of great scope" [18]. Some have used the term to describe projects with many members in a single team, while others are referring to projects with multiple teams over a number of years or a combination of size, distribution and specialization [3].

In order to facilitate discussion of planned studies and identify basic assumptions and knowledge gaps, we suggest a taxonomy of scale for agile projects, and discuss how this taxonomy can be used in future studies of large-scale agile development.

Research on large-scale agile development can include numerous topics, but the research community should emphasize more conceptual clarity and awareness regarding scale and the implications for scalability of agile methods. This would, for example, contribute to effective selection of case studies. To deepen our understanding and develop research-based knowledge, we need in-depth studies that serve as exemplars [7]; they provide a richer description of the projects and help research to connect to relevant theories that can explain the cases and thereby provide lessons for other projects. An agreement upon a taxonomy of scale for agile development projects would make it clearer what topics researchers are addressing, ease discussion of priority of topics in research agendas and make it more evident when studies can provide meaningful lessons for others.

2   A Taxonomy of Scale

A taxonomy may pinpoint differences in various types of large-scale agile projects that could lead to novel research questions. If we are to develop such a taxonomy of scale, the question is then which dimension(s) should we use? Project cost, number of people involved, number of requirements, lines of code, number of teams, additional practices needed? Would large-scale be different in various application domains [14]? In the following, we discuss these possible dimensions:

When focusing on large-scale in relation to development method, the cost is not a sufficient a criterion for large-scale. Costs vary across projects – some may involve hardware procurement or organizational change programs. Furthermore, these cost drivers are different from country to country. The code size is also a problematic factor; code could be generated by tools or be the result of modifications to existing code. Number of requirements, user stories or features to be developed suffers from high variability in the time to implement them. Some domains have a number of non-functional requirements, such as real-time systems in the telecom industry, which leads to additional effort in development. In addition, the size of software in terms of code or requirements is rarely available as comparable measures across technologies and project contexts.

We suggest including generally available and reliable factors. One factor that makes large projects difficult is the coordination overhead that is increasing with size. In management science, there are two general approaches to coordination of work: programming (up-front decisions) and feedback [11]. The nature of software development, being innovative work that is only partially compatible with programmed coordination, requires a strong emphasis on personal communication [9] and tacit knowledge embedded in the team [1]. The common advice in agile methods is to have teams of 7 plus/minus two people in a team[1] to achieve effective teamwork by reducing the number of communication lines.

When more people are required in a project, the work is then divided between several teams. We can identify this as a second type of large-scale project. The use of multiple teams will reduce the effectiveness of communication [17]. Curtis [4] shows how rapid clarification of conflicts is essential to effective software practice. More teams will incur an increase in the number of communication lines, and we can identify a new major change to coordination when we exceed 7 (+/- 2) teams. Coordination forums with many participants will be ineffective, and therefore large projects needs additional fora to coordinate subprojects.

This third type of large projects needs a new level of coordination. A pyramid organization paradigm adds distance between floor and top [15], and distance increases risk of distortion in information and 'knowledge silos'.

Following this line of thought, we end up with a taxonomy as described in Table 1. This is inspired by a taxonomy in requirements engineering [12]. One could criticize that this taxonomy is based on a theoretical model of a project, and in practice one may organize a large project with subprojects that are functionally or technically divided. But distinguishing on number of teams makes an easy and widely applicable taxonomy.

Table 1. A taxonomy of scale of agile software development projects

Level	Number of teams	Coordination approaches
Small-scale	1	Coordinating the team can be done using agile practices such as daily meetings, common planning, review and retrospective meetings.
Large-scale	2-9	Coordination of teams can be achieved in a new forum such as a Scrum of Scrums forum.
Very large-scale	10+	Several forums are needed for coordination, such as multiple Scrum of Scrums.

We suggest that this taxonomy can be used in designing studies in order to be more precise on selection criteria in case studies. Further, the taxonomy could be used in research question design, in order to focus on relations between large-scale projects and topics such as appropriateness of agile practices and when additional practices are required. Finally, the taxonomy can be important in characterizing state of the art of research, in showing the state of research on the different levels of scale. We would welcome a further discussion on the suitability of this taxonomy and whether a taxonomy of scale should include also other dimensions.

---

[1] http://www.scrum.org/Portals/0/Documents/Scrum%20Guides/ Scrum_Guide.pdf

Acknowledgement. The work on this article was supported by the SINTEF internal project "Agile project management in large development projects" and by the project Agile 2.0 which is supported by the Research council of Norway through grant 236759/O30, and by the companies Kantega, Kongsberg Defence & Aerospace and Steria.

References

[1] Boehm, B.: Get ready for agile methods, with care. IEEE Computer 35, 64–69 (2002)

[2] Boehm, B., Turner, R.: Balancing Agility and Discipline: A Guide for the Perplexed. Addison-Wesley (2003)

[3] Bosch, J., Bosch-Sijtsema, P.M.: Coordination between global agile teams: From process to architecture. In: Smite, D., Moe, N.B., Ågerfalk, P.J. (eds.) Agility Across Time and Space: Implementing Agile Methods in Global Software Projects, pp. 217–233. Springer, Heidelberg (2010)

[4] Curtis, B., Krasner, H., Iscoe, N.: A field study of the software design process for large systems. Communications of the ACM 31, 1268–1287 (1988)

[5] Dingsøyr, T., Moe, N.B.: Research Challenges in Large-Scale Agile Software Development. ACM Software Engineering Notes 38, 38–39 (2013)

[6] Dingsøyr, T., Nerur, S., Balijepally, V., Moe, N.B.: A Decade of Agile Methodologies: Towards Explaining Agile Software Development. Journal of Systems and Software 85, 1213–1221 (2012)

[7] Flyvbjerg, B.: Five Misunderstandings about Case Study Research. Qualitative Inquiry 12, 219–245 (2006)

[8] Freudenberg, S., Sharp, H.: The Top 10 Burning Research Questions from Practitioners. IEEE Software, 8–9 (2010)

[9] Kraut, R.E., Streeter, L.A.: Coordination in software development. Communications of the ACM 38, 69–81 (1995)

[10] Lindvall, M., Mutig, D., Dagnino, A., Wallin, C., Stupperich, M., Kiefer, D., May, J., Kähkönen, T.: Agile Software Development in Large Organizations. IEEE Computer 37, 26–34 (2004)

[11] March, J., Simon, H.A.: "Organizations," University of Illinois at Urbana-Champaign's Academy for Entrepreneurial Leadership Historical Research Reference in Entrepreneurship (1958)

[12] Regnell, B., Svensson, R.B., Wnuk, K.: Can we beat the complexity of very large-scale requirements engineering? In: Rolland, C. (ed.) REFSQ 2008. LNCS, vol. 5025, pp. 123–128. Springer, Heidelberg (2008)

[13] Reifer, D.J., Maurer, F., Erdogmus, H.: Scaling agile methods. IEEE Software 20, 12–14 (2003)

[14] Robert, L.G.: Contemporary Application-Domain Taxonomies. IEEE Software 12, 63–76 (1995)

[15] Semler, R.: Managing without managers. Harvard Business Review 67, 76–84 (1989)

[16] Smite, D., Moe, N.B., Ågerfalck, P.: Agility Across Time and Space: Implementing Agile Methods in Global Software Projects. Springer (2010)

[17] Van de Ven, A.H., Delbecq, A.L., Koenig Jr., R.: Determinants of coordination modes within organizations. American Sociological Review, 322–338 (1976)

[18] Webster's, Encyclopedic Unabridged Dictionary of the English Language. Gramercy Books, New York (1989)

[19] Williams, L., Cockburn, A.: Agile Software Development: It's about Feedback and Change. IEEE Computer 36, 39–43 (2003)

A Mapping Study on Cooperation between Information System Development and Operations

Floris Erich, Chintan Amrit, and Maya Daneva

University of Twente, Enschede, The Netherlands

Abstract. DevOps is a conceptual framework for reintegrating development and operations of Information Systems. We performed a Systematic Mapping Study to explore DevOps. 26 articles out of 139 were selected, studied and summarized. Based on this a concept table was constructed. We discovered that DevOps has not been adequately studied in scientific literature. There is relatively little research available on DevOps and the studies are often of low quality. We also found that DevOps is supported by a culture of collaboration, automation, measurement, information sharing and web service usage. DevOps benefits IS development and operations performance. It also has positive effects on web service development and quality assurance performance. Finally, our mapping study suggests that more research is needed to quantify these effects.

1 Introduction

Many organizations which develop and use Information Systems (IS) make a structural division of their IS departments. A popular one is separating IS development and operations. Some practitioners argue that this division has a negative impact. DevOps is a conceptual framework which aims at benefiting IS development by reintegrating development and operations in various ways.

In this paper we try to find empirical evidence that DevOps does indeed benefit IS development. To accomplish this we have performed a systematic mapping study, asking the following main research question: "How does DevOps influence IS development and operations performance?"

2 Research Method

We performed a systematic mapping study [5]. We started our search with the search term *DevOps*. Based on our preliminary findings we also added the search terms *"Continuous Delivery" AND Software*; and *"development and operations" AND software*. We applied the search terms to the databases of Scopus, Web of Science, IEEE Xplore and ACM Digital Library. The first author selected the articles and discussed them with the co-authors. Papers considered for the review were (1) published in 2007 and onward; (2) related to problems found in

A. Jedlitschka et al. (Eds.): PROFES 2014, LNCS 8892, pp. 277–280, 2014.

the intersection of software development and software operations; and (3) mainly considering IS. Because we did not closely study the potential biases authors of the studies might have, and which validity instruments were used, we present our work in progress as a mapping study instead of an SLR.

3   Results

We selected 14 journal articles, 10 conference proceedings and 2 industry reports out of 139 articles found. From the journal articles, 10 originated from special issues on DevOps from the Cutter IT Journal. Summaries of the papers as well as their related concepts can be found online [2]. Following the concept mapping approach [6], we labeled each article based on their primary concerns. This produced the following labels (and the amount of articles labeled as such):

- Culture of collaboration (9): Articles concerning the cultural changes required to reintegrate development and operations.
- Automation (9): Articles describing how the SDLC can be automated, covering both development and operations.
- Measurement (4): Articles describing how measurements can be introduced which cover both development and operations.
- Sharing (5): Articles describing how information sharing between development and operations can be increased and improved.
- Services (4): Articles describing how DevOps supports service development and is supported by existing services.
- Quality assurance (5): Articles describing what role quality assurance plays in a DevOps initiative.
- Structures and standards (8): Article describing how DevOps can be integrated into existing processes and works together with standards.

Regarding study quality, we have classified each study according to the Study Design Hierarchy for Software Engineering [4, p. 13]. We have classified 20 articles to be in the lowest level (5, evidence being limited to expert opinion), 5 articles to be in level 4 (evidence from (quasi-)randomized experiments in an artificial setting or case series) and one article to be in level 3 (in this case a multi-arm study considering a focus group and two cases).

4   Discussion

Until now development and operations have mostly been studied as two different fields. We believe our research shows that there is some merit in studying the combination of both. This is because in industry, many organizations are reintegrating development and operations. We understand that academic research should not primarily be swayed by trends in industry, which are often the subject of hype. But at the same time, academic research should support industry developments by finding evidence which supports or rejects the value proposition of commercial offerings that match the respective market developments.

Our survey of the academic literature available on DevOps shows that there is some interest in DevOps from an academic perspective in three ways: DevOps is considered as (i) the subject of discussion, (ii) a supporting factor of some other subject (iii) a factor supported by some other subject. Yet, we consider the study design quality of the discovered literature to be low.

A problem frequently discovered in the literature is the lack of a concrete shared definition of DevOps. While we have defined it as a conceptual framework, some authors see DevOps as a job description and others see it a skill set. Research could benefit from a clarification by creating a DevOps taxonomy [1]. A good starting point for a taxonomy is the CAMS framework [3]. We suggest that DevOps research can be classified using an extended version of this framework, including the concepts of services, quality assurance and structures & standards.

We believe the different views of DevOps require us to look at DevOps from multiple perspectives. This allows us to unite the conflicting definitions of DevOps under separate names, such as DevOps as a role in the SDLC process, DevOps as a skill set and DevOps as a conceptual framework for supporting IS development and operations.

We hope that by writing this article we have contributed towards creating more awareness and some initial understanding of DevOps.

5 Limitations

One must consider two primary limitations of mapping studies. First, possible selection bias. This bias is reduced significantly, as no author has prior publications in the area nor collaborations with authors of the included 26 papers. Also, our inclusion of English-only papers might mean that we missed out relevant studies in other languages actively exploring DevOps. This could not be avoided since English was the only feasible common language for our team. Second, it is possible that we collectively categorized a paper in a wrong way. The categorization was reviewed by another senior researcher, minimizing this threat's risk.

We think our research is in particular vulnerable to two biases, the argument from authority bias and the publication bias. Most articles selected in the review are based on expert opinion. While we have no reason to doubt these opinions, one should be aware that experts can be wrong. When one blindly follows expert opinion, one is vulnerable to the argument from authority bias. That is why expert opinion should be backed up with other sources of evidence. In our research we have found little evidence of DevOps having a positive effect on IS development besides expert opinion. The research is also vulnerable to publication bias, which means there is a tendency to publish only positive results. Hence, there might be organizations which struggle with DevOps and might have abandoned it, yet nothing is published regarding this. We control for these biases by being aware of them and regularly reflecting on the risks they pose.

We have limited our research to IS development and operations. This limitation follows from our belief that this is the biggest class of systems using structured software development processes, such as agile software development.

Our limitation to academic search engines hides a lot of potential sources of state-of-the-art material on DevOps research and development. DevOps is a concept born in the field, the primary venue for research and development of the DevOps concept are professional conferences and blogs. But professional conferences are hosted in native languages in countries all over the world, making it hard to extract useful information about them. Also, getting a complete overview of which authors have blogged about DevOps is nearly impossible. We have decided to offer a complete study over a smaller population, rather than offer a possibly incomplete study over a larger population. This paper still represents the state-of-the-art of academic DevOps research. We recommend future research to focus on the gap between professional research and development regarding DevOps and the academic research on the topic.

6   Conclusions

We now return to the main research question, which asked how DevOps influences IS development and operations performance. We have discovered that this influence is generated by practices which are considered part of DevOps, as well as how DevOps supports the development of web services and the process of quality assurance. DevOps itself is both supported by structures and standards, as well as allows the realization of structures and standards which are considered beneficial for IS development and operations.

The arguments of DevOps proponents that development and operations could benefit from more integration are quite compelling, yet lack very strong evidence. We suggest further research is needed to discover whether DevOps actually increases IS development and operations performance.

References

1. Bailey, K.: Typologies and Taxonomies: An Introduction to Classification Techniques, 1st edn. SAGE Publications, Inc. (June 1994)
2. Erich, F., Amrit, C., Daneva, M.: Report: Devops literature review (October 2014), http://www.utwente.nl/mb/iebis/staff/amrit/devopsreport.pdf
3. Humble, J., Molesky, J.: Why enterprises must adopt devops to enable continuous delivery. Cutter IT Journal 24(8), 6–12 (2011)
4. Kitchenham, B.: Procedures for performing systematic reviews (2004)
5. Petersen, K., Feldt, R., Mujtaba, S., Mattsson, M.: Systematic mapping studies in software engineering. In: Proceedings of the 12th International Conference on Evaluation and Assessment in Software Engineering, EASE 2008, pp. 68–77. British Computer Society, Swinton (2008)
6. Webster, J., Watson, R.: Analyzing the past to prepare for the future: Writing a literature review. MIS Quarterly, 26(2), xiii–xxiii (2002)

Breathing Life into Situational Software Engineering Methods

Masud Fazal-Baqaie, Christian Gerth, and Gregor Engels

University of Paderborn, Zukunftsmeile 1, 33102 Paderborn, Germany
{masudf,gerth,engels}@uni-paderborn.de

Abstract. Software engineering methods are used to prescribe and coordinate the tasks necessary to plan, build, deliver, and maintain software. There is a broad consensus that there is no one-size-fits-all method and that, e.g., agile and plan-driven approaches have to be mixed sometimes, based on the context of a project. Creating these so-called situational methods and assuring that they cover all necessary details consistently is a challenge. There is also the challenge for the project teams to follow methods as prescribed by the method engineer. Our approach supports the creation of consistent situational methods from a repository of pre-existing building blocks. Moreover, we present means to enact these methods with standard BPEL/BPEL4People workflow engines, automating the coordination of tasks and providing guidance for them.

Keywords: Situational Method Engineering, Method Enactment, BPEL4People, MESP.

1 Introduction

Special attention has been given lately to the need for methods that combine plan-driven and agile philosophies [1] based on the project characteristics. For example, in a previous paper, we described the trade-off between formality and agility in eID projects [2]. Approaches for situational method engineering support the creation of so-called situational methods based on the project context [3], however workflow support to guide project members in following the method is usually not available. Based on the initial idea of process programs [4] other researchers proposed modeling languages expressive enough to execute methods. However, approaches commonly do not support situational method engineering. Instead methods have to be modelled from scratch.

The aim of our approach called *method engineering with method services and method patterns* (MESP) is to support the creation of situational methods and to enact these methods with a standard workflow engine, which coordinates the tasks and provides guidance for the tasks of project members during enactment. We support the novel notion of *method patterns* that describe context-specific quality constraints, e.g., that tasks with specific characteristics have to be part of the method [2]. In this paper, we focus on how methods are enacted with standard BPEL/BPEL4People workflow engines.

A. Jedlitschka et al. (Eds.): PROFES 2014, LNCS 8892, pp. 281–284, 2014.

2   Overview of the MESP Approach

Figure 1 provides an overview of the different roles and tasks that are part of the MESP approach. They are called *meta-roles* and *meta-tasks* to avoid ambiguity regarding roles and tasks defined in a situational method:

The *senior method engineer* is responsible for defining method building blocks based on existing software engineering methods and his project experience (1). First, *method services* describe method content, e.g., a textual description of a task to define a software architecture. Second, *method patterns* describe context-specific quality constraints, e.g., that tasks with specific characteristics have to be part of the method. Method patterns are used to guide *project method engineers* during the creation of situational methods [2]. The senior method engineer also associates services and patterns with situational factors (e.g. project risk or team size) used to identify suitable elements during method assembly and is responsible for the quality assurance of the method base (2).

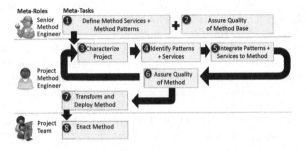

Fig. 1. Overview of MESP meta-roles their meta-activities

The *project method engineer* is responsible for defining a situational method with respect to a specific project. She characterizes a project based on the available situational factors (3) and uses this characterization to identify suitable method services and method patterns from the method base (4). Then she assembles chosen elements to a situational method (5). Once a method is assembled, she is responsible for the quality assurance of the method (6), e.g., that no data flow specification is missing and that there are no contradictions between the control and data flow specification. In addition, the constraints imposed by the method patterns used in the method need also to be fulfilled. These meta-tasks of the project method engineer are carried out iteratively to allow for stepwise refinement. When the method assembly is finished, the project method engineer invokes the transformation and automatic deployment of the method to the workflow engine (7). Here, she assigns individual project members to the roles used in the method.

The *project team* can enact the method by interacting with the workflow engine (8), once it is deployed. The workflow engine creates workflow tasks for the responsible project members based on the process flow defined in the method and presents task descriptions and runtime information about the current state of the method instance.

3   Method Enactment and Transformation to BPEL

Figure 2 is showing an example situational method. It includes among other elements a *phase* "Elaboration Phase". This phase contains an *iteration* called "MonthlyIteration", where first, a *method service descriptor* "HoldStandup-Meeting" is invoked. Afterwards, concurrently "ImplementTheSolution" and "RefineTheArchitecture" are invoked. Method service descriptors reference method services, defined in the method base, which in turn reference tasks using *task descriptors*. Tasks contain among other information a textual description.

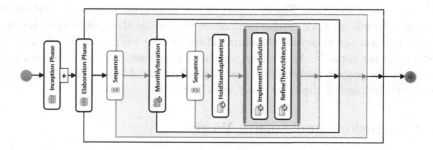

Fig. 2. A situational method referencing the method service "Refine The Architecture"

When the method is deployed on the workflow server, team members can log in to see their open *workflow tasks* according to their roles set up in the system. Once a workflow task is selected, information about it is presented. This description originates from the textual description of the task defined in the method base. In addition, information about the current phase and iteration is shown based on the method execution so far. Also the locations (URIs) of the inputs for this workflow task are presented. Once the owner of the task is finished, she enters the URI locations of the outputs she created, such that they can be retrieved and used in subsequent workflow tasks.

As soon as the workflow task is finished, the workflow engine executes the subsequent tasks based on the specified flow. According to the method shown in Figure 2, the workflow inside the iteration is finished after "Refine the Architecture", assuming that the concurrently executed "Implement the Solution" was also already performed. Based on our implementation of the concept iteration, a workflow task is created at the end of each iteration. This workflow task is basically a yes-or-no decision, whether another run of the iteration "Monthly-Iteration" should follow or not. Let us assume that this workflow task finished with a positive decision. In this case, the workflow engine would execute the contents of the iteration again. According to Figure 2 the first task of the sequence is the task "Hold Standup Meeting". A standup meeting is a short status meeting of the whole project team defined in the method Scrum. The invocation of this task creates a workflow task for the associated role.

In order to enable the described enactment of situational methods, MESP methods are transformed into BPEL4People processes. While, e.g., sequences of MESP can be directly transformed into BPEL sequences, the transformation of tasks descriptors is non-trivial and requires several BPEL `activities`: A task descriptor is transformed into the invocation of a HumanTask (`peopleActivity`) that will trigger the creation of a workflow task. To do this, the invocation parameter variable of this HumanTask has to be initialized, so that the right information is presented to the project member. First, a part of the invocation parameter variable is `assigned` values from the Task that is referenced, e.g., its name, its description and the associated role. Second, a part of the invocation parameter variable is `assigned` values from the process, e.g., the current phase and the current iteration. Third, a part of the invocation parameter variable is `assigned` values of work product variables that store the locations of inputs. After these `assign` activities the HumanTask can be `invoked` with the initialized parameter variable. Afterwards, another `assign` activity saves the provided output by the project member into a work product variable for that output. This way it can be used as input by other workflow tasks.

4   Conclusions and Future Work

In this paper, we presented an overview of the MESP approach and illustrated the transformation and enactment of situational methods. Our approach enables the coordination of tasks during method enactment and incorporates the data flow of input and output work products, which is often neglected. Currently, we work on finishing the implementation of conditional control flow constructs and improving the GUIs as part of a technical validation. Additionally, we are improving our MESP approach in a project with an industrial partner[1]. We are working on the definition of a method base in order to evaluate the approach with first application examples. In future, we want to extend the modeling capabilities to incorporate exceptions and exceptional flows.

References

1. Boehm, B.W., Turner, R.: Observations on Balancing Discipline and Agility. In: Proc. of the Conf. on Agile Development (ADC 2003), pp. 32–39. IEEE Computer Society, Los Alamitos (2003)
2. Fazal-Baqaie, M., Luckey, M., Engels, G.: Assembly-Based Method Engineering with Method Patterns. In: Wagner, S., Lichter, H. (eds.) Proc. of the Software Engineering 2013. LNI, vol. 215, pp. 435–444. GI (2013)
3. Henderson-Sellers, B., Ralyté, J.: Situational Method Engineering: State-of-the-Art Review. Journal of Universal Computer Science (J. UCS) 16(3), 424–478 (2010)
4. Osterweil, L.J.: Software processes are software too. In: Proc. of the 9th Int. Conf. on Softw. Eng. (ICSE), pp. 2–13. IEEE Computer Society, Washington D.C. (1987)

---

[1] http://s-lab.uni-paderborn.de/s-lab-software-quality-lab/
unsere-innovativen-projekte/aktuell/tasq.html

On the Role of System Testing for Release Planning: Industrial Experiences from Comparing Two Products

Michael Felderer[1] and Armin Beer[2]

[1] University of Innsbruck & QE LaB Business Services,
Innsbruck, Austria
michael.felderer@uibk.ac.at
[2] BVA & Beer Test Consulting, Baden, Austria
armin.beer@bva.at

Abstract. In this paper, we highlight our experiences on the important role of system testing for release planning. We do so by analyzing and comparing the release planning in two products which are based on the same underlying release planning process of a public health insurance institution in Austria.

1 Introduction and Industrial Context

Release planning (RP) is an important part of any type of incremental product development [1]. Often, too much emphasis solely is put into functionality when making release decisions, thereby neglecting system testing (ST) and related quality aspects important for the success of the released product [2]. In this paper, we therefore highlight our industrial experiences on the role of ST for RP based on the analysis and comparison of the RP process of two similar products developed at a public health insurance institution in Austria to motivate further research in this field. The process of RP in the studied institution has five steps shown in Fig. 1.

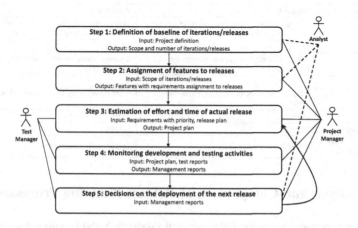

Fig. 1. Release Planning Process of the Studies Institution

A. Jedlitschka et al. (Eds.): PROFES 2014, LNCS 8892, pp. 285–289, 2014.

Each product is developed in an *iterative and incremental development process*, where each iteration contains several releases. The key stakeholders involved in these are the analyst, project manager and test manager. The project manager is also responsible for product management. In *Step 1*, the project manager and the analyst specify the scope and effort of each iteration as well as the number of releases. The definition of the baseline has to be altered in the course of a more detailed analysis in Step 2. In *Step 2*, the analyst has to partition the features of the product which are related to a bundle of requirements. It is considered that dependencies between the different features have to be minimized to avoid redesign of precedent iterations. In *Step 3*, the project manager and the test manager estimate the effort and duration of an iteration taking the priority of the requirements and the risk of use case misbehavior into account. The estimation is based on the experience of the project and test managers and results in a concrete project plan for a release defining its development and test schedule as well as resources. In *Step 4*, the development and testing activities are monitored by the project and test manager based on the project plan and test reports reflecting the ratio of test cases failed as well as new and closed defects. A key issue in monitoring release plans is to assess the quality of a release and to recommend which defects should be corrected in the next release or could be postponed. These recommendations and the underlying test and defect data are collected in management reports. Finally, in *Step 5*, decisions when and what to deploy in the next release are made in change control board (CCB) meetings where the project manager, the analyst and the test manager are involved. These decisions take the management reports and the results of CCB meetings into account. Based on the decision, the next release is estimated in Step 3 or the release process terminates if the product is finally released.

The presented RP process is applied for the development and test of Product A and Product B. The characteristics of these products are shown in Table 1.

Table 1. Characteristics of Products A and B

Characteristics	Product A	Product B
Area	Web application for refunding invoices of medical care and managing these cases	Web application for accounting liabilities and automatically issuing payment orders
Staff	43	23
Duration	3 years of development, operation started in February 2014	2.5 years of development, operation started in February 2014
Iterations	6	4
Size	~ 250 requirements, 45 use cases, 100 business rules	~ 140 requirements, 65 use cases, 277 business rules
Total effort	50 PY	12 PY
System test cases	~ 2.500	~ 3.000
Max. effort of system testing per iteration	40% of overall product effort	60% of overall product effort

2   Analysis and Comparison of Release Planning Processes

We first analyze specifics of the RP process of Products A and B with regard to system testing on the basis of the institution's RP process presented before.

In Product A, two releases were in general planned per iteration. Dependencies between features, which were implemented in different iterations, impeded the development and testing in later iterations. The effort and the schedule of development and ST of all iterations were calculated at the beginning of the project. However, bug fixing and change requests influenced effort and allocation of resources significantly. For instance, an unplanned bug fixing release or the implementation of change requests increased the effort for development and ST to about 30% in a subsequent release and delayed the deployment of an iteration up to 50%. The implementation of feature and change requests was prioritized over bug fixing. Also requests of to add new requirements, shortly before the development of a release was finished, harmed the quality of the released product. The consequence were numerous bugs in the state "new" and "re-opened" (for instance 227 in Rel. 1.6.3 of Product A). These bugs were categorized as "enhancements" and their resolution postponed. For instance, in Iteration 3 the number and severity of failures during system testing required a code freeze and made a complete test cycle, regression tests included, mandatory. Another issue was manual regression testing as well as the fact that effort and time to run tests for the unplanned releases exceeded the effort and time estimated at the beginning of the product. Release decisions were driven by the goal of the project manager to balance the workload of the developers, without taking the release quality into account. Bug fixing was shifted to later releases and new features were implemented instead. Features closer to completion or a small number of defects of severity blocker or critical were prioritized. An extra effort and time of executing added regression test cycles in Iterations 5 and 6 could not be afforded. The situation was even worse, because several external components and services with no integration testing beforehand were added.

In Product B, the original RP with 4 iterations was updated in Iteration 1 and kept until the end of the project. The system test cycles included regression testing and test of bug fixes. The analyst focused on the testability of requirements and features. The iterations are defined according to the business processes. The features are partitioned into components, where no changes are expected, e.g. fundamentals of double-entry bookkeeping, and where updates during the software life cycle are expected, e.g. operating sequences. Components which are stable, important and risky are implemented in the first place. The test manager calculated the effort and duration of the releases to be tested according to an estimation procedure already in place in the organization. A revision of the release plan was needed only once. The test results documented in the test reports influenced release decisions in respect of the correction of defects in the next release. In Product B, the value of early bug fixing was appreciated by the stakeholders and automatic unit and interface testing using mock objects was in place. Change requests shortly before the development of a release was finished caused a tradeoff in quality. In Product B, a mix of test methods, the simulation of external components, the good testability of requirements and the automatic unit tests with the measurement of branch coverage fostered the good quality of a release and enabled the decision when and what to release next.

Based on the analysis presented before, we compare the role of ST for RP in Product A and B and highlight positive and negative influence factors. In both products, number and scope of iterations were planned. One iteration was generally split into two releases. However, in Product B the release plan was rather stable, whereas in Product A it was changed several times. The release plan could be kept until the end of the development of Product B, mainly because bug fixing of critical defects had a high priority. In general, in Product B the viewpoint of the analyst and the test manager influenced release planning more than in Product A. The sequence of releases, the number of executed test cases and the percentage of test cases failed is shown in Table 2. In Product A, seven releases using the test process in place were tested. Thereby, several test cases could not be executed, because functionality or bug fixes were not implemented according to the release notes. For instance, the share of failed test cases would rise up to about 40% in Release 6 of Product A. Six releases had to be deployed after Release 7 (Iteration 5 and 6), one release every 3-5 days. The aim of these releases was to fix the most critical bugs to keep the start of operating in the organization by beginning of February 2014. Systematic regression testing was not feasible any more leading to quality degradation. But in Product B, *system testing and regression testing could be performed regularly, due to a more realistic release planning taking the availability of enough testing resources into account.* The share of the effort for ST was 60% for Product B (Iteration 4), compared to 40% for Product A (Iteration 5). The ratio of all test cases failed throughout the development cycle related to all test cases is 6% for Product B compared to 27% for Product A, despite the fact that more tests were performed for Product B. For this product, the number of failed test cases decreased significantly after Release 2, but stayed high for Product A.

Table 2. Results of System Testing of Products A and B per Release

		Product A				Product B		
		TC executed	% TC not exec.	%TC failed		TC executed	% TC not exec.	%TC failed
Rel. 1	V01.02.00	154	8,50	52,60	V 0.1.1 V 0.1.2	166	13,54	12,05
Rel. 2	V01.02.01	16		31,25	V 0.2.4	675	16,97	20,59
Rel. 3	V01.03.00	79		58,23	V 0.3.0			
Rel. 4	V01.03.01	354		57,91	V 0.3.1	1.414	4,26	7,00
Rel. 5	V01.03.02	169		44,38	V 0.4.0	508	75,63	2,17
Rel. 6	V01.04.00 not testable				V 0.4.1	1.846	0	4,28
Rel. 7	V01.04.00 - hot fix not testable				V 0.4.2	1.921	0	2,19
Rel. 8	V01.04.01	1065	9,50	23,29	V 1.0 Nov.13			
Rel. 9	V01.04.02	872	1,00	12,84				
Rel. 10	V01.05.00	254	62,50	8,66				
Rel. 11	V01.05.0 hf1	637	31,27	27,32				
Rel. 12	V01.05.01 funct.test	886	1,00	21,67				
Rel. 12	V01.05.01 regression test	696	7,69	3,02				
Rel. 13	V01.06.00 funct.test	68	76,00	47,06				
Rel. 13	V01.06.00 regression test	602	64,73	3,32				
	V 01.06.01 - 01.06.04 hot-fixes	Bug testing only, no regr. tests						
	V 1.0	Feb.14						
Sum TCs executed		5852				6530		
Average		450	29	30,12		1088	18	8,05
Median		354	10	27		1414	9	6

The key issues for a release decision in Product A were (1) the priority of the implementation of a new function instead of bug fixing, and (2) a balanced workload of development resources. The key issues for a release decision in Product B were (1) test results and error rates, and (2) coverage of requirements and business rules.

3   Conclusion

In this paper, we presented the RP process of a public health insurance institution and analyzed this process in two products. Experiences from our comparison of the RP process in the two products indicate that it should take the availability of test resources, adequate ST techniques, the viewpoint of the analyst and test manager as well as the quality of a release into account to keep the planned number of releases and the testability of a product. As such, this paper is relevant to product managers, project managers, requirements engineers as well as test managers. In addition, we conclude that additional research on the integration of RP and ST is needed. First, empirical studies are required to provide evidence for our experiences. Then, further decision support for RP is needed that takes testing into account. Finally, requirements engineering and testing have to be aligned to support integration of testing into RP.

References

1. Ruhe, G.: Product release planning: methods, tools and applications. CRC Press (2010)
2. Felderer, M., Beer, A., Ho, J., Ruhe, G.: Industrial evaluation of the impact of quality-driven release planning. In: ESEM 2014, p. 62 (2014)

A Process-Oriented Environment for the Execution of Software Engineering Experiments

Marília Freire[1,2], Gustavo Sizílio[1], Edmilson Campos[1,2],
Uirá Kulesza[1], and Eduardo Aranha[1]

[1] Federal University of Rio Grande do Norte, Natal-RN, Brasil
{marilia.freire,gustavo.sizilio,edmilsoncampos}@ppgsc.ufrn.br,
{uira,eduardoaranha}@dimap.ufrn.br
[2] Federal Institute of Rio Grande do Norte, Natal-RN, Brasil

Abstract. Over the last decade, the software engineering community has been discussing how to better support the planning, execution and analysis of controlled experiments. There is a growing interesting in this topic because it is a mean to meet empirical evidence facilitating the work of researchers. In this paper, we present a process-oriented environment proposed to support the conduction of controlled experiments in software engineering. We describe the desired requirements for such kind of experimental supporting environment and analyze how our experimental environment addresses these requirements.

1   Introduction

Controlled experiments play an important role in science. However, the planning, conduction and analysis of controlled experiments are, in general, work intensive, time consuming and error prone [1] [2]. Besides the importance of experimentation to the area and although there is an increased number of guidelines on the topic [3], there are still a few supporting environments to the conduction of controlled experiments [4]. Arisholm et al. [5] developed a web-based tool that supports management of participants. Its weakness is the data collection and analysis, since it does not provide support to the analysis and interpretation stage. In addition, Travassos et al. [6] provided an environment, called eSEE, with a set of facilities to allow geographically distributed software engineers and researchers to accomplish and manage experimentation processes, as well as scientific knowledge concerned with different study types through the web. It has a prototype and an initial set of tools to populate the eSEE infrastructure has being built.

The lack of supporting environments has hampered the running of controlled experiments with professionals from industry using professional development tools [1], and invalidated experiment results due to planning or conduction problems [7]. The challenges are even greater when considering distributed experiment [8] and experiment replication [9] or meta-analysis [10]. Some of the reasons that contributes to the existing lack of supporting environments are (i) the absence of a conceptual model that precisely represents the experimental planning and (ii) the necessity of an environment customization according to the experiment procedure and design.

A. Jedlitschka et al. (Eds.): PROFES 2014, LNCS 8892, pp. 290–293, 2014.

In this work, we present a process-oriented execution environment to help researchers guiding the experiment participants during the planning, execution and analysis of controlled experiments. It is based on the experiment formalization using a domain-specific language and supports data collection, online execution monitoring, data analysis, reporting and contributes for replication and packaging.

2   An Integrated Environment for the Execution of Software Engineering Experiments

Our environment is part of a larger project that intends to provide a complete infrastructure to support the conduction of controlled experiments in software engineering (SE). In this context, this environment is grounded by a model-driven process-oriented approach, which was presented in [11] [12]. The approach has two main stages: (i) the definition and deployment of an experiment specification; and (ii) the configuration and execution of the experiment.

The first stage of our approach is responsible to support the experiment definition using a domain-specific language (Step 1), which is then used to produce workflow models (Step 2). These workflows have to be deployed in a workflow engine in order to provide the participants guidance during the experiment execution (Step 3).

The second stage represents the proposed environment, a web application powered by a workflow engine. This stage provides the entire necessary configuration before starting the experiment execution. Therefore, in order to execute an experiment, the environment automatically distributes the treatments and configures the participants (Step 4). Then, these workflows can be instantiated in order to be executed for each participant. The workflows are executed in the web application responsible for guiding (Step 5) and monitoring the participants during the experiment execution, including the feedback gathering from the participants (Step 6).

The environment functionalities were developed in order to meet a set of requirements, which are listed and discussed below:

Experiment Formal Documentation – This requirement was addressed by the experiment formalization in ExpDSL. The DSL provides a formal way to specify and document an experiment.

Automatic Treatment Distribution – This requirement is partially supported in the execution environment. It depends on the DoE selected to the experiment. Firstly, the DSL provides an element responsible to define the statistical design of experiment (DoE). The experimental design type in ExpDSL currently supports three types of DoE: (i) completely randomized design (CRD); (ii) randomized complete block design (RCBD); and (iii) Latin square (LS). In case of a not supported type, the researchers responsible for the experiment can distribute the treatments manually using the application environment.

Participant Guiding – The workflows generated from the model-driven transformation (step 2) from the treatment process definition in ExpDSL (step 1) represent themselves the participant guidance. Each ExpDSL process activity is represented as a workflows task in the workflow model generated and is instantiated as part of a web-form in the execution environment. The participants are then guided as the sequence of workflows tasks.

Data Collection - The workflows are responsible by these data collection using the web forms generated for the execution environment (step 6). During the experiment definition, the Artefact Element, for example, is responsible to define the output that the participants have to produce during an activity of the experiment process. It is essential in the data collection procedure to gather the participant output information.

Experiment Monitoring – The participants' interactions as well as their generated artefacts can be monitored by the researcher during the experiment execution (step 6) in our execution environment. The online experiment monitoring also allows researchers to take notes for the experiment and produce historical information.

Integrated Analysis – The environment allows experiment analysis through the integration with the R statistical tool. It is important to emphasize that additional processing (or preparation) of the collected data set can be required. This includes, if appropriate, data transformation, identification and potential removal of outliers, and handling of missing values, as well as the discussion of dropouts. Our environment currently provides support to the analysis of variance (ANOVA) for the three statistical designs supported by ExpDSL: CRD, RCBD and Latin Square.

Report Generation – The reporting generated by the environment contains information about the experiment execution and a summary of analysis results.

Gathering of feedback – The participants can be asked to answer feedback questionnaires when specified in the ExpDSL definition. In our environment, these questionnaires are presented as online web questionnaires before or after the execution.

In order to meet these requirements is needed to organize and formalize all the involved information related to experiment conduction as well as providing a customized environment that can run and analyze different designs of experiments in SE.

3   Conclusions and Future Work

This paper described a process-oriented experimental environment that supports the conduction of controlled experiments in software engineering. We presented the requirements of the environment and how they were addressed. The preliminary execution of some experiments in the proposed environment helped us to identify its benefits and limitations in order to improve it. Our environment is integrated with a model-driven approach [12] and a domain-specific language [13], which enable to specify
and generate formal definition of experiments to be executed and analysed in the environment. Additional details about the environment can be found at http://goo.gl/0VnkKB.

As part of future work of this research, we are preparing two new studies to be conducted: (i) a survey that will be performed and applied to experts from the experimental software engineering community to collect feedback about the current proposal of the environment; and (ii) the usage of the environment to conduct controlled experiments by external researchers in order to assessing the usability and performance of the complete approach.

Acknowledgments. This study is supported by the program "Ciência sem Fronteiras", from Ministério da Ciência, Tecnologia e Inovação (MCTI) and Ministério da Educação (MEC) of Brazil, through CNPq and CAPES. It is partially supported by the National Institute of Science and Technology for Software Engineering (INES), funded by CNPq, grants 573964/2008-4 and 552645/2011-7, and by FAPERN, CETENE and CAPES/PROAP.

References

[1] Sjøberg, D.I., Anda, B., Arisholm, E., Dybå, T., Jørgensen, M., Karahasanovic, A., Koren, E.F., Vokác, M.: Conducting Realistic Experiments in Software Engineering. In: ISESE (2002)

[2] Hochstein, L., Nakamura, T., Shull, F., Zazworka, N., Basili, V.R., Zelkowitz, M.V.: An Environment for Conducting Families of Software Engineering Experiments. Advances in Computers 74, 175–200 (2008)

[3] Jedlitschka, A., Ciolkowski, M., Pfahl, D.: Reporting Experiments in Software Engineering. In: Guide to Advanced Empirical Software Engineering. Springer Science+Business Media (2008)

[4] Freire, M., Alencar, D., Campos, E., Medeiros, T., Aranha, E., Kulesza, U.: Automated Support for Controlled Experiments in Software Engineering: A Systematic Review. In: SEKE, Boston/USA (2013)

[5] Arisholm, E., Sjøberg, D.I.K., Carelius, G.J., Lindsjørn, Y.: A Web-based Support Environment for Software Engineering Experiments. Nordic Journal of Computing 9(4), 231–247 (2002)

[6] Travassos, G.H., Santos, P.S.M., Mian, P.G., Dias Neto, A.C., Biolchini, J.: An environment to support large scale experimentation in software engineering. In: 13th IEEE ICECCS, pp. 193–202 (2008)

[7] Accioly, P.: Comparing Different Testing Strategies for Software Product Lines (Masters Thesis) Federal University of Pernambuco, Recife, Brasil (2012)

[8] Budgen, D., Kitchenham, B., Charters, S., Gibbs, S., Pohthong, A., Keung, J., Brereton, P.: Lessons from Conducting a Distributed Quasi-experiment. In: SEKE (2013)

[9] Solari, M.: Identifying Experimental Incidents in Software Engineering Replications. In: SEKE (2013)

[10] Ciolkowski, M.: An Approach for Quantitative Aggregation of Evidence from Controlled Experiments in Software Engineering (PHD Thesis) Kaiserslautern (2013)

[11] Freire, M., Accioly, P., Sizílio, G., Campos Neto, E., Kulesza, U., Aranha, E., Borba, P.: A Model-Driven Approach to Specifying and Monitoring Controlled Experiments in Software Engineering. In: Heidrich, J., Oivo, M., Jedlitschka, A., Baldassarre, M.T. (eds.) PROFES 2013. LNCS, vol. 7983, pp. 65–79. Springer, Heidelberg (2013)

[12] Freire, M.A.: A Model-Driven Approach to Formalize and Support Controlled Experiments in Software Engineering. In: IDOESE, Baltimore (2013)

[13] Freire, M., Kulesza, U., Aranha, E., Jedlitschka, A., Campos, E., Acuña, S., Gómez, M.: An Empirical Study to Evaluate a Domain Specific Language for Formalizing Software Engineering Experiments. In: SEKE, Vancouver (2014)

Predicting Risky Clones Based on Machine Learning

Ayaka Imazato[1], Keisuke Hotta[1], Yoshiki Higo[1], and Shinji Kusumoto[1]

Graduate School of Information Science and Technology, Osaka University,
1-5, Yamadaoka, Suita, Osaka, Japan,
{i-ayaka,k-hotta,higo,kusumoto}@ist.osaka-u.ac.jp

Abstract. Code clones are similar or identical code fragments to one another in source code. It is said that code clones decrease maintainability of software. On the other hand, all the code clones are not necessarily harmful to software. In this study, we propose a method to identify risky code clones out of all the code clones in source code by using machine learning techniques. Our proposed method learns information about features of code clones which existed in the past and whether they were risky or not. Then, based on these information, we identify risky code clones. As a result of a pilot study, we confirmed that the proposed method was able to predict risky code clones with high accuracy.

1 Introduction

It is said that code clones (hereafter, clone) have bad effects on maintainability of software. For example, when one code fragment is modified, other code fragments that are similar or identical to it also require the same modifications frequently [2]. When multiple code fragments that are similar to one another require similar modifications, there is a possibility of overlooking some of the code fragments that should be modified. If overlooking happens, bugs might occur in the overlooked location. Hence, clones could decrease maintainability of software [1]. On the other hand, all the clones are not necessarily risky. For example, clones are harmless to maintainability of software if they have never been modified since they had appeared. Moreover, it is not realistic that developers manage all the clones because there are a huge number of clones.

It is necessary to take care of only risky clones out of all the clones in order to manage clones efficiently. In this study, we propose a method to identify risky clones out of all the clones by using machine learning (hereafter, ML). In our proposed method, we analyze development histories of software to obtain information about features of clones which existed in the past and whether they caused bugs or not. Then, based on these information, we construct models to predict risks of clones, and identify risky clones out of all the clones in current source code with the models. We have implemented our proposed method, and conducted a pilot study to evaluate the accuracy of predictions with our proposed method. As a result, we confirmed that the proposed method was able to predict risky clones with high accuracy.

A. Jedlitschka et al. (Eds.): PROFES 2014, LNCS 8892, pp. 294–297, 2014.

2   Background and Related Work

All the clones are not necessarily risky. Hence, it is necessary to identify only risky clones in order to manage clones efficiently. The authors thought that it might be possible to predict risky clones with ML. ML is a technique to predict or identify the characteristics of unknown data by learning existing data. Several research uses ML to predict clones that should be taken care of.

Yang et al. assume that judging whether a clone is useful or not varies from user to user [4]. They proposed a method to identify useful clones for each user with ML. Wang et al. proposed a method to predict risks of the clones when clones are generated by copy and paste operation [3].

In Yang's proposed method, users have to classify clones manually beforehand. Wang's method works only under the limited situations. On the other hand, our proposed method does not need any advance preparations by users, and can predict risks of arbitrary clones.

3   Proposed Method

We propose a method to predict risks of clones by using ML. ML learns existing data, and predict or identify the characteristics of unknown data based on learned information. In ML, data for learning are called **training data**, and a model that is constructed by learning training data to predict characteristics of unknown data is called **learning model**. Our method learns information of *clone set* (group of code fragments that are similar to one another) as training data, and constructs a learning model to predict risks of clone sets. Also, our method intends to identify clone sets that will cause bugs in the future. Therefore, we define that clone sets which will cause bugs in the future are risky, and otherwise not risky. Our method takes the development history of the target software as its input, and provides a learning model to predict risky clone sets as its output. The proposed method consists of the following four phases.

1. First, we detect all the clone sets that were generated during past development process by analyzing the development history. Then, for each detected clone set, we obtain its evolutional data since it was generated. The evolutional data of clone set is typically called **genealogy of clone set** (**genealogy**). Fig.1 illustrates an example of it.
2. Then, for each genealogy, we judge whether it was risky or not. We regard a given genealogy as risky if it had undergone one or more bug fixes during its evolution. For example, the genealogy in Fig.1 is judged as risky because there was a bug fix between revision $r + 1$ and $r + 2$. Note that we get information of bug fixes through commit messages. We regard the modifications at the commit as bug fix if the commit message includes any words that imply to fix bugs such as *bug fix*.
3. After judging risks of all the genealogies, our method extracts training data from each genealogy. In our method, we extract the clone sets at the start

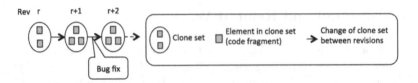

Fig. 1. An Example of a Genealogy

	Predicted	
	Risky	Not risky
Actual Risky	1,501	194
Not risky	117	2,446

Precision = 0.93, Recall = 0.89

(a) J48

	Precidted	
	Risky	Not risky
Actual Risky	1,409	286
Not risky	80	2,483

Precision = 0.95, Recall = 0.83

(b) SVM

	Predicted	
	Risky	Not risky
Actual Risky	1,530	165
Not risky	310	2,253

Precision = 0.83, Recall = 0.90

(c) BayesNet

Fig. 2. Result

revision of each genealogy as training data. For the genealogy in Fig.1, the clone set at revision r is extracted as training data. Subsequently, we judge risks of clone sets extracted as training data. In our method, training data belonging to risky genealogies are considered risky, and training data belonging to not risky genealogies are considered not risky. At the same time, we investigate the status of training data. The status of training data is, for example, the number of the elements that compose the clone set, the similarity between the elements, and so on. In this paper, we call such values and parameters that describe the status of clone set **feature value**. Our method uses 30 kinds of feature values in total.

4. Finally, for each clone set extracted as training data, we learn its feature values and information about whether it is risky or not together to construct a learning model. Our method predicts risk of a given clone set when users give feature values of it to the constructed learning model.

4   Pilot Study

We have conducted a pilot study with an open source project *jEdit* (the number of target revision is 5,292, and the development period is about 11 years) to evaluate our method. As described in the previous section, we detected all the genealogies and extracted their first clone sets from the *jEdit* project. We call the set of the clone sets data set. Note that the data set consists of 1,695 risky clone sets, and 2,563 not risky clone sets. This pilot study adopts the cross validation. The cross validation divides the data set into k blocks, and evaluates the accuracy of prediction by using these blocks. Note that the number of clone sets in each block is almost the same. In the cross validation, we use $k - 1$ blocks as training data, and the remaining one block as test data. Concretely, we construct a learning model by learning training data. Then, we adopt the learning model to test data and measure the accuracy. This process is repeated k times, with each of the k blocks used exactly once as test data. The average of k results is the entire accuracy. We set $k = 10$ in this pilot study. This pilot study uses two indicators below as measure for evaluation.

Precision: the rate of risky clone sets in clone sets that are predicted as risky by the learning model

Recall: the rate of clone sets that are correctly predicted as risky by the learning model in all the risky clone sets

Also, we use three algorithms (J48, BayesNet(Bayesian Network), SVM(Support Vector Machine)) to construct learning models, and evaluate each learning model. Fig.2 shows the results. As shown in this figure, the proposed method can predict risky clones with high accuracy, 83–95% *Precision* and 83–90% *Recall*. The accuracy of J48 is very high, both *Precision* and *Recall* are almost 90%. For SVM, *Precision* is the highest among the three algorithms, 95%, but *Recall* is the lowest. For BayesNet, on the contrary, *Precision* is lower than other algorithms, but *Recall* is the highest. The result of the pilot study showed that the proposed method was able to predict risky clones with high accuracy.

5   Conclusions

In this study, we proposed a method to identify risky clones out of all the clones in source code by using machine learning. As a result of a pilot study, we confirmed that the proposed method was able to predict risky clones with 83–95% *Precision* and 83–90% *Recall*. However, at present, our proposed method cannot rank specified risky clones, which is our future work.

Acknowledgment. This work was supported by MEXT/JSPS KAKENHI 24680002 and 24650011.

References

1. Higo, Y., Kusumoto, S.: How Often Do Unintended Inconsistencies Happen? Deriving Modification Patterns and Detecting Overlooked Code Fragments. In: ICSM, pp. 222–231 (September 2012)
2. Kim, M., Sazawal, V., Notkin, D., Murphy, G.: An Empirical Study of Code Clone Genealogies. FSE 30(5), 187–196 (2005)
3. Wang, X., Dang, Y., Zhang, L., Zhang, D., Lan, E., Mei, H.: Can I Clone This Piece of Code Here? In: ASE, pp. 170–179 (September 2012)
4. Yang, J., Hotta, K., Higo, Y., Igaki, H., Kusumoto, S.: Classification model for code clones based on machine learning. ESE, 1–31 (June 2014)

Maximizing Product Value: Continuous Maintenance

Tommi Mikkonen and Kari Systä

Tampere University of Technology
Korkeakoulunkatu 1, FI-33720 Tampere, Finland
{tommi.mikkonen,kari.systa}@tut.fi

Abstract. A frequent software related claim is that the initial development costs are 30% and that 70% more is needed in maintenance. However we claim that in today's software industry, software maintenance and the development of new features are intimately tangled, and it is impossible to separate them in a reliable fashion. We demonstrate this by showing how some modern software engineering approaches address maintenance and the development of new features, and we describe a concept of continuous maintenance to manage frequent changes both in software and business.

Keywords: Maintenance, agile development, development methodologies.

1 Introduction

A frequent software related claim is that the initial development costs are around 30% and that 70% more is needed in maintenance. These figures, which refer to software development expenditure for 1977 in the USA, are often still used as a rule of thumb [6]. The comment

> "Thank you for your improvement ideas, thus Symbian is in maintenance mode and no new features will be implement without extremely good reason (business case)."

at Nokia's bug tracker[1] inspired the authors to consider what is the investment that is still being made in the Symbian platform by its stakeholders, and what percentage will that be in the total cost of building the platform in the first place in the light of our experiences and earlier claims.

In this paper, we address the resulting ideas regarding software maintenance. The main claims we make are that 1) maintenance is intimately built in agile development methodologies; 2) it is difficult to define beyond all doubt what is maintenance and what is new development; 3) the way of working in modern software development is largely similar what we used to understand as maintenance. Consequently, we claim that only about 10% is truly original work and up to 90% is maintenance, leading us to conclude that today's software development is about *continuous maintenance*.

Jones in [5] also claims that maintenance is an ambiguous term but he considers enhancements (new features) to be substantially different from maintenance (bug

---

[1] http://mynokiablog.com/2012/10/18/symbian-in-maintenance-mode-or-crossed-wires/

A. Jedlitschka et al. (Eds.): PROFES 2014, LNCS 8892, pp. 298–301, 2014.

fixing) and suggests that development of new and maintenance should be separated. We believe that the reasoning of Jones (Table 1 in [5]) might apply to traditional waterfall style development, but in this paper we claim the opposite: in modern software engineering new features and bug fixes should managed together and in a similar, uniform fashion.

2 Defining Maintenance

Like development, maintenance of software has an abstract nature. Maintenance is commonly considered to include all work on the software after it has been taken into use for the first time. Therefore, actions to be taken in maintenance phase are many. Bugs repeatedly require fixing. Reacting to external changes, such as availability of a certain hardware element, can lead to wide spectrum of changes. Improving performance, battery life, or network throughput are common reasons for changes. New needs are frequently discovered, which require changes or totally new code.

The IEEE-ISO Guide to the SWEBOOK [1] is based on standard ISO/IEC 14764 [4] and defines the following activities as a part of maintenance:

1. *Program understanding*: activities needed to obtain a general knowledge of what a software product does and how the parts work together.
2. *Transition*: a controlled and coordinated sequence of activities during which software is transferred progressively from the developer to the maintainer.
3. *Modification request acceptance/rejection*: modifications requesting work beyond a certain size/effort/complexity may be rejected by maintainers and rerouted to a developer.
4. *Maintenance help desk*: an end-user and maintenance coordinated support function that triggers the assessment, prioritization, and cost estimation of modification requests.
5. *Impact analysis*: a technique to identify areas impacted by a change.
6. *Maintenance service-Level agreements (SLAs) and maintenance licenses and contracts*: contractual agreements that describe the services and quality objectives

3 Maintenance in Modern Software Development Models

Scrum. Scrum is a simple, iterative framework for project management [8]. In Scrum, incoming requirements are stored in *product backlog*. Collection of product backlog items are selected for implementation within fixed-length iterations called *sprints*. Each sprint results in a complete, robust system that can at least in principle be delivered to customers. It is important to note that prioritization and selection of the items for a sprint is based on *value* - only items with enough value will be considered. *Maintenance related activities in Scrum.* The only way to introduce a change – regardless of its complexity and motivation – is to include it in the product backlog. This offers two interpretations for maintenance related activities: 1) every sprint improves the original system, so everything that will be done is in fact maintenance; 2) each sprint creates a new, improved system, and there is no need for maintenance as a special activity. Still, it is not uncommon to perform special maintenance actions on already installed customer systems outside sprints, especially in critical situations.

Lean Startup. In Lean Startup [7] Minimum Viable Product (MVP) is a key concept. The goal is to identify the most valuable features by iteratively experimenting the market. The goal of iterations is to learn what features customers are ready to pay for, and which are not interesting. While the lean startup approach defines no particular process or tools fot software development, agile development approaches are assumed to minimize the time from a concept to a prototype that can be experimented with.

Maintenance related activities in Lean Startup. The target of the Lean Startup is iterative improvement of software and business direction together. New features are rapidly introduced, and those that fail are rapidly removed - in essence maintenance. Due to the rapid changes in the feature set, there is a high risk of technical debt.

DevOps. DevOps stresses communication, collaboration, and integration between software developers and IT professionals running the information systems [2]. A key target is to enable rapid development and utilization of the software. To reach this target *continuous deployment* and/or *continuous delivery* [3] are used. Moreover, in order to gain benefits from the capability to release rapidly requires that also business goals are defined in a clear and achievable fashion. Technical requirements for implementing DevOps include release management for and standardized development and product environments, as well as a high degree of automation.

Maintenance related activities in DevOps. In many cases, maintenance is split to maintenance of the software applications (performed by development team) and maintenance of the operations (performed by IT operations). In the DevOps approach the maintenance challenge is shared by development and operation. In essence this means that all changes to the running system, be it new development or an operational modification, are executed similarly.

4   Discussion

In the above examples, implementation of new features (or change) is based on business value compared to the associated cost, similarly to what has been the traditional goal of maintenance. Regardless if the action is "development of new" or "maintenance" in traditional terminology, the decision and development processes are same, and in agile approaches one must embrace change and be prepared to deal with it with minimal extra trouble. Agile approaches also provide control to changes and interrupts change request cause to the process. Agile is thus about bringing structure to maintenance to manage ongoing activities, value-based decisions and feedback mechanisms.

The discussion above was given from point of view of the developer organization, but these changes have implications to the business and customer organization, too. Firstly, is that there should not be any borderline between implementation and maintenance. New products are based on older ones, i.e., source code of the older product is used as a platform for the new. Thus the implementation work of a new product resembles maintenance. The agile way of working amplifies this phenomenon, and continuous deployment makes process of business decisions unified with SW engineering process. Secondly, many customers still think that they first make a contract to buy new SW system, wait until it is ready, and then budget money for the maintenance. However, the best way is to develop a useful system is to participate in the project and give constant feedback. This means that both developers and customers are in the mode of continuous maintenance – and the first main borderline is the date when software is in operational use for the first time.

For the maintenance activities discussed in Section 2, the model of Continuous Maintenance means the following modifications to the standard definition:

1. *Program understanding*: as the same team(s) is responsible for both new development and maintenance, they should already know the code.
2. *Transition*: no transition is needed before the software is considered as too old for new features (as in the case of Symbian platform).
3. *Modification request acceptance/rejection*: done together with development decision, using customer input and value for prioritization.
4. *Maintenance help desk*: only one interface towards the customer.
5. *Impact analysis*: easier and similar to analysis of all changes and additions;
6. *Maintenance Service-Level Agreements (SLAs) and maintenance licenses and contracts*: DevOps type of operation and maintenance means that maintenance is put under the same contract.

To return to *"maintenance mode"* as indicated in Nokia's bug tracker mentioned earlier, the statement can only be taken as a point where the final actions to keep software alive after any active development have stopped, and no effort is made to avoid declining quality. Such event will be followed by the rampdown of the supporting organization. At this point, the cost is only a fraction of what was invested before, no matter whether classical or modern development methodology is used.

References

[1] Bourque, P., Fairley, R.E. (eds.): SWEBOOK, Guide to the Software Engineering Body of Knowledge, Version 3.0. IEEE Computer Society (2014)
[2] Debois, P.: Devops: A software revolution in the making. Cutter IT Journal 24(8) (August 2011)
[3] Humble, J., Farley, D.: Continuous delivery: reliable software releases through build, test, and deployment automation. Pearson Education (July 27, 2010)
[4] ISO/IEC 14764: Software Engineering, Software Life Cycle, Processes, Software Maintenance (2006)
[5] Jones, C.: Geriatric Issues of Aging SoftwareJones. CrossTalk - The Journal of Defense Software Engineering, pp. 4–8 (December 2007), http://www.compaid.com/caiinternet/ezine/capersjones-maintenance.pdf
[6] Lehman, M.M.: On Understanding Laws, Evolution, and Conservation in the Large-Program Life Cycle. Journal of Systems and Software 1, 213–221 (1980)
[7] Ries, E.: The Lean Startup: How Today's Entrepreneurs Use Continuous Innovation to Create Radically Successful Businesses. Crown Publishing (2011)
[8] Schwaber, K., Beedle, M.: Agile Development with Scrum. Prentice-Hall (2001)

Artefact-Based Requirements Engineering Improvement: Learning to Walk in Practice

Daniel Méndez Fernández

Technische Universität München, Germany
http://www4.in.tum.de/~mendezfe

Abstract. Requirements engineering process improvement (REPI) has gained much attention in research and practice. Most REPI approaches are of solution-driven and activity-based nature. They focus on the assessment of company-specific RE reference models against an external norm of best practices, and they propagate an improvement by forecasting the adaptation of the processes and methods in the RE reference model towards that norm. In recent years, we could develop a first problem-driven RE improvement approach that supports an improvement against individual goals and problems of a company putting primary attention to the quality of the RE artefacts (named *ArtREPI*). In this short paper, we briefly illustrate our resulting approach and report on our initial experiences from ongoing empirical evaluations in practice. We conclude with a summary of planned next steps.

Keywords: Requirements Engineering, Artefact Orientation, Software Process Improvement, Case Study Research.

1 Introduction

Requirements engineering (RE) constitutes an important success factor for software development projects. Its interdisciplinary nature, the uncertainty, and the complexity in the process, however, make the discipline hard to investigate and even harder to improve [1]. For such an improvement, process engineers have to decide whether to opt for a *problem-driven* or for a *solution-driven* improvement [2]. In a solution-driven improvement, the engineers assess and adapt their RE reference model, which captures company-specific RE practices and artefacts, against an external norm of best practices. The latter is meant to lead to a high quality RE based on universal, external goals (see, e.g. CMMI for RE [3]). Whereas solution-driven improvement approaches might thus serve the purpose to achieve externally predefined goals (e.g. as part of a certification), they do not necessarily consider company-specific goals that dictate the notion of RE quality within a particular context and, thus, result in an RE reference model that might alien to the organisational culture. A notion of RE quality where individual company-specific goals dictate the improvement is taken by problem-driven approaches. Besides the principle of conducting the improvement, the paradigm in which the targeted RE reference model is structured (and, thus, improved)

A. Jedlitschka et al. (Eds.): PROFES 2014, LNCS 8892, pp. 302–305, 2014.

plays an important role, too. A reference model can either be *activity-based* or it can be *artefact-based*. An activity-based improvement approach focuses on improving the quality of the RE activities (practices) while an artefact-based one puts focus on improving the quality of the RE artefacts.

In a recent systematic mapping study [4], we revealed that the high number of available RE improvement approaches still remains solution-driven. They focus on assessments and benchmarks of a company-specific RE based on external activity-centric norms of best practices. As the notion of RE quality is relative to its context [5], those approaches encounter problems in practice [6] and are, thus, often rejected by practitioners [1]. In response to this shortcoming, we elaborated concepts of an artefact-based and problem-driven RE improvement. In [6], we presented how we inferred its basic concepts from selected REPI projects we conducted in practice. Since then, we extended our concepts to a holistic tool-supported and seamless approach. We call our approach *ArtREPI*. With ArtREPI, we could make first contributions and experiences to support a problem-driven and artefact-based RE improvement [6], but we still have little empirical evidence on the benefits and limitations. In this paper, we therefore provide an overview of ArtREPI and report on experiences resulting from ongoing evaluations. The purpose is to support the dissemination and evaluation.

2   ArtREPI in a Nutshell

Figure 1 shows the simplified structure of ArtREPI. We distinguish two views on the notion of RE quality: an external one (lower part of the figure) and one where the notion of quality is relative to its socio-economic context (upper part of the figure). The external context comprehends external norms of best practices and is not key to solution-driven improvement approaches, but we postulate its importance also to a problem-driven improvement as technology transfer according to context-specific goals is an important facet. The socio-economic context comprehends a set of disciplines that aim at managing software processes and changes therein. A change is performed as part of an RE process improvement project which is in scope of the (cyclic) ArtREPI phases. During the *preparation* phase, we agree on the general improvement plan, define the goals, and infer a set of metrics and measurements which serve to evaluate the efficacy of an improvement. During the *problem analysis*, we create an artefact model that reflects the current practice in an organisation. We call in practitioners to validate the as-is model and identify potential problems and candidates for an improvement. The *improvement design* is concerned with the actual improvement where we establish a model candidate and a first prototypical implementation (e.g. modelling tools to create the RE artefacts). The *improvement evaluation and transfer preparation* finally comprehends the evaluation of the RE model in realistic environments provided by pilot projects, before preparing its release. The full ArtREPI model including its (EPF) process implementation, document templates, and evaluation instruments can be taken from our online sources [7].

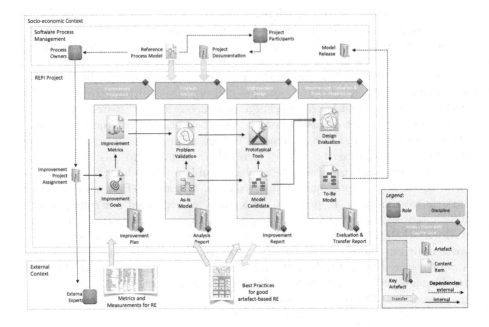

Fig. 1. ArtREPI in a nutshell

3   Ongoing Evaluations and Next Steps

To effectively evaluate our approach, we implemented the process using the EPF Composer, and we made all models and evaluation instruments publicly available [7]. This supports the dissemination, its (technical) validation, and its evaluation in the long run. As an initial evaluation, we applied ArtREPI in two socio-economic contexts via a series of (technical) action research workshops followed by a rating by process engineers and project participants. Process engineers rated the actual approach and project participants rated the improvement outcome after applying it in a series of pilot projects as only they could decide to which extent the improvement outcome eventually achieves their improvement goals. The instruments can be found in our online material. As cases served the companies Wacker Chemie, a German company and works in the chemical business, and SupplyOn AG, a company that works as a software as a service provider. Of particular interest was to know what general benefits and limitations we can expect when applying ArtREPI in a socio-economic context and whether our approach can be used by others if we are not involved at all. For this reason, we conducted the second case study as an independent replication of the first.

Our results indicate, so far, that ArtREPI is well suited to cover the needs of a structured problem-driven improvement while supporting knowledge transfer. The results from pilot project further suggest that the improvement eventually achieved the improvement goals indicating to the problem-driven nature of ArtREPI. Out of scope, however, where long-term investigations. A detailed analysis of our case studies and a longitudinal study are in scope of future work.

We see the biggest benefits of case studies, however, not in providing evidence on what works, but in revealing limitations and eventually fail conditions for an ArtREPI. The limitations include, inter alia, that we, as researchers involved in the development of ArtREPI, seemed to lower the efficiency and effectivity of an improvement due to long preparation phases to explore the domain and the terminology used. Our initial assumption that the success of ArtREPI strongly depends on us conducting the improvement thereby seems to be wrong.

Also, there are a plethora of subjective (social and political) factors important to the success of an RE improvement of which only some might be tackled by methodological aspects; for instance, by involving project participants early in the improvement process to mitigate a missing organisational willingness to change. However, many factors might not be tackled by an improvement approach, nor by an RE reference model that, by nature, abstracts from those aspects important to RE, such as desires, beliefs, experiences, and expectations.

To elaborate to what extent the application of an artefact-based and problem-driven RE improvement eventually leads to an improvement, and how to measure the success of an improvement, we therefore need to:

1. increase our understanding on the variables as there are many facets that we did not measure, that are not measurable at all, or that do not depend at all on the chosen process model (see also [5] for richer discussions). This also supports conducting longitudinal studies.
2. further scaling up to practice to come close to a generalisation.

We support the latter as we made all our material publicly accessible [7], but we need to take new perspectives and conduct further independent case study replications. We therefore encourage researchers and practitioners to join us to fully understand the broad spectrum of possibilities and limitations in ArtREPI.

References

1. Méndez Fernández, D., Wagner, S.: Naming the Pain in Requirments Enginering: A Design for a global Family of Surveys and First Results from Germany. IST (2014)
2. Pettersson, F., Ivarsson, M., Gorschek, T., Öhman, P.: A practitioner's Guide to light weight Software Process Assessment and Improvement Planning. JSS (2008)
3. Beecham, S., Hall, T., Rainer, A.: Defining a requirements process improvement model. Software Quality Control 13 (2005)
4. Méndez Fernández, D., Ognawala, S., Wagner, S., Daneva, M.: Where Do We Stand in Requirements Engineerign Improvement Today? First Results from a Mapping Study. In: ESEM 2014 (2014)
5. Méndez Fernández, D., Mund, J., Femmer, H., Vetrò, A.: Quest for Requirements Engineering Oracles: Dependent Variables and Measurements for (good) RE. In: EASE (2014)
6. Méndez Fernández, D., Wieringa, R.: Improving requirements engineering by artefact orientation. In: Heidrich, J., Oivo, M., Jedlitschka, A., Baldassarre, M.T. (eds.) PROFES 2013. LNCS, vol. 7983, pp. 108–122. Springer, Heidelberg (2013)
7. Méndez Fernández, D.: ArtREPI Online Resources (2014), http://www4.in.tum.de/~mendezfe/openspace.shtml

Security and Privacy Behavior Definition for Behavior Driven Development

Takao Okubo[1], Yoshio Kakizaki[2], Takanori Kobashi[3], Hironori Washizaki[3], Shinpei Ogata[4], Haruhiko Kaiya[5], and Nobukazu Yoshioka[6]

[1] Institute of Information Security, 2-14-1, Tsuruyamachi, Kanagawa-ku, Yokohama, Japan
[2] School of Science and Technology for Future Life, Tokyo Denki University, 5, Senjuasahimachi, Adachi-ku, Japan
[3] Computer Science and Engineer Department, Waseda University, 1-104 Totsukamachi, Shinjuku-ku, Tokyo, Japan
[4] Shinshu University, 4-17-1, Wakasato, Nagano City, Japan 380-8553
[5] Kanagawa University, 2946 Tsuchiya, Hiratsuka-shi, Kanagawa-ken, Japan
[6] GRACE Center, National Institute of Informatics / SOKENDAI, 2-1-2 Hitotsubashi, Chiyoda-ku, Tokyo, Japan

Abstract. There is an issue when security measures are implemented and tested while using agile software development techniques such as Behavior Driven Development (BDD). We need to define the necessary levels of security and the privacy behaviors and acceptance criteria for the BDD. A method for defining the acceptance criteria (BehaveSafe) by creating a threat and countermeasure graph called the *T&C graph* is proposed in this paper. We have estimated the efficiency of our method with a web based system.

1 Introduction

Agile software development techniques such as the spiral and incremental types of development have been popular for developing small applications such as web applications. The threat analysis in the design phase of this type of development techniques requires designing detailed specifications such as data flow diagrams [1] and activity diagrams [3]. However, with agile software development, developers do not produce many design specification documents.

We put the following research questions.

RQ1: Is there any threat analysis method suitable for agile development?
RQ2: What kind of security testing is suitable for agile development?
RQ3: How to create test cases for such testing?
RQ4: Is the testing method sufficient for each release?

We propose a method for defining the acceptance criteria by creating a threat and countermeasure graph called the *T&C graph* and specifying the method for the security behavior *BehaveSafe* by using an attack scenario defined by the threats in the T&C graph relation to answer to these questions.

A. Jedlitschka et al. (Eds.): PROFES 2014, LNCS 8892, pp. 306–309, 2014.

One of our contributions is that the proposed *T&C graph* makes use of the proper implementation of security countermeasures when using an iterative and incremental development technique. The countermeasure related to the architectural choice for each iteration is specified in the *T&C graph*. Another contribution is that the developers or testers can verify the security level of the countermeasures they implemented by using the acceptance criteria generated by using the attackers' attack scenarios.

2   Threat Analysis and Behavior Specification

For BDD, we need to identify and define the specifications for the security and privacy functions. We propose a process with security and privacy requirements analysis and threat and countermeasure analysis. We use a conventional misuse case [4] approach for the former analysis and our analysis method called *T&C graph* for the latter analysis to answer RQ1. Moreover, for specifying the behaviors and acceptance criteria for security countermeasures, we propose a novel behavior definition method called *BehaveSafe* to answer RQ2.

2.1   Requirements Analysis

In this step, the analysts should identify any threats and then specify the security (countermeasure) requirements that mitigate these threats. The analysts can use the misuse case or the MASG approach [2] for this analysis. The threats decomposition or detailed security design specification should not be done in this step. They are issues for the next step.

2.2   T&C Graph

Threat and Countermeasure graph (T&C graph) provides security countermeasure decomposition in addition to the threat decomposition like a threat tree [1]. Fig. 1 represents the metamodel of the T&C graph. Each threat has multiple children who are actually decomposed attack methods or conditions. The threats are linked to multiple countermeasures, which means the threats can be mitigated with countermeasures linked to them.

The relation links between the parents and children have "and" / "or" values. "And" means that in order to achieve the parent threat (countermeasure), all the children linked with the "and" value are required. Otherwise, the children with the "or" value are independent from the other children. Each relation also has the "architecture" property value that represents the architecture specification that the children require. The "scenario" property of a threat and the "behavior" property are explained in the next section.

The proposed *T&C graph* makes a proper implementation of the security countermeasures using iterative and incremental development for each iteration or sprint, and the countermeasure related to the architecture choice is specified by the "architecture" property of the relation in the *T&C graph*.

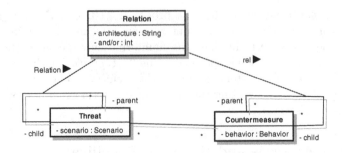

Fig. 1. Metamodel of T&C graph

2.3   BehaveSafe

The security countermeasures contain two types of behaviors. One is a functional behavior and the other is a non-functional one. The functional behavior can be specified just like other non-security function since it only represents the functional requirements. Although the non-functional behavior is more important for security and privacy reasons, it is more difficult to specify since it cannot be retrieved directly from the functional requirements.

BehaveSafe focuses on specifying the non-functional behavior. BehaveSafe uses the relation of the T&C graph. The developers or security analysts define the attack scenarios for each threat identified through the threat decomposition process using the T&C graph. The attack scenarios are written on the "scenario" property.

The acceptance criteria of each countermeasure can be generated from the attack scenarios of the threats linked to the countermeasure. The acceptance criteria are defined so that they do not satisfy the post condition of the attack scenario: If the attack scenario fails due to a countermeasure, it satisfies the acceptance criteria. In other words, we can create test cases not being satisfied from the attack scenarios, that is our answer to RQ3.

2.4   Testing Countermeasures When Using Agile Software Development

As mentioned in the section 2.2, there is a parent-child relation in the threat graph and the countermeasure graph. Therefore, the acceptance criteria must inherit the criteria of the parent countermeasure.

There is an issue when security needs to be implemented and tested while using spiral agile software development. When a countermeasure is implemented at an iteration or sprint, the countermeasure is tested using its acceptance criteria including all the inherited ones. However, there is an exception. When a countermeasure has multiple children linked by "and" relations, the parent's acceptance criteria cannot be satisfied until all the children are implemented. In this case, the testing of the parent's acceptance criteria is postponed until the iteration when all the countermeasures of all the children are implemented. Alter all, the structure of a T&C graph tells us how many security tests we need for each release. This might imply an answer to RQ4.

More comprehensive testing such as testing using black box tools is preferable before finishing creating the software.

3   Discussion

This section discusses the effectiveness of the proposed method using the T&C graph and BehaveSafe. We used an actual application being developed at the author's institute called *EMS (Enrollment Management system)* for the evaluation of our method. EMS is a web application for universities.

One of the developers of EMS has succeeded in identifying 26 threats and designed 39 countermeasures using the T&C graph for one day as a part of agile software development. Security experts verified the results and confirmed it is sufficient. Another developer created acceptance tests using BehaveSafe and tested EMS in another day. In this case, we can create proper test cases for a release. This is why we can say the T&C graph and the BehaveSafe might be suitable for agile development, which are answers to RQ1, RQ2, and RQ4.

It, however, might take more time when the number of use cases increases. On the other hand, since it takes more than a day for the analysis and testing, our approach may not match the development style for a short span iteration (every day release). For future work, we need additional experiments, because we have not enough evaluation for verifying RQ4.

4   Conclusion

A method for threat analysis and countermeasure specification using threat and countermeasure graphs called T&C graphs is proposed in this paper. A novel method for specifying the acceptance criteria for agile software development such as Behavior Driven Development (BDD) is also presented here. We have evaluated our methods using the development of a typical software problem called EMSsec. The evaluation results indicated two key points. One is that the T&C graph and BehaveSafe are useful for defining the acceptance criteria for the security level, and also the specified criteria are useful for verifying the security level for BDD and the iterative developments.

References

1. Howard, M., Lipner, S.: The Security Development Lifecycle. Microsoft (2006)
2. Okubo, T., Taguchi, K., Kaiya, H., Yoshioka, N.: Masg: Advanced misuse case analysis model with assets and security goals. IPSJ Journal of Information Processing 22(3), 536–546 (2014)
3. Sindre, G.: Mal-activity diagrams for capturing attacks on business processes. In: Sawyer, P., Heymans, P. (eds.) REFSQ 2007. LNCS, vol. 4542, pp. 355–366. Springer, Heidelberg (2007)
4. Sindre, G., Opdahl, A.L.: Eliciting security requirements with misuse cases. Requir. Eng. 10(1), 34–44 (2005)

The Challenges of Joint Solution Planning: Three Software Ecosystem Cases

Danielle Pichlis[1], Mikko Raatikainen[1], Piia Sevón[1], Stefanie Hofemann[1], Varvana Mylllärniemi[1], and Marko Komssi[2]

[1] Aalto University, Helsinki, Finland
[2] F-Secure, Helsinki, Finland
{firstname.lastname}@aalto.fi, marko.komssi@f-secure.com

Abstract. Software ecosystems are increasingly involving multiple companies to collaboratively propose value for an end user. When planning a joint solution however, there are challenges for companies. In this paper, we study the experience of joint solution planning in three different kinds of ecosystem settings, highlighting the nature of collaboration and the challenges that arise. The results suggest that the key challenges are not of a technological nature, but instead concern the process of value creation and collaboration.

Keywords: software ecosystem, solution planning, value, case study.

1 Introduction

In order to succeed in the market, companies are opening up their businesses to third parties [2]. Recently, software ecosystems (SECO) are becoming increasingly common among software development organizations [6] to effectively build large systems utilizing the contribution of multiple parties [11] beyond what is possible for a single organization [1]. SECOs diverge from traditional software development in that the development and the ownership of the software is decentralized [4]. A SECO enables development that can harness open innovation [13] and can significantly increase the value to the end user or customer, thereby contributing to the success of all stakeholders [11]. Central characteristics of a SECO include the use of a common technology; collaboration with the keystone player (who is primarily responsible for the common technology), third party developers and users; and shared value proposition [1][3][5][7,8]. In addition, there are a number of secondary characteristics which can be used to classify or differentiate SECOs in a more detailed manner, such as governance model [5][7] and entry conditions [2][7,8].

Throughout the planning of the joint solution, the participating companies face several challenges: For example, identifying the value proposition for each stakeholder as well as the responsibilities. This paper addresses the research question: *What are the challenges of joint solution planning in different kinds of software ecosystems?* The contribution of the paper is to give an account of three different SECOs elaborating their peculiarities and the challenges that

A. Jedlitschka et al. (Eds.): PROFES 2014, LNCS 8892, pp. 310–313, 2014.

arise during the planning of a joint solution, especially in light of the identified peculiarities.

This research employs the case study approach [12], covering three different cases, each involving the collaboration between two industrial companies. The unit of analysis within these cases is joint solution planning, and especially the challenges arising from it. The data collection relied primarily on workshops, in which we observed the joint solution planning. The workshops were recorded and notes were taken. Furthermore, additional data was based on more informal discussions.

2   Results

2.1   Case A: Companies Alpha and Beta

Companies Alpha and Beta aimed to initiate collaboration to provide services for other ecosystems operating in the cloud, such as those of Amazon or Google. The products of Company Alpha could be utilized in such ecosystems as services, while Company Beta provides consulting services for the cloud, utilizing Company Alpha's products. Thus, neither of the companies are actually a keystone organization but provide specific services for existing ecosystems. The common value for both would be more extensive usage of their services in the cloud.

The challenge here, for the success of this collaborative solution depends upon the service design of Company Alpha's product offering, in terms of business model and value proposition. In fact, only minimal tweaks would be required on the technology level, as technical prototypes of this kind of offering have already been evaluated.

2.2   Case B: Companies Alpha and Gamma

Company Gamma is a small company operating in a niche market and consisting of only two founders. Company Alpha has developed an ecosystem platform, which Company Gamma is eager to utilize in order to extend their own offering. Company Gamma has developed an application, which could be integrated with the platform of Company Alpha.

One major challenge for this particular collaboration concerns who is driving the joint solution development and taking responsibility for its progress. In this case, a common value proposition does not yet exist, there is no common business model and the companies are not equally interested in investing resources. For Company Alpha, the solution with Company Gamma represents only one of many possible applications for their ecosystem platform. The collaboration has an unknown impact; although, as a keystone organization, Company Alpha would benefit from the application of its ecosystem platform in the new domain. Thus, there is no strong wish to adapt the platform, especially considering the uncertainty surrounding the business case. Company Gamma has a strong interest in the collaboration; however, they are small and lack the resources for the development. As a result of these challenges, the collaborative solution planning is currently lacking a clear vision, and the parties are unevenly committed to its progress.

2.3   Case C: Companies Alpha and Delta

Company Delta has developed a prototype service that could complement their current offering. However, in order to be a viable product and not just a prototype, the service needs to be integrated with various external heterogeneous data providers. Furthermore, this service, and Company Alpha's platform could complement each other.

Two major challenges exist in this case. First, the parties, and specifically Company Alpha, doubt the market potential. Second, neither of the involved parties seemed to be interested in taking leadership of developing the collaboration or joint solution further, as it would be outside the core business for both companies. Even though the platform of Company Alpha has been launched already and Company Delta only has a prototype, no major imbalance in terms of potential benefits of a joint solution and potential resources to be invested from both sides seemed to exist.

3   Conclusions

An examination of the SECO cases reveals only a minimal amount of technological uncertainty, whether or not something can be done, and even development seems easy and fast. The main reason for this seems to be that SECOs combine the competences of its participants and the platform of the SECO provides many technological solutions. However, a SECO can also be restricting, e.g., by requiring certain architectural styles.

Instead, the challenges are more about defining the value for each stakeholder. This includes what each actor brings to the SECO, their individual and combined business value, and value for the customer. The concerns that the case companies highlighted dealt with understanding stakeholders and their relationships. Furthermore, the responsibilities and relationships are more complex when several organizations work together within a SECO. Consequently, the difficulties lie not in technological uncertainty, but relate more to market uncertainty [10].

The challenges were emphasized due to the fact that in all cases the companies also had other existing businesses. Consequently, the novel joint solutions were competing with those core activities for attention and resources. Nevertheless, SECOs are a means to find new business opportunities for companies that cannot do everything by themselves. The joint planning seems to benefit from holistic, cross-functional competencies. In the aforementioned cases the user experience design and business model planning could have been more present in the collaborative workshops. A means to tackle the challenges would have been to operate in an internal start-up or joint venture [9] manner that would have provided the required ownership and resources, separate from the existing business activities.

As demonstrated by the three cases, SECOs differ largely regarding the participating actors, their roles and value within the SECO. Even within one SECO there can be major differences, as exemplified by Case B and C, where the keystone organization and technological platform were common to both. Consequently, whenever designing a joint solution for a SECO, these differentiating characteristics need to be considered and accounted for.

Acknowledgments. We acknowledge the financial support of TEKES as part of the Need for Speed (N4S) and FinnCloud2 programs of DIGILE.

References

1. Bosch, J.: From software product lines to software ecosystems. In: 13th International Software Product Line Conference, pp. 111–119. Carnegie Mellon University, Pittsburgh (2009)
2. Bosch, J.: Software ecosystems: Taking software development beyond the boundaries of the organization. Journal of Systems and Software 85(7), 1453–1454 (2012)
3. Bosch, J., Bosch-Sijtsema, P.: From integration to composition: On the impact of software product lines, global development and ecosystems. Journal of Systems and Software 83(1), 67–76 (2010)
4. Ghazawneh, A., Henfridsson, O.: Balancing platform control and external contribution in third-party development: The boundary resources model. Information Systems Journal 23(2), 173–192 (2013)
5. Hanssen, G.K.: A longitudinal case study of an emerging software ecosystem: Implications for practice and theory. Journal of Systems and Software 85(7), 1455–1466 (2012)
6. Hanssen, G.K., Dybå, T.: Theoretical foundations of software ecosystems. In: Forth International Workshop on Software Ecosystems. CEUR Workshop Proceedings, vol. 879, pp. 6–17 (2012)
7. Jansen, S., Cusumano, M.A.: Defining software ecosystems: A survey of software platforms and business network governance. In: Forth International Workshop on Software Ecosystems. CEUR Workshop Proceedings, vol. 879, pp. 40–58 (2012)
8. Jansen, S., Finkelstein, A., Brinkkemper, S.: A sense of community: A research agenda for software ecosystems. In: 31st International Conference on Software Engineering, Companion Volume, pp. 187–190. IEEE (2009)
9. Komssi, M., Pichlis, D., Raatikainen, M., Kindström, K., Järvinen, J.: What are hackathons for? IEEE Software (PrePrints, 2014)
10. MacMillan, I.C., McGrath, R.G.: Grafting R&D project portfolios. Research & Technology Management 45(5), 48–59 (2002)
11. Manikas, K., Hansen, K.M.: Software ecosystems — A systematic literature review. Journal of Systems and Software 86(5), 1294–1306 (2013)
12. Yin, R.K.: Case Study Research, 2nd edn. Sage, Thousand Oaks (1994)
13. Yoo, Y., Henfridsson, O., Lyytinen, K.: Research commentary — The new organizing logic of digital innovation: An agenda for information systems research. Information Systems Research 21(4), 724–735 (2010)

A Benchmark-Based Approach for Ranking Root Causes of Performance Problems in Software Development

Mushtaq Raza and João Pascoal Faria

INESC TEC and Department of Informatics Engineering,
Faculty of Engineering, University of Porto
Rua Dr. Roberto Frias, s/n 4200-465 Porto, Portugal
uomian49@yahoo.com, jpf@fe.up.pt

Abstract. In previous work we proposed a performance analysis model for automatically identifying potential root causes of performance problems in personal software development. In this paper we present an approach for automatically ranking those potential root causes based on a cost-benefit estimate that takes into account historical data. The approach was applied for the Personal Software Process, taking advantage of a large data set referring to more than 30,000 projects, but can be replicated in other contexts.

Keywords: Ranking, Root causes, Performance problems, Personal Software Process.

1   Introduction

High-maturity software development processes, such as the Team Software Process (TSP) and the accompanying Personal Software Process (PSP) [1, 2], can generate large amounts of performance data that can be periodically analyzed [3] to identify performance problems, determine potential root causes and devise improvement actions. The manual analysis of such data is problematic because of the lack of benchmarks, the amount of data to analyze, and the expert knowledge required.

To overcome the lack of support in existing tools for such type of analysis [4, 5, 6, 7], in previous work [8, 9] we developed a performance model and a prototype tool, tailored for the PSP, validated and calibrated based on a large PSP data set referring to more than 30,000 projects, to enable the automated identification of performance problems of individual PSP developers and their potential root causes.

In this paper we propose a novel approach to rank the identified root causes, based on a cost-benefit estimate that takes into account historical data, so that subsequent improvement actions can be focused on the highest-ranked root causes.

The rest of the paper is organized as follows. Section 2 presents the proposed raking approach. Section 3 presents an example to illustrate the application of the approach. Section 4 presents the conclusions and points out future work. Due to space limitations, further details about the approach can be found in a technical report [10].

A. Jedlitschka et al. (Eds.): PROFES 2014, LNCS 8892, pp. 314–317, 2014.

2   Proposed Ranking Approach

The model [9] developed in our previous work for analyzing the performance of PSP developers contains a set of performance indicators (PI) organized hierarchically, starting from three top-level PIs (for productivity, quality and predictability), and descending to lower level PIs that affect the higher-level PIs according to formulas or historical data. For each PI, the model contains performance ranges for classifying its values as suggesting a clear (red), potential (yellow) or none (green) performance problem. The performance ranges and dependencies between PIs were calibrated and validated, respectively, based on a large PSP data set from the Software Engineering Institute with data from 31,140 projects. Having such a model as input and some PSP project data to analyze, our PSP PAIR tool automatically indicates performance problems (top-level PIs with 'red' values) and their root causes (lower-level PIs with 'red' or 'yellow' values), but does not indicate the relative importance of those causes.

Here we propose to order the lower-level PIs $(X_1, ..., X_n)$, or factors, that affect a higher-level PI (Y) according to the value of a *ranking coefficient* ρ_i, computed for each X_i as the product of a *sensitivity coefficient* σ_i and a *percentile coefficient* π_i.

The *sensitivity coefficient* σ_i estimates the impact on Y of a small change in the value of X_i, whilst keeping all the other factors unchanged, and is computed by [11]:

$$\sigma_i = \frac{\partial Y}{\partial X_i}\left(\frac{X_i}{Y}\right) \qquad \left[\approx \frac{\Delta Y/_Y}{\Delta X_i/_{X_i}}, \text{for small } \Delta\right] \tag{1}$$

Here we assume that: (i) the relationship between Y and the factors $X_1, ..., X_n$ can be described by a function $Y=h(X_1, ..., X_n)$, representing an exact formula for deriving Y or a regression formula [12] calibrated based on historical data; (ii) the higher order partial derivatives of h are negligible for small variations; and (iii) there is no correlation between the factors, so that one factor can be changed at a time [13].

The *percentile coefficient* π_i is an indicator of the 'cost' to improve the value of each X_i. Intuitively, the closest a value is to the optimal value, in terms of percentiles, the more difficult it is to improve it. Let x denote an actual value of X_i, let $F_i(x)$ denote the approximate cumulative distribution function of X_i, let $f_i(x)=F'_i(x)$ denote the approximate probability density function of X_i, let o_i denote the optimal value of X_i, and let $P_i(x)=F_i(o_i)-F_i(x)$ denote the percentile distance of x to o_i. Our base hypothesis for deriving a ranking coefficient is that equal relative variations in the P_is have equal cost. Then, the percentile coefficient is:

$$\pi_i = \frac{\partial X_i}{\partial P_i}\left(\frac{P_i}{X_i}\right) = \frac{F_i(x)-F_i(o_i)}{x f_i(x)} \qquad \left[\approx \frac{\Delta X_i/_{X_i}}{\Delta P_i/_{P_i}}, \text{for small } \Delta\right] \tag{2}$$

The approximate cumulative distribution function $F_i(x)$ can be obtained by computing a theoretical distribution that best fits the historical data, or by linear interpolation between a few percentiles computed from the historical data.

The overall ranking coefficient is a composite sensitivity coefficient, representing a ratio between a benefit estimate (a relative variation in the value of Y) and a cost estimate (a relative variation in the percentile distance of X_i to the optimal value):

$$\rho_i = \frac{\partial Y}{\partial P_i}\left(\frac{P_i}{Y}\right) = \frac{\partial Y}{\partial X_i}\left(\frac{X_i}{Y}\right) \times \frac{\partial X_i}{\partial P_i}\left(\frac{P_i}{X_i}\right) = \pi_i\,\sigma_i \qquad \left[\approx \frac{\Delta Y/_Y}{\Delta P_i/_{P_i}}, \text{for small } \Delta\right] \tag{3}$$

3   Example

In the PSP, the size of the delivered program (measured in functions points, lines of code or other size unit) and the effort spent in each process phase (Plan, Design, Design Review, Code, Code Review, Compile, Test, and Postmortem) are among the base measures collected by developers with tool support. From these base measures, we can compute the overall productivity (*Prod*) in a project, as a ratio between the program size and the total project effort, as well as the productivity per phase $Prod_k$ (where k denotes a process phase), as a ratio between the program size and the effort in phase k. The overall productivity is affected by the productivity per phase according to the formula $Prod = \frac{1}{\Sigma_k \frac{1}{Prod_k}}$. From this formula we can derive the sensitivity coefficients $\pi_k = \frac{Prod}{Prod_k} = \frac{effort\ in\ phase\ k}{total\ project\ effort}$. This formula basically tells that $Prod_k$ will be ranked higher for the phases that consume more effort.

Table 1 presents productivity values from a concrete project (out of the training data set), as well as all the calculations performed to rank the factors (productivity per phase) that affect the overall productivity. Regarding the sensitivity coefficient, the phases that consume more effort (i.e., with lower productivity) - Design and Unit Test - are ranked at the top 2 positions. However, the productivity in Unit Test is significantly closer to the optimal value (in terms of percentiles) than, for example, in Design Review, so, when computing the combined ranking coefficient, the productivity in Unit Test goes down to the 4th position. In the final ranking, the top two phases which productivity should be improved (for improving the overall productivity with the best cost-benefit ratio) are the Design and Design Review phases. In our previous work [9], all the phases with a value in the red range (percentile below 33%) - all but the Code phase in this case - would be indicated to the user as equally important for improvement.

Table 1. Ranking calculations for the factors that affect the overall productivity

i	Variable	Value (LOC/ hour)	Percentile (F_i) [1]	Probability Density (f_i) [1]	Percentile Coefficient $\pi_i = \frac{F_i(x) - F_i(o_i)}{x f_i(x)}$	Sensitivity Coefficient $\sigma_i = \frac{Prod}{Prod_k}$	Ranking Coefficient $\rho_i = \pi_i \times \sigma_i$
0	Productivity	8.63	7%	0.00936	11.45		
1	Plan Productivity	73.5	10%	0.00223	5.48	0.117	0.64 (3rd)
2	Design Productivity	19.4	3%	0.00172	29.11	0.446	12.98 (1st)
3	Design Review Prod.	100.0	7%	0.00066	14.26	0.086	1.23 (2nd)
4	Code Productivity	87.8	45%	0.00693	0.91	0.098	0.09 (7th)
5	Code Review Prod.	163.6	18%	0.00211	2.39	0.053	0.13 (6th)
7	Unit Test Prod.	67.9	18%	0.00353	3.42	0.127	0.43 (4th)
8	Postmotem Pord.	120.0	20%	0.00220	3.03	0.072	0.22 (5th)

(1) Computed by liner interpolation between a few percentiles computed from the training data set.

(2) The optimal value assumed here is $o_i = \infty$, so $F_i(o_i) = 1$

4 Conclusion and Future Work

We proposed an approach for ranking the root causes of performance problems, based on a cost-benefit estimate, combining an estimate of the cost to change each factor and an estimate of the benefit (impact) on the affected PI. We illustrated its application with a real world example in the context of the PSP. For space limitations, a case study conducted to show the adequacy of the approach can be found in [10].

As future work, we intend to extend our Performance Analysis and Improvement Recommendation tool [8], build a comprehensive catalogue of improvement actions to recommend for the highest-ranked root causes, conduct further experiments, and extend the approach for analyzing data produced in the context of other processes.

Acknowledgments. The authors would like to acknowledge the SEI for facilitating the access to the PSP data for performing this study. The work of J. Faria is partly funded by FEDER through the Portuguese ON.2 Program, under project reference SI IDT - 21562/2011. The work of M. Raza is partially funded by the Portuguese Foundation for Science and Technology, under research grant SFRH/BD/85174/2012.

References

1. Humphrey, W.: PSP^{sm}: A Self-Improvement Process for Software Engineers. Addison-Wesley Professional (2005)
2. Davis, N., Mullaney, J.: The Team Software Process (TSP) in Practice: A Summary of Recent Results. CMU/SEI-2003-TR-014 (2003)
3. Burton, D., Humphrey, W.: Mining PSP Data. In: TSP Symposium 2006 Proceedings (2006)
4. The Software Process Dashboard Initiative, http://www.processdash.com/
5. Hackystat, http://code.google.com/p/hackystat/
6. Shin, H., Choi, H.-J., Baik, J.: Jasmine: A PSP Supporting Tool. In: Wang, Q., Pfahl, D., Raffo, D.M. (eds.) ICSP 2007. LNCS, vol. 4470, pp. 73–83. Springer, Heidelberg (2007)
7. Nasir, M., Yusof, A.: Automating a Modified Personal Software Process. Malaysian Journal of Computer Science 18, 11–27 (2005)
8. Duarte, C., Faria, J.P., Raza, M.: PSP PAIR: Automated Personal Software Process Performance Analysis and Improvement Recommendation. In: Proceedings of the 8th Int. Conf. on the Quality of Information and Communications Technology, pp. 131–136. IEEE (2012)
9. Raza, M., Faria, J.P.: A Model for Analyzing Estimation, Productivity and Quality Performance in the Personal Software Process. In: 2014 International Conference of Software and System Process, pp. 10–19. ACM (2014)
10. Raza, M., Faria, J.P.: A Benchmark-based Approach for Ranking Root Causes of Performance Problems in Software Development. TR-PROCPAIR-2014-01, FEUP (2014), http://www.fe.up.pt/~jpf/TR-PROCPAIR-2014-01.pdf
11. Saltelli, A., Chan, K., Scott, E.M.: Sensitivity Analysis. Wiley (2008)
12. Navidi, W.: Statistics for Engineers and Scientists, 3rd edn. McGraw-Hill (2011)
13. Hamby, D.M.: A Review of Techniques for Parameter Sensitivity Analysis of Environmental Models. Environmental Monitoring and Assessment 32(2), 135–154 (1994)

An Evaluation Template for Expert Review of Maturity Models

Dina Salah, Richard Paige, and Paul Cairns

The University of York, York, UK
{dm560,richard.paige,paul.cairns}@york.ac.uk

Abstract. This paper describes an evaluation template for expert review of maturity models. The template addresses the different aspects involved in assessing both the construct and instruments of maturity models. It was produced via an extensive literature review of principles of design, development and evaluation of maturity models. This template can be beneficial to creators of maturity models since it provides them with a road map of the issues involved in evaluating maturity models via expert reviewers. The results of the expert evaluation can lead to the evolution of the maturity model into a number of subsequent versions.

Keywords: Maturity Models, Expert Review, Evaluation, Assessment.

1 Introduction

Maturity Models are normative reference models [5] that embrace the assumption of predictable evolution and change patterns. The main purpose of maturity models is to assess the current situation in order to evaluate the strengths and weaknesses and then prioritize and plan for improvement [5]. This is achieved via evolutionary successive stages or levels that signify step by step patterns of evolution and change designating the desirable or current organisational capabilities against a specific class of entities [3,7]. Those maturity levels form a path from initial state to maturity that can describe logical, anticipated, or desired evolution and change path(s) [3,1]. Although maturity models represent assessment tools yet maturity models are also subject to evaluation and improvement activities [4]. Maturity model assessment focus on comprehending and enhancing the process under investigation whereas the evaluation focus is to understand and improve the maturity model itself [4].

The purpose of this paper is to propose a template for maturity model evaluation that can be utilised by expert reviewers as a checklist for evaluating maturity model constructs and instruments. The result of the expert evaluation can lead to the evolution of the maturity model into a number of subsequent versions.

The rest of this paper is structured as follows: section 2 discusses maturity model components. Section 3 discusses the evaluation methods of maturity models. Section 4 discusses the proposed evaluation template. Section 4, presents the planned evaluation and section 5 discusses the conclusion.

A. Jedlitschka et al. (Eds.): PROFES 2014, LNCS 8892, pp. 318–321, 2014.

2   Maturity Model Components (Instruments)

Maturity models are composed of three components; first, **Reference Model:** a set of dimensions that represent fundamental elements that should be examined in an assessment. The results of the assessment can help organisations assess their current status and identify weaknesses and strengths in order to pinpoint improvement areas. Second, **Performance Scale:** that helps the assessors to rate organisational performance in regards to the examined elements included in the reference model. Third, **Assessment Procedure:** that provides guidance to assessors and is composed of a maturity recording sheet, maturity levels performance rating, and typical quotes.

3   Evaluation of Maturity Models

A systematic mapping study on maturity models' evaluation and assessment proposed three types of maturity model evaluation [4]. First, **Author Evaluation:** that is conducted via the maturity model authors who evaluate the maturity model's processes for its intended use or compare it with other similar maturity models. Second, **Domain Expert Evaluation:** this evaluation occurs via experts in the type of process that the maturity model intends to improve, but who were not involved in the maturity model development. This evaluation is usually performed via surveys, interviews, or simulated assignments. Third, **Practical Setting Evaluation:** this evaluation involves using the maturity model in practical settings. This method is considered to be the most costly, however, the evaluation results is used to analyse and improve both the examined process and the maturity model [4].

4   Evaluation Form for Domain Expert Evaluation of Maturity Models

Maturity model testing should focus on two aspects: the model's construct and the model instruments [2]. Maturity model constructs should be tested for completeness, simplicity, understandability, ease of use, operationality, efficiency and impact on the environment and users [6]. Whereas the model instruments need to be tested for validity and reliability [6]. Maturity models should also possess a number of qualities, for example, flexibility, understandability, implement-ability, correctness, and relevance [8]. Maturity models should be tested to ensure the presence of those qualities as well.

There is an absence of a study that provides concrete guidance on how expert reviewers can conduct evaluations of maturity models and what aspects of the maturity model constructs and instruments needs to be examined during that evaluation. Based on extensive literature review of principles of design, development and evaluation of maturity models an evaluation form was designed in order to evaluate the various aspects related to expert review of maturity model construct and instruments.

Figure 1 shows the proposed domain expert evaluation form.

Maturity Model Domain Expert Evaluation Forms

Expert Information					
Date					
Name (Optional)					
Organization/Institute					
Position					
Email					
Criteria	Strongly Disagree	Slightly Disagree	Neither Disagree Nor Agree	Slightly Agree	Strongly Agree
Maturity Levels					
The maturity levels are sufficient to represent, all maturation stages of the domain (Sufficiency)					
There is no overlap detected between descriptions of maturity levels (Accuracy)					
Processes and Practices					
The processes and practices are relevant to the domain (Relevance)					
Processes and practices cover all aspects impacting/ involved in the domain (Comprehensiveness)					
Processes and practices are clearly distinct (Mutual Exclusion)					
Processes and practices are correctly assigned to their respective maturity level (Accuracy)					
Maturity Model					
Understandability					
The maturity levels are understandable					
The assessment guidelines are understandable					
The documentation is understandable					
Ease of Use					
The scoring scheme is easy to use					
The assessment guidelines are easy to use					
The documentation is easy to use					
Usefulness and Practicality					
The maturity model is useful conducting assessments					
The maturity model is practical for use in industry					

Q1. Would you add any maturity levels? If so please explain what and why?

Q2. Would you update the maturity level description? If so please explain what and why?

Q3. Would you add any processes or practices? If so please explain what and why?

Q4. Would you remove any of the processes or practices? If so please explain what and why?

Q5. Would you redefine/update any of the processes or practices? If so please explain what and why?

Q6. Would you suggest any updates or improvements related to the scoring scheme? If so please explain what and why?

Q7. Would you suggest any updates or improvement related to the assessment guidelines? If so please explain what and why?

Q8. Would you like to elaborate on any of your answers?

Q9. Could the model be made more useful? How?

Q10. Could the model be made more practical? How?

Fig. 1. Maturity Model Domain Expert Evaluation Forms

5 Testing

The testing phase for the proposed template for expert review of maturity models will involve inviting a set of maturity model domain experts to evaluate the proposed template. The domain expert evaluation process will include a number of steps: choosing domain experts, inviting them to take place in the evaluation, evaluating the template by maturity model expert reviewers and then the results of the evaluation will lead to the evolution of the template into subsequent versions as a result of the experts feedback. The selection of the expert panel occurred via preparing a preliminary list of potential candidates who are experts in the development, design, and evaluation of maturity models.

6 Conclusions

This paper reported on the development of a template for evaluating the constructs and instruments of maturity models via expert reviewers. This template provides maturity models creators with a road map of issues involved in evaluating maturity models via expert reviewers. The results of the expert evaluation can lead to the evolution of the maturity model into a number of subsequent improved versions. The changes to the model's maturity levels, key practices, scoring scheme as a result of the evaluation and the reasons behind these changes should be recorded and analysed.

References

1. Becker, J., Knackstedt, R., Poppelbus, J.: Developing Maturity Models for IT Management. Business and Information Systems Engineering 1, 213–222 (2009)
2. DeBruin, T., Freeze, R., Kaulkarni, U., Rosemann, M.: Understanding the Main Phases of Developing a Maturity Assessment Model. In: Australian Conference on Information Systems, New South Wales, Sydney, Australia (2005)
3. Gottschalk, P.: Maturity Levels for Interoperability in Digital Government. Government Information Quarterly 26, 75–81 (2009)
4. Helgesson, Y.Y.L., Host, M., Weyns, K.: A Review of Methods for Evaluation of Maturity Models for Process Improvement. Journal of Software: Evolution and Process 24(4), 436–454 (2012)
5. Iversen, J., Nielsen, P.A., Norbjerg, J.: Assessment of Problems in Software Development. ACM SIGMIS Database - Special Issue on Infomration Systems 30(2), 66–81 (1999)
6. March, S., Smith, G.: Design and Natural Science Research on Information Technology. Decision Support Systems 15, 251–266 (1995)
7. Mettler, T.: Maturity Assessment Models: A Design Science Research Approach. International Journal of Society Systems Science 3, 81–98 (2011)
8. Poppelbub, J., Roglinger, M.: What Makes a Useful Maturity model? A Framework of General Design Principles for Maturity Models and its Demonstration in Business Process Management. In: European Conference on Information Systems (2011)

Do Open Source Software Projects Conduct Tests Enough?

Ryohei Takasawa[1], Kazunori Sakamoto[2], Akinori Ihara[3],
Hironori Washizaki[1], and Yoshiaki Fukazawa[1]

[1] Waseda University, 3-4-1 Okubo, Shinjuku-ku, Tokyo, Japan
[2] National Institute of Informatics, 2-1-2 Hitotsubashi, Chiyoda-ku, Tokyo, Japan
[3] Nara Institute of Science and Technology, 8916-5 Takayama, Ikoma, Nara, Japan

Abstract. Do open source software projects provide and maintain tests?
What metrics are correlated with the test success? This paper answers
these questions by executing tests of 452 open source software projects
in GitHub and measuring 13 metrics from 77 projects. Only 117 projects
passed all test cases. Additionally, the results are correlated with the
comment density, public documented API density, and test coverage.

1 Introduction

The number of Open Source Software (OSS) projects is increasing [1]. Because
the source code in OSS is more readily available than commercial software,
empirical studies on OSS are being actively conducted. For example, Hars et al.
analyzed the reasons why developers participate in OSS projects [2]. Schryen et
al. compared OSS and Closed Source Software (CSS) in terms of vulnerability
[3], while other studies have examined OSS from various viewpoints. However,
little is known about the test activities on OSS.

It is unclear what percentage of OSS projects pass all their test cases and
then how carefully we should treat OSS projects in general. Moreover, executing
tests is a simple and good way to evaluate OSS projects, but such tasks are
time consuming. It is also unclear whether there are useful metrics to estimate
test quality such as test results (passed or failed) and test coverage without
execution.

Thus, we conducted large-scale analysis of OSS projects by collecting 791
Maven projects from GitHub, executing tests of 452 projects and measuring 13
metrics from 77 projects. As a result, only 117 projects passed all their test cases
and comment metrics (comment density and public documented API density)
and test coverage are useful metric to estimate test results.

The research questions (RQs) of this paper are following.

RQ1. What percentage of OSS projects pass all their test cases?
RQ2. Which metrics are useful to estimate whether OSS projects are well tested
without execution?

A. Jedlitschka et al. (Eds.): PROFES 2014, LNCS 8892, pp. 322–325, 2014.

The contributions of this paper are following.

- We show only 14.8% OSS projects passed all their test and we recommend users and contributors to treat OSS projects carefully.
- We find comment metrics are useful to evaluate OSS projects quickly without execution.

2   Experimental Setup

We collected projects in GitHub[1], a famous project hosting service. We targeted projects that use Maven[2], which is the most poplular project management tool for Java, because it automates projects' build, reporting and documentation, including testing and measuring. We used Maven to test projects and measure metrics through SonarQube[3], a metrics management platform.

We collected all the found projects with a search query indicating that target projects contain the pom.xml file which is a build file for Maven. We limited the size of the pom.xml file is 8,798-8,894 or 9,001-9,189 or 9,501-9,562 bytes in order to avoid the limitation of the search result of GitHub, which shows 1,000 projects at a maximum.

We chose 13 metrics[4] : lines of code, number of statements, number of files, comment density, lines of comments, cyclomatic complexity per files, total cyclomatic complexity, line coverage, branch coverage, public documented API density, duplicated lines density, violations, violations per file.

Lines of code, number of statements and number of files are a popular index of the scale of a project. In this paper, lines of code exclude comments. Comment density is defined as the ratio of the lines of comments from the lines of code and comments. Line coverage and branch coverage are the ratio of the executed program elements (line or branch) in testing. Public documented API density is defined as the ratio of public APIs with document from all public APIs which are public classes, interfaces, methods, constructors, annotations and fields. Duplicated lines density is defined as the ratio of duplicated lines from all lines. Violations is defined as the number of issues found in static code analysis.

3   Experimental Results

Although 791 projects were gathered from GitHub, the metrics in some projects could not be measured due to build failures, especially failures caused by omissions of the dependency on the configuration file. Therefore, the experiment included 452 projects (57.1%) that were built without errors.

Next we executed tests, which are included in the targeted projects, and collected the metrics from these 452 projects. Test cases were not run in 276

[1] http://github.com/

[2] http://maven.apache.com/

[3] http://www.sonarqube.org/

[4] http://docs.codehaus.org/display/SONAR/Metric+definitions/

projects (34.9%), it means there were no test cases, or misconfiguration. In 59 projects (7.46%), tests cases were run but failed. Only 117 (14.8%) passed the tests.

In order to measure meaningfully, we targeted projects which have 10 or more test cases and 1 or more files. Then we analyzed the averages of the metrics values for the 51 projects that successfully passed all the test case runs (successful projects) and the 27 projects that failed some test cases (failed projects).

Table 1 shows the results. Although successful projects had higher values of most metrics than failed projects, only 4 metrics listed in Table 1 had statistically significant difference in the average values ($p < 0.05$).

Table 1. Results of metrics

	Comment Density		Documented API Density		Line Coverage		Branch Coverage	
	Success	Failure	Success	Failure	Success	Failure	Success	Failure
average	18.9%	10.8%	52.4%	35.0%	50.5%	31.0%	43.6%	23.2%
dispersion	0.0102	0.0100	0.0957	0.103	0.107	0.0704	0.0918	0.0727
p value	0.00121 (< 0.05)		0.0223 (< 0.05)		0.0170 (< 0.05)		0.00769 (< 0.05)	

4 Discussion

Surprisingly, 14.8% of projects have test cases and pass all of them (RQ1). Pham et al. found that projects with test cases have more contributions from outside developers than those without test cases [4]. Speaking in terms of psychological aspects [5], not fixing failed test cases can be harmful because their presence may cause developers to ignore future failed test cases, increasing the number of failed test cases.

Thus, a method to aid developers in writing test cases should improve OSS projects. We recommend that users of OSS projects pay attention to the existence of test cases and the OSS quality. Because most OSS projects lack the ability to test the contributions from outside developers, we also recommend that contributors write test cases to assure the quality of their contributions.

Although reviewing and executing existing test cases is a simple and effective way to evaluate the quality of OSS projects, it is a costly task. Arafat et al. mentioned that successful OSS projects are consistently well documented and commented [6]. Our results show that the comment metrics and test coverage are strongly correlated with the test results. Because the comment metrics can be measured without execution, it is useful to evaluate OSS projects quickly (RQ2).

5 Threats to Validity

The experiment only used Maven projects, which may cause limitations. However, measuring metrics or running test code is difficult without using tools. Consequently, this issue is unavoidable when studying metrics or testing.

There are other repository hosting services besides GitHub (e.g., SourceForge[5] or Google Code[6]). The difference of the service may affect the experimental results, thus, we will conduct more experiments on other services.

6 Conclusion

Herein we mined OSS projects in GitHub, and we found that most of projects do not have test code. Furthermore, we found a correlation between the testing results and metric values.

The answers (As) to the research questions are as follows:

A1. Only 14.8% of the projects passed their test cases. Thus, users should pay attention to the quality of OSS projects and contributors should write their own test cases.

A2. The comment metrics and test coverage are correlated with the test results, thus, the comment metrics can be used as lightweight metrics to evaluate OSS projects without execution.

We plan to publish our data set and create a platform to search specific characteristics of OSS projects. For example, users can search projects by the percentage of successful test cases. This platform may make it easier to conduct studies on OSS projects.

References

1. Deshpande, A., et al.: The Total Growth of Open Source. IFIP Advances in Information and Communication Technology 275, 197–209 (2008)
2. Hars, A., et al.: Working for Free? -Morivations of Participating in Open Source Projects. International Journal of Electronic Commerce 6, 25–69 (2002)
3. Schryen, G., et al.: Open source vs.closed source software: towards measurring security. In: Proc. of the 24th Annual SCM Symposium on Applied Computing, pp. 2016–2013 (2009)
4. Pham, R., et al.: Creating a Shared Understanding of Testing Culture on a Social Coding Site. In: Proc. of the 35th International Conference on Software Engineering, pp. 112–121 (2013)
5. Wilson, J.Q., Kelling, G.L.: Broken windows. Atlantic Monthly 249(3), 29–38 (1982)
6. Arafat, O., et al.: The Commenting Practice of Open Source. In: Proc. of 24th ACM SIGPLAN Conference Companion on Object Oriented Programming Systems Languages and Applications, pp. 857–864 (2009)

---

[5] http://sourceforge.net/

[6] http://code.google.com/

Author Index